TIPS FROM 65 OF THE FIELD'S TOP EXPERTS:

JANET DAILEY • BARBARA CARTLAND • BER-TRICE SMALL • ELEANORA BROWNLEIGH • PATRICIA MATTHEWS • JENNIFER WILDE • ANNE GISONNY of Candlelight Ecstasy • JACQUI BIANCHI of Harlequin • and more

"Comprehensive . . . a book for realists that is witty, wise and ambitious . . . one of the best around!"
—*Philadelphia Inquirer*

"Every possible directive needed to turn amateurs into slick professionals."
—*The Phoenix*

"An informed how-to book . . . a very interesting guide for anyone thinking of writing a romance."
—*Boston Herald*

"The definitive aspiring romance writer's self-help book . . . lively, interesting, thorough."
—*New York Daily News*

KATHRYN FALK was herself a fan of romances before realizing that the vast, unorganized audience of similar fans needed a guiding force. A resident of Brooklyn, New York, Kathryn created *Romantic Times*, a newsletter which she publishes and which has become the bible of romance writers throughout the country. She is the author of LOVE'S LEADING LADIES and is currently at work organizing the Third Romantic Book Lovers Convention, to be held in England next year.

Kathryn Falk

How to Write a
Romance
and Get It Published

*With Intimate Advice from the
World's Most Popular
Romantic Writers*

Kathryn Falk

Illustrations by Ignatius Sahula

Ø
A SIGNET BOOK

NEW AMERICAN LIBRARY

To Kenneth,
who took me off to his castle in Brooklyn,
where I have lived happily ever after . . .

NAL BOOKS ARE AVAILABLE AT QUANTITY DISCOUNTS WHEN USED
TO PROMOTE PRODUCTS OR SERVICES. FOR INFORMATION PLEASE
WRITE TO PREMIUM MARKETING DIVISION, NEW AMERICAN LIBRARY,
1633 BROADWAY, NEW YORK, NEW YORK 10019.

Published by arrangement with Crown Publishers, Inc. The hardcover
edition was published simultaneously in Canada by General Publishing
Company Limited.

SIGNET TRADEMARK REG. U.S. PAT. OFF. AND FOREIGN COUNTRIES
REGISTERED TRADEMARK—MARCA REGISTRADA
HECHO EN CHICAGO, U.S.A.

SIGNET, SIGNET CLASSIC, MENTOR, PLUME, MERIDIAN and NAL BOOKS
are published by New American Library,
1633 Broadway, New York, New York 10019

First Signet Printing, May, 1984

1 2 3 4 5 6 7 8 9

PRINTED IN THE UNITED STATES OF AMERICA

Contents

Acknowledgments   xiii

List of Contributors   xiv

Introduction   xvii

PART ONE

1 Introduction to Category Romances   1

Recommended Romance Reading List   2

Classification of Romance Novels   5

Types of Category Romance   12

Publishers' Directory   13

Examples of Tip Sheets   14

What Every New Romance Author Should Know
Interview with Jacqui Bianchi   22

The Meaning of Romance: Notes on the Writing
of the Romantic Novel
by Violet Winspear   25

Finding the Formula
by Judy Sullivan   33

Interview with Janet Dailey: America's Queen
of Category Romance   35

Image Making for Romance   39

Research Methods for Category Romances:
The Notebook System   42

Phyllis A. Whitney's Remarkable Notebook   43

Organizing Research Material for Category Romances
by Sara Orwig   44

CONTENTS

What You Need to Get Started: Creative Corner 4

Stimulating Sensuality
by Vivian Stephens 5

The Practical Side of Romance Writing
by Eleanora Brownleigh 5

2 Plotting the Category Romance 6

The TORTE System 6

Mixing Fact with Fiction
by Carolyn Thornton 6

The Use of Theme
by Suzanne Simms 6

How and Why
by Anne N. Reisser 68

Determining the Situation
by Jennifer Blake 71

Obstacles to Love
by Brenda Trent 76

The Third-Person Viewpoint
by Marisa de Zavala 81

Breathing Life into Your Characters
by Maggie Osborne 87

Creating the Hero and Heroine
by Casey Douglas 91

Finding the Right Names, Titles, and Careers
by Debra Oxier 97

Let the Character's Words Flow
by Ginger Chambers 102

3 Polishing the Prose 107

The Dialogue of Love
by Bonnie Drake 109

In the Beginning . . .
by Jayne Castle 115

Humor in Dialogue Is Tricky
by Bonnie Golightly 118

A Pinch of Humor
by Elaine Raco Chase 120

CONTENTS

Narrowing the Narrative
by Lois Walker   123

The Romantic Setting
by Susanna Collins   127

Suspense in Romance
by Nelle McFather   132

4 Between the Sheets   135

Why Women Prefer Steamy Romances   135

A Market Analysis of the Romance Reader for
the Romance Writer (One Man's Opinion)
by Richard Flaxman   136

Building Sexual Tension
by Donna Kimel Vitek   141

Full-Blown Eroticism
by Alice Morgan   150

5 Style and Usage   159

Beware of the Pillaging Mouth
by Donna Ryan   159

Tips from a Copy Editor
by Donna Ryan   162

Caveats and Don'ts
by Renée Rubin   164

The Aches and Pains of Writing Your First Romance Novel
by Erin Ross   168

Questions to Ask While Plotting
by Serita Stevens   172

Testing Your Story   175

Writing Ethnic Romances   176

6 Category Romance Mini-Course   180

Preparing for Your First Romance Novel   180

The Romance Formula   182

The Romance Plot   184

The Romance Heroine   187

The Romance Hero   190

PART TWO

7 *How to Write a Historical Romance* 19

Historical Romance Novels Before 1950 19:

Historical Romances 1940–71 200

Recommendations for Beginning Writers
by Fredda Isaacson 20.

Improving Your Historical Romance Plot
by Kay Meierbachtol 205

Getting Organized
by Miriam Pace 207

Researching History
by Roberta Gellis 216

Casting the Part of Your Reader in Historical
Romance Novels
by Joan Dial 219

Channeling Feelings into History
by Julia Fitzgerald 223

Writing the Erotic Love Scene, or Sex Sells!
by Bertrice Small 226

Building a Novel
by Patricia Matthews 232

How to Write Like Rosemary Rogers
by Rosanne Kohake 236

Jottings from My "Castles in the Air" Notebook-Journals
by Patricia Gallagher 239

How I Create My Heroes and Heroines
by Cynthia Wright 244

Writing the Sensual Novel
by Tom E. Huff (a.k.a. Jennifer Wilde) 250

The Tapestry of Historical Romance
by Maura Seger 253

How I Outlined *Highland Velvet*
by Jude Deveraux 257

The Magic Touch
by Celeste De Blasis 260

How to Write Like Kathleen Woodiwiss
by Rosanne Kohake 265

Planning a Multivolume Saga
   by Kathryn Davis   267

The O'Hara Dynasty
   by Mary Canon   271

Writing Series and Sagas for Book Creations, Inc.
   by Lyle Kenyon Engel   273

An English Historical Novelist's Writing Views
   Interview with Malcolm MacDonald   277

PART THREE

8   **Introduction to the Other Romance Genres**   281

Sigh, Spy, Cry, Sci-Fi   281

Confessions of a Regency Romantic
   by Megan Daniel   289

A Lighthearted Plot
   by Marion Chesney   292

An Explanation of the Regency
   by Elizabeth Mansfield   294

How to Write Today's Gothic
   by Virginia Coffman   297

The First Gay Gothic: *Gaywyck*   301

The Contemporary Romance Novel: The Woman Who
   Breaks Reader's Hearts   303

How to Write Like Danielle Steel
   by Rosanne Kohake   305

Advice on the Contemporary Romance Novel
   Interview with Pamela Strickler   308

Romance in Science Fiction and Fantasy   310

My First Sci-Fi Fantasy
   by Carole Nelson Douglas   311

9   **Can a Man Write Romance?**   314

How Can a Man Write Romance Novels?
   by Mike Hinkemeyer   317

10   **Teaming Up to Write Romances**   323

Half the Headache, Double the Fun   323

How We Write Together
by June Hayden
                                                                        326

11   *How to Write Teen Romances*   330

The Teenage Formula
by Audrey P. Johnson
                                                                        333

Turning Teenage Fantasies into Fiction
by Suzanne Zuckerman
                                                                        337

PART FOUR

12   *Love's Literary Labors*   340

Manuscript Preparation
by Marianne Lopriore
                                                                        340

Synopsizing a Novel
by Marion Chesney
                                                                        346

The Outline Hurdle
by Bonnie Golightly
                                                                        347

What Happens To Your Manuscript When It Arrives
at a Publishing House
by Hilary V. Guerin
                                                                        349

Romance Jargon   353

The Romance Novel Route   357

The Literary Agent and the Book Contract   362

The Author-Agent Relationship
by Denise Marcil
                                                                        365

List of Romance Literary Agents   368

Writing Tools   368

How to Write a Best-seller on a Dictaphone Word Processor
by Janelle Taylor
                                                                        371

Advice to Husbands: Don't Bite the Hand That Writes
by George Small
                                                                        376

PART FIVE

13   *An Interview with Barbara Cartland*   381

PART SIX

14 *Keeping Fit While Writing*   390

A Writer's Regimen   390

Creative Writing Tips
   by Dr. Lonnie MacDonald   394

To Thine Own Self Be True   396

PART SEVEN

15 *How to Promote a Romance Novel*   397

Love Is in the Air: TV, Radio, Media Lists,
   and Publicity Agents   398

Tips for TV
   by Velma Daniels   409

The Author-Publicist Relationship
   by Joan Schulhafer   411

PART EIGHT

16 *Pink Ink*   416

Listing of Major Romance Publishing Houses   416

A Publisher Talks About Romance Fiction
   by Ron Busch   433

Appendix   437

   Publications   437

   A Recommended Reading List   442

   Researching the Historical Novel: A Bibliography   455

   Researching the Edwardian Novel: A Bibliography   463

   Bibliography of Contributors   464

   Index   480

Acknowledgments

A most grateful thank you to all the authors, editors, and *Romantic Times* subscribers who contributed to this project. I hope that our efforts will assure a talented new generation of romance writers. Acknowledgment is also made to the following publishers for the excerpts from the contributor's own books used in their articles contained in this book:

JOVE PUBLICATIONS, INC., 200 Madison Avenue, New York, N.Y. 10016 for *Scream of the Parrot* by Marisa de Zavala, 1983 • HARLEQUIN AMERICAN ROMANCE for *Kiss Goodnight and Say Goodby* by Marisa de Zavala, 1983 • SUPERROMANCE™ for *Proud Surrender* by Casey Douglas, 1983, Copyright © 1983 by Casey Douglas. Reprinted by permission of the publisher, Worldwide Library, 225 Duncan Mill Road, Don Mills, Ontario M3B 3K9. Superromance is a trademark of Harlequin Enterprises Limited • CANDLELIGHT ECSTASY for *Passion and Illusion* by Bonnie Drake, 1983 • SILHOUETTE for *Fast Courting* by Billie Douglass (a/k/a Bonnie Drake) © 1983 by Barbara Delinsky • CANDLELIGHT ECSTASY for *The Silver Fox* by Bonnie Drake, 1983 • SILHOUETTE for *Sweet Serenity* and *Beyond Fantasy* by Billie Douglass (a/k/a Bonnie Drake) both 1983. Copyright © 1982 by Barbara Delinsky • SILHOUETTE DESIRE for *Affair of Honor* by Stephanie James (a/k/a Jayne Castle) 1983. Copyright © 1982 by Jayne Krentz • CANDLELIGHT ECSTASY for *Spellbound* by Jayne Castle, 1982 • CANDLELIGHT ECSTASY for *Conflict of Interest* by Jayne Castle, 1983 • SILHOUETTE DESIRE for *Battle Prize* by Stephanie James (a/k/a Jayne Castle), 1983. Copyright © 1982 by Jayne Krentz • DELL for *Diamond of Desire* by Lois Walker (as Candice Adams), 1983 • BALLANTINE for *Exploring* by Lois Walker (as Candice Adams), 1983 • CANDLELIGHT ECSTASY for *Passion's Price* by Dona Kimel Vitek, 1983, Copyright © 1983 by Dona Kimel Vitek. Reprinted by permission of Dell Publishing Company, Inc. • CANDLELIGHT ECSTASY for *Dangerous Embrace* by Dona Kimel Vitek, 1983. Copyright © 1983 by Dona Kimel Vitek. Reprinted by permission of Dell Publishing Company, Inc. • CANDLELIGHT ECSTASY for *Morning Always Comes* by Dona Kimel Vitek, 1982. Copyright © 1982 by Dona Kimel Vitek. Reprinted by permission of Dell Publishing Company, Inc. • CANDLELIGHT ECSTASY for *Masquerade of Love*, *Sands of Malibu*, and *The*

List of Contributors

AUTHORS

Jennifer Blake
Eleanora Brownleigh
Shirlee Busbee
Mary Canon
Barbara Cartland
Jayne Castle
Ginger Chambers
Elaine Raco Chase
Marion Chesney
Virginia Coffman
Susanna Collins
Janet Dailey
Megan Daniel
Kathryn Davis
Celeste De Blasis
Jude Deveraux
Joan Dial
Carole Nelson Douglas
Casey Douglas
Bonnie Drake
Julia Fitzgerald
Patricia Gallagher
Roberta Gellis
Bonnie Golightly
June Hayden
Audrey Johnson
Roseanne Kohake

Marianne Lopriore
Nelle McFather
Malcolm MacDonald
Elizabeth Mansfield
Patricia Matthews
Alice Morgan
Sara Orwig
Maggie Osborne
Miriam Pace
Anne N. Reisser
Erin Ross
Vanessa Royall
Maura Seger
Suzanne Simms
Bertrice Small
Serita Stevens
Janelle Taylor
Carolyn Thornton
Brenda Trent
Donna Kimel Vitek
Lois Walker
Jennifer Wilde
Violet Winspear
Cynthia Wright
Marisa de Zavala
Suzanne Zuckerman

List of Contributors

EDITORS AND PUBLISHERS

Introduction

Welcome to the wonderful and exciting world of romantic fiction.

I'm pleased that all the information in this paperback edition of *How to Write a Romance and Get It Published* is still relevant, and indicative of the present-day romance market.

I have updated the information on series, editors, and publishers because a few changes have taken place. Two series (Love and Life and Finding Mr. Right) are no longer in print, and Harlequin, Silhouette, and several smaller publishers have introduced new series. The recommended reading list has also been updatd, so you can study some of the currently most popular writers and titles.

If I add any additional advice it is only this: Stay abreast of the unusual new titles. They may be indicative of trends and continuing defining of the genre. Study the top reviews in *Romantic Times* and talk to readers at your local bookstores. Discover which writers and titles are creating a lot of talk, which novels are fresh or have unusual new plots or characterizations. It's no coincidence that many romance readers turn into writers; they have kept up with the books and understand what readers are ready for *next*. So must you!

Today *more* than 24 million women are reading all types of romantic fiction. Readers include single and married women and range from stay-at-homes to professionals. They all find romantic fiction a healthy and relaxing distraction.

So who are your readers today? Everywoman. That is why publishers now have a complete spectrum of romance reading, ranging from explicitly sensual books to the new sweet inspirational romances. You just have to choose your type of romance and turn your fantasies into fiction.

I wish you luck and I hope you write a bestselling romance. Let me hear from you anytime.

Kathryn Falk
Spring, 1984

PART ONE

— 1 —

Introduction to Category Romances

> *Romance is not truth but a delightful and neces-*
> *sary holiday from common sense.*
> LETTERS ON CHIVALRY AND ROMANCE (1762)

People everywhere dream of putting their stories on paper, and usually they involve . . . ROMANCE.

One such dreamer was Rosie, but she didn't know where to start.

She knew that romance novel writing had become the biggest cottage industry in the country, making small fortunes for women and men who had never published a word before they sat down to record their romantic fantasies.

Rosie had the needed aspiration and plenty of ideas, but "how to" was a mystery. Her inability to get started led her to write to me.

Maryland Avenue
Royal Oak, Michigan
From the den of
    dungarees and dreams . . .

March 23

Kathryn Falk
<u>Romantic Times</u>
163 Joralemon Street
Brooklyn Heights, NY 11201

Dear Kathryn Falk:

I read your publication, <u>Romantic Times</u>, with great interest, and have decided that I too want to become a romance writer, even

1

though I'll be a "late starter" (I'm thirty-five, married, and have two children). Ever since I read <u>Gone With the Wind</u> I've been hooked on historical romance novels, and now I'm reading some of the contemporaries.

Could you please help me to write a romance? I'm ablaze with ideas, but I don't know where to begin. Writing even one romance novel would satisfy a life's ambition.

Respectfully,
Rosie Reynolds

From the Desk of Kathryn Falk

April 19

Dear Rosie:

I used to be from your part of the world. Hearing from you is like being back home again. Dens and dungarees, indeed!

If you're sincere about learning how to write a romance, I'll be happy to get you started. I give a class on the subject in New York and will send you some of my material.

But first, you should know that as an avid reader you have the best chance of getting published. When I researched my book, <u>Love's Leading Ladies</u>, I discovered that most of the popular romance authors are readers turned writers. Their average age for getting published is the late thirties and early forties, most are married with children, and their education and background vary widely. One day they said either "I don't have anything to read" or "I can do it too," and they did.

Now, with the market expanding, writers from other fields are trying to write romance, but the avid reader is still the best candidate.

If you haven't a preference as to the kind of romance you want to write, perhaps you had better get started by studying the different subgenres. I've enclosed a general reading list of popular authors and notes on various classifications of the romance genre.

Hoping you always have romantic times,
Kathryn Falk

Recommended Romance Reading List

The following names are a compilation from a questionnaire filled out by *Romantic Times* readers. Due to the short shelf life of books in some of these categories, only authors' names are given.

Category Romances

Mary Burchell

Jayne Castle (a.k.a. Stephanie James)

Elaine Raco Chase

Susanna Collins (Sue Ellen Cole)

Jasmine Cresswell (a.k.a. Jasmine Craig)

Ann Cristy (a.k.a. Hayton Monteith, Helen Mittermeyer)

Janet Dailey

Anne Hampson

Robin James (a.k.a. Laura London, Tom and Sharon Curtis)

Penny Jordan

Flora Kidd

Charlotte Lamb (a.k.a. Laura Hardy)

Amii Lorin (a.k.a. Joan Hohl)

Ann Mather

Carol Mortimer

Diana Palmer (a.k.a. Diana Blayne)

Anne Reisser

Nora Roberts

Rachel Ryan (a.k.a. Laura Jordan, Erin St. Clair, Sandra Brown)

JoAnn Robb

Essie Summers

Donna Vitek

Violet Winspear

Historical Romances

Lynn Bartlett, *Courtly Love*

Jennifer Blake, *Love's Wild Desire*

Shirlee Busbee, *Gypsy Lady*

Jude Devereaux, *The Velvet Promise*

Patricia Gallagher, *Castles in the Air*

Roberta Gellis, *Bond of Blood*, Roselynde Chronicles

Sergeanne Golon, Angelique series

Lisa Gregory, *The Rainbow Season*

Victoria Holt, *Mistress of Mellyn*

Johanna Lindsey, *Captive Bride*

Norah Lofts—everything she writes!

Laurie McBain, *Tears of Gold*

Margaret Mitchell, *Gone with the Wind*

Jean Plaidy, Plantagenet series

Rosemary Rogers, *Sweet Savage Love*

Anya Seton, *Katherine*

Bertrice Small, *Kadin, Skye O'Malley*

Jennifer Wilde, *Love's Tender Fury, Once More Miranda*

Kathleen Winsor, *Forever Amber*

Kathleen Woodiwiss, *The Flame and the Flower, The Wolf and the Dove*

Cynthia Wright, *Caroline, Touch the Sun*

Contemporary Romances

Janet Dailey, *Touch the Wind, Ride the Thunder*, Calder Series

Carolyn Fireside, *Anything but Love*

Judith Krantz, *Mistral's Daughter*

Esther Sager, *Only 'Til Dawn*

Danielle Steel, *The Ring, The Promise*

Charlotte Vale Allen

Helen Van Slyke

Regency Romances

Joan Aiken

Diana Brown

Marion Chesney (a.k.a. Jennie Tremaine, Ann Fairfax, Helen Crampton)

Catherine Coulter

Megan Daniel

Claire Darcy

Georgette Heyer

Elsie Lee

Elizabeth Mansfield

Janet Louise Roberts (a.k.a. Janette Radcliff, Rebecca Danton)

Joan Smith

Patricia Veryan

Joan Wolf

Romantic Suspense

Isabelle Holland

Victoria Holt

Elsie Lee

Barbara Michaels (a.k.a. Elizabeth Peters)

Mary Stewart

Phyllis A. Whitney

Science Fiction and Fantasy

Jean Auel

Carole Nelson Douglas

Anne McCaffrey

Read for enjoyment and recognition of writing style, not to copy. Otherwise, you end up a bad imitation of Janet Dailey that no one will like. *Read—but don't copy.*

Classification of Romance Novels

Category Romances

Short, contemporary novels.

These follow the "romance formula," a set of rules also known as the "Cinderella legend." They are the hottest thing in publishing, and several publishing houses print more than one line of category romances.

The category romance rules (in brief): female meets devastating man, sparks fly, lovers meld, lovers are torn apart, get back together, resolve their problems, and commit themselves, usually to marriage. The heroine is the reader's eyes, ears, and heart. Very simple to follow; very tricky to write.

Publishers print two lengths, the very short 192-page books (60,000-word manuscripts) and approximately 256-page books (80,000-word manuscripts).

Category romance falls into the sensual mode, but even at its most steamy a romance is never soft-core pornography. A romance is sex with commitment, pornography is sex without commitment.

Pseudonyms are usual. Many publishers require an author to take up a new or prettier pen name, particularly if she or he writes for more than one publisher.

Historical Romances

Medium-length or long novels (set in any period prior to World War I).

Emphasis is on romance, not history ("sex in hoop skirts"). Good storytelling is the main requirement, providing adventure, excitement, and titillation.

The historical romance rules (in brief): accurate historical research, erotic sex scenes, one woman/one man or one woman/many men relationships, and usually a happy ending. Readers' protests about rape scenes have cut back on the violence in "bodice rippers."

Contemporary Romances

Medium-length problem solvers.

These are in a contemporary setting with modern and realistic characters. The romance rules may or may not be applied. Sentimentality is evoked; readers may shed a tear. The emphasis is on the woman's emotional and romantic experiences.

Danielle Steel, one of the most successful contemporary romance novelists today, varies her storytelling, but usually follows this specific formula: woman meets man, man dies, woman meets another man, and he may die too. Patricia Matthews favors this formula: woman meets two men, one a charmer and one a rogue, she falls for the first but ends up with the second when he shows redeeming qualities. Contemporary authors have a leeway of subject matter and number of pages not available to category romance writers.

Regency Romances

Short and medium-length novels of manners; witty, light.

Set during the Regency period in England (1811–20), a time of affluence and elegance. They capture the flavor of a Jane Austen novel, and emphasize the repartee between the hero and heroine, rather than a sexual relationship.

The Regency romance rules (in brief): similar in form to the category romance except for the absence of sexuality, the addition of history, and a real literary style. A few authors have recently added sex to their plots, but this is not the norm. A Regency heroine is pure until her wedding day, unless she's a widow. A thorough reading of Georgette Heyer's Regencies and the histories of the Regency period should be followed.

Regency novels are not being published in as great numbers as in the past. St. Martin's Press, Walker and Co. (hardcover), and NAL/Signet, Avon, Berkley/Jove, and Ballantine still print original stories.

Romantic Suspense/Gothic

Medium-length novel.

A romantic suspense novel is always a mystery, full of action, intertwined with romance, and the background is contemporary.

A gothic follows the *Jane Eyre* plot, often implies the occult, and has elements of terror: gloomy mansion, creaking staircases, and a light in the attic, plus an eerie setting, such as the north coast of England in an earlier period.

For a time these romance novels, with the exception of those

Why Pseudonyms?

In some cases an author has several writing styles. She may opt for one name for her historicals and another for contemporary romances. Many publishers feel that men's names and unromantic-sounding women's names don't look fetching on a book cover. Therefore, Tom E. Huff writes as Jennifer Wilde and Rhoda Cohen writes as Eleanora Brownleigh. Many authors share the feeling that a romantic name is enticing and invent pen names such as Rosalind Foxx, Vanessa Royale, and Fern Michaels. Last but extremely important is the fact that many publishers want to "own" their author's name, especially when they have launched and developed the author. They don't want to risk losing it to another company if the author changes publishers. This safeguarding is completely understandable, as books are business.

written by Victoria Holt or Phyllis A. Whitney, were not in demand at all, but new authors are being developed for series.

Science Fiction and Fantasy

Medium-length novel.

It is doubtful that the avid romance fan will become addicted to the entire science-fiction world, but she is buying romances about intriguing heroes who could come from this milieu. Making love in a space ship or a mountain resort hotel on the moon will be possibilities in future novels.

Office of the Editor
Bantam Loveswept Romances
New York

April 23

Dear Rosie,
When Kathryn told me you were interested in writing a romance

and that she's trying to help you, I was intrigued, and I thought I'd throw in some of my own advice—I'm always looking for promising new writers.

Read! Read! Read! When a book strikes you as simply wonderful, go back to it and read it again. But this time read it analytically, figure out what the author did—exactly—to excite you, to make you respond to the story she wrote. Take notes. Try to see how you can use the techniques you discovered in that book in your special way.

Another word of advice is to learn everything you can about every line of romances—and submit your manuscript to the right line! Each line has a "personality" beyond its guidelines. You should make your book match that personality.

I love 60,000-word category romances because they demand the most exquisite discipline on the part of the writer. The so-called formula isn't restrictive, it's a framework. And the craft of writing one of these novels is very important. Why do editors harp on point of view? Because you only have 60,000 words for a very small canvas on which to work, so you must use a number of techniques that

---

Finding the Word Count

WANTED: 75,000-Word Manuscript

In the romance field you will always hear that one romance line wants 60,000-word or 80,000-word manuscripts.

One method of figuring the approximate number of manuscript pages is to count the words you type double-spaced on a page, then divide the number into the requested word length and come up with the required manuscript pages you will hand in.

A 75,000-word manuscript is approximately 300 double-spaced manuscript pages. If your average page is filled with approximately 250 words:

75,000 words ÷ 250 words per page = 300 pages

For 10 lines, count characters on a line and get an average. Skip chapter breaks; multiply the average number of characters by the number of lines on a page. Multiply this figure by the number of pages in the book and divide by 6 (which is the average number of characters in an English word).

make the work strong, forceful, and coherent. In that respect, it's very much like the craft of short story writing, with the telling detail. You paint pictures.

You don't have room to thoroughly background, so you must do it very deftly, and this demands a high level of skill. The best romance writers are truly excellent writers, with a great deal to be proud of. They can tell a rich and passionate story in a short, and dramatic way.

I'm looking for writers who can move the emotions of the readers to the point of laughter or tears or both. And the stories should be very sensual and exciting.

Viva romance novels! Hope to see your manuscript one day.

Regards,
Carolyn Nichols

Maryland Avenue
Royal Oak, Michigan

May 1

Dear Kathryn:

Wow! My mind is steaming.

It was so wonderful to hear from a real editor. Thank her for me. And thank you for the reading lists. My husband is wondering why I'm particularly passionate these days (and nights), and it's due to my reading of Ecstasy, Desire, and Rapture. He recommends a lot of cold showers until he gets home. (Little does he know I'm secretly modeling my hero after him!)

I wish I could bring characters to life like Janet Dailey, write sex like Sandra Brown and Alice Morgan, invent situations like Elaine Raco Chase, and live like Danielle Steel! Do you think I ever can?

Our local book stores are humming with women customers grabbing up the category romances by the handful. They are obviously the market for future writers and I see that I wouldn't have as many pages to fill or as much history to research if I could write a short contemporary tale myself. I like all the types of romances though, and would appreciate your making a suggestion on which type I should write and how to get started.

Still respectfully
and very hopeful . . .
Rosie

From the Desk of Kathryn Falk

May 9

Dear Rosie:

You've obviously hit the nail on the head with the observation that category romance research is minimal compared to that necessary for a historical romance. Also, there's much less work when a new writer tackles writing 60,000 words versus 120,000 words.

If you do like reading category romances, by all means concentrate on their form as your first project. You should always write what you enjoy reading. (However, if you're still hung up on <u>Gone With the Wind</u>, then start thinking about which period of history you want as the setting.)

Writing category romance is a wonderful discipline that will help you even if your ultimate goal is to write a historical romance. I suggest it for a beginning writer, and an approximate 250-page manuscript isn't too overwhelming. Think of it this way—if you write one page a day, you'll be finished before the year is out.

I've enclosed the latest publishing report on category romances and a publisher's directory. Most of the category romance lines have a free writer's tip sheet available. Send a SASE (self-addressed stamped envelope) to the publisher you want to write for. In addition, I've included two sample tip sheets to give you the idea.

Don't let them frighten you, they're just guidelines so you won't stray from their requirements. You should begin studying your favorite romances, with the publishers' tip sheets beside the book.

Keep this in mind, category romances are first and foremost a female's first awakening. You will be recording "first love."

It helps to keep feeling romantic as you develop your writing skills. Sharpen all your sensual feelings. You might want to try this on your next dinner or breakfast tray. Take the crusts off thin white toast and cut out a heart with a cookie cutter. It's great with caviar at night or jam in the a.m. (One of Danielle Steel's fondest recipes, since she doesn't cook.)

Best wishes,
Kathryn

Category Romance Lines (Published Monthly)

Adult

HARLEQUIN

Romance (6)
Presents (8)
Superromance (4)
American Romance (4)
Temptation (4)

SILHOUETTE

Romance (6)
Special Edition (6)
Desire (6)
Intimate Moments (4)
Inspiration (2)

CANDLELIGHT ECSTASY

Romance (8)
Ecstasy Supreme (4)

BERKLEY/JOVE

Second Chance at Love (6)
To Have and To Hold (3)

NAL

Rapture (6)

AVON

Velvet Glove (1)

BANTAM

Loveswept (4)

Total
82

From England

MILLS & BOON

Romance (16)

Teen

SCHOLASTIC

Wildfire (1)
Windswept (1)

SILHOUETTE

First Love (3)

BANTAM

Sweet Dreams (3)

Total 8

Historical Series

POCKET BOOKS

Tapestry Romances (2)

NAL

Scarlet Ribbons (1)

Total 3

Types of Category Romances

The current series of category romance are becoming more confined to two kinds of stories:

1. Fun, light, charming, and sensuous.
2. Hot, steamy, and perhaps issue-oriented.

A more exact breakdown is impossible because changes constantly occur.

Two considerations are certain: (A) Sex is either (1) *virginal or sweet,* (2) *spicy* (some sensual action above the waist), or (3) *steamy* (no holds barred, sexually). (B) Manuscript lengths are either (1) *short,* 50,000–60,000 words (around 200–225 typed manuscript pages), or (2) *longer,* 70,000–100,000 words (250–300 manuscript pages).

Here is a very general look at the current types of romances. Lines may subtly change from season to season regarding plot points or word lengths. To be prepared, keep abreast of the market and get the most current tip sheets.

Short Category Romances (50,000–60,000 words)

Candlelight Ecstasy—
    steamy
Harlequin Presents—spicy
Harlequin Romances—
    sweet
Loveswept—sensual
    and/or steamy

Rapture—spicy or steamy
Second Chance at Love—
    spicy or steamy
Silhouette Desire—steamy
Silhouette Romance—sweet

Longer Category Romances (70,000–100,000 words)

Harlequin American
    Romance—sensual,
    mainstream fiction
Harlequin Temptation—
    steamy
Silhouette Special Edition—
    spicy or sensual, issue-
    oriented

Silhouette Intimate Moments
    —steamy
Superromance—spicy

Category Romance Print Run

A new writer should understand that it is good business to know the print run of each publishing company. At this time, Harlequin prints the largest number of romances (200 million worldwide every year). They have foreign editors who translate the manuscripts into some eighteen languages. A Harlequin author will make the most money in royalties because of the publisher's book club and worldwide distribution.

Silhouette is the second biggest publisher, and their book club is growing along with their sales. They print between 300,000 and 450,000 copies of each title and have foreign sales. Candlelight Ecstasy is up to a 300,000 print run.

The rest of the romance lines are currently averaging 200,000 copies per title. The teenage lines are approximately 90,000.

The above figures may grow in the months ahead. Publishers do not reveal returns (except on your royalty statement), and you are paid only on the number of sales. Returns may be as high as 50 percent.

Publishers' Directory

This publishers' directory lists the current senior editor of each line but is subject to change. (Check to verify before submitting a manuscript.) The editor's name is important for the day that you're ready to send in your query letter, synopsis, and/or manuscript. Directing it to an editor's attention may prevent it from getting shuffled about on other desks.

Many manuscripts are rejected because they don't conform to the guidelines or the word count. Publishers don't have the time or money to revise manuscripts, no matter how well written your story may be. If you haven't understood that the line prefers older heroes and experienced women, the editor probably won't buy your virginal heroine even if you are a potential Janet Dailey or a Danielle Steel *wunderkind*.

Publishers' Tip Sheets

Category romance publishers print writers' tip sheets that explain the general editorial requirements. You should read several books from each line to know which suits your style of writing.

To obtain one, send a self-addressed stamped envelope to the publisher (see listing that follows).

Candlelight Ecstasy
Dell
1 Dag Hammarskjold Plaza
New York, NY 10017
(Anne Gisonny)

Harlequin American Romance
919 Third Avenue
New York, NY 10022
(Hilary Cohen)

**Harlequin Presents and
  Harlequin Romance**
Mills & Boon
15-16 Brook's Mews
London W1A 1DR
England
(Jacqui Bianchi)

Harlequin Superromance
Harlequin
225 Duncan Mill Road
Don Mills, Ontario, Canada
M3B 3K9
(Star Helmer)

Harlequin Temptation
Harlequin
225 Duncan Mill Road
Don Mills, Ontario, Canada
M3B 3K9
(Margaret Carney)

Loveswept
Bantam
666 Fifth Avenue
New York, NY 10103
(Carolyn Nichols)

Rapture Romance
NAL
1633 Broadway
New York, NY 10019
(Mary Anne Gartland)

Second Chance at Love
Jove Books
200 Madison Avenue
New York, NY 10016
(Ellen Edwards)

Silhouette (all lines)
1230 Avenue of the Americas
New York, NY 10020
(Alicia Condon)

Torch Magazine
8353 A Greensboro Drive
McLean, VA 22102
(Elizabeth Brandon-Brown)

Velvet Glove
Avon
Packager: Denise Marcil
316 West 82nd Street
New York, NY 10024

Examples of Tip Sheets

Mills & Boon/Harlequin

A FINE ROMANCE . . . is hard to find!

EDITOR seeks manuscripts for publication in women's category romance market. Manuscripts should be between

50–60,000 words long and concerned with the development of true love (with view to marriage) between lady, 17–28, and gentleman, 30–45 (must be rich and/or powerful). Exotic location preferred, happy ending essential. Applications in writing to *Jacqui Bianchi, Editorial Director, Romance Fiction, Mills & Boon Ltd., 15-16 Brook's Mews, London W1A 1DR, England.*

If only it were as easy as that! Every Harlequin reader and very aspiring Harlequin writer has a very clear picture of what makes our books so successful; some people have even tried to educe it to a formula which, in its essentials, would look very like the fake ad above. But in order to keep up the high reputation which rests at the core of Harlequin's success we have to be lot tougher than that.

We believe that the so-called formula is only the beginning, and that originality, imagination and individuality are the most important qualities in a romance writer. Any competent novelist an follow a detailed recipe for success, but we want writers who have the sort of star quality that makes their books instantly recognizable as *theirs*. The Mills & Boon editorial office, which originates every HARLEQUIN ROMANCE and every HARLEQUIN PRESENTS, receives nearly 4,000 manuscripts for consideration every year from aspiring authors. If a dozen new authors are selected for publication in that time, we reckon we are having a bumper year!

In a very short space of time, the world of romantic fiction has grown into a big business, and it's not easy to stay businesslike and romantic. However, we still believe that quality is more important than quantity—that romance readers deserve the best we can find. A book that simply "makes the right noises" will not make a Harlequin.

What do we look for when we read a manuscript for the first time? Many would-be authors have tried to find exactly the right note, but have had to admit defeat in the end. Surprisingly, we don't worry too much about flawless presentation; a book that has been written with genuine feeling can be forgiven a few typing mistakes. What is more important is a genuine love of storytelling, combined with a freshness and originality of approach. Sincerity, and belief in the characters as real people, communicate themselves to the reader; if a writer is less concerned about conveying her heroine's innermost thoughts, so that the reader

understands and sympathizes, than making sure the hero fi
kisses her on page 18 as laid down by the tip-sheet, that preoccu
pation will show up on the page. Similarly, although imitation
the sincerest form of flattery, we don't want new authors who
work echoes the style of our readers' current favorites. Each
our authors must possess an individual touch, her own particul
way of telling a story, and this quality is vital. The great artist
not simply someone who can paint a human figure with the rig
number of arms and legs, and the great musician does more tha
hit the correct notes in the correct order! In the same way, it
what a romance writer creates with her material that makes h
special (and successful); a good book is not simply a questio
of constructing a plot with a hero, a heroine, two quarrels and
happy ending, and spinning it out for 200 pages.

The story doesn't necessarily have to be complicated—in fac
a simple tale introducing only a few characters besides the her
and heroine is often very successful. Make sure, however, th
the characters are convincing in both their actions and the
words. If the hero is meant to be a man of authority, used
being obeyed, he should be shown as such and the other charac
ters should react to him accordingly. With such clues of behavio
too, it is not always necessary to state bald facts; you can affor
to keep the reader guessing by stimulating his/her imagination
For instance, if you include a scene in which the heroine quarrel
violently with someone, there is then no need to state that sh
has an unpredictable temper! If such behavior is unusual, th
reason for it (nervous strain, a headache, a feeling of apprehension
immediately gives the reader a deeper understanding of th
heroine's character, and one that has been arrived at by guesswork
the reader who guesses about a character in a book is an inter
ested reader.

In general, the dialogue should be completely unstilted.
would-be writer should be aware all the time of everyday pat
terns of speech, and should try to make the characters as true t
life as possible.

Equally important is the background against which the princi
pal characters are set. It is vital that this should be as accurate a
research allows, although there is no substitute for an author'
personal knowledge of a particular background. All Harlequi
authors spend a good deal of time checking the material used i
their books, because they realize how quickly the recognition o
a fault or inaccuracy can spoil the reader's enjoyment of a scene

This care should be extended to small details, as well as the more obvious points such as foreign locations and customs; if, for instance, a would-be writer has no idea about office life, it is a mistake to make the heroine a secretary! A working knowledge of the practical details is essential at such points. All this may sound like obvious common sense, but it is surprising how often the obvious is ignored!

When attempting at Harlequin novel, concentrate on writing a good book rather than a saleable proposition. A good book sells itself and is good indefinitely, while a "saleable proposition" tends to be based on what is saleable *at the time of writing*—even if a publisher snaps it up, the world will have moved on by at least nine months by the time it finally appears. Think of what you, as a reader, would like to read, rather than what you think an editor will buy—the one will lead to the other if all goes well.

A Harlequin has a standard length of about 192 printed pages—between 50,000 and 60,000 words. From a purely practical angle, any manuscript which differs so greatly that its author cannot reduce or expand its size to fit this requirement is unsuitable. The most important consideration in accepting or rejecting a manuscript is, however, whether the story lives up to the high standard that Harlequin readers have set for us. We know from their letters what they like and dislike about our books, and their opinions matter to us. Maybe we can't please every one of our readers all the time, but it isn't for want of trying!

Rapture Romance

Rapture Romance is a line of 55,000-word contemporary romances aimed at the reader who wants more romance, more passion, more sensuous and sensual detail than is found in traditional romances. It will feature provocative situations that explore any of the possibilities that exist when today's men and women fall in love. The heroine and hero will become intimately and intensely involved early in the plot and will make love several times throughout the course of the romance, and each passionate kiss, each tender caress, each earth-shattering climax will be described at length, in lavish, specific (though not clinical) detail. The plots will be sophisticated and modern, but they must remain wonderful fantasies with no grim or tragic elements and no elements of mystery or suspense.

Of course, although more emphasis, and therefore space, is

taken up by the physical expression of the hero's and heroine['s]
love and desire, the most important element is still the lo[ve]
story. The relationship must develop in a believable way, pr[o]
ceeding logically from first encounter to first kiss to love-makin[g]
we do not expect the hero and heroine to jump into bed t[he]
minute they meet, and careful thought should be devoted [to]
setting up a situation in which rapid intimacy is plausible. T[he]
plot of a Rapture Romance should be believable in terms [of]
today's lifestyles, and we expect the problems that come b[e]
tween the hero and heroine to be of the kind that occur betwe[en]
adults with well-defined opinions, ambitions and morals, and t[he]
misunderstandings to have supporting evidence that couldn't [be]
set aside simply by asking the loved one a few questions. An[d]
when all conflicts are resolved, the solution arrived at will be a[n]
equal compromise, or a change of mind based on new information–
for example the discovery of true love would make a hero wh[o]
doesn't want to be tied down propose, most likely to a heroin[e]
who can accompany him on his expeditions into uncharted jungle[s]
Needless to say, while the heroine and hero may or may n[ot]
continue to make love while misunderstandings and conflic[ts]
remain unresolved, when they are ready to admit that they lov[e]
one another, and believe in each other's love, they will agre[e]
to marry (or if separated, renew their vows).

The heroine will be youthful, but will have a sense of maturit[y]
that manifests itself in her dedication and goals. She will b[e]
attractive, but not necessarily ravishing, and she does not dwe[ll]
despairingly on her looks. If she is indeed ravishing, she know[s]
it and enjoys it as she would any other natural gift, and if merel[y]
attractive, takes pride in her good points (thick, shiny hair, fi[rm]
and athletic body), and makes the most of herself, then forget[s]
her appearance—other things are more important. She is capabl[e]
and resourceful, but never strident and domineering, and coul[d]
conceivably be shy or of quiet nature. She will not be a timi[d]
shrinking violet or bumbler who has to be rescued constantly
although the hero can smooth over a rough moment for her, a[s]
the heroine will do for him. We wouldn't, for instance, b[e]
surprised to see the heroine's knowledge of first aid used to hel[p]
the hero when he sprains an ankle. However, she may at times
be overconfident, and certainly she should be able to laugh a[t]
herself or admit to a mistake. Finally, it is important that the
heroine not be simply a passive object of the hero's attentions o[r]

he plot's twists, but contribute actively to the plot's development. The heroine is always American.

The hero is older, not necessarily fabulously wealthy, but uccessful at what he does. He is attractive in a masculine way vith an athletic but not muscle-bound build. Although strong-willed and determined, he is not a bully and can, when necessary, be gentle and supportive. He not only loves the heroine for her beauty and desirability but respects her abilities. In fact, he comes to realize that he would be unhappy with a weaker, less-accomplished woman. This respect may come grudgingly. The hero may or may not be American.

Since the emphasis in Rapture Romance will now be placed heavily on the physical expression of love, it is important that each love scene (and a love scene can be something as simple as the look two people exchange, the unexpected electricity that flares between strangers, a quiet moment of unspoken sharing) be an integral part of the plot development and contribute something new to the relationship, that it have its own mood. Foreplay and afterplay, with descriptions of what the heroine thinks and feels, what the hero says and does, before, during and after making love can provide this, as can a change in setting (i.e., outside in the afternoon rather than in the bedroom at night); a switch in the seducer/seducee roles; a change in the level of experience or attitude of one of the participants: an infinite number of distinctions can be made. And the love scenes should be described in full and lavish, though not clinical, moment by moment detail. We don't want to know that he is handsome, we want to know that he has cripsy curling black hair with just a touch of gray at the temples. We don't want to know that the moonlit night was romantic, we want to know that the sky was a dark velvet canopy over their heads, and as they walked barefoot at the edge of the ocean the cool water tickled their bare feet and the rush and roar of the ocean seemed to echo their own heartbeats. We don't want to know that his touch aroused her, we want to know that the rough feel of his callused fingertips as he wonderingly explored the outline of her face with featherlike caresses set her trembling as no arrogant and inescapable embrace could have. It is important that the reader at all times feel the strong mutual desire of the hero and heroine, their constant awareness of, and fascination with, each other.

Of course, physical attraction is not the only thing that brings the heroine and hero together. We should see, not be told about,

the reasons why these two people are unique, and uniquel●
suited to one another—in short, they not merely desire, but lov●
each other. There should be little if any reliance on alcohol as ●
reducer of inhibitions—though we have seen emotional crise●
which worked well for that purpose—and *no* rape or coercion●
These are normal, healthy adults who love each other and kno●
what they want. When appropriate, their relationship may als●
include a sense of fun—gentle teasing, mock wrestling matches●
etc. However, this does not preclude the darker side of passion●
as long as it does not become abusive.

Finally, the important thing to keep in mind about writing ●
Rapture Romance is that you should enjoy creating it. Write●
about things you know, things that interest you, things you find
romantic, and men you could fall in love with. The little details
will make the story rich and more real than any formula story.
Do not try to copy other people's plots or characters, but, while
keeping in mind our general rules, make your story unique. If
the characters live in your imagination, and the story touches
you, your sincerity will show to an overworked editor or a reader
bombarded with choices!

We look forward to hearing from you—for further information
contact:

> Editor
> *Rapture Romance*
> New American Library
> 1633 Broadway
> New York, NY 10019

Maryland Avenue
Royal Oak, Michigan

June 21

Dear Kathryn,

The tip sheets I requested from the publishers came back pretty
speedily. In the meantime, I've read six new Silhouettes and
Loveswepts, eight different Second Chances and Harlequins, fourteen
Ecstasies and Desires, and two Raptures. (It's not possible to
overdose on love!)

I realize that not all the romance writers are studying the Kamasutra
and writing about it. I also like the "sweet" style—especially books
by Mary Burchell and Violet Winspear. They're good writers. I wonder

I'm going to have some trouble writing "steamy" sensuality? (I'll face that decision later.)

I really understand the wild popularity of these new romances. I get a wonderful "rush" from them! I keep reminding myself that I should be studying them, not enjoying them.

The tip sheets are a little overwhelming. I've gotten a writing lesson already just by reading them.

I'm itching to get going. Paul is lending me his electric typewriter, and since I took two semesters of typing in high school, I'm ready!

I don't want to get off on the wrong foot. What should I do next?

Eagerly,
Rosie

P.S. I'm writing this at midnight. The kids are asleep and Paul is watching Johnny Carson. I tried the heart-shaped-toast bit—with Spam—I'll forgo caviar until I'm as rich from writing as Danielle Steel (I'm not holding my breath).

From the Desk of Kathryn Falk

July 1

Dear Rosie,

Forget about Paul's typewriter for the moment, you've got a long way to go . . .

To begin with, honestly, the publishers' tip sheets are not hard and fast rules "taught to the tune of the hickory stick," as the old song went. They are guidelines so you won't choose a virgin as a heroine for a romance line that wants experienced women.

Although you're rarin' to get going, I'd like you to stop and do some additional thinking about what you're getting into—a craft. And if you're really good, an art form.

I correspond with several editors and authors who are concerned that new writers are not sufficiently aware of the literary responsibilities they should be facing. One of the top English romance writers, Violet Winspear, believes in maintaining true tenderness in category romances. What she says should be taken to heart for perfecting skills.

And finally, I don't think any new writer to the field could be better encouraged than by talking to the editor of Mills & Boon/Harlequin Romances. Of course, this is not feasible, as Jacqui Bianchi is far too busy, but enclosed is the next best thing—an interview with her.

Enjoy!
Kathryn

Romance Writer's Creed

1. *Be true to your feelings.*
2. *Write only your overwhelming emotions.*
3. *Write all that you have to give—intelligence, memories, sensibilities, innermost feelings, talent.*
4. *Remember, this is an art form and a craft.*
5. *Express yourself in a controlled way and tap your basic bedrock of human emotion.*
6. *Only by expressing your personality and talent will you write a good book.*

What Every New Romance Author Should Know

AN INTERVIEW WITH JACQUI BIANCHI

Mills & Boon/Harlequin Editor

Miss Bianchi, I've read many of your romances, and I would like to begin a career of writing them. What advice do you have to give someone in my position?

First you have to believe in the values that you're writing about. If you don't fall in love with your hero, then nobody else will. And if you don't passionately desire a happy ending to your

story, then nobody else is going to care what happens to your
characters.

The start of every story is the characters themselves. And you
have to visualize them so clearly that they become independent
people—it can be like having a baby. Quite often the characters
will begin to behave in a way you never imagined, if the book is
working.

Always remember that the heroine is your reader's eyes, ears,
perceptions, and her heart. Center your whole story on how she
feels and how she is affected by everything around her. And
that includes the plot, the setting, and, most importantly, the
hero.

What exactly in your opinion is a romance novel?

A romance novel is a love story. It concerns two people who are
drawn out of their normal existence into a totally new life
because of the power of their feelings for each other. That
newness is often reflected in a writer's choice of an exotic
setting, or glamorous trimmings. But it is the power of emotion,
and the universally recognizable sensation of falling in love, that
give the books their strength and appeal.

Is there a philosophy behind romantic writing?

The romance writer's creed is the same as that of every worthwhile writer in literary history: writing as well as she can. There
are many tricks to the trade and you're fortunate that there are
many tip sheets and guidelines and people who will give you
advice about the forms of the romance books. But there's no
substitute for sincerely felt high-quality writing. If you have
talent, and are willing to put everything into a story that you'd
like to get out of it as a reader, then you are more likely to
succeed than somebody who follows all the tips with no other
emotions than the desire for hard cash.

Whatever the line you choose to follow, whether it's a category romance, historical, or gentle romantic, or the more realistic passionate books of the current climate, never forget that
you're writing about love—about its beauty, its force, and all the
facts of its expression. How you choose to convey these things
will be part of your personality as a writer. But, whatever you
do, don't copy other writers' phrases and expect them to work as
well for the second time. It's originality and the uniqueness of

your use of langauge that will make your style instantly recognizable to romantic readers.

How do you see the evolution of romantic novels through the years?

Well, we've been publishing romance novels since 1909 (*Arrow in the Heart* by Sophie Cole was the first). And what is very clear is that public taste is a pendulum that swings between sweet romance and explicit passion. With that experience, we would never advise a writer to go so far in one direction that she loses touch with the mainstream. We choose writers with strong personalities in order to spread our net as widely as we can and capture the readers who are fond of both extremes, so that if we can't please all the people all the time, we will please all the people some of the time. We think it's better than pleasing some of the people all the time.

At the moment we are at the extreme point of a phase of permissiveness in romantic writing, and some not-so-good writers are using titillation in place of craftsmanship to sell their books. I'm sure you'd never do that!

I can't press too strongly that you should write as you feel, and presentation and technique can be taught or supplied by a good editor. But the gift of storytelling and the ability to hook a reader's interest is God-given. And it's the one thing we cannot teach anybody. Occasionally a writer can learn it by herself, but as an editor I can only cross my fingers and agonize along with her.

You make writing these books sound very hard, but they seem easy enough to read, almost simple.

That's because you haven't written your first one yet. I think that to be simple is the most complicated thing in the world. You spot a mistake in a Japanese flower arrangement sooner than you will in a whole greenhouse. Our books are embodiments of the dream and fantasy of three generations of readers. And that's a pretty big responsibility, so they've got to be good.

The Meaning of Romance:
Notes on the Writing of the Romantic Novel

BY VIOLET WINSPEAR

author of sixty-six category romances

The romantic novel is a form of entertainment that has its roots firmly in the nineteenth century. It was brought into prominence by writers such as the Brontë sisters, and every aspiring romanticist should make the effort to read *Jane Eyre* and *Wuthering Heights* and absorb their brooding passion and atmosphere. Both novels are supreme examples of the genre; both heroes love with an intensity beyond the merely sexual. There are scenes in which the reader can almost hear the walls of their hearts breaking.

There have also been films that have explored romance in a way we no longer see in the cinema. *The Seventh Veil* was pure romance, with James Mason interpreting perfectly the smoldering passion beneath the cold surface: a man afraid to reveal his love until that love broke free of its own accord and swept the heroine into his arms.

To be the center of another person's existence is the perfect dream, and the romantic novel sets out to provide this dreamlike experience. The reader is no fool. She has the security of husband, lover, or career, but deep in most feminine (and masculine) hearts there is this dream of being loved until the end of time, with a great and caring passion that never falters.

What woman hasn't dreamed of being wanted as Rhett wanted Scarlett? What woman wouldn't want to stand on a tarmac and have Rick say to her, "Here's looking at you, kid"? Who did not sigh at the finale of *Casablanca* and wish to be loved so gallantly?

The English definition of the word *romance* is a tale, written in the popular tongue, celebrating the exploits of love (or war) of a chivalrous hero. A tale of feeling, of moral atmosphere; of the marvelous, mysterious, picturesque, and fanciful.

Romance does *not* apply to loveless, heartless sex. Romance resides in the heart, and to deny its existence is to deny one's humanity. If writers cease to write of love from the heart, without sincere respect for their hero and heroine, then "love" will become so diminished that it will be no more than a form of pornography.

Sex is easy to obtain, and we all know it. Love is the hardest thing in the world to win. It's the glittering prize. Love includes the act of love, but let it be the tender, laughing, heartfelt secret of two people in love. I define love as a secret society with just two members.

When we grieve, we do so from the heart. When we laugh with a lover, the heart is as pleased as the head. When we see that certain other person come toward us, the heart seems to fill the chest, and even when it's raining, the sun is shining.

So when you sit down to write your romantic novel, let the heart rule you. Don't be ashamed of sentiment, and shout hooray when you feel moved by what you have written, because if *you* are moved, then the reader will react in the same way. The fact of the matter is that the reader picks up on sincerity very quickly. It's like a friend who welcomes her with open arms.

It seems to have become the fashion to deride writers of romance who, like myself, draw a veil over the lovemaking. I do this because I have respect for my hero and his girl; I feel they are entitled to their privacy when they want to be alone to express their love. I won't provide a peephole for the reader to peer through, but I will leave the reader the means by which she can use her imagination.

If you pour a power of feeling into your story, then it will come alive of its own and there will be no need to fill up the pages by resorting to the easy ploy of describing sexual activity. Enough of that and the book is soon written . . . if you can call it a book! I call such books sex manuals. I call such writers love cheats.

They are cheating the readers out of the suspense and conflict of a real love story. They are palming off on the readers a sexual lollipop, and it leaves a sickly aftertaste in the mouth.

Jane Eyre is one of the most passionate of romantic novels; it throbs with the sensuality of a woman's growing love for a man; there is the deep longing of the lonely heart in its every line.

In all the true heroes and heroines of romance, there is a loneliness that speaks for all of us. There is this reaching out for love . . . for just one person in the world to love with every beat of the heart, so that even the act of holding hands is more rich and full than a dozen acts of sex *sans* love.

In writing my books, I've chosen to respect this need in the man and the woman I am writing about, and so they in turn have allowed me into their world and have shown me how to represent them to the reader—in the way they meet, in the way they come into conflict, in the way they reveal their love in the finale of the book.

Thus the meeting of Marny and Paul in *House of Strangers:*

Her jockey cap was poised jauntily over one eye, but she wasn't being given much chance to exhibit herself in it, for a group of very much larger people were jostling her toward the nearest exit and she had to battle her way clear of them. In the process she got herself entangled with a couple of bowler-hatted office types who were ready to be a bit too friendly, and then with a woman pulling a dog on a lead, neither of whom had the friendly dispositions of the two office types. Finally a careless arm knocked her jockey cap clean off her head.

"I never did!" Her green eyes flashed with exasperation. She made a dive for her cap, but a slender masculine hand was there before her and scooping it off the ground.

"A green and black jockey cap and red hair," drawled a slightly grating voice, and Marny found herself gazing into a pair of amused gray eyes—very light, almost silvery eyes, set in a face which immediately struck her as being at once hard and yet humorous; attractive and yet ugly.

"You're Marny Lester without a doubt," he said, and he plonked her cap on her head and imperiously swung her suitcase out of her hand.

"Just one moment!" Marny hung on the handles of her case. "Are you from the Stillman Clinic?"

"Very much so." His lips twitched amusedly. "I'm Paul Stillman."

"Oh!"

"Oh?" He mimicked her startled expression rather unkindly. "What were you expecting, someone creaking with distinction and frosty at the temples?"

Thus in the conclusion of *The Strange Waif*:

He drew back from her a little and she saw that he was biting his lip. "I've almost got the courage in this moment to let you go," he said.

"No!" In sudden fear that he would do this, she crept close to him and he felt her tremble. "Don't put me out in the cold! Don't condemn both of us to any more loneliness —please!"

The whispered, pleading words broke him and the giving in to her was wild and sweet and complete. He held her in silence, against his heart, and the rowan tree waved its feathery foliage in the fresh clean wind off the moors.

"It was meant to be, wasn't it, Lygia?" Robert said at last. "We could never have forgotten one another if I had found the courage to walk away from you. Your funny little face would always have haunted me, and I'd have died each night, wanting you in my arms. I'm not a solitary man at heart."

It's important to establish the characters in that very first meeting; their impact upon each other must also affect the reader. The girl and the man must be people whom the reader can *like*, for when the story foundation is established she will become part of the conflict and drama and will be drawn along with them. But in no way is it necessary to make the girl too sweet, or the man too nice; a dash of spice and vinegar does for the relationship what it does for a good salad.

Thus in the meeting in which Sabrina falls for the eponymous Black Douglas:

Eyes wide and startled she faced the man who was to be her patient . . . he was dark, almost swarthy, and taller than Ret, with shoulders in proportion to his height. He wore a smoking-jacket with a spill of ash on the velvet, and his black hair was untidy above his dense black brows.

Black Douglas . . . his left hand gripping tensely the handle of the white walking-stick.

Realization struck at Sabrina like a blow. The eyes that seemed to look right through her, cutting her to the core with their cold brilliance, were the sightless eyes of a blind man. Douglas Sanit-Sarne sensed her standing there but he could not see her. The nostrils of his rather imperious nose twitched slightly, as if he breathed the delicate perfume she was wearing. His powerful, almost noble head reared back slightly, like a stallion in blinkers.

"Ret?" The voice was deep, stern, cultured. "You have arrived back from the harbor with my latest Nightingale?"

"Yes, the nurse is with me."

"Does she speak?" queried the man, who could not have been much older than Ret yet who looked as if suffering had matured him. Deep lines grooved his face. He was sardonic, harsh with the world he could no longer see.

"It would be a trifle confusing for a blind man to be led about by a nurse without a voice," he added in his sardonic drawl.

A dash of mystery also adds to the romance, as in *The Loved and the Feared:*

He was wearing a black domino which added a kind of menace to his face and she recognized him instantly, but this time he wasn't going to permit her to get away from him so easily. His fingers caught her by the wrist and she felt the strength in them. "Come, you may not know the music they are playing, but they play it tonight in memory of a certain famous Italian who long ago went to America and became the embodiment of every woman's secret dream."

The lean fingers took hold of the silver mask and Donna found herself submitting to the dark stranger as he adjusted the mask over her face. Through the slits she looked at him, but she didn't tell him that she did know what the music was called. Without a word she let him lead her on to the dance floor and there she entered his arms to the romantic strains of "Dream Lover."

Donna danced with the dark stranger until the ballroom emptied. They didn't exchange names and he wasn't in the dining room the following morning, but there on her table was a single white rose and a note in a sealed envelope. "In Italy we say *che sera, sera*. Perhaps one day we may dance together again, perhaps without our masks."

As I have stated, lovemaking in the romance should be romantic. Thus in *Time of the Temptress:*

Her fingertips touched Wade in the water and she felt the shock of it vibrate through him . . . then he somersaulted with hardly a splash, a gleaming body that was moonlit, with a dark clouding of hair that brushed Eve as he swam up beneath her and wrapped his arms all the way around her. It was incredibly sensuous, wonderful, the feel of his hands gliding over her wet curves.

"Eve, you little devil," he groaned. "God, how lovely you feel, like a slim white fish with soft, velvety scales all alight and trembling. I'm mad for you, you wicked child. I want you till you cry the jungle down—but I'm damn not going to do what Adam did!"

"Scared?" she taunted, slipping her arms around him and feeling his body taut and burning through the cool water. "Is the great big hero a mouse at heart? Oh, love me, love me, Wade, so I'll have something I can't forget!"

"You'd have it all right!" He scooped her into his arms and ploughed out of the water with her and dropped her to her feet on the riverbank. His hand slapped out and stung her wet bottom. "Now stop being a pretty strumpet and behave yourself. I've been a gentleman with you for the first time in my inglorious life and I'm not spoiling the sheet."

Again I stress that the lovemaking can be sensual without being spoiled by explicit wording. Thus in *Desire Has No Mercy:*

"Rome—please—"

"I like it when you plead with me."

"I—let me up!"

"Not yet, my sweet." He leaned down until his face touched hers and his lips vibrated against her skin as he whispered something. Instantly she tried to struggle out of his arms, but they refused to release her and her movements only caused her tunic to ride up and reveal a little more of her bareness. She realized that if Rome was aroused she had only herself to blame for not being completely dressed, and even as she caught at his hair in an attempt to pull him away from her, she felt the tunic come open and his lips were against the curve of her breast. *"Santo dio,"* he said huskily.

"I must have you, Julia. You can yell at the pitch of your lungs but no one will take any notice. I've given orders that we aren't to be disturbed—do you hear me?"

"Don't hurt me—" She said it pleadingly.

"Hurt you?" His hand moved on her body and she gasped, but not with pain. "Have I ever hurt you? You know the answer even if you won't admit it—ah, *mia,* you smell of the sea and you feel like satin—sweet satin doll, let me—"

His words died to incoherency, passion was released in him and there was no restraining it—it swept over both of them, and distant yet close Julia heard the sea as it came and went in the groin of rock.

These passages from some of the books I've written demonstrate my technique more fully than if I set out to try and explain it. I can only repeat that first and foremost I respect my hero and heroine; I tell their love story but I refrain from invading their most secret moments. Love between two people is a wonderful experience, and if the romantic novel brings a little of that into the lives of the readers, then it hasn't done any harm at all.

It has, I hope, intensified the message that *who loves wins*.

> Maryland Avenue
> Royal Oak, Michigan
>
> July 8

Dear Kathryn,

I'm taking a new look at this "craft" I'm so enthusiastic about. I must admit that when I first wrote to you, I began to hear tales about all the fabulous money these writing ladies make, so it does whet my appetite.

But above all, I do want to write good, honest books that other women will enjoy. And thanks to Ms. Winspear, I'm not going to be afraid of being "tender," instead of just sexy.

What a sane, discerning woman Jacqui Bianchi is! You bet I'd like to talk to her!

> Rosie the Impatient One

From the Desk of Kathryn Falk

July 13

Dear Rosie,

Now it's time for your Romance Writing Lesson, Number 1. (You didn't know there was such a thing as a Romance Correspondence School, did you!)

Always keep in mind this additional definition of the "formula" of a category romance—it's the story of a woman's first sexual awakening.

Whether she is eighteen or eighty, a virgin or a widow, when she sees the hero she has <u>never</u> felt like this before. (The destiny of star-crossed lovers unfolds!)

Your readers want the story of a great romance so they can share the experience for a few hours, not a travelogue or a fashion show. That is the <u>background</u> of a romance.

The <u>romance rules</u> should become as imprinted on your memory as the words of your favorite love song.

1. Woman meets devastating man, sparks fly.
2. Motivation for their attachment is established, along with a conflict.
3. They are torn apart.
4. They are drawn back to each other. (Steps 3 and 4 may be repeated.)
5. They reconcile their problems.
6. They commit themselves to marriage.

Category romances are told from the viewpoint of the heroine. We are inside her head and we see, hear, and feel what she is experiencing. The idea is for the reader to identify with the heroine and fall in love with the hero.

If you're going to write romances, you have to continue reading them. But start reading critically. Make notes in the margins, or try my "rainbow" method: Buy several colored felt-tip markers and underline dialogue with blue, sensuality with purple, erotic sex with red, description with yellow, humor with orange, and so on. This will give you a very visual picture of the ingredients of a romance novel. Also, observe the spacing of chapters. (Janet Dailey always writes twelve chapters, and Mary Burchell writes ten.) Notice how many words in a chapter, how much action in a chapter, <u>where</u> the romance rules unfold.

Romances are fun to read and can be fun to write, <u>if</u> you follow the rules.

But color me pink,
Kathryn

*Finding the Formula**

BY JUDY SULLIVAN

What the Formula Contains:
Definition of the main characters: the age, personality, and appearance of the hero and heroine
Minor characters: to use or not to use central casting

The Focus of the Action:
Balancing the romance within the framework of the story and background

Length:
This influences plot and character development

The No-No's:
Rape and violence, bed-hopping, extramarital affairs, and sundry other miseries
Hidden agendas

What the Formula Does Not Tell You:
How not to repeat or compete too closely with what's currently on the market or coming out soon
Poisonous settings, names, situations, politics, and religion

Why Publishers Use a Formula:
To deliver what the reader wants to read
To avoid clearly unsuitable submissions

Why a Formula Changes:
Editors' instincts
Competition
Changing values in American life

Differences in Formulas:
Contemporary versus historical
From publisher to publisher
From editor to editor
From agent to agent
From writer to writer

*From a lecture (Finding the Formula) delivered by Judy Sullivan, Editor, Gallen/Pocket romances, at the Romantic Book Lovers' Conference.

Who Has the Formula and How to Get It:
  All the category romance lines
  Send a SASE and ask for tip sheet

What to Do When You Have a Formula in Hand:
  Know how a manuscript should look and why
  Pay attention to spelling and syntax
  Give vivid descriptions of clothes, furniture, and houses
  Use natural dialogue forwarding the action

Maryland Avenue
Royal Oak, Michigan

July 20

Dear Kathryn
  Underlining the important parts of romances really helps. Just as you said, the books do look like rainbows.
  I feel like I'm understanding how the rules work. I must have heard "boy meets girl" a million times and never knew what it really meant.
  By the way, I've made a rhyme that sticks in my head. If you like it, pass it on to your students in New York.

> Woman meets man, she catches his eye
> They get together and the sparks really fly.
> Then something goes wrong and the breakup occurs
> She says, "It's your fault," but he thinks it's hers.
> Fate, hope, and love can't keep them apart
> So Fate intervenes and they make a new start.
> However, it's rocky, filled with tears, but much laughter
> —And so forth, but of course it's "happy ever after."

Rosie the Rhymer

P.S. When can I get started writing other than doggerel????

From the Desk of Kathryn Falk

August 1

Dear Rosie,
  The class loves your verse.
  This is a short short—I'm off to Europe for my yearly visit to England and B.C. (Barbara Cartland). Before I go, I'm sending you a piece on imagery. I think you're about ready for it.
  Before I forget, and most important of all, I'm including Janet

Dailey's terrific method of implanting every scene firmly in her memory. It's called "The Filmstrip." So read it, and produce a Rosie Romance Filmstrip.*

Au revoir for now . . .
Kathryn

*And be sure to smell the flowers and feel the raindrops.

Interview with Janet Dailey:
America's Queen of Category Romance

How does she do it? Everyone wants to know. Eighty titles in seven years, and her 100 millionth book rolled off the presses in spring of 1983. She also made the jump from Harlequin, to Silhouette, to Pocket Books (mass market and then trade edition), and finally to the niche in which she wants to stay—contemporary novelist. Her first hardcover contemporary is from Poseidon Press, a division of Simon and Schuster.

The remarkable leapfrog literary journey, engineered partly by Pocket Books president Ron Busch, came about because he feels Janet could be the next Edna Ferber.

That's all fine and impressive, you say, but how does she write? How can any human being write a category romance in eight days and maintain the precision and regularity of a General Motors production line? Unlike them, Janet doesn't have bad days; the quality of her work doesn't vary from Tuesday to Friday. Yes, some readers prefer her early category romances to some of her recent ones that were being written at the same time she was also writing her first best-selling contemporary novels, such as *Ride the Wind* and the Calder Range series.

Eight days to write a category romance? Let's see, divide 60,000 words by eight and you get 7,500 words per day (approximately). Here's how Janet paces herself. She always stops at page twenty every day (even in midsentence), and she takes approximately twelve hours to write those twenty pages. Translated that means: one and a half hours a page. These daily twenty pages constitute her one and only typewritten draft. This is the pacing, she says, that best suits her energy and keeps her creative juices flowing.

Janet's longer books take up to six weeks to complete (the same time period required by Danielle Steel, who writes only the longer contemporary romances). But Janet's research and planning may require several months.

The amazing style of Janet Dailey is the result of knowing the formula and having total concentration when she's writing. In order to avoid distractions, Janet is one writer who doesn't take any breaks during the day.

She gets up at the crack of dawn and works until nearly suppertime. And nothing intrudes upon her. Husband Bill Dailey keeps the rest of her life running smoothly, overseeing the domestic and business details so she is free to concentrate only on writing.

After reading many Harlequins, Dailey sent her first manuscript to the Canadian company that had never published an American author. She received an advance of several thousand dollars and was asked to submit more. The rest is romance novel history. It was Bill Dailey who suggested that each of her Harlequin novels be written in a different state, which will soon make her eligible for the *Guinness Book of World Records*. The fifty-second book in her "states" series was printed at the end of 1982.

Fine, fine, you're saying, but how does she do it? How can anyone write one category book in a week, and produce some sixty in her first five years of writing, plus the big contemporary novels, adding up soon to another ten titles?

Here comes the lesson from Janet Dailey. She was more than willing to offer it.

"I carry what I call a 'filmstrip' in my head. I'm the director and the people already have their scripts. I tell them where to move. I can even reverse the film strip when I'm writing to see when they stood up and sat down.

"The filmstrip is running even when I'm not writing. I may not be thinking about how I write, but it remains in my mind. Technically, I shut it off when I get up from the typewriter. But that process by which it continues to create is on going.

"The most important advice for new writers is to *learn the format*. Follow it explicitly and be original.

"For a long time I wasn't able to verbalize how I write. I know that I took six months to learn the format. And I'd read many Harlequins for years. One thing I've realized is that I never call my people 'characters.' *Never*.

"When I talk about my stories with readers, I notice that I'll say 'Do you remember Chase Benteen?' I think of them as real people always.

"I rely on my husband to keep notes for me. If I need to know the name of a saddle or a rifle, he has the facts for me. And we keep a book of names to keep track of my people in the books.

"My contract is finished with Silhouette, and I'm going to be writing only the longer contemporary romances. Someone recently said, 'Well, then there's an opening for another Janet Dailey in the category romance field.' I laughed and said, yes, if they get up at the crack of dawn and follow the format, and write a book every other week."

That was when her husband Bill added, "But few can write them in only eight days, and I mean good ones."

"Also," added Janet with a grin, "they can't do anything else except eat and sleep while they're writing. My back usually hurts me, but I live with the pain. When the fever of writing possesses me, I don't leave the typewriter."

What is her opinion of the category romance writing techniques?

"They are excellent training for any new writer. I will miss writing the little romances. But I want to find out where I can go from here. I wrote two screenplays that Bill produced, and if everything goes well, I'll be writing a lot more. But my heart is now with the six big contemporary romances I'm planning to write.

"I put together these tips for new category romance writers. I wish everyone the best of luck. Being a romance writer is a wonderful career."

Janet Dailey's Tips

"Follow the Format but Make the Book Different"

1. *Start with weather, location, plus how, when, and where, all the basics, and depend upon strong, fine details.*
2. *When woman meets man, create an instant awareness. Sparks should embellish the situation; you must have a chemical reaction.*
3. *Create motivation for why sparks are flying, why they should be in close quarters. If it's an angry beginning, why does it continue? Be able to justify why they are going to continue into a relationship, particularly if it's a negative beginning.*
4. *Establish the reason for the source of the conflict. They are together, but inevitably they are apart.*
5. *Resolve source of conflict in a logical way when you are past the part of the hero and heroine in danger. Usually a compromise occurs, if he wants her home when she wants to work, etc.*
6. *Description of hero: Choose four or five adjectives to describe hero, choose a mannerism for reinforcement. Keep description to a minimum, pull out his physical description and awareness, try to establish a flow. Is he arrogant, too sensitive, vulnerable?*
    Some favorite mannerisms: Curling his lip when he talks implies annoyance right away; male dimples—boyishness; arching of an eyebrow—aloofness; wicked grin—playboy; hands, rough or smooth—sensuality. (Chins are not my forte.)
7. *Description of heroine: more difficult to describe than hero, because she is wholesomely attractive; you end up writing of "fire in her eyes," which means she is frisky, and "softness in her lips," which indicates gentleness. We are not as concerned with her mannerisms. We are reading her impressions of him.*
8. *I recommend writing the same number of pages every day. I do twenty pages a day, at approximately the same hours. I don't do more; I don't do less; I don't burn out!*

Image Making for Romance

No one can say "this is the way to get started writing," but several theories have emerged in interviews with the popular romance writers, and the ability to conjure up images seems to be of foremost concern.

Janet Dailey is not the only writer who puts her story on a "filmstrip." Rosemary Rogers sees all of her major scenes as in a movie. Bertrice Small sees a "gigantic movie screen, complete with conversations and special effects."

Some authors rely on just the filmstrip, while others work also from carefully detailed outlines. Marie de Jourlet, who wrote the Windhaven series, makes a detailed outline in addition to the filmstrip, with every little point and descriptive detail to be included, and the outline is sometimes longer than the finished manuscript. (From this she dictates the material and punctuation into a Stenorette, and the material is later transcribed by a secretary.)

Many writers were born with or have developed a colorful image-making process in their brains. They can close their eyes and evoke a vivid scene that is like real life.

Beginning writers sometimes have their impressions and ideas of romance bottled up intellectually. They need some help to evoke pictorial images with richness of detail.

If you are having trouble putting down your story, take heart! It's probably due to the fact that you aren't *seeing* it. To develop this power of the imagination, a few exercises can help.

1. Closing your eyes and concentrating on a place you have seen or visited, or saw in a film, is a starting point. Pretend your mind is a sound camera taking in a scene. Are you getting all the sensations the camera can get? The weather, the noise level, the colors of food, flowers, clothes, people, their complexions, body language, and conversations? Then give your camera the ability to catch scents: grass, perfumes, fresh paint.

   Keep your eyes closed and go over this type of exercise every day to get better at this conjuring. The imagination is like a muscle, and it's important to give it a workout every day, preferably at the same hour.

   Finding which time of day is your most relaxed and/or

productive is important for your writing schedule. If you know when it is, you might schedule your imagination exercise at this hour. It's not exactly what Pavlov had in mind, but starting the muscle's performance as soon as possible is the best aid for developing discipline.

2. Let's go on the assumption you're getting pretty good at scene evocation. Now let's add some flame to your fire. Focus in on the people in your scene; overhear a couple talking, and pretend they are your hero and heroine. Often a scene brings the characters together for a purpose, which is a nice uncontrived way to have them meet and even have some kind of work or hobby in common.

3. Looking at the rules of romance, set a scene, which will be your major one, at each plot point. For example: (a) see a scene of heroine's background (her apartment, and you meet her roommate); (b) see a scene of her at work, meeting the hero, sparks flying, even though they're immersed in a conflict, a misunderstanding, or whatever keeps them from getting together; (c) see the scene where they work things out—usually another career involvement situation/scene; (d) see the scene where they resolve their misunderstandings and commit themselves, usually to marriage plans.

4. You can choose only three or four vivid and important details from the scenes to write down and depict the moment to the reader. The impressions must seem strong and vital to you; if they aren't, don't choose them.

Example: The way his hand trembles as he tentatively offers her the engagement ring, then, realizing how very much he desires this, firmly grasps her hand himself and tenderly, gently slips the ring on her finger.

Start practicing now! Roll the film . . .

Camfield Place
Hertfordshire, England

August 4

Dear Rosie,

Having a grand time at La Cartlandville. Eating cucumber sandwiches, sipping tea, and indulging in meringues.

B.C. wishes you jolly good writing . . .

Kathryn

Maryland Avenue
Royal Oak, Michigan

August 10

Dear Kathryn,

Life is _so_ exciting and _romantic!_ Imagine getting all this encouragement from the very heads of romantic state! Thanks to Janet Dailey's filmstrip method, I can just visualize to perfection Kathryn taking tea with B.C. (How's that for being creative?)

I've also started keeping notes on my favorite fantasies, such as: What would happen if someone gave me a million dollars and lopped off my age by thirteen years? I'd be twenty-two. And lovely, of course. So I would go to New York and have a romantic adventure with my true love. We'd ride in a hansom cab, go to Regine's (isn't that where the jet set dances?), stay at the St. Regis hotel, and have breakfast at Tiffany's.

Is this the kind of dream list I should be making to put on my filmstrip?

Rosie (or Cecil B. De Mud)

P.S. Maybe all this heady stuff is the result of buying my first long dress! Had to, as Paul is taking me to a dealership dinner dance at the Detroit Boat Club. Glitzy!
P.S. again. Can't wait for you to get back from England. Hope this letter will be on top of your mountain of mail.

Maui

August 19

Dear Kathryn,

Paul won the grand prize at the dinner dance—a week's trip to Hawaii! I'm soaking up sun and atmosphere and have actually started to write!!! (What about? Hawaii, of course!) More later . . .

Aloha,
Rosie

From the Desk of Kathryn Falk

August 25

Dear Rosie,

I just returned and found your letter and card. Very glad you and Paul won the prize.

But I was astonished, Rosie, to hear you had "actually started to write." I hope you mean a piece on travel, not your romance, because it's best "to stay in your own backyard" for your first book. That's the number one tip for a beginner.

Your area has lovely spots you may not know . . . so make some visits . . . gourmet restaurants . . . art galleries . . . the "mansion rows" in the suburbs.

After you go to these places, make notes on those that had the strongest impact on you . . . get info on office buildings, too.

Your heroine might work in a fashionable office. If so, find out what "in" spots are nearby. The same applies for singles complexes, upper-strata housing, etc.

Romance novels are fantasy within the realm of reality. Readers appreciate settings out of the ordinary, as long as they're genuine. (Meaning you've been there!)

Authors use various methods of organizing research material, but I recommend Phyllis A. Whitney's plan for the beginner. Sara Orwig, who writes fine category romances, heard you were starting out, and she suggested her plan as another alternative.

Think sensuous,
Kathryn

Research Methods for Category Romances: The Notebook System

Learning an efficient method of researching and organizing your material is really necessary. There is no greater frustration than searching for tiny scraps of paper, or worrying about some forgotten fact or good idea that didn't get written down or filed. The more preparation you do, the better the writing will be when you finally write the story.

Some authors use colored file cards for research. But if you have ever dropped a stack of cards, you know the disadvantages. Writing furiously in various notebooks and on random pieces of paper is not any help at all. You'll be left with scribblings in meaningless piles. Don't be self-defeating and think you can carry all the facts in your head. You cannot. No one can (not even Truman Capote).

Collect as much pertinent information as possible on plot and characters and keep the notes together and labeled. You can do this in any way that is comfortable for you, from expansion alphabetical folders to notebooks, to yourself on taperecording cassettes, but *do be organized*.

When the moment comes to sit down and write, you must be free of having to "remember" facts, such as hair color or mother's name or title of a magazine. These details will be at your fingertips, and seen at a glance when you are writing. Just lean over and examine the notebook or whatever repository you choose. All research should be completed and neatly arranged by the time you begin writing.

Phyllis A. Whitney, author of twenty-eight romantic suspense novels, has devised a notebook system that is one of the best systems I know. As she says: "Being able to keep constructively busy on some phase of my notebook, whether I'm actually writing or not, is wonderfully stimulating to my imagination, and it keeps the creative flow high."

Studying her system will provide the control of the materials you need as a beginning romance writer. It could prove to be the foundation of your writing.

Phyllis A. Whitney's Remarkable Notebook

1. Buy a looseleaf binder with large rings that will hold a thick stack of paper (preferably unlined and 5½-by-7).
2. Divide notebook into sections and label with gummed tabs.
3. The Calendar Section: for keeping tabs on your work schedule.
4. The Title Section: for selecting possible names for your manuscript.
5. The Chronology Section: for listing completed pages and controlling chapter lengths.
6. The Characters and Story Events: for collecting details of characters' biographies and accurately coordinating background or historical details.
7. The Theme: for expanding the ultimate meaning and "point" of your manuscript, which will be broken into several phases of your growing novel.
8. The Situation: for the details of the basic situation; and thoughts that come to mind for another story while you're working.

More on Phyllis's notebook and her techniques of writing fiction is found in her textbook *Guide to Fiction Writing* (The Writer, Inc., 1982).

Organizing Research Material for Category Romances

BY SARA ORWIG

author of eight romances

Thumbing through a magazine, I noticed a picture of a small oak table. Beside the picture was an explanation that this table had recently been returned to Washington by a family whose ancestor carried it away when the British burned the White House during the War of 1812. From this small picture and my large imagination came the idea for a novel.

When I get an idea, I begin my research. Research is fascinating; the world is filled with marvels, excitement, and challenges. History is full of intriguing events. Any facts used should be extremely accurate. Editors will immediately catch an unusual point and ask about it. For instance, in one of my romances the hero used coconut oil as insect repellent. The editor wanted to know how the hero extracted the oil, so I added a scene where the hero splits open the coconut, places it on a rock in the hot sun, and lets the oil drip out. This was easy to include because I had researched jungle survival and kept records about it.

So, after research, how do you get a jumble of information organized to use in a category romance? I have found a formula that has proved to be very successful for me. With each novel I utilize four basic methods of organizing research material. I have (1) a card index file of information from library books, (2) marginal notes in books and magazines that belong to me, (3) a regular file drawer for pictures, brochures, etc.—anything too lengthy to go into the card file—and (4) a spiral notebook that is a quick reference for all the research.

First, the card index file consists of references from library books. People keep bits and pieces of information and don't organize them. One small piece of information can contain an idea for a story, and it's frustrating to be unable to find where it came from. I jot down things I want to remember on index cards. These are filed alphabetically according to the first letter of the subject of the information (a note about Brazil would go into the file under *B*).

In order to know the source of these bits of information without repeatedly writing the name of the book and author on each card, I've devised a simple method: I assign a number to each library book. This basic information goes into a separate file. When researching material for *Love's Trace,* a Masquerade historical for Mills & Boon, Ltd., I found a library book on Mississippi. On an index card I wrote the title of this book, author's name, catalogue number, and library. I then assigned it a number, #64, and put it in a numerical card file. In this book was the fact that pirates and highwaymen made the Natchez Trace perilous to travel, information I wanted to remember, so I made a note of it on another file card. After this notation I wrote, "#64, page 13."

I put this card in an index file behind *T* for Trace. This way I can simply glance at the number, #64 in this instance, and look in the numerical file to see what book that number represents.

It isn't necessary to look up every number because some are easily remembered; for example, the *Encyclopedia Britannica* is #1 and any reference from it will get "#1" on a card. This eliminates continually writing down the source of each note.

I've found it easier to keep separate card index files for each novel. If it's necessary to know something about weapons during the nineteenth century, it doesn't take long to check the *W*'s in several files, rather than keeping all the information together in one large file.

If a particular heading will have many references, such as the subject "Natchez Trace," a tab is made specifically for it. That way, all cards mentioning the Trace are together. The tabs of these small index files are easy to read at a glance.

My second method in organizing material is marginal notes in books and magazines that belong to me. I keep as complete a library as I can because it's more convenient to have a book on hand when you want it and to be able to make notes in it. Reference notations on index cards rarely are made for books and magazines I own.

Anything important is underlined with a colored pen and brief notations are written in the margin. I keep these books and magazines close where they will be handy all the time I'm working on the novel.

Sometimes I work on more than one novel at a time or I expect one back later with editorial changes. In order to quickly find the books used for a particular novel, small color-coding labels are placed on the spines of my books and magazines.

Any office supply store carries self-adhesive color coding labels, small colored dots that can be peeled off and attached easily. For a Harlequin Superromance, *Magic Obsession*, set in Brazil, bright red coding labels were used.

Later, in *A Flame in Winter*, a Bantam novel set in Chile, I referred to some of the same books on South America that were used for research on the Superromance. Yellow coding labels were then attached to the books for *A Flame in Winter*. At a glance, I can spot these books on the shelf. When they are no longer needed, these coding labels can be peeled off without damage to the book.

Third, in addition to small index files, books, and magazines, I keep other research material, information too lengthy to jot on an index card, in a file drawer within easy reach. These are pictures, notes from taped interviews, correspondence concerning the novel, brochures, maps, and newspaper clippings. For all this information I use file folders, and now keep different color folders for various publishing houses—beige for Mills & Boon, Ltd., yellow for Bantam, pink for Jove, and blue for Harlequin.

When I am finished with a novel, I gather all the folders and put them in another file cabinet, keeping them together. This clears the drawer beside my typewriter for folders for the next novel, yet keeps the last where I can locate them easily for editorial purposes.

Usually I have several maps on hand and file these with rochures, pictures, etc., but one map is placed where it's visible rom my desk all the time. While writing *Temptation's Flame* for ove, I pinned an enlarged map of downtown New Orleans on a ulletin board in front of my typewriter.

Fourth, the most important and useful item in organizing esearch material is simply a spiral notebook. This is my main eference for all the information compiled.

Using colored plastic tabs, I make my own headings. Some re used each time, such as *Research, Dates, History,* and *Miscellaneous,* and some are unique to a particular book, such as *Guanacos* for *A Flame in Winter.*

While researching the novel, information that is important is isted in the spiral notebook under *Research,* and this becomes a handy checklist during the development of the romance. This includes eferences to material saved in the card files and regular file, with orief notations of all research facts that should go into the novel.

This spiral notebook takes little space and is kept beside the ypewriter. When something is jotted down from research, such as that there are now approximately 100,000 guanacos in South America where there used to be millions, note is made of this under the section labeled *Guanacos.* Also, I put the page number from my novel where the reference is made, in this case page 13. In addition, the source of this information is listed because it may be necessary to look it up again. Later in the novel, if another reference is made about the number of guanacos, I can quickly open the spiral notebook and see what was written before and what page it's on. This second mention about guanacos goes into the notebook along with its page number. At a glance I can find this number again.

When the novel is finished, the spiral notebook contains all this information, a list of the major research items, sources of information and references used in the novel.

Although research may sound like a chore, it's a great boon. I can advise any writer that it will have more than one benefit. It gives you a well-rounded education and broadens your outlook on life. All this work on research has another advantage. It gives a wide range of topics for conversation at parties. Now I can discuss a 400-pound catfish in the Amazon; Dolley Madison standing on the roof of the White House to watch for President Madison's return; a glacier's calving; the months-long fast of Emperor penguins; and the recipe for a very powerful home brew.

Maryland Avenue
Royal Oak Michigan

September 3

Dear Kathryn:

I loved the notebook and research ideas, and I'm beginning to figure
out my own. And I am looking in my "own backyard." (I don't
want you mad at me again!) I just read a romance set in Detroit and
Canada, and the heroine jumped into a cab and sped through the
Windsor Tunnel? Without stopping for customs? (Now I see what you
mean by having to be there.) Anyone knows there's a customs stop
on both sides of the border.

I took my kids for a drive along Lake Shore Drive to see an old
mansion being torn down. There was a large sailboat anchored at the
dock and "the skipper" invited us aboard, but one of the kids is
afraid of water, so I declined. We got out of the car and stood on the
sweeping lawn, watching the demolition progress. Sad. For those
moments, I was the lady of the manor and I felt the scene as sharply
as possible. My mind even skipped to think what if this was my
land and my children would inherit this magnificent estate. Again,
sad.

I put all this on my filmstrip, and practiced running it back and
forth on the way home, but I had trouble reexperiencing the weather.

Oops! I almost forgot, I am planning to write a short category romance,
not a family saga!

Rosie, Michigan's next Janet Dailey

From the Desk of Kathryn Falk

September 20

Dear Rosie,

I'm dashing this off at the printer's—we're putting the next issue
of Romantic Times on the press.

You're getting into the swing now. Good piece of observation and "what
if" in your last letter about your "backyard." I feel sure you will
be able to handle the imagery well, but keep working on developing
your five senses. (Touch, feel, see, smell, and hear.) A romance
writer has to have heightened sensuality for her book.

Hurriedly,
Kathryn

Maryland Avenue
Royal Oak, Michigan

September 25

Dear Helpmate,

Again, help! Now that you feel I'm making progress with my
imagination and filmstrip, what next? Am I finally ready to round up
some ideas and sit down to write?

Anxiously,
Rosie

From the Desk of Kathryn Falk

September 28

Dear Rosie,

Yes, you're ready—but not quite.

Enclosed are a few practical suggestions on getting started and
keeping your creative corner neat and romantic.

At this point, due to the enthusiasm of my New York classes, I'm
going to seriously start collecting essays from the leading romance
authors explaining their specialties. I'll keep you supplied. Must close
now—it's so late . . .

Kathryn
2 a.m., <u>alas!</u>

What You Need to Get Started: Creative Corner

Where you write can help your writing, so the romance authors
say. They advise a setting to fit your own personality.

Having at least a "corner" to call your own is necessary.
Amii Lorin and Rosemary Rogers got started by writing at the
kitchen table late at night, which proves it's possible to write
anywhere and get published. However, writers also believe that
writing romance is made easier and more sensual by turning the
creative corner into an area with romantic atmosphere. Soft
lights, scents, sultry music pouring from the stereo, even special
loungewear add to the ambience of romance.

One historical romance writer, Parris Afton Bonds, always
slips into her most seductive negligee when she writes love
scenes, and claims it's "inspiring."

Bertrice Small, who also started out writing on the kitchen

table years ago, now has graduated from a little den in her hous to a real writing studio—a room added to her house. "It's like job," she claims. "I go there every morning and I'm home fc supper." The studio has one area just for her books, which sh sells to interested readers via the mail, and for copies to accompan any publicity she sends out. The books are displayed in dumps as in a bookstore, and are attractive storage. The scheme is whit and green, and very feminine. In the center is a cozy conversa tional area, complete with a couch and a coffee table for inter views and guests; to one side are her desk and research materia and a wide curtained window to let the sunshine stream in Overhead is a poster of Tom Selleck, "for inspiration," sh says.

In the back of Bertrice's studio is a "secretarial corner," witl file cabinets, and here a typist or researcher can work comfortably

Roberta Gellis's creative corner is a large library, filled witl books, and the main decoration is a floor-to-ceiling picture window that gives the effect of letting in the wooded acres outside he house. Malcolm MacDonald works in a cluttered "olde English" atmosphere, with bookshelves reaching to the high ceilings and requiring sliding ladders for access. His word processor sits nea a window with a view of his Irish property.

The beginning writer should give considerable thought to hei creative corner. Depending on your budget, make it as pretty efficient, and personal as possible. An uninviting writing space can invite writer's block—just like bad weather. Try to see to i that your writing "climate" is always full of sunshine.

Give yourself a room, a corner, or even turn a closet into an alcove. Be certain to know if you need a window to be comfortable, and arrange things accordingly.

Attach your phone to an answering machine, or just turn it off until you're finished writing for the day. A corner is not creative if you're constantly being interrupted. Once you turn on that filmstrip, or enter your fantasy world in your own way, don't be interrupted; it's like breaking a trance.

Invest in a great secretary's chair, one made for typists. A cheap chair will make you feel like a cripple. And sit on a cushion; this helps the circulation through your lower body and may counteract varicose veins, which can become a problem for writers. (Many see veins appearing behind their knees, where the hard rim of their chair hits.)

Sitting in the same position for more than three hours is

dangerous to your health. The aches and pains of writing and the soreness in the neck are caused by lack of exercise and too much sitting in the same position.

One last note on a creative corner. Try to concentrate here at the same hours, whether you're dreaming, planning your filmstrip, arranging your notebook, or actually typing. Your imagination is a muscle; let it know it has a time and a place.

A colorful note: Some authors use different colored typing paper for their second and third drafts. When Jacqueline Susann followed this system, she made her final copy on her Tiffany stationery. It is easier to follow your changes and revisions this way.

Items in Your Creative Corner

1. Nontoppling vase
2. Desk/filing cabinet space
3. Good secretarial chair
4. Cushion
5. Pens and pencils
6. Typewriter or word processor plus a substitute machine, probably a portable typewriter
7. Plenty of typing paper, maybe colored paper for drafts.
8. White-out and erasers; art gum
9. Scissors, ruler, Scotch tape, felt-tip markers
10. Notebook and paper
11. Tapes or stereo for background music, if preferred
12. Tape recorder for practicing dialogue
13. Telephone-answering machine
14. Reference books, dictionary, thesaurus, etc. (in reference book section)
15. Folders for pictures and material
16. Bulletin board and calendar
17. Scent—potpourri, incense, perfume
18. Pitcher of water and glass (so you don't have to use thirst as an excuse to get up)
19. Address books (for friends and business)
20. Personal stationery, mailing envelopes, and stamps
21. Scenic pictures for stimulation and reference to project

Stimulating Sensuality

BY VIVIAN STEPHENS

Editor, Harlequin American Romance

Vivian Stephens, editor of Harlequin's American Romance line, is a firm believer that romance writers must be either born or trained sensualists. She has some suggestions that can help writers to stimulate sensuality, and therefore eliminate *flat* romance writing.

"Writers really have to get in touch with life," she insists. "Their five senses must be aroused. They should eat food they really like; listen to music that can be so poignant it makes them cry; enjoy the feel of wonderful fabric against naked skin, be it silk, satin, or fur. Anything that is tactile and will stimulate the senses can then be translated into words. When a writer enjoys these feelings herself, she can then translate the emotions into words and share these beautiful thoughts with the readers."

A problem manuscript is one that will have a scene that has gone flat. Usually, the editor says, there is a scene of a man and a woman walking in the park, not touching, and not seeing the beauty of nature around them. They are involved only in naked thoughts. To enhance a scene like this, a hint of sensuality is necessary. A touch of the hand. A smile. A glance. An indication that soft words are spoken, in low tones. A description of characters reacting to nature around them (sunshine, rain, coldness, etc.).

"It's important to realize that the sensuality you're sharing will be between you and the reader. You are making her vulnerable by letting her share these feelings, so you aren't telling her what is happening, you're sharing what you're feeling in these moments," adds Stephens. "Sensuality is not just sex. It can be a brush of the lips, a caress, a touch. If you're not feeling the tremors and excitement, there is no way you can transport your readers to that heightened awareness they all love."

Music

Classical and semiclassical: Schubert, Brahms, Rachmaninoff

Accessories

Scented candles in a softly lit room

Write in bed with beautiful bed linen (spray sheets with toilet water)

Fresh cut flowers

Sip something cool (your own type of ambrosia)

Personal Care

Long baths in scented waters

Luxurious bath sheets in beautiful colors: emerald green, pale melon, soft salmon

Lace, silk, or satin negligees and robes

Clothing

Go into a department store and try on:

—silk garments

—fur coats (turn up collar; feel the softness against the face)

—scarves (let them flow down the neck and arms so you can feel the sensuousness of the material)

This whole exercise is to provoke thoughts that have been generated by the emotions, that have been set off by the sensuality of (1) *touch*, (2) *scent*, (3) *seeing*, (4) *hearing*, and (5) *taste*.

Flower Power

Flowers and the power of scent have always been associated with love and romance. Depending on your budget, plants and fresh flowers are very stimulating to the aura of romance. Even one beautiful rose can be a daily presence.

Taking the time for more romance in your own life is really a labor of love, if you're not accustomed to the tasks. Here are some hints on flowers and plants, to get you started. This effort may seem silly but the majority of romance writers claim it's an important stimulation to feeling and, therefore, writing great romance.

Keeping Flowers Fresh

A simple routine will prolong the vase life of flowers. Make sure the container or vase is clean. Flower stems should be cut at an angle with a sharp knife and put in tepid water. Repeat this procedure every other day.

Many gardeners swear by floral preservatives. Their value should not be underestimated—they do work. Most of the commercial brands consist of sugar and acid, which many flowers benefit from.

The Amazing Geranium

If you have trouble getting geraniums to bloom properly, it may be they are not potbound. This condition must exist before they put on a good show.

Geranium cuttings can be taken year round if you have a good mother plant.

Scented geraniums have pretty flowers and interesting foliage. They come in a wide variety of fragrances to suit every nose, such as rose, apple, pine, spice, lemon, cinnamon, and many more too numerous to mention.

Scented geraniums are easy to care for. When potting, simply use ordinary soil with an extra dish of perlite (for good drainage). They hate "wet feet." They must dry out between waterings.

Use scented geraniums for potpourri and sachets. Add a leaf of peppermint geranium to applesauce. A leaf of the rose geranium in a jelly jar (just before adding the jelly) adds a just-right sweetness.

The Practical Side of Romance Writing

BY ELEANORA BROWNLEIGH

author of two historical romances

We all have to begin somewhere with our first book, and I belong to the school that says it's better to take one's time and, figuratively speaking, browse around until both style and pace are developed. I'm a meanderer of the first order, hate flash, and think that if you rush you miss half the fun, so the following suggestions are strictly my own personal idiosyncrasies (if you're sure you can write your book in the next three weeks, my observations aren't going to help you *at all,* so just dash on to the next informative section).

Suggestion one is *start small.*

How terrific if you own the latest model IBM Correcting Selectric (frankly, I'm green with envy; these words are being typed on a 1978 Smith-Corona Coronet Super 12—my first, and so far only, electric typewriter), and if you can operate a home computer without either wiping out a day's work by pressing the wrong key, or accidentally blacking out your neighborhood (or both), you're already several steps ahead in your writing career. But if you don't, remember you can begin work without either of the above aids.

Buying a typewriter is a highly personal thing, so all I'll say on the subject is that a decent electric typewriter runs about two hundred dollars, and once your books sells—even if it's a year or two later—it becomes a tax deduction, so save those receipts. IBM typewriters and home computers are big-ticket items, and you can wait to acquire them until you have your first multibook contract. Besides, if you make a big purchase like that now and decide later that you *don't* want to write, you won't have that expensive mistake around staring you in the face and reminding you about your grounded flight of fancy and seriously injured bank account.

Yes, all those guides on how to prepare your manuscript for submission are right—you do need the best-quality paper you can afford for the original copy, but you can cut costs when it comes to second sheets, and whether it comes from the best stationery store or Woolworth's, carbon paper is carbon paper. In my own case, when I began to type my first romance, *A Woman of the Century,* the carbon paper I used was what was left of the 200-sheet package that saw me through assignments and term papers at fashion school—seven years earlier.

What else will you need when getting started? Not too much more. Unless your typewriter has a built-in correcting ribbon, several bottles of Liquid Paper and a package of Ko-Rec-Type are necessary, as are a good paperback dictionary, folders to keep your work in, and mailing envelopes.

Suggestion two can best be termed *loving hands at home*.

Pounding the typewriter is one way to work, but if this is your first book you might want to consider starting out using another technique—writing by hand.

I wrote every word of what became *A Woman of the Century* (as well as the books that are following it) by hand, in ink—either ballpoint or felt tip—in eight-by-five-inch spiral notebooks because I knew that no matter how terribly I wanted to write, if I sat down in front of the tyewriter it would never work. Working with notebooks gives me mobility. I write in the Metropolitan Museum of Art, in the Frick Museum, in various libraries, and in an armchair in my living room. When I do sit down at the typewriter, it's to *transcribe,* meaning another chapter is complete, the corrections made, and I have a finished product to turn out.

But no matter how you get to work, suggestion three is *keep a low profile*.

Particularly in today's booming romance market, there's the rage to tell everyone that you are too trying to become more than just a consumer of this popular reading matter. *Don't.* With few exceptions, family and friends aren't going to say how bright and clever you are; they're going to say you're cracked, and will drag out overworked, clichéd, and generally incorrect advice about the publishing industry. True, you might tell a friend and find out that her old college roommate is now an editor at Silhouette, or her second cousin's wife is a literary agent and will want to help you contact those potentially helpful people, but it's more likely that either you'll be told "first books never sell" or you will waste an hour of your time listening to her family history because "it would make a wonderful book."

Tell those few closest to you and no one else until that wonderful day when you hear that a publisher wants your book and is drawing up the contract.

Of course you like to think of yourself as a cheerful, open person, but be secretive on this one topic. Look at it this way: On those ghastly days when the chapter you're revising for the third time still won't come out right, or your manuscript has just come back in the morning's mail, rejected for the fourth time, you won't have to walk into the hairdresser's or the supermarket and have to answer the question "How's the book coming?"

All right now, you've begun to write your romance, but writing means research, and research means reading, which brings us to suggestion four, that being, *you are what you read.*

You can't write a romance on love scenes alone, and that means you have to start with basics—*Publishers Weekly.* No, it doesn't have that much to do with romance, but it does tell you what's going on in the world of publishing, and without that information you're at a real loss, so subscribe.

As for other reading that is more related to your writing . . . well, the other night I was watching television when an ad came on selling an over-the-counter medication. In it, a "mailman" was complaining that he threw his back out delivering fifty pounds of magazines, and my first thought was that he must have been carrying my mail!

Well, not really, but if I list all the magazines I subscribe to, there won't be space for anything else. Suffice to say that *Time* and *Newsweek* can be great sources for story ideas, *Savvy* and *Working Woman* for insight into what today's businesswomen really think, *Vogue* and *Harper's Bazaar* so you can "dress" your characters, and *House and Garden* and *Architectural Digest* so they have appropriate places to live.

This leads rather naturally into suggestion five, *research.*

If you want to write a historical romance—and don't let anyone tell you that they've "had it," because they *haven't*—you might consider setting your story in the Edwardian period. (Technically, that's 1902 to 1910, but it can be stretched to include 1900 to 1914.) True, the idea of setting your story in Elizabethan England or at the court of Louis XIV or during the days following the American Revolution may have more allure, but unless you already have some background in those areas, the research can get very tedious and technical. On the other hand, the Edwardian era is much easier to delve into. You can read old issues of *Vogue* and *Harper's Bazaar* and the *Illustrated London News* instead of dusty old tomes, flip through books on the history of the automobile, and read about daily life from the plethora of books about the period generated during the run of the television series *Upstairs, Downstairs*.

My own historical romances are set in that period not because the background is easier to learn about, but because I wanted to have my characters travel on great ocean liners and wear beautiful clothes and go to grand parties and drink champagne and do it all in the twentieth century. The way we live now, as well as many of our ideas, were formed back then, and besides, you may not be able to stay at the Ritz in Paris, but your characters can!

When writing the contemporary category romance, research is equally important, and don't let anyone tell you otherwise.

I've had the misfortune to read category romances set in New York in which the author felt it was her duty to reinvent the city. Imagine a New York without Saks Fifth Avenue, without "21" or Windows on the World, without the Plaza Hotel. I've also read romances set in Boston with nary a mention of the Ritz-Carlton Hotel and Harvard University, as well as romances where the characters—who were all involved in the movie industry—were so ethnically pure they could have been given instant membership in the Grosse Pointe Country Club.

All of the above gaffes are unforgivable, and saying that you don't live in those cities is an excuse that won't wash. What do you think guidebooks are for? The point is, no museum or restaurant or department store or theater is going to sue you for placing your characters within its four walls. Mystery writers have known this for years, and some of the classiest, most entertaining thrillers have taken place in famous spots. The Metropolitan Opera House (both the old and new locations),

Elaine's (the well-known celebrity restaurant), and the Stork Club (a once-famous nightclub whose heyday went from the 1920s to the 1950s) have all been backgrounds for popular books. Even the Ritz in Paris has been used as the scene for a murder mystery. (For all you mystery buffs, the book is *Whatever Became of Anna Bolton?*)

True, you're writing romance, not mystery, but the rules still apply. Let your characters meet at the National Gallery, dine at Lutèce, make love at the Beverly Wilshire (French floor, new wing), shop at Bergdorf-Goodman and Brooks Brothers, and live in the Olympic Towers. It doesn't hurt anyone, and readers love stories that are set in *recognizable places*.

The best place to begin your research is by reading the "city" magazines. *New York* began it all, and it's hard to think of a major city in America that doesn't have its own glossy to record its pitfalls and pleasures. Another aid is a city's convention and visitors' center. They're generally full of brochures that describe everything from a boat tour around Manhattan to a shopping guide to Beverly Hills to the summer schedule at Tanglewood. All provide mail service, and a letter describing what information you need will probably net you the information.

The final word on research is still *reading*. Becoming an "armchair traveler" is the best way possible to research your contemporary romance, short of actually getting on a plane or train and going to New York or Boston or New Orleans.

No one wants to write in a vacuum, and suggestion six covers *courses*. Some of them can be helpful; others have the well-deserved reputation of being run like abusive encounter sessions, and romance writers make a great target. A course run *specifically* for women and men interested in writing romances is different; there's a real camaraderie and sense of fun in these classes, quite unlike the overearnest atmosphere of the more traditional writing groups.

A course on publishing—or how to get published—is also good for the beginner. You may be writing romance but you're in the business of publishing, and it behooves you to learn all you can about that fascinating, fast-changing world.

To sum up, romance writers have made a definite change in the publishing industry, and we've forced people who only a few years ago either smiled indulgently or else made snide remarks to take us very seriously indeed. Romance novels are now advertised on television and radio and in the print media; publishers are rushing to print newsletters so that readers can have up-to-the-minute information about their favorite authors; and Kathryn Falk has given us *Romantic Times*, whose every issue is a source of information for both readers and authors of romance.

We're improving every year, and for the first-time writer, taking your time and not wanting to be a whiz kid the first time out does pay off in the end. Know your market, your research, and the sort of book you want to write, and before too long you just may be joining our ranks. Welcome.

Maryland Avenue
Royal Oak, Michigan

October 10

Dear Kathryn,

Paul is exhausted. Not only did he fix up a tiny office for me, complete with fresh flowers (he buys me a few carnations every week now!), but my attempts at increased (heightened!) sensuality are keeping him further exhausted (ho ho).

It's great in my own creative corner, having my books neatly stacked in front of me. (As Carolyn Nichols suggested, read the good parts over and over, and I do.)

My notebook is gradually filling up. It's alongside the typewriter (which I have not really touched yet).

I'm keeping my mood romantic. I think pink (and Paul)!

Ready-to-go Rosie

P.S. I found Eleanora's first book—what fashion details!

2

Plotting the Category Romance

From the Desk of Kathryn Falk

October 16

Dear Rosie,

Enclosed are the first "essentials of love" (Lesson 2 of this correspondence course!). My collection of essays increaseth.

I'm passing on a "torte" drawing to pin on your bulletin board. You do have one, don't you? Everyone needs a reminder board. (More about that later.)

Best wishes,
Kathryn

The TORTE System

The TORTE symbol is a reminder to new writers as they learn the plotting steps of a category romance novel.

What follows are explanations of the necessary fiction techniques by the very authors who have adopted them best in romantic literature.

There are scores of books on the art of writing fiction, and most new writers are familiar with them, but this is the first complete reference book and writing guide devoted to the current romance novels.

There are several important differences between writing popular fiction for mainstream novels of romance and category romance. For one, category romances are small, with fewer pages for expanding beyond the boundaries of the formula. Therefore, like a short story, they must be little compact jewels of fiction; a writer uses words as the Japanese use brushstrokes, to paint a scene in one of these small books.

Everything revolves around one theme: a woman falling deeply in love. The reader wants the heroine's emotional turmoil directly on the pages, with the guarantee that it is a great love that will end in commitment. Once the writer understands this, she must devise ideas to avoid banality, sameness, and these are solely up to the author's skill and talent. They come about through fresh appraisals and surprises for the reader—all having to do with falling in love in a believable, engrossing way.

And regardless of what type of romance you write, even the longer, less restrictive types, the TORTE system must be there, ready to be adapted to the story.

By having complete, original explanations for each section of the TORTE, you won't be forgetting the essentials. You will avoid giving the romance readers a small slice, or even half a pie; you'll give them the *whole thing*.

Mixing Fact with Fiction

BY CAROLYN THORNTON

author of four category romances

Loving—as I'm struggling to understand it—demands a certain vulnerability, laying yourself open to another person, risking rejection. It's a lot like writing.

The only unique thing I feel I have to offer my readers is myself. In that, I strive to make my romances a reflection of my life's experiences, blending minor realities with major fantasies. At the heart of these stories are issues I'm dealing with today— how to juggle a career and still have enough time and energy to devote to a personal life; how to deal with dating in the 1980s when you still think in terms of Ozzie and Harriet; how to make a relationship work.

Silhouette Special Edition romances, the line I write for, are about real women dealing with real problems today. In sharing my search for the ideal romantic man and all the frustrations and excitement that go along with that, I'm hoping to create books that meet that need. Seeds of truth are planted throughout my novels—some more heavily scattered than others. Most of my plots develop out of a "what if?" approach that helps me turn reality into fantasy.

For instance, as a journalist writing about cruises, I spent a good part of six months bobbing between land and sea in research. The sea is a natural setting for a romance, and most ships follow the "Love Boat" theme. What if I had a shipboard romance? What would happen when the boat finally docked back in Miami? Enough people in my interviews had told me stories of romances begun aboard ship that ended happily ever after. Others told me stories of relationships that sank as soon as the gangway touched solid ground. I decided to explore what the routine of everyday real living would do to a begun-in-the-moonlight romance that started aboard a sailing fantasy island. The result was *Looking-Glass Love*.

It doesn't take such exotic circumstances to apply the "what if?" technique to your story. What if that handsome stranger in a restaurant asked you to join him for dinner? What if you had to find a husband in three days, and had only strangers to choose from? What if you had to arrange for the marriage to take place without your new husband knowing about it until after the fact? Similar thinking led to my romance *For Eric's Sake*.

Sometimes the simplest things happening around you can bring your story alive. Whenever I hit a block with the plot, I'll throw in anything I'm doing just to get the story moving again. Later I can come back and edit that segment out, or find that it was just the spark needed to bring the story to life. Whatever I use, it serves its purpose in getting the words to come out of the typewriter. Use anything at hand—like the burning pot of soup that turned up in *The Heart Never Forgets;* the menu at the Miami Fontainbleau Hilton for *By the Book;* the designer dress I couldn't afford but my heroine wore for the Mardi Gras ball in *By the Book*. You build your story out of details.

Everywhere you go, take notes about interesting occupations of people you meet, funny things your neighbor's toddler says, or interesting points raised in an article or book you've read. I keep a collection of these odd bits of information in a file folder and pull it out to mull over before beginning to write.

When I start a book I have a general theme in mind, my characters pictured in front of me—based on someone I may have met even briefly, or a clipping out of a magazine, or my favorite soap opera hero, who became Adam Anastasia in *The Heart Never Forgets*. Once the opening scene is clear and I have a hazy idea of where the ending will be, I start writing. The characters and the plot develop as I go along. Outlines don't work for me, but the little bits and pieces of information spread out around my typewriter can sometimes inspire an entire chapter.

When you start with things in your own backyard of experience, you'll find the entire story mushrooming around you. If you think you have a dull life, it's only because you're not looking closely enough at it. Take the places you've been, characters you've met, funny incidents that have happened to you, and embellish them with your imagination. It's up to you to decide how much of yourself you want to put into your plots. But a good rule is to mix well with a lot of fiction, because factual incidents, told exactly as they happen, are never as convincing as the way real events can be embellished. Remember the game of "Rumor," where one person whispers something to the one next to him? By the time the statement has made the rounds of everyone in the circle, the result is totally different from the initial fact.

Lately I've found my romanticized plots turning into reality. With *By the Book* I was writing my ideal fantasy. The hero falls in love with the heroine, a romance writer, by researching her books to know how to treat her. When I was halfway through the writing of that book, that actually happened to me. You can read about my real-life hero and how we met in *Male Order Bride*, but I'll leave it to your imagination to figure out where the reality ends and the fantasy begins.

The Use of Theme

BY SUZANNE SIMMS

author of eleven category romances

When I first begin a new manuscript, it is a "theme" I have in mind rather than an actual plot. I seek the motivation behind the story, the point I wish to make, before I even begin to visualize the characters and the plot. With the greater freedom afforded romance writers today, I have enjoyed exploring some of my own ideas and thoughts about men and women.

I like to develop a philosophy, an attitude with each romance novel I write. I prefer the inevitable conflict between the heroine and the hero to develop logically out of a conflict between their lifestyles, their attitudes, what they seek from life itself, rather than introducing an outside force or the "other man" or "other woman" as the source of contention between them. I used that convention in some of my earlier books, but I deliberately avoid using it in the romantic fiction I now write. The reason is simple. It is much more difficult to come up with a fresh approach while employing plot devices that have been frequently used in the past.

In developing a theme for a book, I spend several weeks sorting through ideas in my head, bouncing them off my editor, my husband, or a good friend. This preliminary step is vitally important to the book that will eventually emerge.

The next step is finding a plot and characters that will illustrate the theme I have chosen. I begin to write at this point, making a detailed outline of the two main characters, from the shape of their eyes to the size of their shoes, from their favorite flower to their childhood passion for candy. I use only a small percentage of this background information in the actual finished manuscript, but it is an extremely useful writing tool. I try to create real people in my mind. I want their actions and thoughts to be consistent with their personalities.

Once I have outlined the heroine and hero, I begin the search for their names. This is always a rather odd experience—but I know, I sense, when I have found the right names.

With the theme developed, the two lead characters named and outlined in detail, the next step is selecting the location for the book. I use the location only to further the atmosphere or the "feel" of the story. The obvious use of location in terms of travelogue is no longer recommended by most publishers.

Since 1981 I have been concentrating on themes centering on the conflict between the lifestyles and attitudes of my hero and heroine. Beginning with *Moment in Time,* I have explored the professional woman, usually in her late twenties or early thirties, who has her own career and who meets a man's ardor with an equally strong passion of her own.

I have now written about the college professor, disdainful of the business world, who falls in love with a businessman; the civil engineer who contends with a lonely rancher; the teacher who falls in love with a former student ten years after their last meeting; the cartoonist who despises sports and, you guessed it, falls in love with a sports promoter. Currently, I am writing about an aggressive art dealer who has met her match in a sculptor uninterested in either fame or fortune.

In all of these books I explore people's attitudes about their jobs, their approach to love and marriage, what they find is important in their lives—being very sure not to forget that it is romantic fantasy I'm writing.

One writing device I often use and thoroughly enjoy employing is the "reversal." If the reader would normally expect the dialogue to go in one direction, I will deliberately turn it in the opposite. If one would ordinarily expect the man to make a certain kind of statement, or take a particular action, I will have just the reverse happen. It's switching the roles of hero and heroine in subtle ways.

The reversal works well for me because I consider myself a fairly liberated woman. I find the role reversal idea healthy in life as well as in romantic fiction. One's femininity, one's masculinity, should not be based on who does the dishes or who takes the lead in lovemaking, or who brings home the paycheck. The mature, confident adult does not rely on such extraneous props to ensure his or her sexuality.

And yet that "fine line" must still be maintained in romantic fantasy. Yes, we want a three-dimensional man, with strengths and weaknesses—but he must still be heroic. Yes, we want an aggressive, intelligent heroine—but she must still be a sympathetic character, the one we identify with.

I believe this to be the future of romantic fiction—to work within the broad boundaries of what constitues a romance while we explore all the ideas and attitudes and situations that can exist between a man and a woman.

I do not write to a formula. I write my books my way, with the help of those around me. Writing romance has certainly provided me with the means to say what I think about the most important event in anyone's life—falling in love! As one of my characters said in *A Wild, Sweet Magic:* "Falling in love is easy, *being* in love is the difficult part." And that is one of my favorite themes.

How and Why

BY ANNE N. REISSER

author of six category romances

I don't suppose that there's a writer alive (or dead, for that matter) who hasn't been asked how and why he, she, or they (in the case of writing teams) began to write. The how and the why vary widely, but every writer I've ever talked to, including myself, started out as a reader. I'd go further and generalize by saying that almost all writers were (and still are, of course) readers first, although the reverse is obviously not true. I had better define a reader, however, as one who reads for pleasure as well as for information. I'd also better add that the female reader-turned-writer most probably didn't confine herself to one particular genre for her reading pleasure.

I read incessantly and "omnivoraciously" (to coin a useful word): books, both fiction and nonfiction, magazines, newspapers, cereal boxes . . . I'd rather read than do housework, which, as those who know me personally realize, isn't saying much, because I'd rather do *anything* than do housework. Be that as it may, my long, if not distinguished, career as a reader does have a great bearing on the particular *why* that resulted in my own writing career.

Over the years I had read a large number of then current romance offerings, both historical and contemporary, and said, as so many before me have said, "I can do better than *that!*" My attempts to "do better than that" thus far consist of six books published by Candlelight Ecstasy, and I'm still trying, with each new book, to "do better" than the previous book.

Before I started writing, I spent my time trying to keep at least one step ahead of my three children, at least even with my checkbook balance, and not more than a mile or two behind on my list of household chores. Since I've started writing, I do pretty much the same thing, but now I have a valid excuse for being a perpetual no-show in the contest for Housewife of the Year. Writers are allowed eccentricities. Mine is laziness, if such a state (even advanced) is eccentric.

And laziness brings me to the next topic: how I sold my first book. I like to write stories, always have. But, strangely enough, I hate to write letters. To sell a book yourself, you must write a lot of letters. To me that's work, and lazy people avoid work. Ergo, the smart lazy person finds someone to write the letters for her. I found an agent. Three weeks later, she sold my first book. I thought that was a fair division of labor: I wrote the books, she sold them. After all, even a lazy person doesn't mind being paid for having fun. It takes remarkably little effort to endorse an advance check. Even the most dedicated proponent of indolence as a way of life can summon up enough energy for that.

To sell a book, however, you must first write a book, and that requires a plot. Plots come in all sizes and shapes. Some may be old standbys that have been given a new twist by an exasperated writer who, as an equally exasperated reader, has screeched, "Horsefeathers! Real, adult people wouldn't act in such an idiotic manner."

For the first book I had published, *The Face of Love*, I took standard plot #123 (it was just such a plot that maddened me to the point of proving that there are *different* ways to illustrate that "there is nothing new under the sun"), containing the classic philandering father (who was also embezzling company funds), the hero who uncovers the father's peccadilloes, and the heroine who is the daughter of aforementioned father. The hero, having a yen for the heroine, and having previously made no headway in his campaign to clasp her to his manly bosom, decides that a spot of judiciously applied blackmail is in order, i.e., marry me or your father's sins will come back to haunt him.

In the course of such a standard plot, the heroine selflessly sacrifices herself on the altar of filial duty. Then she and the hero lead an excruciatingly improbable married life for a period of time—sometimes even as long as a year!—before finding out that they loved each other all the time and it's all been a big *misunderstanding*. They then live happily ever after. Dear old Daddy either (a) reforms or (b) doesn't reform, but the dutiful daughter understands and forgives, whichever the case may be. By the time I had read the third book that featured that particular plot, I was screaming "I *can* do better than that!" at the top of my lungs.

You can read *Face* yourself to decide whether I *did* do better or not, but at least she doesn't marry him. She informs the hero that Daddy would do well for a spot of jail. Of course, if I'd left it there, the book would have been over on page 99, but the wily hero has an ace up his sleeve, in the shape of the heroine's invalid mother, who, inexplicably, still adores the philandering father. The heroine can't trump that ace, but she does the logical thing—she becomes the hero's mistress. Yes, she really does, and believe me, at the time that was an innovation for the genre. Naturally, true love eventually triumphed—it is a romance, after all—but the hero really had to work for it.

The moral of that illustration? Old plots can be fun, as a starting place, but only as a starting place. As a writer, you've developed an individual character, given her (or him) certain personality traits, and placed that person within the framework of the plot. Now you must allow that unique individual to take on life and depth, to direct the action according to the dictates of her nature. If your character is mischievous, let her make mischief. If she is of a primarily logical turn of mind, her actions should reflect that facet of her personality, and lo and behold your tired old plot will take off in new, and probably unexpected, directions.

You'll still get to the same place in the end—girl *does* get man—but the trip will cover new landscapes, entertaining both you and your reader along the way. No living beings react in exactly the same way to an identical stimulus or situation. Neither should your created characters. If you allow your characters to act according to the logical necessities of their personalities, your plot will be both internally consistent and entertaining.

A plot can also stem from a character. Instead of starting with a full-blown story idea, sometimes I begin with a mind picture of a particular character, who has one or more distinctive personality traits or problems. Then I build the plot around her. I devise a career, one that is consistent with her personality; I develop a family background, which may, depending on the person, be either a source of strength or a source of problems; and I create a complementary male character, one who I think will make an interesting foil for the heroine. In this type of plot, the conflict may be internally derived, stemming from the developing relationship between the two main characters, or the pressures may be external, derived from the events and people surrounding the heroine and her hero.

Fresh, exciting plots and characters constantly present themselves to a writer, begging, "Tell *my* story. Make *me* come alive!" Plots flutter up to our eyes from the pages of our daily newspapers. They whisper in our attentive ears as overheard bits of conversation. We transform them into a colorful and richly textured fabric of narrative. New, attractive characters, their unformed personalities awaiting our delineating pens, present themselves to us as intriguing faces glimpsed in passing, on a street, in a car. The writer's indispensable tool, "What if?", her sense of the potential implicit in the raw material of our daily lives, is the key to an inexhaustible warehouse of material. Fill your shopping cart, writers, with plots and characters. They're all around you, just waiting for you to pick them up and mold them to suit your personal taste.

Determining the Situation

BY JENNIFER BLAKE

author of twenty-four romance novels

Stated simply, a situation is a factor or set of factors that pits a man and a woman against each other in a given environment. Some of the most famous examples of these are the Woman

Abducted by a Stranger, the Man and Woman stranded on a Desert Island, the Arranged or Forced Marriage, the Pretended Engagement or Marriage, the Angry Woman Who Seeks Revenge, the Lady Mistaken for a Woman of the Streets, the Woman Who Assumes Another Identity, the Woman under the Protection of a Man of Superior Position. There are many others, and each has been used, with variations, hundreds of times.

The situation is different from the plot in that it is the vital idea, the central core, that sparks the beginning of a story. The plot, on the other hand, is the series of constructed scenes, crises, and final climax that is then built around this core.

The importance of having a clear-cut situation cannot be overemphasized. From it stems the basic conflict, the tension and excitement of the story. These are the very elements that are most often missing from the work of beginning writers. Without them, you can write with the stylistic perfection of a Henry James and not find acceptance; with them, there is a good possibility that you will interest an editor.

It may sound as if the use of well-known situations will guarantee acceptance to books without originality, all of a stultifying sameness. It can happen that way, but it should not. It is up to you, the author, to use your imagination and talent to create characters, devise settings and scenes, invent dialogue, and uncover new psychological insights that will not only breathe new life into an old situation, but so disguise it that only someone searching for the basic situation will recognize it for what it is. More, it is a truism that there is no such thing as original fiction, that any story you can concoct must be based on human qualities, which are limited. In essence, then, all stories are twice-told stories.

Another possibility in the use of situations is to combine two or more. This often gives excellent results, heightening the level of excitement and drawing the reader deeper into the story.

To gain some idea of how using a situation works, let's look at a few of them. Perhaps analyzing some that I have used in the past will also be helpful. The different descriptive titles given to them are my own and, like the order in which they appear, are purely arbitrary.

The woman Abducted by a Stranger has long been a favorite. The famous Valentino move *The Sheik,* based on Ethel Dell's book of the same title, comes immediately to mind. Several authors have taken the exact same theme for their books, Barbara

Cartland, Violet Winspear, and Joanna Lindsey among them. A couple of my own contemporary romances feature the same idea, but with a different treatment. In *The Abducted Heart*, the woman is accidentally abducted in the private plane of a Mexican millionaire, a man who refuses to believe that her presence wasn't deliberate. The hero of *Bayou Bride* is a French Creole tycoon from New Orleans who spirits the heroine away to prevent her from interfering with his brother's engagement, then decides to keep her for himself. The prince in *Royal Seduction,* a sensual historical, mistakes the heroine for her look-alike cousin, who was the mistress of his murdered brother, and kidnaps her with the intention of forcing her to reveal what she supposedly knows of the deed.

The Man and Woman Stranded on a Desert Island is another that sees frequent use. Not too long ago, I read a fascinating Harlequin Presents tale about a couple who were shipwrecked. The man claimed they were husband and wife, but the marriage had not been consummated; the woman had amnesia. Now that was original!

Stories of men and women stranded together in other settings, however, partake of the same idea. Esther Sager's *Only 'Til Dawn* is the story of a woman forced to accept the hospitality of a man during a snowstorm. Unhappily married to an older man, she submits to one night of love, then disappears.

In my own book *Snowbound Heart,* the heroine takes shelter in a snowstorm in a mountain chalet she thinks is unoccupied, and finds herself trapped for three days with a famous reclusive actor whom she has always admired, and who thinks she is a snooping reporter. *Captive Kisses* is about a woman who is held prisoner at a house on a secluded lake because she has seen an old man who is a witness in a protective custody case who is scheduled to testify in an important murder trial that will expose a corrupt political machine.

The important thing about this kind of situation is that it allows the couple to remain together in forced contact for much of the book. It is this aspect that readers especially enjoy. Let me enter a warning, however, that because of the limited number of characters, these are not the easiest books to write. Most keep the hero and heroine together for a while, then let them move to another setting.

The Arranged or Forced Marriage has been getting a lot of attention in contemporary romances lately, primarily because it allows immediate sexual intimacy without the danger of having the heroine seem lacking in moral character. It has long been a staple of historical fiction, but is somewhat out of favor in that category because of its predictability. An older story of an arranged marriage is Norah Loft's *The Silver Nutmeg*, about a glove-marriage (arranged marriage) in the Dutch East Indies. Others are Georgette Heyer's *Arabella* and *The Convenient Marriage*. My third sensual historical, *The Storm and the Splendor*, uses this ploy, as does an older romantic suspense tale, *Bride of a Stranger*.

The Abducted Heart, previously mentioned, combines the Pretended Engagement or Marriage and an Abduction by a Stranger. In many cases, the agreement to the pretended engagement or marriage is undertaken for the sake of someone who is ill and particularly requests it. There are exceptions. One that lingers in the mind is the famous screenplay *The Man Without a Face*, about a federal agent who takes the place of a diplomat who has disappeared in Eastern Europe under suspicious circumstances, then falls in love with the diplomat's wife.

The Angry Woman Who Seeks Revenge is the basis for my sensual historical *Tender Betrayal*. The heroine, positive that the hero is the source of the rumors of treason and dereliction of duty stemming from the Mexican War that kills her grandfather, honors her relative's dying request to make the man pay. This story also includes elements of the Forced Marriage, plus that of the next category:

The Lady Mistaken for a Woman of the Streets. Kathleen Woodiwiss deserves the credit for bringing this situation into popularity in recent years, though it, too, has a long history. In Woodiwiss's first book, *The Flame and the Flower*, the heroine finds herself in that position. In my own historical *Love's Wild Desire*, the hero fights a duel with an old enemy over a woman he takes to be a quadroon. The heroine, afraid of the repercussions should her masquerade be discovered, keeps quiet until it is too late. A similar arrangement is the catalyst for my historical *Golden Fancy*. The hero rescues the heroine on the plains after she has been left behind by a Mormon wagon train because of an unfounded charge that she is a prostitute. He is unable to believe her protestations of innocence, and forces her to become his kept mistress in the gold camp where he is heading.

The Woman Who Assumes Another Identity is an interesting situation, and one challenging to write. I have used it twice, though in completely different ways. In my romantic susense tale *Dark Masquerade*, the heroine takes the place of her widowed sister who died in childbirth and travels to the plantation of the deceased husband's family because she had no place else to go and refuses to part with the baby her sister died bearing. Since the marriage took place in Texas, and he was never informed of it, the husband's brother is suspicious on all counts.

Night of the Candles, on the other hand, is a supernatural story of possesson. One woman, killed by her lover, possesses the body of her cousin who comes to visit. In her thirst for life and love, and in her desire to vindicate her husband who is suspected of the murder, she nearly drives the heroine mad, especially when she attempts to seduce her husband once more.

The Woman under the Protection of a Man of Superior Position is the base of any number of Regency novels, including Georgette Heyer's *The Grand Sophy*, the story of a flamboyant and independent young woman who must accept the guardianship of a handsome but strait-laced and rather priggish man. The same format, but with a different twist, is that of my own *Notorious Angel*, wherein the heroine, caught up in the fighting in a filibuster campaign, is forced to become the mistress of the military second-in-command. The events in *Embrace and Conquer* are similar, except that the heroine is made the colonel's mistress out of revenge for what he considers to have been an attempt upon his life, and because of the chance of saving her father from being hanged as a traitor during the transfer of Louisiana from France to Spain in the eighteenth century.

The examples above should be enough to give you an idea of the value of working with a basic situation, and of how to go about it. There are many others: the Woman Who Challenges the Woman-Hater, the Woman Who Masquerades as a Boy, the Lovers Caught in a Feud. These are only a few of the most common; if you try, you can easily think of others. They are there for everyone.

Obstacles to Love

BY BRENDA TRENT

author of seven category romances

In a romance novel, the primary conflict is the romantic tension and the obstacles between the hero and heroine. Since the entire plot revolves around the conflict between the couple, the problems that separate them and the solutions that bring them back together are critical.

No matter how strong the plot, the book won't work unless the obstacles are serious enough to keep the lovers apart. Equally important is the manner in which the author handles the reconciliation.

Making the conflict work well is a complex and delicate process. It is difficult to sustain tension and excitement when the conflict revolves around a single obstacle that is stretched to the end of the book—then conveniently explained away so that the couple can live happily ever after. Some people complain (and rightfully) that in many of these books the heroine and hero could clear up their misunderstanding with one sentence. The writer's job is to make sure that this problem is licked by providing substantial tension and obstacles—a job growing more complex as writing competition increases and readers become more selective.

There should be a major difficulty and several minor ones. In many cases, the major conflict is hero versus heroine; they are uncertain of each other's love right to the end of the book. The complexities of character—the shadow in the hero's past, for example—keep the tension strong. Because of a past painful love experience, he is reluctant to commit totally. Although the major conflict continues throughout the book, there are periods of relief when the couple are shown in agreeable situations; otherwise, the happily-ever-after won't be believable. In some of the newer books, the hero and heroine admit their love early, but there must be something that keeps them from total commitment.

The minor problems should run throughout and should be solved as the book progresses; this keeps the level of conflict high and the reader's interest alert.

Conflict is both internal and external. Since most of the books are written from the heroine's point of view, the reader sees her engaging in a lot of introspection—internal monologues—exploring and questioning her situation. The reader also sees her responses and reactions in detail.

As the books have become more sophisticated and realistic, so have the conflicts; however, there are time-honored devices that will always be used to separate the couple. Jealousy is one of them. In the past, it has been utilized in romance books most frequently as the heroine's envy and passionate resentment of the traditional "other woman."

I used this device in *Runaway Wife*. The hero takes his secretary to his home in Mexico City on Christmas Eve, leaving his wife, the heroine, in their New York home, and the complications arise from there.

In the future, jealousy will be used in more complex ways. In my *Hold Love Tightly* (under the pseudonym "Megan Lane"), the hero and heroine have a conflict of careers, and the heroine accuses the hero of being jealous because she's the more successful performer.

The idea is to try to come up with something original, more challenging than the traditional devices, but don't rule them out completely. If they can be used in innovative and entertaining ways, they are still viable.

In *Run from Heartache,* my heroine has amnesia, the result of a car crash, which is certainly seen often enough in these books. This case, however, is a little different, as neither the hero nor the heroine without a memory is sure whether or not the heroine is married right until the end of the book. She has a man's wedding band in her hand, and a blond man from the past keeps flashing into her mind at all the wrong times.

The forced marriage has stood writers in good stead for a long time, and it can, and most probably will, still work in the light romances. *A Stranger's Wife* utilized this device. I want to use this novel to illustrate the handling of major and minor obstacles. The plot involves a heroine desperate for money to find her missing fiancé, who was accused in a bank crime and presumed drowned, victim of suicide.

The heroine is determined to prove that he wasn't cupable and that he wouldn't have taken his own life, so she engages the services of a private detective. She is so in need of money to continue the search that she agrees to pose nude for the hero, a portrait artist. She's "forced" into his marriage bed when her fiancé is found—with another woman.

The conflict here briefly: The heroine has a fiancé to whom she feels intensely loyal; consequently, she must fight her attraction to the hero. Her inability to fulfill an agreement to model nude for him results in a deal whereby she will marry him under certain circumstances. She mistrusts him because he has a woman who is actively pursuing him, and he also has a line of women in and out of his apartment, posing for him. When the heroine meets the "other woman," it appears that the hero is married to her and treating her most abominably. Later, when the hero and heroine marry, the hero's father, as well as the woman in the hero's past, become obstacles.

The heroine's conflict: her loyalty to her fiancé versus her compelling attraction to the hero, her awareness of his treatment of the woman in his past, and her own embarrassment over finding her fiancé safe—and with another woman.

The situation is further complicated by the hero's internal conflict: He feels guilty over his mother's death, he mistrusts women because of Elleen, the woman in his past, and is aware of how devoted the heroine is to her fiancé.

The major conflict, hero versus heroine, continues throughout, of course, but I resolve the first primary minor conflict of the heroine needing money by having her attempt to pose nude for the hero. When this is unsuccessful, she enters into the agreement by which she will marry him under given conditions.

I resolve that conflict by having the fiancé, on the run from the law, be found with another woman. The heroine feels obligated to marry the hero. (Of course, by this time she wants to.)

They go to Monterey, where more conflicts arise because the hero installs his new wife in his home with his father and his stepmother—the other woman, Elleen. Not only is Elleen still pursuing the ero, but now the hero's father evinces interest in the heroine.

By this time the heroine is very much in love with the hero, who doesn't appear to return her affection. To add insult to injury, the other woman drags out a nude portrait of the heroine and displays it before dinner guests—a portrait the hero painted from memory, which embarrasses the heroine horribly. She thinks that the hero told Elleen about that little episode, and she is humiliated.

Of course we know that they live happily ever after, but you can see how the conflict works through the book, with minor problems being solved and major ones actually increasing as love increases between the couple.

Occasionally they are swept up in their desire for each other, as they find themselves in pleasant interludes, and the obstacles appear less important; however, when the passion subsides, or the idyllic times end, the conflict once again dominates.

In my longer, more complex book *Stormy Affair*, the heroine falls in love with her dead husband's brother. Needless to say, this affair seems literally doomed because of various complications: The hero believes that the heroine drove his brother to his death, and the heroine is appalled to learn that the singer to whom she is so attracted is, in fact, her dead husband's brother.

Both are driven by private demons—the heroine because her husband accused her of being frigid, and the hero because he separated his brother from the woman he *really* loved.

This couple has an incredibly stormy affair; however, as in all romances, the conflict must be resolved. The hero learns the truth from his brother's mistress and realizes that he misjudged the heroine.

Whenever possible, try to resolve the conflict by some method other than the hero and heroine confessing all. In *Bitter Vines*, the heroine sees the truth when she goes to the house the hero purchased for her before she left him. In *A Stranger's Wife*, the portrait is actually the device that triggers the resolution of the couple's problems. In *Run from Heartache*, the blond man reappears in the heroine's life and the conflict begins to be resolved.

The solutions can be as varied and interesting as the problems, so be creative, use your imagination, and the reader will race ahead. All's not well with love unless the path is rough and the way to the happy ending treacherous.

Maryland Avenue
Royal Oak, Michigan

October 25

Dear Kathryn,

The material on situations and theme was mind-boggling at first, but I think I've got my plot! However, it might jinx me if I tell you what it is.

I'm in the process of filmstripping the major scenes, but I don't know if my characters (whoops—Janet Dailey never calls them that!) my people are springing up alive yet.

Wish I were Dr. Frankenstein, but I don't want to create monsters. Got anything to help me with making my people "nice and human"?

Rosie

From the Desk of Kathryn Falk

November 1

Dear Rosie,

You might have to go back to first base again, or have I misunderstood you? Do you mean you have a skeleton plot, à la your "rhyme" (woman meets devastating man), with just the time, location, house, and furniture in place, and no flesh on the bones, no brain in the head, no smiles on the lips, and no beating heart? I can hardly believe it. Skeletons don't make very good filmstrip stars or great star-crossed lovers!

Give the hero a birth certificate. You should know everything about him, as if he were Paul—his mother's name, where he went to school, was he good in sports, etc. Some romance authors fill up fat notebooks just giving their hero "life." (You should have gathered such an accumulation in your research notebook.)

The essays I'm enclosing now will be added to those you have already read for a possible book by me on How to Write a Romance and Get It Published. Try to conquer the "point of view" lesson immediately.

So from now on, I probably won't have time to be writing many letters to you, but I will keep sending pieces on romance writing that I think will be helpful.

Sincerely,
Kathryn

From the Desk of Kathryn Falk

November 1

Dear Rosie,

Started my TV show and I'm in a dither. Forgot enclosures in this morning's letter, so here they are ... and a few others.

Let me emphasize again just how important the hero is. He's the main reason for the story. You should be creating a wonderful and unusual man who is also very sensitive and vulnerable, meaning very real. Sort of a Paul Newman who finds you can tame him. Or a Burt Reynolds who succumbs to your charms alone. Or a Prince Charles who needs only you.

Rosemary Rogers kept a photo of Clint Eastwood on her bedroom wall when she wrote her first novels, and Bertrice Small has Tom Selleck's poster above her desk as a constant reminder of male magnetism.

Kathryn

The Third-Person Viewpoint

BY MARISA DE ZAVALA

author of two category romances

Beauty is in the eyes of the beholder. Romance beats in the heart of the beloved. In category romance, that beloved is the heroine. Through her eyes we behold the central drama of her heart's experience that changes her life.

Using a single main character as the center of consciousnes through which all events and ideas are seen, analyzed, an reordered is called third-person limited point of view. By limit ing the point of view to one character's perceptions, the autho limits the reader's point of view and the reader's sympathies a well.

Such a limitation has advantages and disadvantages, as doe any one of the various narrative points of view commonly use in fiction. For instance, the first-person participant point of view in a Victoria Holt gothic or a Mary Stewart romantic suspense opens with the "I" who invites us to share her confusion, he terror, and finally her solution to the mystery that has baffled and plagued the characters from the start of the book. This approach has the tremendous advantage of immediacy—we are there! Where? In the heroine's turbulent mind, in her terror, in her beating heart. And finally in her dramatic triumph over the forces that had threatened to overwhelm her. How can we be so sure? Because as narrator of her tale she has told us so: "People wanted to see the spot where the bones had been found. I was one who wanted to see," explains Karensa of *The Legend of the Seventh Virgin*.

Category romance shuns this immediacy. It opts instead for greater distance between reader and heroine that is maintained by the narrator's reference to the character as "she," by the narrator's refusal to allow the heroine to refer to herself as "I." Why would a category romance novelist choose to establish their distance, you ask? Because in referring to my heroine Ana María de Luna (*Golden Fire, Silver Ice,* an Ecstasy romance), as "she," not "I," the hero, Carlos Garcés y Lorca, becomes "hers," not "mine." He is thereby made accessible to the reader. He is not the exclusive property of the heroine. In direct proportion to the degree to which one can identify with the heroine of a third-person narration, the reader is then able to call the hero "hers," not the heroine's anymore (at least, not exclusively the heroine's).

Once having resolved to write in a third-person limited point of view, the author must bend her efforts toward overcoming that distance, compensating for the loss of immediacy. This the author does by creating a character with whom the reader can be integrated, a heroine who will stand as the reader's idealized self—bright and bold, witty and charming, self-reliant yet flexible—all done in the expectation that the heroine's lover will become the reader's model lover. In her love affair is yours. In her emotional fulfillment, you are fulfilled. In her heart's ease, your own is eased. When Ana begs Carlos never to leave her, he is stunned by her fear. " 'How could I leave you?' he asked incredulously. 'What good would it do me to leave you when you live in my heart? Wherever I go, I take you with me.' " What woman does not feel reassured by love? And falling in love with the hero and being loved by him in return is what category romance is all about.

The author develops reader identification to make possible this emotional fulfillment by using the third-person point of view to advantage. One method of development is to paint a picture of the heroine as others see her. "The bright silver glaze" of Ana's blue-gray eyes "were the envy of many of her friends, as was the coal-black hair that fell like shining silk down her straight back to her small waist." In *Scream of the Parrot* the face of Lydia Belmares is described: "with its wide and generous mouth, its well defined cheekbones beneath which were the deeper shadows of its hollows, there was a dramatic beauty that in her youth had frightened off young boys and now revealed a sophisticated poise that frightened off even worldly men." With a third-person approach, the narrator is able to tell the reader what the heroine knows without having the heroine admit, "People think highly of me."

Because I usually write about Mexican-Americans whose familial ties are strong, I favor developing a subordinate character who stands in a familial or near familial relationship to the female protagonist. As a confidante whose judgment has proven to be reliable, this subordinate character comments on the protagonist. Her favorable comments are readily embraced by the reader, who sees in the confidante a woman well qualified for her role because she carries not only the allegiance of the protagonist but, in a more subtle way, the allegiance of the narrator as well—a double endorsement possible only through a third-person point of view.

As Ana Maria's confidante, Consuelo Delgado realizes that her friend has met her match in the golden-eyed Carlos, who refuses to be frightened off by a glacial look and an arrogant dismissal:

> Consuelo added almost apologetically, "You know it was bound to happen."
>
> "What was?" Ana quickly asked . . .
>
> "You were bound to meet someone who could break through your iron reserve to reach the emotions you put in cold storage."

Like Consuelo, Ofelia López acts as a confidante to her cousin and business partner, Lydia Belmares. Her assessment of Lydia's determination to succeed—'' 'Aren't eighty-hour work weeks enough for you? Do you have to make it one hundred hours without time off for good behavior?' ''—is the push that drives Lydia to vacation in the Amazon jungle and into the arms of the hero, Ramiro Inclán. He fulfills the prophecy Ofelia had earlier announced to Lydia:

> "Someday you're going to attract someone whose will is as strong and whose nature is as passionate as yours, and it's going to be a spectacular affair. . . . He's going to see beneath the sophistication to the . . . generous heart . . . [I] know is there."

Similarly, Juanita fills the role of confidante to Alejandra Carerra *(Kiss Good Night and Say Goodbye),* who has schooled herself to believe that it is better to be unloved and alone than to have been loved and then abandoned. Andra insists that her rage against Marques Montemayor as a possible new artist in her gallery is justified because he is conceited and patronizing:

> "And absolutely charming, ironic and compellingly good looking, not to mention talented," Juanita parried. "Believe me, once you get to know him, you're going to . . . fall under his spell. Everybody does."

All three women, acting as character foils to the heroine, assist her in her search for self-awareness and love even when she does not recognize what she is searching for. Endorsed by the narrator, the confidante speaks for the hero, pleads his cause, reinforces his view when within the narrative framework he cannot speak for himself. In this capacity the confidante carries the reader forward on the same quest the heroine undertakes, and for the same reward.

The narrator must also develop reader identification with the heroine by showing and telling the reader how the heroine is responding to her situation. In a book of only 60,000 to 75,000 words, the author cannot allow the reader to forget whose story is unfolding, cannot allow the reader to transfer sympathy or allegiance even for a short time. With the focus on the heroine's emotional response, all other characters' responses are proportionately minimized and the heroine's proportionately maximized.

Nowhere is this showing and telling more crucial to the success of the category romance than in the scenes of sensuality and passion. The reader must feel as though she is awakening to her own deepest sensual urge coupled with an emotional love to last a lifetime. The narrator describes this physical and emotional awakening, which Ana experiences with Carlos on their wedding night:

> Ana was overpowered by a new awareness of her body as the feminine counterpart to his masculinity. Where he was hard, she was soft; where he was insistent, she was yielding. Under his expert care, her body was coaxed to an even deeper realization. She allowed her hands to enjoy his body at first tenatively, then more confidently, and urged him toward herself, never reckoning the full scope of her power to thrill and excite. When he could bear no more, with an agonized cry he was upon her and her body accepted his. She felt herself drowning in an ocean of previously unimagined sensations whose tides were a deluge of torment both unbearably savage and unutterably sweet.
>
> Suddenly she arched her back in wondrous astonishment as a volley of sensations burst in upon her with the exploding force of falling stars. He clasped her quivering body to himself and a cry of pain escaped her lips that in the same breath became a cry of pure pleasure whose intensity sent a shudder through her newly awakened self.

" 'Ramiro,' " cries Lydia in the intensity of their lovemaking: "It was more a sigh than a word left quivering in the space between his lips and hers, between her nakedness and his." Ramiro responds to her need with skillful teasing, which the narrator must describe as the heroine absorbs it:

> Expertly he pulled the lace bodice down to her narrow waist, exposing the lovely fullness of her high breasts. He stroked the rose-hued tenderness until it hardened beneath the fluttering caress of his experienced hands, intentionally inciting riotous demands he would not gratify—not yet.

The reader must so closely have become one with the heroine by this point that she too is "rewarded by the feel of the lean hardness of his chest beneath her fingers . . . the sinewy strength of his back." In his tormentingly slow, immeasurably sensuous love play, the reader luxuriates "in the sexual manhood she discovered and the convulsive spasm that shuddered through his great frame."

Identifying with Alejandra, the reader abandons her inhibitions in favor of a desire for Marques too long denied: "With a velvet touch she moved her hand over his hip and down his muscled thigh." Urgently the heat of his body enters hers, and in this consummation the narrator must satisfy the reader's emotional expectations, which the narrator has purposefully cultivated. " 'Marques!' " Andra called.

as she fell into a world of spinning light and soundless space, clinging to him, digging her nails into the hard flesh. . . .

Was that her voice or his she heard crying its sweet torture into the distance? Then she heard him call her name and inexpressible pleasure burst in anew and she embraced the thief who had stolen her mystery, sheltering him within the deep warmth of her feminine self.

None of these passages would carry the same impact in a first-person point of view, for then they would appear to be a violation of the privacy of the "I" narrator, or conceivably make the narrator appear to be of an exhibitionist persuasion. By contrast, third-person narration makes it possible for these passages to be enactments of sensual privacy tastefully enjoyed.

By the close of the final chapter, the heroine has moved away from her reluctance to engage in an affair of the heart. This transformation the reader animatedly endorses, since she has had a personal stake in the happy resolution of the conflict. The reader has known all along that the heroine will find the completion of her life's circle in *romance tan divino*, for the reader has been in silent communication with the narrator of the third-person narrative. Together they have watched the heroine come to know herself as she comes to know the hero. And together they have seen her do what they have wanted her to do all along—embrace the hero in a sensual and emotional commitment that fulfills.

In the heroine's embrace is the reader's fulfillment.
In her heart's ease is your own.

Breathing Life into Your Characters

BY MAGGIE OSBORNE

author of five historical romances

Scarlett O'Hara, Amber, Jane Eyre, Madame Bovary—who can forget these ladies once having met them? We smiled at their antics, raged at their blunders, hurt when they hurt. We cared about them. We cared enough to continue until the last word had been read.

Readers are interested in plot, certainly, and in well-drawn stories and unfamiliar settings. But unless the characters are fully developed—characters the reader can care about—the work is unlikely to be memorable. Engaging characters comprise that magical element that sustains the reader's interest until "The End" appears.

So how do we as writers transfer the Scarletts and the Ambers from our minds to paper and bring them vividly to life?

1. *Know Your Characters*. Know more about your major characters than you will ever reveal to the reader; know them totally. Compile a list of tough questions, questions to reveal your character's major traits, faults, and virtues. What childhood diseases or emotional traumas did your heroine suffer? How did she feel about her parents then? Now? Her siblings? Who is her best friend/enemy and why? What is

she most proud/ashamed of and why? What are her immediate goals? Her long-term goals? What does she like/dislike
about herself? Has she been in love, and what happened?
What would she do if she found a fortune and no one knew?
And so forth.

A thorough questionnaire will help develop well-rounded,
complete characters. And when a plot crisis comes up, a
quick glance at the character's questionnaire reminds you
of your heroine's background, her strengths, talents, and
vulnerabilities.

Tricks: Need an instant characterization for a secondary
character? Consult an astrology book. You'll find a ready-
made character described for each astrological sign, complete with virtues and vices, preferred colors and jewelry,
profession, and occasionally a physical description.

2. *Names.* Characters' names should never be chosen frivo-
lously but selected with care to subtly suggest the traits
you've assigned that character. Harsh consonants hint at
strength and perseverance. Softer names suggest a more
gentle personality. Make the character's name work for you.

When selecting names, consider the following: time period,
geographical location, ethnic background, age. An unusual
name suitable for a contemporary romance may be jolting in
a historical. Each era has its popular and fashionable names.

Don't overlook the characterizing possibilities of nicknames. The way one character addresses another can quickly
establish the relationship between the two.

Vary names. Several characters sporting names beginning
or ending with the same letter can be confusing.

Tricks: Keep a name-your-baby book near the typewriter
and add to it for possible future use. Maintain lists of French
names, German names, etc.

When researching, note the names and titles of actual
historical figures, then mix and match to create fictional
names authentic for period and setting.

3. *Appearance.* While readers want to form a mental image of
your characters, it isn't necessary to dwell on more than a
few significant features. Most readers would prefer to learn
what is transpiring underneath the heroine's coiffures than
read a description of it.

When clothing is mentioned, select apparel that makes a statement about the character. The heroine wearing a tailored business suit is rarely the same personality as a heroine draped in lace ruffles.

Don't dress your heroine to match her eyes; dress her to match her circumstance and mood. A sunny nature is easier to sell when clad in yellow or pink than when presented in gray or navy.

Tricks: Clip pictures that resemble your characters in coloring and general appearance and tack them near the typewriter. Draw in any moles, scars, mustaches, beards, etc. When working with a lengthy manuscript over a long period, it is devilishly easy to inadvertently transfer a beauty mark from one cheek to the other or to provide the hero with a mustache on page 10 and present him cleanshaven on page 100.

4. *Action.* Reaction to action and stimulus help reveal your character's substance.

5. *Thoughts.* Nothing fixes personality more quickly than taking the reader inside your character's mind. Sharing the character's thinking forms rapid reader identification. The character's thoughts transmit emotion, conflict, and his/her point of view.

Warning: When a character is thinking, your story is not proceeding. The action stops. Do share the character's thoughts, but not at the expense of your story. Intersperse thinking with action.

6. *Dialogue.* Characters take on reality when they speak. But don't let all your characters sound alike—provide secondary characters with occasional verbal mannerisms, such as a habitual pause before speaking or a repetitive phrase special to that character. Dialogue should reflect the character's age, background, education, interests, and emotions.

Present conflict in dialogue. Use dialogue to heighten contrasts between characters. Dialogue is an excellent instrument for illustrating feelings and relationships.

Tricks: To be fully effective, each section of dialogue should ideally do at least three of the following: (1) Aid characterization through content and presentation. (2) Develop your story line. (3) Show your characters' state of mind and temperament. (4) Provide new information to the

reader. (5) Interrupt lengthy narrative and pick up the pa
of the story.

Read your dialogue aloud to test for flow and natur
expression.

7. *Viewpoint.* Presenting your story through a single viewpoi
deepens characterization, as all events are perceived throug
your major character. Reader identification is quickly esta
lished and maintained.

While it is necessary to restrict yourself to a single view
point presentation in a category romance, care should b
taken in a historical romance not to present too many view
point characters. Each time you introduce another viewpoi
character you ask the reader to switch her identificatio
bond, thereby weakening the original tie.

8. *Emotion.* The emotional content of your story keeps th
reader turning pages. Develop your character's reaction
through thoughts, dialogue, and movement. It is not enoug
to simply show the heroine reacting; the reader wants t
participate, wants to share what is in your heroine's hea
and mind.

Tricks: Don't stop revising until your sad scenes mak
you weep and your amusing scenes make *you* smile. If you
emotional scenes do not affect you, the writer, they will ne
stir your reader.

9. *Your Heroine.* Allow her to be human, which is to allow he
mistakes and the freedom to be less than perfect. Give he
areas of vulnerability, areas of doubt.

Resist the natural urge to protect your heroine, lest sh
become a narrator standing outside the action. But don
make her a victim.

Provide believable motivation for her actions and reactions

By all means allow your heroine to grow, but maintain
consistency of major personality traits.

Tricks: If in doubt as to your heroine's response in a pl
situation, act out the event. When acting the scene, note you
gestures, body language, voice inflections, emotional responses

Become your heroine—crawl into her skin, perceive th
world through her eyes and experience. The better you know
your heroine, the more your scene and word choices wil
reflect an actual scene.

0. *Final Suggestions.* The best writing instructors in the world are waiting and willing to help you—you'll find them on the shelves of your personal library. Select one of your favorite author's books and study it. How did the author present physical description? Why does the dialogue work? How much or how little background information is offered? Underline the elements of characterization: thought, dialogue, viewpoint, description, action. Tear apart and study the examples your favorite writers offer.

Challenge yourself. Compose a biographical sketch of someone you know, then ask a mutual acquaintance to identify the character. To make it tougher, rewrite the piece providing no physical description.

Write two pages of dialogue, using no narrative or tag lines, striving to create dialogue so distinctive that a reader will experience no confusion between the two speakers.

Most important—keep writing. Good luck and good fortune!

Creating the Hero and Heroine

BY CASEY DOUGLAS

author of six category romances

Though the plots I contrive are fairly complex, they begin from as little as one or two words. A particular geographical locale or a certain career may ignite my imagination and spur me to build a story around it.

That's precisely how my superromance *Proud Surrender* began. Because I adore animals and wildlife, I thought it would be fun to make my heroine a veterinarian. And where could I find a more abundant and colorful wildlife backdrop than in the ruggedly beautiful safari country of East Africa? *Voilà*, my female protagonist is born: Katherine (Kit) Shannon, a newly graduated veterinarian from California whose goal is to establish a game preserve for endangered species in Kenya.

So far it's all very straightforward and simple. But what do we do about a hero? I knew that he had to be British: (a) because swoon over Anthony Andrews, Jeremy Irons, and all the other English heroes who populate TV's elegant *Masterpiece Theater* and (b) because I knew that Kenya's modern history was one of British colonial development and that one could logically expect to find Britons there now. (I should interject here that I do my research concurrently with my plotting, not only for accuracy in developing story line but because research provides many ideas for individual scenes within the book.)

So we have in mind a ruggedly attractive British hero to go along with the ruggedly exotic landscape. But now what? What possible business could this Briton be in that he's making life hell for our heroine Kit while fighting off the inevitable hot sparks of attraction that fly between them from the first moment they set eyes on each other?

What we need is a believable, divisive, potentially explosive source of contention between hero and heroine that, in the end, will be totally reconcilable. Doug (my co-plotting husband) and I mulled the problem over for a week with no satisfactory answer.

Who would be so mean and lowdown as to fight a lovely young veterinary doctor because she wanted to set up a preserve? Either there could be no common meeting ground (i.e., the hero might be a big-game hunter—macho enough, to be sure, but a character who probably wouldn't find much sympathy with today's readers) or the hero might run the risk of being altogether too nice and pleasant (i.e., a doctor with the U.N. working on projects of his own on the continent). Our hero had to fall somewhere in the middle—tough and uncompromising in the position he is defending against our feisty veterinarian, yet one who eventually can compromise with her.

What was born out of the joint labors of our imaginations was a tough, brooding third-generation coffee plantation owner, whom we duly christened Devin Michaels. Naturally, his property would djoin that of our heroine, Kit. Do you see the seeds of conflict eing planted? Good, because without conflict you have the ame thing as a car without gas. Your characters may be strong nd compelling, your setting magnificent, but if you don't have everal convincing reasons for them to be at each other's throats or 95,000 words, you're in trouble.

I know, because I've been in trouble like that myself.

Some time ago we began to plot out a romance novel that eemed to have exciting possibilities. But two weeks down the ine (after I'd read ten books and filled two dozen five-by-seven ards with research notes and we'd redone a plot draft for the hird or fourth time) we came reluctantly to the conclusion that or all the excitement of our protagonists' careers, and their nerry romp through the antique auction houses of Europe, the conflict between them simply wasn't strong enough. We didn't compound our error by plunging ahead doggedly with the allur- ng theme (which would probably have fallen apart two thirds nto the manuscript). We dropped it and started afresh on some- hing totally new.

So, note well, your story must have a credible conflict. To be complex and sustaining enough, I think the plot must have a "physical" as well as an "emotional" basis for conflict.

You've probably already guessed at the source of "physical" conflict in *Proud Surrender*. Tender young coffee bushes and gamboling wild animals aren't exactly ideal neighbors. To this situation we added another twist: The Kenyan highlands are in their third year of drought, and the vital dam used to irrigate the coffee trees on the plantation is situated on Kit's property.

Now that we've set our protagonists on a metaphorical powder keg, you might think it was enough for us to begin and ring the bell for round one. But you're wrong. We've barely just begun to plot.

Logical questions of how a California woman would magically gain access to a prime, water-supplied highland property eight thousand miles from her home led Doug and me off on another fruitful tangent. Once again, as we spent several evenings mull- ing over ideas, we came up with what would turn out to be the central theme of the novel—the classic one of the characters' pasts spilling over to haunt the present.

Hero and heroine are still fighting over the land and water rights, though now the contested dam is nestled on a piece of property Kit inherited from her recently deceased mother. The

land had been a wedding gift to the woman who'd left her firs
family (Kit and her father) to marry a wealthy, handsome wid
ower (whose son happens to be our hero). For twenty years tha
land has been in the de facto possession of the Michaelses. No
the legacy of that distant past begins to simmer as Kit returns t
Africa to claim the land that was bequeathed to her.

From this we began to build an interlocking story line that w
hoped would be sufficiently believable and tense to grip th
reader for some 380-odd pages.

Now we have our emotional conflict, which will be fueled b
several undercurrents: (a) Kit is the living image of her dea
mother; (b) Devin as a young man had been attracted to a
beautiful but deceptive woman; (c) Kit herself is a divorce
escaping a desperately unhappy marriage.

So you see the plot has evolved so far from one fragmente
idea—a vet in Africa—to a convoluted story that can be de
scribed in a long paragraph.

The next step before writing out the plot in terms of a chapter
by-chapter breakdown is to make lists: of potential characters
major and minor, who can contribute to the development and/o
resolution of the conflict; of the reasons why hero and heroin
don't get along; of scenes and possible snippets of dialogue
From these sketched notes and lists we begin to build a story
with as many twists and turns as possible (including in *Prou*
Surrender an unexpected marriage of convenience in which ou
heroine does the proposing. The hero agrees, but not withou
exacting some clever demands of his own in exchange!).

Often I will have the first chapter and the last chapter plotted
in detail before there's anything in the middle, but perhaps that's
for the best: You know where you're starting from and you have
a clear idea of where you're ultimately heading.

I suppose we can conclude by saying that the key to a marketable plot is conflict—with major and minor themes that cross over
and interweave with one another. Your novel becomes a symphonic
variation that provides endless opportunities to fight, resolve that
particular conflict (temporarily or permanently), have a tender love
scene, build to another conflict, and repeat the whole cycle. This
is the basic ebb and flow of any romance novel, short or long.

Once you have your plot formalized, let your characters begin
to interact among themselves. While I wouldn't think of beginning a novel without a detailed plot outline, I rarely note anything special about my characters.

Perhaps the true miracle of writing is to see the protagonists take on a solid three-dimensional form, until it seems as if they're controlling me at times rather than vice versa. Have one guiding idea when you throw your characters together in a scene: dramatic impact. Is it going to be exciting, unnerving, sensual, hilarious each time they collide?

Additional Notes on the Hero

What makes our heroes "heroes" is their machismo, that overwhelming maleness that calls to the heroine's blood even when she's madder than hell at him.

The trend (fortunately) is to create feisty, independent heroines who will be matched pretty evenly in any contest of wills with the hero. By comparison, the hero's character has changed little over the years.

As the twelve-year-old daughter of one avid romance reader put it: "Sure, I know what those guys are like; they're always tall, dark, and sardonic." Or as one British editor more bluntly put it: "We want our heroes to be the very antithesis of our gentle, kindly, and understanding English husbands!"

Heroes are harsh, impatient, proud, daring, successful, stubborn. (These are not exclusively male prerogatives, to be sure. In fact, it will help your story if the heroine shares many of these qualities with him.)

The challenge to you, the writer, in creating a specific male character is to make him as three-dimensional as possible, so that he's something rather more than a chess piece you move around in accord with the story line. Like the most fascinating real people you know, your hero will be complex and paradoxical. He will be a product of the setting in which he lives and the past that molded him, a man whose prejudices and loyalties, desires and hatreds will collide with those of the heroine.

We can take another look at *Proud Surrender*, focusing on the hero Devin Michaels. From the very opening sentences of the prologue we learn what kind of man he is: a third-generation British Kenyan whose land is his lifeblood, whose land is so intrinsic a part of him that he would ruthlessly fight any threat to it. The threat, of course, is our heroine Kit, presaged in the newspaper photograph that the elder Michaels shows his son.

Born to a harsh, unforgiving land, Devin shares those characteristics. He is hard and self-sufficient (a man who hunts and flies planes expertly), a man accustomed to flirting with danger. This last quality will feed the sexual tension between him and Kit, whom he sees as a danger/attraction. That very duality of his character lends excitement:

> She'd felt contempt emanating from him like a silent raging torrent . . . beneath it a dark brooding sensuality.

Devin is a cynic. He saw his father remarry, watched the woman trade on her beauty to manipulate both father and son, and then came to hate her after she'd gone, "leaving emotional wreckage behind her." Out of that experience has come his inability to trust women.

Tempering these qualities are his basic fair-mindedness (as evidenced in his willingness to deed a huge tract of land to a local farming cooperative) and an underlying generosity of spirit (as shown in his concern for the happiness of Sattima, a young woman whom the Michaelses brought into their home after her parents died).

You can hint at the hero's character through physical description:

> Though his face was bronzed from long hours beneath the equatorial sun, he wasn't as dark as she'd imagined him to be the night before. . . . Kit sensed that the darkness was more a reflection of some brooding inner quality than physical delineation.

And you can let other characters describe him:

> "Did you teach Devin to shoot?" she asked. A short bark of laughter escaped Ford's lips. "Yes, beginning when he was a lad of six. He was proud and tough even then, and stubborn, too."

The heroine may measure him against others:

> But she needn't have worried about Ali guessing at her inner state. He had none of Devin's cool yet watchful intensity, that unnerving capability to reach out and respond to her in uncharted emotional depths.

Most important, the hero's character will reveal itself through his interactions with the heroine:

> "But all that I see is another beautiful woman bent on conquest—the past reshaping itself. You've drawn Ford into your gleaming web. Am I to be the next?"

The same fierce undercurrent that she'd sensed in him broke through to the surface, but she had no idea of how to tame it. With tentative fingers she reached out to trace the line of his hard jaw. "How could I ever hope to conquer such a stony heart?" she whispered.

But Devin was too absorbed in his own anger to notice the wounded, vulnerable look in her eyes and he took her words as another piece of calculated coquetry. He jerked his head from her gentle touch and stood up. "You won't," he whispered down at her harshly with eyes that glinted like beaten gold. "I swear it, dear Katherine."

Remember, the hero is yours—first, last, and always. You're the one who has so lovingly fashioned him. Make him everything you'd want a man to be in real life: a strong, multifaceted individual who ultimately brings out the best in your heroine—and in you.

Finding the Right Names, Titles, and Careers

BY DEBRA OXIER

a romance reader

Romantic Names

When I was asked to make a list of some of romance's favorite masculine names, I immediately thought of Janet Dailey, who has a knack for using unusual, character-fitting names for all her heroes. As I began to recall a few, I suddenly realized that, unlike many authors, Janet seldom, if ever, repeats a name when creating all new characters. To give you an idea of what I mean, here is a list of fifty-one names from fifty-one different Janet Dailey books:

Bay, Blake, Brant, Brock, Brodie, Chance, Choya, Cody, Cole, Colter, Cord, Dane, Deke, Dirk, Flint, Gabe, Jace, Jake, Jared, Jett, Jock, Jonas, Jordan, Josh, Judd, Lije, Linc, Luck, Mitch, Morgan, Race, Rad, Rans, Reese, Reilly, Rhyder, Rian, Roarke, Rolt, Rome, Ruel, Seth, Shad, Sin(clair), Slade, Tell, Travis, Wade, Whit, Zachary, Zane.

Going through my myriad books in search of suitable names, I noticed that several very common names were never used unless it was as the antagonist in the story line. Bob, Rick, Steve, Bill, Warren, Paul, George, etc., only serve to create problems for the hero and seldom, if ever, come out ahead in the end. Once in a while David or Ben wins the heroine's heart, but they were usually portrayed as tender, gentle lovers rather than those possessing fire and passion.

The following list comes from a variety of well-known category authors. In each case the hero possessed a domineering personality, self-confident, assured, successful. Naturally good-looking, they projected that masculine aura that causes a woman's blood to boil. At times full of loving tenderness, their love more often than not culminated in an eruption of blazing passion.

Picture yourself locked in the arms of:

Drake, Lance, Mac, Jed, Locke, Nick, Gareth, Griff, Rafe, Derek, Steele, Wolf, Stone, Luke, Vance, Clint, Cam(eron), and Zeke, to name a few.

Several authors delight in setting their novels in foreign countries. The hero is often of foreign descent, resulting in the use of foreign names. Anne Mather is one such author, having several books located in Spain or one of the Latin American countries. Upon researching her novels, I discovered such names as Dominic, Rafael, Manuel, Raoul, Luis, Vincente, Andre, and Santino. Anne Hampson has had great success with Greek locales, utilizing such names as Nico, Leon, Stephanos, Lukas, Dion, etc. And who can forget the Vikings: the Swedes? the Russians? with names like Erik, Kurt, Alexi, and Swen.

Growing up in an era of *Snow White, Cinderella,* and *Sleeping*

Beauty, I often dreamed of the day when a handsome prince would come dashing forth on his white charger. However, as I matured into adulthood I discovered that fairy tales seldom come true. Yet in spite of this fact, my love of a good romance never diminished. If anything, it has been enhanced by the Janet Daileys, the Barbara Cartlands, the Danielle Steels, and all those other authors whose books fill the racks in the romance section of my local bookstore.

What's in a name? Let's face it, if it weren't for Wade, Brock, Jake, Dominic, Drake, Leon, Erik, Swen, etc., something would be missing from my life. Each a creation of some author's vivid imagination, these characters have provided many hours of enjoyable reading and relaxation to me and thousands like me.

And it all began with a name. For at the same time the author thought of that name, a character began to take shape along with it. This character was projected into a story line or plot, whose image became more vivid with each new page. When at last the final page is turned, we, as readers, have shared in the privilege of knowing these characters. We were partakers of their sorrows and joys, relished their laughter, endured their tears. We lived right alongside them, just as surely as the author who carried them from page to page, or stage to stage. For a little while, they belonged to us, and though the story is over, the precious memory lingers for days on end.

It all began with a name.

While searching through shelf after shelf of category romances, I discovered it quite difficult to respond positively to most feminine names. Perhaps, being female myself, the sound of the everyday names for heroines just didn't turn me on, so to speak.

However, I did see a trend by several authors toward the more unusual-sounding names. I fell to comparing the heroine's name with that of the hero. Did the names match well? Could I easily picture the rough, rugged male breathing the heroine's name in a delightful sigh of passion? Based on these thoughts, I came up with the following list of favorite feminine names. If you will, for a moment, place yourself in the man's position. Can you picture yourself whispering sweet nothings to:

Amii, Brandi, Britt, Camera, Cassie, Corinne, Courtney, Danielle (Dani), Daran, Gidian, Glenna, Jesse, Jodi, Jordan or Jordanna, Lacey, Lissa, Michaela, Morgain, Raine, Rhea, Sacha, Shannon, Skye, Storm, Tish?

If so, then I guess we're in business. If not, then either we just plain don't see eye to eye (or name to name), or you aren't the romantic you claim to be! Whichever, next time you're browsing through a bookstore, or sifting through your own collection of romantic fiction for something to read, take a moment to study the names.

Just for fun, make a list of those that catch your interest. Compare them with the hero's name to see if they match up. Then narrow your choices down to one or two that seem really intriguing. Now decide for yourself if it's a name you might use in a novel of your own. You'll probably be amazed at what you come up with!

Catchy Titles

The first time I really paid any attention to titles was when Harlequin produced a series of one-word titles authored by Charlotte Lamb. These eye-catching titles included: *Temptation*, *Seduction*, *Retribution*, *Crescendo*, *Heartbreaker*, *Sensation*, *Possession*, *Obsession*, *Abduction*, *Frustration*, *Illusion*, *Compulsion*, and *Fever*.

Rachel Ryan (a.k.a. Sandra Brown) came up with some memorable titles—memorable because they fit in so well with her story line that it was almost impossible to forget them. For instance, in *A Treasure Worth Seeking*, the hero was a U.S. Treasury agent, while *Eloquent Silence* concerned the care and education of the hero's deaf daughter.

Several Janet Dailey novels clued the reader in to their location. Among them were *Fiesta San Antonio*, *The Indy Man*, *That Carolina Summer*, *Dakota Dreamin'*, and *That Boston Man*.

Except for the above-mentioned books by Charlotte Lamb, it was difficult to find any specific patterns for title choices by category romance authors. Unlike the historicals, with Patricia Matthews' Love's series, or Janelle Taylor's Ecstasy series, category authors seldom write sequels, or use catchall phrases to gain reader attention. Perhaps this is due in part to the shorter length of their novels or the fact that so many categories have flooded the market in the last couple of years. Due to the vast numbers of titles available each month, many of us have been forced to be very selective in order to remain within our book budgets. A difficult task, but necessary.

Because of this, I have deliberately paid less attention to new titles in recent months. Instead, I first select my reading material by author, then turn to the back cover for a brief synopsis of the story line. Occasionally, however, a title on the book rack will catch my eye if it suggests that the story within is on a favorite subject of mine. Since I love ranch stories, any title containing the word *Texas* immediately draws my attention. Not that all books set in Texas are located on ranches, but that one word is enough to make me investigate further. One lady buys anything and everything connected with Australia. In her case, any book title with the word *outback* is worth a second look.

If I am reduced to picking several novels on title alone, not knowing the author's name or anything about the book at all, I select those titles that hint at what lies between the sheets. *Passion, fire, desire, danger* are all words that touch off a spark of interest in my own romantic heart. Therefore, on title alone, I selected the following as some of the best-*sounding* category romances: *Stormy Reunion, Passionate Encounter, Untamed Desire, All the Fire, Duel of Desire, Dangerous Enchantment, The Flame of Desire, Again the Magic, Intimate Strangers,* and *Seduction,* to name a few.

The list is endless, and with the ever-changing trends in romantic fiction, I look forward to new ideas and even more exciting titles (if that's possible) in the months to come.

Favorite Careers

Several years ago, when I first began reading romantic fiction, English governesses and schoolteachers could be found in abundance. In addition, a married woman instantly became a homemaker, her husband generally insisting she adopt that role upon her marriage.

Today's trend in romantic "employment" reveals the changing mores in our own modern society. Job selection expanded as women became more independent. The hero is no longer required to be the dominant force in today's romance.

Upon researching the wide range of category romance, I found it difficult to narrow the heroine's employment to any given areas. Therefore, I have simply made a list of careers found in these romances, rather than attempting to pinpoint a particular direction for the authors' favorite choice. These are:

secretary, nurse, lawyer, doctor, airplane pilot, computer programmer, journalist, writer, model, actress, teacher, clothing store manager, proprietor, clerk, real-estate agent, librarian, social worker, photographer, artist, singer, dancer, pianist, caterer, veterinarian, hair stylist, waitress.

Let the Character's Words Flow

BY GINGER CHAMBERS
author of five category romances

To a great many people first attempting to learn the craft of writing, dialogue is a major stumbling block. Telling a story in narrative form is easy for them, but when it comes time for a character to speak, they freeze. Instead of letting the character's voice come through naturally, the writer imposes his or her own words. As a result, the character sometimes sounds as if he is giving a speech rather than taking part in a conversation. The writer, sensing this stiffness, is dissatisfied but doesn't know what to do about it.

The best solution I can recommend is to relax! Don't tighten up. Let the character's words flow. Get into his mind and let *him* do the talking.

Often a major key is to use contractions. In contemporary life people do use them, and it's amazing how some of the stiffness disappears when a few word combinations are sprinkled into sentences. Also, don't hesitate to use some slang. If the terms are in accepted usage, take advantage of them.

The next hint, which assures a naturalness to dialogue, is to listen. Hear the way people talk and imitate it. In all situations, keep alert. Standing in a grocery line is wonderful. So is an elevator, an airport, a bus, a plane, a hair salon, a shopping mall, a restaurant—anytime you are among people, absorb what is said, how it is said, the rhythm. Jot some of it down if you need to.

Another suggestion is to read your work out loud, preferably to someone else. But if no one is available, read it to yourself or a tape recorder. Hearing your words, both dialogue and narrative, is a tremendous help. It especially aids dialogue, because the areas with problems—where the flow is not smooth—can be easily spotted and remedied.

Now, two cautions. One is to be careful in using regional dialects. A little can give flavor; too much can confuse. The second is to be careful about repetitions. Once, as a prank, my young son taped about fifteen minutes of my family's day. When he played it back for us, we were amazed at the number of times we repeated certain words. So the warning is this—do not use the same expression too often. This is one time a writer should not reflect life.

Which brings us to something else: Don't be afraid to rewrite. What a character says is not written in stone. If the sound is not quite right, don't feel that you can't change it or make it better. You can. Keeping firmly in mind your character's personality, rework your dialogue until you get it right. And at revision time, carefully check for repetitions. Use a thesaurus or synonym finder to discover other ways of saying the same thing.

Good dialogue writing accomplishes two main purposes: It reveals the essence of your characters and it makes the plot move forward. Telling a fact in narrative is not nearly as effective as letting a character's voice show it.

As an example, in *Call It Love*, the basic misunderstanding between my hero and heroine, Luke Morgan and JoAnna Davis, occurs immediately and is handled entirely by dialogue. Preceding the following scene, Luke has just prevented JoAnna's ex-boyfriend from raping her on the beach. Now they are in her beach house and JoAnna is shaken both by her experience and by the virile presence of the man she has just found out was her new neighbor on an isolated stretch of Galveston Island.

    "Was he your boyfriend?"
    "I thought he was."

"Under the circumstances, I don't think it would be a very good idea for you to see him again."

JoAnna shuddered slightly at the understatement. "I won't," she assured him.

"He may not agree with that."

"He'll have to!"

The man's pale eyes narrowed and he spoke slowly, carefully. "From what I saw last night, he might have cause to think you're playing with him—and that maybe you didn't like it that I interfered today." JoAnna gasped but he went on as if unaware of the shock his words had dealt. "Do you always do your lovemaking on the beach? . . . I'm not condemning, mind you. Making love in the out-of-doors can be very . . . stimulating. I'm just asking if you ever do it conventionally—in a bed."

Understandably, JoAnna was outraged, which catapulted the plot forward, while at the same time disclosing a part of each of their basic characters.

In *Sweet Persuasion*, Blake Michaels, the hero, is determined that Cindy Thomas, the heroine, come around to his way of thinking and admit that she is more than just a little attracted to him. But Cindy has other ideas and has agreed to work for him only because she is a professional and has a commitment.

"You want me to work for you, remember? Or was that just another . . . deception. I'll use that word since you seem to be allergic to 'lie.' "

"There's work to be done—plenty of it. But I also counted on a little time off for play . . . a chance for us to get to know one another."

Cindy snorted. It was inelegant, but it was what she did. "Did you ever stop to think that maybe I don't *want* to get to know you?"

"You're fighting me, Cindy." His brown eyes were filled with amusement.

"You're damn right I am. I also think you're crazy!"

"Only about you."

Do you see how much more effective words are than the previous narrative summation of this scene? The stated words come to life through the dialogue of the characters. If a person is selfish, generous, sarcastic, or filled with humor, let his words reveal this about him.

Still, after taking all of what has been suggested into consideration, probably the most important aspect of writing dialogue is to have fun with it. Enjoy your characters. Let them dictate to you. And definitely be open to surprises. To me, a great part of the magic of writing is the unexpected things some of my characters say. Often new sides of their natures are revealed that I knew nothing about, and the story takes wing and flies in a direction I didn't plan.

Spontaneity, flow, rhythm, relaxation, and enjoyment—these are the secrets I have learned over the years. When they work well, my characters speak and all I have to do is write down what they say.

Try it. You'll be surprised how easy it is.

> Maryland Avenue
> Royal Oak, Michigan
>
> November 25

Dear Kathryn,

All those essays you sent me spurred me into a white heat and I did go back to first base. I made a complete dossier on my hero, and if he walked in the door right now I wouldn't be surprised. Honestly, he's that real. I feel like I gave birth to another child.

I must admit I was upset because you sounded so exasperated with me, but I realize how busy you are and how much of your time you'd shared with me and I feel sheepish. Thanks a million.

I put my hero and heroine back on the filmstrip and now I've taken to the typewriter (with Peter Duchin music playing in the background)—I have a bit of a preppy atmosphere going when they meet. I've almost finished the first draft of <u>Sterling Silver Love</u>, with my typewriter smoking from speed and exhaustion.

Kathryn, I was so proud of it! And the typing was near perfect, too. But then I read it . . . Janet Dailey, Danielle Steel—it wasn't even a good steal from them.

Again, what shall I do?

> Rosie the Wretched

P.S. Shall I send you the manuscript? No, I won't. Not until you have time and ask for it yourself.

From the Desk of Kathryn Falk

December 5

Dear Rosie,

I do sympathize. Yes, writing your first romance is a little baffling, but let me quote what a Mills & Boon editor says: "The most saleable thing for a writer, even in a field like category romance fiction, is originality. Anybody can write like somebody else and copy a formula. We call it 'clone writing.' We try to be sure that each of our writers has her own individual characters and personality. A writer should do her thing and be concerned with the formula afterward."

So, Rosie, do your thing, and then cut and expand it to the right formula size. You've got what you need—inspiration, talent, red pencil, scissors, Scotch tape, a fresh ream of paper, and your typewriter. And seated at the latter (on a cushion, please) you will produce your nicely tailored, but highly original, romance—all seams fitted, stitches fine. You will be the author of a stylish, chic novel, the envy of the <u>haut monde</u> romance writing-reading set everywhere.

Onward!
Regards, as always,
Kathryn

3

Polishing the Prose

Once the formula is intimately comprehended, when all the techniques of romance fiction are balanced together, what else must the writer do? Polish the prose.

She or he can check for predictability, analyze the prose for tightness of plot, smoothness, good characterization, and above all, freshness.

Heightening sex appeal, pulling out all the stops on sensuality, can make for a really stunning category romance.

As one way editors study manuscripts and make decisions is by reading a synopsis, the following is a look at Alice Mogan's plot for *Masquerade of Love*—chosen because she is able to grab her readers in the solar plexus at once with her startling treatment of lusty love.

So here is a short analysis of that book with its delightful surprises numbered:

1. The story opens with the hero sitting in a plush Las Vegas casino considering his present celibacy, counting the number of months he's been in this state. (That's unusual right off, and sets the reader's erotic interests to instant boil!)

2. Who appears at the door but a young gorgeous blonde who catches the hero's eye. Before he can make a pass, she stares at him as if she recognizes him. She walks over and sits down. He notices a white circle on her ring finger, as if a wedding band has been recently removed. He surmises that she's probably married and out for a free night on the town. She propositions him immediately, to his amazement, and he accepts. (That's pretty quick for the lead-up to the first sex scene!)

3. The warm-up (more like heat-up), or foreplay, takes place on the dance floor, as his hands travel up and down

her back until she's a quivering mass of flesh. In bed that night, he discovers she's wearing a wig and demands she take it off. (That scene is hilarious, and certainly was a first in category romances.)

4. When he starts to make love, he finds he has on his hands a virgin, wedding-ring mark or not. The hero, being the perfect lover, naturally, starts all over on his lovemaking, and the devirgination night becomes the night of nights.

5. However, the lady has a problem. (If she didn't, they'd just live happily ever after and no story.) She disappears from his bed while he sleeps, and the reader soon learns that she's rich, and trying to get pregnant by someone who resembles her husband, who died—with her small child—in an automobile crash. (How can she have had a child we wonder?) Her godfather (also her husband's grandfather) is dying over the tragedy, and a grandchild is one way she may give him the heart to live.

6. The lady, her godfather, and the family valet are quite excited when she tells them she is pregnant. A vacation is in order, so the godfather picks a place from a prospectus he's recently been sent for investment purposes. The little group drives there, and guess who owns the luxurious resort? The handsome rogue in the casino. The father of the baby. He has tracked down the heroine through her wig, bought at Neiman-Marcus, and sent the grandfather the brochure to lure her into his lair. Will he blackmail her—or what?

The plot thickens, leaving the romance reader of the steamy type enthralled. To any romance devotee, such a fresh plot is intriguing.

As an aside, the author, Alice Morgan, winner of the first Pearl Award for this steamy first category romance, is herself a sensual woman who enjoys tapping her libido and transferring her feeling to the "hot" pages of her brand of romance writing. (It's rumored that Alice never sleeps on white sheets, just black silk!)

Humor is always a bright and airy addition to a category romance. Bringing a smile to the lips is as necessary as bringing a tear to the eye. Minor characters are sometimes the most convenient ways to convey humor. One of the mistakes that new writers make is being so overly concerned with the hero and heroine that they end up very dull, while the minor roles of housekeeper or best friend, having not been overworked, end up light and amusing because they've escaped the new writer's nervousness.

In a category romance there's barely room for more than three or four minor characters, but they do serve the purpose of supplying information that the hero and heroine can't relay—such as what their youth or college days were like, or a relationship with a past flame. A category romance doesn't give much information on the heroine's past, because of lack of space, but it's enough to establish her according to the *W*'s—who, what, where, why, and when.

The ins and outs of polishing the prose should be the most enjoyable part of writing. It is up to each writer to learn as much as possible from the reading and analyzing of what is stimulating, and apply the techniques to her/his own book.

Each part of the romance TORTE can be polished. All it takes is a little time and patience.

Here are some more suggestions from the category romance writers who have become popular with readers for their special techniques.

The Dialogue of Love

BY BONNIE DRAKE

author of eighteen category romances

To speak of the category romance is to speak of a modern-day love affair, a relationship between a man and a woman that embraces and combines the intellectual, the emotional, and the sexual. To write the category romance is not only to write a story that contains these elements but to present it in such a way that the reader is intimately and inextricably drawn into the characters' midst. Dialogue is the perfect means for accomplishing this purpose.

Times have changed. No longer do readers want page after page of flowery description or showy travelogue. Nor do they want unending chapters of introspection. Rather, the emphasis has shifted toward action, toward getting the hero and heroine together, toward letting the reader experience the story as it unfolds, as the main characters themselves experience it.

Likewise, the days of the noncommunicative hero and heroine seem numbered. In today's world, with fiction mirroring reality, characters are more forthright than ever, speaking their thoughts freely, tending to express themselves openly and honestly. Hence . . . dialogue.

There is nothing new about the presence of dialogue in fiction, nor have its fundamental functions changed. But since Hemingway's innovative use of it, dialogue is now more heavily relied upon to strengthen a story. It has always been used to reveal the nature of characters, just as it used to illustrate the growth of their relationship. Additionally, it is a means of telling about the past, describing the present, planning the future—in short, a means of furthering the story line.

But dialogue is particularly critical in category romance, where the author must struggle to fully construct a story within a prescribed number of pages. The hero and heroine must be thrown together as *quickly* as possible and kept that way for as *long* as possible, so the reader can know the nature and depth of their relationship. All communication between them must have its purpose; there isn't time to waste on meaningless jabber.

It goes without saying that to write effective dialogue, the writer must know the characters as intimately from the start as they will eventually know each other. Just as different situations call for differently paced dialogue, different characters call for different speaking styles. A character's words are a reflection of his personality and must always be consistent with it.

The earliest conversations between hero and heroine are especially important in establishing both their and the reader's initial impressions.

One look at herself in the mirror caused Monica to gasp, grow apprehensive, then lean in for a better view.

"It's quite a gash, isn't it?" came the deep voice at the door.

She bolted in fright. "Oh! It's you!" she cried, having somehow expected to be given this modicum of privacy.

"I thought you might need some help," he returned calmly, studying her bruised temple. She turned back to examine it herself.

"Why didn't you tell me it was this bad?"

"There was nothing you could do about it there on the sidewalk. Here, let me take a look. Have you got a washcloth?"

Monica knelt to the vanity below the sink, fished out a clean cloth and handed it to him. "What's your name?" she asked as he began to sponge the bruise at her temple.

[Passion and Illusion]

Monica is quickly established as a woman of spirit, Michael as a compassionate if commanding fellow. Though the characters become far more complex as the story progresses, these aspects of their personalities will remain stable.

Once the characters have been established, dialogue provides a vehicle for furthering the romance itself. The many sentiments associated with love are easily expressed through dialogue. Take tenderness:

Daniel took her arm and drew it through his, holding her close to his side as they walked.

"You know that you've done it again, Daniel, don't you?" Nia teased him begrudgingly. If only his shoulder wasn't so inviting. . . .

"Done what, babe?"

"Gotten me to talk about me. You do it every time. I think you'll be a counselor one day."

"Perhaps," he said with a smile.

"You're very good at it. You make me feel so comfortable that I can't seem to stop the flow once it begins."

"I'm glad." He cast her a sidelong glance that held a tenderness far beyond "glad." Nia was enthralled.

[Fast Courting]

Or easy companionship:

"What do you do for *fun?*" Justine said and squealed, as much in desperation as in curiosity. Once again he'd hit too close to home, and she wanted nothing to spoil the time they shared.

His breath was warm, fanning her forehead. "I ravish fair maidens," he said with a growl, disguising frustration in mischief.

"No, seriously, Sloane. You must have some hobby, side interest, sport . . . ?"

"Bingo!" he squeezed her tightly. "Sport. Specifically handball, I play as often as I can."

"Ah, that explains 'em, then."

"Explains what?"

"Your muscles." Rolling onto him, she stretched to admire the subjects in question. "There had to be some work involved in building those. Regular exercise type of thing. . . ."

Suddenly she found herself on her back, looking up at the handsome face that hovered close above. "Right now I have a very different type of exercise in mind," he drawled, a return of huskiness in his voice. Just as Justine's senses came to life, however, he levered himself off her. "I believe I'll take a run into town. To pick up something to eat. . . . I'm famished."

[The Silver Fox]

Or even a seemingly insurmountable conflict:

Daring to come to his side, she put a hand on his arm. "Why, Michael? I have a right to know."

His head swung around. "*What* right?" he shot back. "Or is this the feminist talking? Woman power?"

Stung by his bitterness, Monica recoiled. Then, as her own anger flared, she faced him. "You know, Michael Shaw, you're a bull-headed man. You ask me to understand your work—work that I detest—and I'm actually trying to understand. But when it comes to *my* feelings as a woman—a modern woman—you refuse to accept that there may be something worth understanding. We're not all *that* bad!"

"Oh?" he growled. "I'll take an old-fashioned girl in my bed any time."

"Passive? Is that what you want?"

"I want sweet and warm and receptive."

"But what about active and curious and eager?" she countered. "Can't I want your body as much as you want

mine? Don't *I* have the right to express myself sexually—
rather than merely being an outlet for *your* expression?"

[Passion and Illusion]

Yes, dialogue can indeed be the means of expression for any
number of sentiments. But what about form? Certainly there is
well-written dialogue, just as some is poorly written. For as
many authors as there are trying their hand at it, there will be
that many different styles. I can only speak of what works for
me.

There is a critical relationship between dialogue and narrative
that demands a weighing and balancing of the two. Dialogue
must flow from narrative, and vice versa. When writing a passage dominated by dialogue, such as we're concerned with here,
one must determine how much narrative to add between the
lines.

Unfortunately, there is no hard and fast rule to follow. Certain
scenes are more thought-provoking and by necessity require
dialogue that is slower, more soulful, more heavily couched in
narrative.

Given my choice, I prefer to write faster-paced dialogue, crisp
sequences of give and take that I feel emulate real-life conversation.
However, to continue for a stretch without so much as a "he
said" or a "she answered" may become tedious for the reader,
as he tries to remember who is speaking. Conversely, there is
nothing more annoying, more distracting, than lines of dialogue
that are so widely dispersed by blocks of private reaction and
reflection that the question is forgotten by the time the answer
appears.

The key is to find a happy medium, a conbination with just the
right rhythm. After three or four, perhaps five lines of straight
bantering dialogue, I feel myself facing a runaway conversation.
At that point I stop, interject just enough narrative to enrich the
thoughts expressed, then throw it all open again.

He squirmed in an almost boyish way. "Well . . . ?"
"What?"
"Your dates? *Are* there a string of them?"
She lowered her voice. "Jealous?"
"You bet."
"Well, you needn't be."
". . . Elaborate."
When she feigned distraction and glanced lazily off to-

ward another table, Tom reacted with a quick growl. "Serena
. . . tell me about them."

[Sweet Serenity]

Further, it is imperative to differentiate stylistically between
dialogue and narrative. Particularly in the field of romance,
where narrative may often tend toward the poetic, a character
shouldn't be allowed to *speak* poetically unless he actually *is*
poetic.

The average person speaks more simply than the average
writer writes. If dialogue is to be realistic, believable, *and*
contemporary, it must capture that simplicity. Indeed, there is no
better exercise in the world in preparing to write dialogue than to
listen.

Dialogue offers the ultimate in intimacy, and for that reason,
among others, I love writing it. There is nothing more rewarding
for an author than to sit back and let her hero and heroine come
alive and have a go at each other. If a man and woman are able to
enjoy a spontaneous verbal rhythm through the ups and downs of
their relationship, I have to believe in their chances of living
happily ever after.

His arms tightened convulsively around her. "Oh, Deanna,
I love you." He moaned with such depth of feeling that she
had to believe him. "You're all I've ever wanted in a
woman."

"And you really cancelled your appointments today on
my account?"

"Sure did. . . . But you sound surprised. Isn't that what
you did for me when I abducted you for a weekend in the
mountains?"

"Hmmmmm. Different types of appointments . . . but I
suppose you've got a point." She burrowed closer against
the firmness of his chest. "That was a wonderful weekend."

"Want to go back?"

She sat up. "Say when."

"When," he said with a rakish grin.

"Really?"

"Sure. I'd say you could use a good weekend's rest what
with all this unplanned excitement." He darted a glance at
his watch. "We could leave right after lunch if you can be
ready by then."

"I'm ready now."

"I thought you felt sick."

"Not any more."

"Speedy recovery?"

"The best medicine in the world."

[Beyond Fantasy]

In the Beginning . . .

BY JAYNE CASTLE

author of seventeen category romances

I write opening scenes the way I like to read them, plunging myself and the reader immediately into the situation that will shape the story. The way I look at it, there's always plenty of time to get the details in later. As a reader I tend to be impatient. I want to have my attention grabbed right from the start. As a *writer* I'm after the same quick thrill.

Perhaps it's even more important to me as a writer, now that I think about it. I want the story to hit the ground running because it gives me the sense of excitement, the sheer impetus I need to start the thing and get through that first chapter (one of the hardest to write). A fast-moving opening chapter is better than several cups of coffee when it comes to getting my fingers moving on the keyboard.

Given that the genre in which I'm writing is that of contemporary romance, it follows that one of the most stimulating ways for me to start a tale is to throw the hero and the heroine together as soon as possible in the first chapter, preferably within the opening paragraphs. Mechanically speaking, there are only two choices available for doing this: dialogue or prose. Dialogue can be a quick grabber, as in the following from *Affair of Honor:*

> "Don't stop now. This is just getting interesting." The voice out of the darkness was as cool and deadly as the sound of a revolver being cocked. It had precisely the same effect on Brenna Llewellyn. She froze, one jeaned leg already swung over the sill of the window. She was trapped.

The second choice for that smashing opening line, of course, is a sentence that immediately paints a scene of conflict. The following is the opening paragraph of *The Silver Snare:*

> The clash of wills occurred within hours after the commuter plane shuddered to a jarring halt on the floor of the desert canyon. Jessica Travers lost the battle. Decisively.

Whether one uses dialogue or straight prose as a grabber for the opening paragraph, the goal is the same: involve the reader at once. In so doing the writer is also forced into the momentum of the story. One trick that is useful for getting the reader's attention is to have that opening line be a comment about the hero.

> "You were supposed to be much taller!"
>
> *[Spellbound]*

> "Kali, for God's sake, do something! He's going to ruin the evening!"
>
> *[Conflict of Interest]*

How does one go about finding that perfect, socko opening line? I examine the scene in my head from a variety of angles. It's possible to enter the story from an almost infinite number of avenues. I look for the route that will intrigue the reader and myself the most. For example, in *Battle Prize* I knew I was going to have the hero and the heroine meet each other for the first time in a shop that specialized in military miniatures, the kind used by war-gamers and hobbyists. I thought about having the hero simply walk up to the counter where the heroine was working and introduce himself. I considered having her cleaning the glass of the shop's front door as the hero walks up to face her from the sidewalk. I considered the notion of having her drop a box of toy soldiers on his toe.

But this was a story that would be about the war of love that would take place between these two people, and here I was with a scene filled with the miniature paraphernalia of war-gaming. What could be quite as dramatic as the encounter of two opposing commanders on the field of battle? The heroine, then, is laying out a famous battle in order to display the miniatures she is trying to sell when the hero walks through the shop door. The first lines of *Battle Prize* thus became:

> She first encountered him in the chilled dawn of an English morning. Rani Cameron looked up suddenly to find his sapphire-gray gaze studying her intently from the opposite stretch of high ground which framed the old road from Hastings to London. It was the fourteenth of October in the year 1066 and some feminine instinct warned Rani that the day was going to be as fateful for her, personally, as it was for England.

The scene begun above then goes on to have the two very modern warriors refight the Battle of Hastings. The results presage the outcome of the novel.

Regardless of how I choose to open that first chapter, I use the remainder of it to weave in the primary details of the conflict that will keep the hero and the heroine apart until the end of the tale. I also use that first chapter to give the reader a firm mental image of the two people around whom the story revolves. By the end of the first chapter the pace and direction of the book should be well established. With any luck, the reader will turn the page to Chapter 2.

To accomplish that trick, it is necessary to feed in the vital information without killing the fast momentum set by the opening lines. The spark of excitement that has been struck must not be allowed to die amid the morass of description that has to be completed. This is sometimes easier said than written.

It helps to keep the hero and the heroine together for the better part of that first chapter. Let the last lines of the chapter be as tantalizing as the first. Following are a few closing sentences from the books mentioned above:

> "Isn't it obvious?" she murmured with a flippancy she didn't feel. "I want you to compromise me. Subtly, you understand, but . . . sufficiently."
>
> *[Spellbound]*

Then she turned on her heel and started for the door of the restaurant. Even though she was moving swiftly, however, she still caught Gage's last growl of sardonic warning. She had been meant to catch it.

"Discipline, Rani. Always remember: Discipline. You're going to lose the war without it, you know."

[Battle Prize]

It should be noted that not everyone likes to read or write the kind of opening chapter I have described. Some prefer to be eased gently, thoroughly into a story. It is, I suppose, a matter of personal preference. There is definitely something to be said for the slower, more detailed beginning in which the stage is completely set before the introduction of the hero. It allows time, for example, for the reader to get to know a lot about the heroine and her background. In fact, there are several arguments that could be made for the slower, mellower beginning—which brings us back to my one, cardinal rule for opening scenes:

Write 'em the way you like to read 'em.

Then hope there's an editor and an audience out there who agree with you!

Writing Tip

The most common mistake of the beginner is that the first three chapters are unnecessary and can be cut from the manuscript without harming the story one bit. Other mistakes are letting secondary characters enter a story and take it over, overdescribing minor characters who are never used in the rest of the book and don't forward the plot in any way, and falling into the trap of switching points of view. New writers usually do this unconsciously because they don't realize they are letting us into the minds of all kinds of characters in the book, and that fractures a short novel.

Carolyn Nichols, editor, Loveswept romances

Humor in Dialogue Is Tricky

BY BONNIE GOLIGHTLY

An author may be tickled pink with a bit of funny dialogue she has put in the mouth of a character, but it is fatal to take it for

ranted that the reader will split her sides over this sally. Here is
an example of this fatality:

> "You are a voodoo-done-it," he remarked with his typi-
> cal unmatched wit.
> Marlaina Mae could not control her mirth. She screamed
> with laughter until the tears rolled down her cheeks.

What's wrong here? First of all, the reader may not get the
point of "voodoo-done-it," or if she does, she may think it a
little peculiar, tiresome even, out of place—anything but amusing.
Therefore, to read the author's "he said" substitute in which it is
clearly indicated that the author considers the quip "typical
unmatched wit" can easily make the reader irritated. Then to
read on and find that the author's other character is equally
bowled over by this hilarity is enough to make Dear Reader
become Dear Ex-Reader. The author, by visibly, audibly admiring his own cleverness, has unconsciously asked for rejection
and loss of credibility.

How could it be fixed so that the reader might agree that the
voodoo-done-it speaker is pretty funny? Just leave out the author's
editorializing; omit everything after "he remarked"—and tone
down Marlaina Mae's appreciation. It is quite sufficient to say
that she reacted with "startled laughter" and let it go at that,
immediately giving her some snappy rejoinder.

This "editorializing" warning also applies to grief, or any
other strong emotional reaction, as well as humor.

Then there is the matter of "he said" "she said" substitutes
in general.

Dialogue is speech, and a physical reaction such as " 'You
are hilarious!' she laughed" is an impossibility. Try saying it
and laughing at the same time. Nobody can squeal or choke or
moan dialogue. The right way: " 'You are hilarious!' she
exclaimed, and laughed.

Dialogue has to do solely with the spoken word, *not* with the
bodily comment to it. "He said" must always be inserted, or
implied, directly after the speech, and only then may the "stage
direction" of physical response be added.

A Pinch of Humor

BY ELAINE RACO CHASE

author of eleven category romances

What is 99 percent fat-free, has no cholesterol, can't be smoked, drunk, or eaten, yet is definitely habit-forming? Humor!

But humor *and* romance? You bet. What's more fun than making love? Maybe some rollicking pages of witty foreplay that turn into romantic comedy.

While the ingredients are standard, the mixture is quite delicate. One person's humor may not be another's. What *sounds* funny may read blah. While all my novels are liberally laced with humor, three feature romantic comedy teams: Brandy Abbott and Griffen St. Clair from *Designing Woman;* Virginia Farrell and Alex Braddock from *No Easy Way Out;* and Vikki Kirkland and Daniel Falkner from *Video Vixen.*

Let's start with the main ingredient:

Heroines

They were sharp, sassy, seductive scamps—and quite the vamps: Brandy, Virginia, and Vikki. In creating the character sketches on these ladies, I gave them each a purpose, each a goal.

Brandy wanted to pierce the age-old notion that a woman,

especially an attractive woman, couldn't design a building; Virginia was a genius, a robotics expert with a Mensa IQ, but couldn't keep house if her life depended on it; and Vikki, quiet, shy, and unassuming at night, during the day reigned as the TV soaps' most evil woman—the vixen, able to drive men wild with a bat of her false eyelashes.

Care had to be taken to make the reader and the downright unruly heroine allies. It's very important to create a bond between the two, so that whatever your vampish heroine does, no matter how deceitful, the reader keeps cheering her on.

It is also important to make sure the heroines are mature. My ladies were between twenty-seven and thirty-one—no quivering virgins with girlish antics. All were late bloomers, with their attractiveness derived from cosmetics, fashions, and hair styles—the "after" in the makeup ads, something that again the reader could identify with. Inner beauty was stressed. I took care to show the heroines were normally nice and sane, but when situations were altered, they were given the opportunity for some naughty fun—perhaps another "fantasy" the reader could embrace.

Heroes

The romantic comedy hero is *never* the butt of the joke. Griffen, Alex, and Dan knew what was being perpetrated—although not right away—but each chose to continue because of fascination with his respective lady. What began as lust quickly turned into love. The men were being attracted by the intangibles that seem to defy definition—style, panache, intrigue, to name just a few.

Why would these men be drawn to such women? Probably because the "new" woman doesn't apologize for being experienced, and the "new" man doesn't feel the need to be "first" —just the *last*. Brandy, Virginia, and Vikki were "fantasy" ladies, and what normal, red-blooded hero wouldn't want to take part in a fantasy?

The heroes were slightly "fantasy" creations, too. No strong, silent types. They showed depth and range in their emotions, they had thoughts, they had lines, they played their parts as if they were in a tennis match—giving as good as they got!

Dialogue

This is the backbone of humor writing. The words create an illusion, and the illusion you're after is fun. You must take care to give your characters clever, witty, acerbic voices. I use lots o double entendres:

When Griffen orders Brandy to be on the job for May Day she responds that he'll be the one yelling "mayday" shortly.

Vikki plays her Vixen Mallory TV role for real, telling Dan she's just like Will Rogers—never met a man she didn't like.

Virginia finds the way to Alex's heart with a big plate of seductive flattery, a side dish of verbal foreplay culminating in a mental climax for dessert that would lead to a physical one.

Fun, too, is taking what's normal and making it slightly absurd. Vikki suggestively taunts Dan—who has a head of silver hair—with an old wives' tale, wondering, if there's snow on the roof, can there still be a fire in the hearth? Her favorite songs are "Endless Love," "Let's Get Physical," and "Make a Move on Me"; she dresses only in scarlet or black; her fragrance is Zen—just as mysterious as she!

Virginia is a true Gemini, playing "twin" sisters—one who gets turned on by the navel in an orange, the other nonorgasmic. By day she's glasses, bun, and a lab coat; at night her metallic halter moves with provocative buoyancy, literally ravishing Alex on their first date.

Brandy just embellishes Griffen's fantasy that she was having an affair with her married boss and is now looking for another fish. Here the comparing was done with food—more dessert and fluff than meat and potatoes. Every aphrodisiac known to man was used: from Casanova's favorite oysters, to olives, champagne, and a sausage snuggled between two halves of a baked potato. Symbolism abounded, and since Brandy was an architect and Griffen a builder, it was fun searching up groin vaults, geodesic domes, and tunnels!

Plot

Plot is like a chess game—opening gambits, check, counter-check, and the ultimate mate. Revenge on revenge breed fun. A battle of wits rages, putting the readers in the middle, anxiously waiting to see who does what to whom. Yes, sometimes I get confused, too!

I seem to lead a very funny life—Murphy's Law is constantly at work. I never consciously set out to make a book funny, it just evolves, and so far (knock on wood) this has worked. I would love to do something deep, something heart-wrenching, something tragic.

If you believe that, I have a bridge I'd love to sell you!

Narrowing the Narrative

BY LOIS WALKER

author of eleven romances

Narrative is the writer's time to give background information, describe the scenery, or, best of all, share secrets with the readers. Narrative is also a painless way to carry us through transitions to another time and place. We can move the story forward or sneak into flashbacks. Of course, the writer must be careful in balancing the use of dialogue with narrative. Too much description of surroundings or background information and impatient readers will begin to skim, looking for some *action*.

Most books begin with more narrative than dialogue. This is because the writer is "setting the scene"—that is, telling the reader where we are, what the characters look like, and something about them. These are all things the reader needs to know. However, they don't need to know everything at once. A lot of description at the beginning of a book can rapidly become tedious. It is often better to slip in details between dialogue. In my book *Diamond of Desire*, a historical set in South Africa at the turn of the century, the book opens with:

Davina felt a sense of panic overtake her as the carriage neared the liner and she saw its smoke stacks rising up above the Southampton buildings like an ominous sea monster. Turning to her father, she bargained desperately, "If you don't make me go to South Africa, I promise never to see Maxwell again."

Through a mixture of narrative and dialogue, the reader has been told where the characters are, where Davina is going, and that she doesn't want to go. An in-depth description of Southampton is unnecessary, since she is leaving there. However, once she arrives in South Africa, the readers want to have the country laid out before them. We see it through Davina's eyes as she rides through the streets:

She saw that the people on the city street represented every possible shade of human skin. There were fair-skinned and fresh Dutchwomen who looked as if they could have posed for a Rubens painting alongside men and women of deep black skin. Even the natives' clothes were something she had not seen the likes of before. The black women wore full, bright dresses of pink, green, blue and lilac with bodices of a different color. Their heads were wrapped with gay scarves of yet another shade.

Turning her eyes upward at the buildings she saw that the structures lacked the uniqueness of the people. They were Classical Greek buildings that soared several stories high and would not have been out of place in an English city. Neither would the electric lights that lined the streets nor the electric street cars. On the corners flower sellers vended their wares of orchids and colorful proteas.

There is more description about Cape Town later, but never in large doses. It is a fact that most writers do an enormous amount of background research. But that work should never *show*. Sensitive readers don't want to be given a lecture on history, or scenery. They're reading for a story. Any other details should be skillfully woven in; the action should not stop so that they can be inserted.

While dialogue makes a book live, without strong supporting narrative it is only an invalid. We all know that the characters don't reveal everything in conversation. They keep secrets from each other—but less often from the reader. In *Diamond of Desire*, Davina never mentioned Maxwell's name to her aunt. In fact, she never discussed him with anyone except Lenore and Rachel. And even with them, she did not dare share the secret that Maxwell would be coming to Cape Town as soon as he had the money.

Another instance where we are given a glimpse into unspoken thoughts is in *Exploring,* my contemporary in Ballantine's Love and Life series:

Her gaze was arrested by the sight of a tall man in jeans and an oxblood red knit shirt. His blond hair was wind blown and he had a tired slump to his shoulders. Conflicting emotions of apprehension and pleasure flitted through her as Blythe recognized Drake Renford.

Narrative transitions also allow us to leap across time and place. Again in *Diamond of Desire,* ''Maxwell had tasted the briny breezes for nearly three weeks when he spied the peaks of the mountains that hemmed in Cape Town.''

Three weeks have passed, and six thousand miles, but it was done in brief narrative transition. Such transitions keep the reader from becoming bogged down in events that don't move the story forward.

As well as going forward, we can rewind the tape and go backward. Flashbacks allow us to see something that happened before the book opened. In *Exploring:*

Blythe stirred in her seat as the noise penetrated to a level below her consciousness, making her restless and vaguely frightened. In the back reaches of her mind, she could see the hospital corridor stretching out indefinitely and hear the doctor's words, ''I'm afraid that Jon has ... .''

For the romance writer, narrative is particularly useful during love scenes. The writer is able to describe the heroine's feelings and thoughts. In *Diamond of Desire:*

Anthony's kisses seemed to have the power of a potent drug and, as he continued to inundate her with them, she was becoming limp and pleasantly drowsy. He fitted his body closer to hers while his fingers inched down from her bosom to her waist. He was opening the camisole, she realized, and waited with bated breath for him to touch the bare skin beneath.

And in *Exploring:*

> Gradually they drew together, their bodies complementing each other. She felt like someone who had been stranded in the desert too long without water. Her thirst for him increased with each wild kiss, and she inched herself ever closer to him, straining toward the river of fulfillment she sensed in the distance.

Now that we have seen some of the uses of narrative, let's take a peek at when not to use it. One form of narrative to especially beware of is the deadly summary narrative. It isn't enough to simply *say* that a character is "bright and witty"; the readers want to see instances of it in the story. Neither is it wise to go into a long narration describing some past event if a flashback can be used. Flashbacks give us a sense of seeing what happened rather than being told about it. And, again, it is intimidating to see pages and pages of paragraphs without dialogue. Try to splice narrative description and background information between pages of dialogue.

There is much about narrative, and all phases of writing, that can be learned only by doing. But you'll have fun, and a little frustration, in the learning. Good luck on becoming happily published.

The Romantic Setting

BY SUSANNA COLLINS

author of seven romances

Making a setting as exciting and enticing as the hero is something I strive to do in each of my novels. I want my heroine to feel as passionately about the place as she does for the hero.

Places, like people, can be boring, or they can have an irresistible charm that makes you love them forever. There have been several places like that in my life, places that I cherish as friends, and these I write about. I've actually lived in some of them, like Hawaii, Belgium, and Mexico; others, like Spain and the Santa Ynez Valley in California, I've visited again and again, and each time discover some new, endearing quality about them.

I am never without a notebook when I travel. Here is a sample from a recent trip to Santa Ynez, where I was researching background for *Breathless Dawn*:

Clouds like whipped cream topping on mountains—sunsets here so beautiful because missiles from Vandenberg AFB leaving lovely trails of ethereal light streaking across sky—screech of black crow—black and white magpie sitting—perched on white fence, crickets chirp when sun goes behind cloud—pigtailed child feeding clumps of grass to black-faced sheep—purple lupine flowers—fluffy.

Of course, you're not always going to be able to use everything you jot down. The lovely Santa Ynez sunset, for example, would lose some of its romantic aura when added to the image of Air Force missiles.

Not only are your own impressions valuable, but sometimes someone close by might say something so apt and striking that it brings an entire scene alive. When I was in Belgium, an artist friend said to me one day, as we discussed the unique landscape, "our country is so flat that it brings the sky down to us and we live intimately with the clouds." I gave that line to the hero in *Hard to Handle*. What I especially liked was that it said something about the Belgian people as well.

Which brings me to another good point. Setting, to me, doesn't mean just a description of the landscape, but the people who inhabit it. In *On Wings of Magic*, for example, the heroine is unable to get reservations for a flight from Acapulco to Mexico City, and she calls to tell the hero. He answers her:

". . . I'll tell you what you do. Go out to the airport Friday morning and flash your smile at one of the ticket agents. This is Mexico. There are men who would give their lives for a smile like yours. . . ."

Is it any wonder our heroine *adores* Mexico?

It also helps if you can use the setting to describe a character. In *On Wings of Magic*, I describe Raul's house in the Zona Rosa district of Mexico City, and in doing so, something comes through about the man who lives there:

His four-story Spanish colonial-style home, with wrought-iron balconies, was nestled defiantly between two towering buildings. "At one time most of the district looked like this house, but we have had progress," he told them. "And I don't really mind the change. There's so much life here."

One of my favorite techniques for enhancing a setting is to use the folklore and legends of the place. For *Breathless Dawn*, I immersed myself in Chumash Indian legends, with the help of the lovely ladies at the Santa Ynez Historical Society. (Librarians, you will discover, are at the top of a writer's pantheon. Typewriter repairmen are down there with the dregs of humanity.)

Chumash lore is rich in natural images. One story that particularly enchanted me was about a "Dawn Maiden" who appeared to an Indian chief during a drought. The lovely apparition led him up a steep canyon to a hidden water source, then disappeared through the mist, her dawn dress shimmering in the first rays of sunlight, into the morning star.

In the Chumash religion, the sun is a male force, the earth female, so I decided to combine the legend with the belief in the setting where they took place, and use the sunrise and legend as the catalysts that finally impel Juliana into Scott's arms.

They are at Yelysey Lake, site of an ancient Chumash village. Awake at dawn, she tells him the legend of the "Dawn Maiden." Then:

> The eastern sky lighted into rose, painting the clouds a golden-hued pink in anticipation of the impending sunrise. The whole world was tense, pulse racing, waiting for the curtain to rise.
>
> Suddenly, as though there had been a trumpet blast, the sun's rays shot out in golden spikes from behind the mountain.
>
> Juliana caught her breath. As the light touched Scott's flame-red hair, she was wracked by a desire to touch it, too. She longed for him just as passionately as the dark earth longed for the sun's life-giving rays.
>
> He was watching her without moving. "Juliana." His breath was ragged, but controlled. "Do you know what you're doing?"
>
> "Yes," she whispered, moving her lips close to his.
>
> His strong hands caught hers and held them still before she could encircle his neck. "There will be no turning back."
>
> She knew what he was saying, but Robert didn't matter anymore. Nothing mattered but the rising sun and her own feverish need to leap into the sky and wrap herself around its flaming body.

This was an unusual opportunity to use the setting to help create sexual tension. What I do frequently, and to me very creatively, is to mix images of the setting with the love scenes.

In *Breathless Dawn* I described a harrowing horseback ride up to Yelysey Lake through the steep canyon where the trail was slick from a spring storm. The heroine's horse lost its footing and slipped over the side, nearly plunging into a 300-foot ravine. Later, when Juliana and Scott make love, I reprise the heart-stopping incident on horseback.

Forces beyond them as primitive and dark as the verdant canyons clutched them and commanded abandonment of civilized behavior. Secret valleys were uncovered and ravaged into a frenzy of tremors. Rocks disengaged and slid down damp ravines pounded by the thundering violence of a spring storm.

Red manzanita bushes, heavy with fruit, rushed by her as they tumbled down the steep canyon into bowers of wild mint and lilac.

The words "I love you" echoed in and out of consciousness like a pagan chant that groaned and howled on the nightwind.

They were whirling and swirling in a fireball disk, mouths touching skin with lightning bolts, engaging, disengaging as their bodies entwined in complex configurations of growing passion.

The pounding, like heartbeats, slapped and drove. Fingers dug into flesh, grasping, clutching futilely at the anchoring earth as the windstorm bore them up to the morning star.

When you are as bound by euphemisms as I feel we romance writers are, it is helpful to have a well-established setting from which to fashion your sexual images.

One of my lushest settings was the tropical island of Naupaka for *Destiny's Spell*. The heroine sees the hero as a sea god, and while they make love she imagines herself:

. . . drifting down with him below the rolling waves, plunging deeper into the blue silky darkness . . . hurling them into the emerald depths, crashing down with crystal white breakers.

And in another scene:

Her mind raced along the valleys and gorges of the tropical jungles and elfin caves hidden behind thick primeval ferns. Her legs wrapped around his back like the clinging violet morning glories that twisted around the kukui trees.

His lips were caressing hers, whispering her name as though it were the sound of a breeze rustling through the palm fronds. . . .

In all my novels, the setting has an important role. In *Breathless Dawn*, it becomes almost another character, exerting a powerful influence on the heroine. I establish this early in the novel when she first sees the Santa Ynez Valley after a long absence:

> Bright sunlight streaked through the clouds, casting playful lavender shadows on the green pastures below, and sparkled silver lights off Cachuma Lake as the Santa Ynez Valley spread out before her in a glorious tableau.
>
> Emotion welled up inside Juliana's chest and spilled out her eyes. She knew, as she always did at that particular spot, that her ancestor, Salvador Cardona, had once stood there, looking very gallant in his blue Spanish uniform trimmed with red, and had been overcome with the same profound emotion.
>
> This was home.

And at the very end:

> The sun finally slipped behind the mountain and somewhere up in the dark canyon toward Yelysey Lake a coyote howled.
>
> "Yes, Scott," she whispered. "This is where I belong. I love you."

It is that sense of belonging to a place that I think is every bit as important to a woman as the marvelous hero who's going to share it with her.

Romantic Setting Checklist

1. *Woman meets devastingly attractive man (of her dreams and/or destiny).* **Where?**
2. *Sparks fly and will never die out.* **Where?**
3. *Something plausible separates them.* **Where?**
4. *Something brings them together (optional but good for second love scene).* **Where?**
5. *Something pulls them apart again (optional but good for additional love scene).* **Where?**
6. *Something brings them together and they resolve their problems.* **Where?**
7. *Something makes them commit themselves to marriage.* **Where?**

Suspense in Romance

BY NELLE MCFATHER

author of six romantic suspense novels

Suspense in the good romantic novel is like the garlic in the *boeuf bourguignon*. It enhances the flavor and changes an ordinary stew into an exciting *pièce de résistance*.

Suspense keeps the reader turning the pages. Ask a successful author what she loves hearing most from a fan. Chances are, she'll tell you the refrain she relishes most is "I couldn't put your book down!"

Since you are now or want to be a writer, it's assumed that you have a lively imagination. So put that asset to work right now. Imagine a long hall stretching ahead of you with a door at the end. Walk slowly toward that door (observing details along the way), and picture it either open or closed.

Which would be more intriguing—the open door or the closed one? Beyond that, how would you react to a door that was slightly, enticingly, tantalizingly *cracked*?

My guess is that you'd find it irresistible to take a peek!

That's what leads me to suggest that building and sustaining suspense is a matter of providing a progression of "cracked doors" through which our readers are invited to peek and enter. We hope they'll be delighted, chagrined, intrigued, or satisfied enough to continue turning the pages of our novel.

No one could write about suspense without mentioning its wonderful purveyors in the earlier gothic novels. Though the old-fashioned gothic novel is no longer the rage it once was (at least with editors!), classic tales by those mistresses of magic such as Du Maurier, Seton, Stewart, Holt, Whitney, Eden, and countless others have greatly influenced today's romance writing. Some of those stories of imperiled heroines trapped by circumstances and their own emotions offer splendid examples of top-notch writing.

Wise romance writers often include gothic elements of mystery and suspense, while remaining within the boundaries of straightforward stories of the heart. After all, what could be more mysterious and suspenseful than the developing relationship between a man and a woman?

Let's look at some of the specific ways a writer can add suspense to her novel.

Hook your reader at the very beginning. You've heard this over and over in writing classes and conferences, but I'll mention it again. The "hook," or bait dangled effectively to catch a reader up in your story, is an effective way to build suspense. You may want to use it as a beginning line, in a prologue, or at the end of the chapter—pulling the reader irresistibly on to the next chapter.

Allow plenty of time for anticipation and intensity to build. Remember the romance novel *you* couldn't put down until you'd finished it? Whatever it was, I'm willing to bet it had almost unbearable sexual suspense and intensity between the two main characters. I think readers are disappointed by romance novels that don't sustain the exciting intensity that's promised when the hero first enters the picture.

(If you're having trouble sustaining sexual suspense, read Kathleen E. Woodiwiss's *The Flame and the Flower*. But don't plan to do any writing until you've finished reading the entire book!)

Don't overtell or explain too much or otherwise underestimate your reader. All right—you, the writer, have created suspense in your romantic novel that has your reader's emotional interest at the high end of the Richter scale. Don't spoil it by switching on little light bulbs over her head. Most readers have great imaginations, too (otherwise, they'd be glued to TV instead of reading our books). Allow them the freedom to let that imagination go wild; let them create their *own* suspense as well as swimming in yours.

There are many other ways to bring suspense to your love stories. As you develop your writing skills and read the good romantic novels of others, you'll find your own effective techniques. Just keep in mind that suspense is an important ingredient of *all* good novels—not just mysteries.

If you've done your job and kept your reader turning the pages, you might want to consider rewarding the person who is more important to a writer's success than even the editor or agent. After all, this person has held her breath as you've led her down an emotionally exhausting (if satisfying!) corridor, through one cracked door after another. The best way you can reward her is by leaving her with a gratifying ending to all that romantic suspense. Leave her feeling ebullient, happy that things turned out well—but sad that she's finished your wonderful, exciting book. The suspense is over, but so is her affair with your story!

It's an intimate moment, the ending of a romance novel, and it shouldn't be rushed. A best-selling romance writer friend, Frances Patton Statham, tells me she likes to leave her readers with a "kiss"—an extra "something" that leaves them feeling caressed and special. I think that's a delicious way to reward a reader whose family is going without the evening meal because she couldn't put your book down.

Reading a romance novel that doesn't offer some type of suspense is like a flat bottle of champagne. Half the fun is uncorking it yourself to get to that luscious, bubbly liquid. Holding your breath, waiting for that cork to pop . . .! That's suspense.

But wait until you finish reading this book, complete that romance novel you're working on, and send off your manuscript to a publisher.

That, my writing friends, is *real* suspense!

4

Between the Sheets

Christmas Greetings

Dear Rosie,
Happy Holidays and May You Always Have Romantic Times

   Thought these articles might be useful for understanding more about the reader.

Fondly,
Kathryn

Why Women Prefer Steamy Romances

As Al Lieberman, Silhouette's marketing director, explains, "Millions of women are now very sexually liberated. They go to male stripper performances, buy enticing Frederick's of Hollywood lingerie to please their boyfriends or husbands, and attend Tupperware-type parties for sexual products. Many of these same women are also buying Silhouette Desire books as fast as they come into the stores."

Al should know. Silhouette ships 300,000 copies of *each* of six Desire titles every month. There are plans to increase the print run to 450,000, if the boom continues. (Of the 22 million women who buy 320 million romances worldwide, approximately 9 million are the avid readers who may buy up to forty romances a month.)

Category romance lines named Desire, Ectasy, Intimate Moments, Loveswept, and Rapture are quite a publishing curiosity, though it's really not surprising that they outsell the old-fashioned sweet romance. The tamer varieties enjoy quite credible sales, particularly among older and younger readers, but their sales can't compare to the skyrocketing success of the steamy brand. The women's sexual liberation movement has removed a lot of inhibitions, and for the first time women have their own variety of stimulating reading material. It's not like the male "naughties," or *Playboy* and *Penthouse* girlie magazines, but the writing does perk the erogenous zones.

There is one big difference, however. Romance readers don't want to read of the sex act in graphic terms. Without going into repression and guilt, suffice it to say here that you will not find the words *penis, cunnilingus, sodomy,* or any textbook term in a category romance. You will find a flurry of adjectives surrounding nouns that mean the same things. Many romance writers collect pretty ways of describing anatomical parts, the clichés now being *temple of love, creamy thighs, mound of Venus,* etc. Many imaginative new terms and one-liners are being created to keep sex pretty.

Women also expect their writers to sweep them into an exciting, loving, and breathless encounter with a Prince Charming, but once in his arms the readers want their own fantasies to take over.

Are these steamy romances soft-core pornography, as their critics say?

Yes and no. Yes, they are quite heady, stimulating. Readers and editors know immediately if a title is a "hot-pants" or a "cold-shower" book. Women do read the steamy romances in bed (and every other place); many couples read and enjoy them together. But are these books pornography? It depends on the reader.

Romance is sex with commitment; pornography is sex without commitment.

Steamy romances are safe and pretty sex, all wrapped up with the Cinderella story . . . getting your cake and eating it too.

A Market Analysis of the Romance Reader for the Romance Writer (One Man's Opinion)

BY RICHARD FLAXMAN

marketing analyst for romance books

As a writer of romance novels, the first question you have to know the answer to is, Who is buying the product? Who is your consumer? Who is the target market you are attempting to reach?

In the case of romance novels the answer is not quite as predictable as one might first imagine. After all, you know that the writing is based on a formula. The heroes and heroines are drawn from men and women who could hardly exist by today's standards, and the book endings must be happy. These are the ground rules.

What you may not know and understand are your readers: By and large, they are not mindless, unsophisticated, and naïve. They are in many cases well educated, literate, and verbal. While working for romance publishing companies as a market researcher, I've spoken to nurses, librarians, professional women, and other successful people who devour the novels with the same enthusiasm as the most limited uneducated clerk in a grocery store.

When I was first asked to help Silhouette launch their romance line against Harlequin, I created a picture in my mind of a foolish woman spending hours devouring these books, hiding ashamed in her bedroom or bathroom, never to admit to the outside world that she bought, never mind read, these 192-page novels.

Well, first of all, this woman is not necessarily stupid or ignorant but usually has a lot of sense. She considers what she reads to be literature, not garbage. She believes she is more literate than most because she reads more than do her acquaintances. She also feels she knows more about Europe or Australia because the Harlequins are mini-travelogues. Instead of hiding the books and her enthusiasm for them, she is proud.

So the reader is obviously not the same person I first visualized. She can range in age from fifteen to eighty-nine. Put a teenager in the same room as a grandmother, and if they both read romance novels they will communicate comfortably for hours. The books create a common bond between women of all ages.

Where does your reader live? All over the country. Perhaps there are more readers in the Southwest, Midwest, and South, and fewer in the more urban areas, but they exist in every city and suburb across the country.

Is she well educated? Thanks to the novels she reads, she is *better* educated than one initially imagines. As I said before, she has been all over the world, thanks to her books. Many readers have attended college, most are high school graduates, and *none* are illiterate. (You can't be illiterate if you can read.)

Most important, your reader is a Romantic with a capital R. And a Romantic believes that love is the key element in life.

Also, in many cases, romantic love is what is lacking in most romance readers' lives. They read because they get romance vicariously via books, rather than from husbands or boyfriends.

Your reader is in most cases married or was married at one time. She had a family, and much of her life revolves around them. She derives pleasure from them rather than from who she is. Being a mother and wife is the single most important part of her existence. She believes in traditional values and would be more comfortable in the 1950s than she is in the 80s. Her politics and her morality are conservative. Marital fidelity is preached and practiced. Sex before marriage for her or her children is sinful.

She spends much time watching soap operas but is becoming uncomfortable about the story lines, which now include sex and infidelity. Situation comedies are more palatable. She is a church-goer and probably belongs to a bowling league, but she is mainly a homebody.

If you ask her about her own happiness, she is reluctant to admit anything is amiss. But if pressed, what she lacks is love. Her marriage has lost its luster and she has nowhere to turn . . . except to her romance novels. Her reading is vital to her lifestyle. It is what she calls "my time," and she resents intrusion on it by anyone.

Why does she read romance instead of finding it? It provides the escape she needs, harmlessly. She can escape into a make-believe world of beautiful people without leaving the sweet but too familiar ones behind. A fantasy world of love stories that stress relationships and feelings fuels her for everyday life. Love is powerful and conquers all. This in most cases is diametrically opposed to her real life. What she actually lives is a restricted life of sameness and disappointments, with a distinct lack of romance.

Once upon a time the worldwide marital complaint lay with the husband confiding to his mistress, or would-be mistress, that his wife didn't understand him, hence his infidelity. Nowadays it's the wife who complains that her husband rarely understands *her*. But whom does she bring her grievances to for mending? To her romance books, of course! What could be a healthier, less hurtful solution than an escape into the pretty, idealistic fantasy world that you, the romance authors, have created for her? Her gratitude is apparent in the booming sales of romance novels.

And how does she define the books you write? First, they are not depressing. What they are is uplifting and easy to read. They touch her heart. Most of all, they enable her to derive immediate satisfaction. After each read she feels renewed, better about herself, and relaxed. What she receives is an emotional high. She is like a junkie. The books get her high on emotion—an outlet she desperately needs to eliminate the drudgery of her life.

I won't bore you with exact statistics about the romance genre, but before we put the matter of romance readership aside, a few numbers about the market size should be noted.

If you take the total of all paperback books sold in a given year—and I mean *all*, not just romance—the total exceeds 575 million. That includes everything in paperback. Have you any idea how many of these are romance? And by romance I mean contemporary, historical, romantic suspense, Regency, etc.

Well, the romance portion of the paperback market is about 40 percent of the total, and that means over 200 million books. That's just in the U.S. How about Canada, Japan, Europe, and who knows where else? A lot of books . . . but the penetration of romance novels is still slight. Less than 20 percent of women currently read one or more. It's really a small, well-defined group of consumers who read what you write.

One more aspect that is interesting. The romance category is relatively new and undeveloped. It was only in 1974 that Harlequin recognized the potential and began a real marketing effort against the target group. Until 1979 they had the market to themselves. That situation limited writers' chances of being published in this country, as the Harlequin line is English in origin, and had only English writers.

Now that's all changed. Most major publishers, led by Simon and Schuster (Silhouette), have entered the field and are competing for good manuscripts. The question that remains unanswered is, Will all these new entries expand the romance segment of the paperback book market, bring in new readers, and make money for lots of publishers and writers? Or is the market restricted to the same readers, the 20 percent, who now have more choices but are limited by having only a specific amount of time to read and just so much money to spend on books?

Will competition deflect the romance buyership, cutting the 20 percent total picture into smaller pieces, or will the increase of higher-quality romance publishing result in attracting a wider consumer public, as hoped? You, as romance writers, bear a lot of responsibility for the future failure or success. If that 35 percent share of the market grows to even 45 percent, and the 20 percent total of *avid* readers increases, all of us will have more romantic times.

If *expansion* is the magic word, then new readers will flock to the category. If not, a lot of investment from some significant publishing houses will have been for naught.

Maryland Avenue
Royal Oak, Michigan

January 4

Dear Kathryn,

The market analysis was fascinating. I found out that I'm a romance junkie!

I showed my first three chapters to my sister, a junior-high English teacher, and she thinks that the "voice" of my story doesn't have enough impact. I'm concentrating on telling everything through the heroine's viewpoint and trying to shorten the narrative, so I don't slow down the action too much.

Any suggestions on writing love scenes?

Plodding along,
Rosie

From the Desk of Kathryn Falk

January 28

Dear Rosie,

I want to picture you swaddled in mauve, stroking a cat, smelling the roses, and scribbling in bed à la Colette as you study the enclosed articles on "love scenes." (You did know that Donna Vitek writes in a satin nightie?)

Busily,
Kathryn

Building Sexual Tension

BY DONNA KIMEL VITEK

author of fourteen category romances

The spellbinding exchange of lingering gazes, an accidental touch of fingertips against fingertips, a first irresistible kiss that leads to another—these are some of the initial progressions in the building of sexual tension in the romance novel.

Today, more than ever before, romance authors are permitted to provide their readers with believable and arousing love scenes, and because of this new realism, women *and* men who would turn up their noses at the typical "sweet" romance are reading and enjoying those books that more honestly describe the physical relationships of men and women falling in love. In a sensuously exciting romance, mutual sexual attraction between heroine and hero usually begins at the moment of their first meeting. Even if this first encounter brings hero and heroine into conflict, both of these characters are normal healthy people and are naturally aware of attractive members of the opposite sex. Often, the heroine will conceal her first involuntary response, but a suitably aggressive hero probably will not attempt to hide his appreciation of her femininity. Thus, the initial stirring of sexual tension is introduced. Hero makes heroine vaguely uneasy, and often, to her chagrin, she soon realizes that despite the conflict between them, she cannot ignore the awesome power of his male magnetism.

The building of sexual tension in the romantic novel should be a gradual process. First kisses are exchanged, and although these may be electrically charged experiences, the physical relationship between hero and heroine cannot realistically proceed much further without one vital ingredient—the respect, however grudging, that the man and woman have begun to feel for each other. Actually, this reluctant mutual admiration considerably heightens sexual suspense, because physical attractiveness is enhanced in a character who is also a personable human being. Despite the seemingly insurmountable problems between heroine and hero, both must soon begin to glimpse in each other qualities that make them more than simply "sexy" people. Heroes and heroines who constantly hurl verbal abuse at each other, then end each fight in a passionate clinch, seem involved in nothing more than a lustful relationship, and lust is shallow and fleeting. In other words, the deeper the emotional involvement between hero and heroine, the stronger the tension becomes as they continue to confront the problems that divide them while simultaneously succumbing to the ever-increasing desire to be together. Both characters, therefore, should be likable individuals. Readers would not understand either how a heroine would want to share a sexual experience with a man who treats her brutishly or how a hero would want to make love to a woman who behaves like a shrew. And unless the reader can admire both hero and heroine, there can be no tension, because no one will really care what happens between these two.

Anticipation is also vital in maintaining sexual tension. As Tom Huff, who writes under the pseudonym "Jennifer Wilde," states in an article in *Romantic Times:* "When the heroine is laid every few pages or so . . . I, for one, find it a bit tedious." Most readers will agree, because romances are, after all, *love* stories, and love must grow. A heroine who jumps into bed with a man after one kiss will not appear to readers as a woman searching for a permanent, meaningful relationship. Readers want romance, not lust. Glances *lead* to touches, then to kisses, until even passionate embraces are not enough for either hero or heroine. The writer is weaving a spell of irresistible desire between them, desire that has a chance to simmer.

To add fuel to sexual tension, the romance author must continue to heighten evocative love scenes. "They kissed passionately" simply will not do. The captivated reader actually feels the rush of desire and sexual suspense experienced by the characters. This

fect can be achieved by an exploration of heightened senses—
r example, by having the heroine detect the minty taste of the
ro's mouth as her lips are possessed by his; she inhales the
int fragrance of clean male scent; her breathing quickens as she
tens to whispered endearments; in ecstasy she strokes taut
nooth masculine skin. She trembles as her every nerve ending
mes alive. She gazes up into fiery emerald-green eyes.

She is caught up in a world of sensuous feelings. Even the
cale's beauty becomes more vividly enhanced. The colors of
owers become more vibrantly red, yellow, blue. The breeze
comes more caressingly cool, drifting over passion-heated flesh,
d takes on an incredible sweetness. Swaying branches whisper.
ater cascades softly in a fountain, and senses are inexorably
oused; the reader is drawn into the scene and *feels* the sexual
xcitement and tension.

A writer who yawns while typing her or his love scenes will
kely create the same response in the reader. Those who wish to
onvey sexual suspense in a story must write love scenes that are
veting and arousing, not only to their readers but to themselves.
or example, I interrupted the writing of the following scene in
assion's Price to seduce my husband:

Laine padded barefoot across the beach with Nick. As he
spread the blanket, she dug one foot into the cool sand and
lifted it, allowing the fine grains to trickle between her toes.

For several moments, Nick watched her before reaching
up to take her hands and draw her down beside him. A
salt-scented breeze caressed them. The pale light of the
crescent moon shimmered on the surface of the Intracoastal
Waterway. To the south, in the distance, Sapelo Island was
silhouetted against the night sky, its ancient live oaks standing sentinel over a band of salt marshes. . . . When her
hands came up to cup his neck, he slowly pulled her to him
. . . her mouth opened slightly to receive his kiss. Deliberately teasing, he brushed firm lips slowly back and forth
across hers until her breathing quickened and her arms
slipped around his neck.

With a muffled murmur of triumph, Nick bore her down
onto the blanket, his mouth devouring hers. As their ardor
deepened, a thrill of delight shot through Laine, so intense
that her limbs went weak. . . . He moved his hand over
her, following the swell of her hips into her waist and

onward to the rapid rise and fall of firm cushioned breasts. His palms brushed over one then the other, bringing them to life with exquisite sensations. With Laine's soft gasp of pleasure, he traced a fingertip around the hardening peaks outlined against the fabric of her dress.

Laine strained against him again and again, the long searching passionate kisses seeming to demand total surrender. . . . She offered no murmur of protest as he slowly lowered the back zipper of her dress. The night air cooled her skin as Nick pushed the dress from her shoulders. Laine shivered as the top of her slip fell away, and when Nick arched her to him and his lips explored the fragile contours of her shoulders, scattering hot kisses into the enticing hollows, her entire body was suffused with warmth again. Her arms went eagerly round his waist, her hands wandering beneath his shirt over his broad back. His heated flesh seemed to sear her fingertips, kindling a consuming fire inside her. She liked to touch as much as she liked being touched by him. Even when her bra was unhooked and the lace cups were slowly peeled away, Laine didn't resist. She caught her breath, overwhelmed by a sense of utter vulnerability. . . .

Here the reader should be sharing that sense of vulnerability that tension that comes when the heroine's fevered desire warring with caution, caution that is warning her that because the differences between them she must not become intimately involved with the hero. She is already too intimately involved with him.

Intimacy was not actually achieved in the preceding scene. was written to heighten reader anticipation by increasing the sexual emotion between hero and heroine. Although such scene are meant to be provocative, they should be logical, too. Characters involved in ardent love play simply cannot slam the brakes on desire for no good reason. Occasionally the reason that it interrupted can't be revealed until later in the story, but usually the writer gives the justification for the cessation. Sometimes the heroine simply feels compelled to control her aroused passion, a in this later, more intense, scene in *Passion's Price:*

. . . his hand slipped beneath the khaki fabric and glided possessively across her flat abdomen. Through the sheerness of her panties, his skin scorched her own but, though his touch was an unbelievable pleasure, she tensed when his hand slid downward. She caught his wrist and brought the hand back up to her waist, where she held it still.

"Nick," she said breathlessly, fighting her desire and his as she pulled away from him. Her eyes flickered open as his did and she felt impaled by the glint of passion ablaze in the green depths. Yet, she resisted the need to surrender to him. Innate caution and wariness ingrained after years of standing on the sidelines combined to strengthen self-restraint. She took a deep breath. "I . . . it's late. Time for bed, don't you think?"

"God, I hope that's an invitation," he muttered huskily, his jaw hardening as she shook her head. There was more than a hint of reluctance in his arms as he released her. "Then run away, Laine."

She scrambled up from the chaise and he lay back on it, and one arm covered his eyes. Gathering her clothes up from the deck's planking, she wanted to say something, anything, to him, but could think of nothing to say that would suffice. At last she put a hand over his in silent apology and rushed inside, across the darkened greatroom, and down the long hall to the lonely sanctuary of her bed. . . .

It is not always the woman who brings about a premature end to a love scene. Sometimes the hero exhibits an endearing perceptiveness (one of those qualities the heroine must admire in him) and halts lovemaking before intimacy is achieved, as in this example from *Dangerous Embrace,* in which former lovers are reunited and sexual suspense is especially intense:

She wanted him, so much that she could hardly stand it when his fingers slipped between hers and he raised her hands above her head, denying her the pleasure of touching him. Even teeth nibbled the hardened nubs of her breasts; his tongue flickingly explored the ruched hot skin of her nipples, making her nearly wild with desire. Through half closed eyes, she gazed down at his dark head. Remembering all he had once meant to her, she knew instantly that he still was and always would be everything to her. She loved him still; she had never stopped and her heart was certain of that fact now. Compared with her love for him, her feelings for Joe paled to insignificance. Only with Nathan did she feel complete and when he released her hands, they cupped his face, urging his mouth up to hers again.

Plundering lips ravished the softness of hers as the control Nathan had exercised over his own desire ceased to exist. He moved above her. . . . "Sweet Katie," he groaned. "Let me love you."

"Oh yes, Nathan, love me now," she whispered, pain intermingling with her need to give. She knew he meant love in the physical sense while she meant so much more than that. But a woman's love, too long denied, eventually has to find release and, even when it's not returned, has to be properly given. Kate was ready to give and tried to blink back the tears of conflict that sprang up to her eyes. A few escaped to trickle downward and as Nathan trailed a strand of feather-light kisses across her cheeks, he tasted the saltiness of damp skin.

"God, Katie, don't do this to me now," he muttered roughly, brushing away a fat tear with the edge of his thumb as he leaned on his elbows over her. And seeing the moisture that glistened in her eyes, he clenched his jaw tight and lifted himself up to sit on the edge of the sofa. "Get dressed," he commanded harshly. "I've never resorted to taking a weeping woman to bed and I'm not about to start now."

Such an unfulfilling conclusion to a flaming episode has to intensify sexual suspense and is one of those scenes that must conclude before consummation is achieved because either the heroine or the hero—or both—instinctively realizes the moment is not right. There are other methods employed to delay complete intimacy, but love scenes interrupted by a third party or an unexpected occurrence usually seem rather contrived and become mere frustrations to the characters and the readers. I prefer to use the stronger emotional considerations of one of the characters as the justification for halting a torrid scene so abruptly.

Today, in many romance novels, an intimate relationship is established between a man and woman sometime before the resolution of their major conflict. This turn of events does *not* bring about the end of sexual tension in the story. In actuality, intimacy serves to sharpen the suspense, especially for the heroine, through whose viewpoint most romances are written. When the hero becomes her lover, she is more defenseless where he is concerned. She has already faced the realization that she loves this man, and by committing herself physically, she deepens her emotional commitment. Now she knows she is far more susceptible to the pain and loneliness that will result if their relationship, fraught with uncertainty as it is, completely deteriorates.

In this variation of the romance novel, hero and heroine should share a rapturous intimate relationship, one that is physically and, to a certain extent, spiritually satisfying. The man should be a potently demanding yet tender and patient lover, and the woman should respond by almost wantonly participating in their lovemaking. This ecstasy they find together lends more poignancy to the moments after the act is over when they are forced to recognize that their major conflict remains unresolved. Something as innocent as an inopportune statement can reerect the barrier between them. For example, in *Passion's Price*, Laine, who is allowing her thoughts to wander in the warm afterglow of lovemaking, asks Nick a pertinent question at the worst possible time:

> She lifted a hand to touch light fingertips to Nick's lean cheek. "Nick," she murmured, "you are going to give Latham the grant, aren't you?" And she would have given the world to have been able to recall the words the instant they were out of her mouth and she felt him go tense beside her. Her eyes flew open and she saw the implacable set of his strong jaw and the muscle ticking with ominous regularity there. The planes of his face were now forebodingly hard beneath her fingers and she moved her hand away in a futile gesture of apology. "Nick, I didn't mean . . ."
>
> "I knew virginity was a rare commodity these days," he muttered through clenched teeth. "But I had no idea you'd put a million-dollar price tag on yours."
>
> "Nick, please listen. I . . ."
>
> "Anything for 'Father.' Right?" His voice was low, his tone harsh. "Right?"
>
> "No, that isn't right!" she said urgently, feeling his anger in the taut inflexible line of his body, feeling her own heart react to that anger with wild palpitations. Sensing danger, she tried desperately to explain that she had been half asleep and the question had simply popped into her mind.
>
> "Don't bother talking, Laine. We have no time for that,"

he interrupted her midsentence, in no mood to listen. With the awesome swiftness of a tiger pouncing, he turned over, imprisoning her beneath him. . . . Green ice shards glittered in his eyes as his gaze raked over her face and he muttered, "A million dollars, hmmm? Well, now that I know what a high price I'm expected to pay, I think I should get my money's worth, don't you agree?"

Laine gasped, her face going pale as a hard knee thrust downward and parted her legs. Facing for the first time in her life the absolute proof of a man's overwhelming physical superiority, she panicked. She threw her hands against his broad chest. . . .

Sexual tension is accentuated here, and it does not abate as Nick determinedly proceeds to arouse Laine's physical need of him to a feverish obsession, despite her useless efforts to resist him.

Sometimes misstatements cause more pain than anger, as in this scene from *Morning Always Comes,* in which the heroine is reunited with her baby's father, to whom she is not married:

Warm and content, Devon lay quietly, feeling Ryan's heartbeat beneath the hand she rested on his chest. After a few minutes, she breathed a tremendous sigh. Ryan was very still beside her, so still that she thought he must have fallen asleep. She smiled. Very gently, she kissed his bronzed skin where it hardened over his collarbone. "Oh, Ryan," she whispered.

"God, Devon, I'm sorry," he suddenly groaned, unaware that he startled her by speaking. "I'm so sorry. I never meant for this to happen."

Devon stiffened. Raw pain exploded like fire in her chest. He had sounded so contrite, so *ashamed* that she shrank away from him, humiliation washing over her. He was sorry tonight had happened! She hadn't been sorry at all. But he was and she could hardly bear knowing that. Excruciating despair knotted her muscles but she forced herself to respond. "No need to apologize," she muttered, miraculously steadying the tremor in her voice. "These things . . . just happen sometimes, I guess."

"But Devon," he began raggedly, "if I've made you pregnant again . . ."

"Oh, surely you won't be so unlucky a second time," she retorted with defensive and vehement sarcasm, slipping

quickly from his bed and grabbing her robe up off the floor.
She rushed to the door. . . .

Sexual tension has been reestablished in this scene and is
sustained as Devon resolves not to risk further humiliation by
allowing Ryan to get close to her again.

When a heroine, because of emotional considerations, does
determine not to continue an intimate relationship, the hero may
become just as determined to prove to her that he can arouse her
passion to such a burning intensity that she must surrender to
him. He usually succeeds in proving this, and it soon becomes
apparent that despite their serious and realistic problem, these
two cannot resist the delight that they give each other when they
make love. Though it may seem that they should walk away
from each other, they simply can't. This is the pinnacle of sexual
buildup, a friction that becomes unbearable and must be eased.
Heroine and hero are compelled to confront openly the problem
between them. By compromise or by some other turn of plot,
they are able to resolve their differences. Mutual love declared, a
lasting commitment made, they discover the one element that
had been lacking in their lovemaking—trust: a very necessary
faith in each other. Intimacy takes on a new and more wonderous
significance, and both characters now know that only together
are they complete.

To make such an ending as satisfying as possible for the
reader, the writer has tried to emphasize the sexual suspense
between a man and woman who are irresistibly drawn to each
other despite the intrusion of an underlying conflict. With believable characters who can glimpse admirable qualities in each
other and begin to really fall in love, with a gradual building of
sexual fascination between these two people depicted in exquisitely sensuous love scenes, and with the creation of an equally
sensuous atmosphere resulting in an aura of quickening anticipation,
an author can write a realistic and tremendously stirring romance.

And the reader can turn the last page, sigh dreamily, and
think: "That's really the way love is. What a good story. I can't
wait to read another one like it."

Full-Blown Eroticism

BY ALICE MORGAN

author of five category romances

Boredom with reading romance books that took the hero and heroine to the bedroom door only to shut it abruptly in a reader's face was my original reason for purchasing two hundred sheets of typewriter paper and a Coronet Super 12 Smith-Corona. If the writers of my favorite brand of paperbacks didn't want to, or weren't allowed to, share their characters' intimacies with the reader, then I would plot my own story, without restrictive house-style editing. (Easily said when a novice, and not aware that publishing companies have their own strictly adhered-to guidelines.)

It wasn't enough for me to read the hero kissed and caressed the heroine and eventually—often after the book ended—consummated the relationship. I wanted to know how he kissed her, where he caressed her, and what he did when they made love. Was he tender? Harsh? Brutal? Loving? Solicitous? Concerned about her pleasure more than his own?

Developing a story with a passionate hero eager to enter a receptive heroine's irresolutely barred boudoir—later interspersed with whirling hot tubs, warm beach sand, grassy glens with cool, tree-shaded pools, luxury automobiles, alpaca fur rugs spread before a fireplace filled with burning, pungent eucalyptus logs, early morning sun-drenched hillsides, secluded gazebos, etc.—came easy. The surroundings are limitless, usually bounded by some privacy for the couple involved, and an author's imagination.

With enthusiasm I proceeded to guide my heroes and heroines through a continuing series of romantic little romps. Not only could I have my hero look as I wanted him to, I could let him react the way I wished . . . always undeterred in his pursuit. I could even assure the reader that he knew he wanted the heroine from the moment of first contact—something most often left in doubt, or ignored, until the last pages of a book.

Sensuous love scenes were usually the most enjoyable part of writing, though not necessarily the easiest. It became patently more obvious that passion developed without any flaring buildup between characters was merely information. Sexually implicit words alone do not make a physically exciting love scene. More important are the couple's constant interaction throughout the story, creating a mood for lovemaking when the occasion arises.

I strive to fabricate plots with romantic sensuality permeating the entire story. This prevents the need for using sex for the sake of sex because a particular publishing company requires three erotic scenes per book. I have found no need to fantasize about my characters' libido. When writing about a virile male in the prime of his life encountering a modern, mature, progressively receptive female, the problem is toning their desires down enough not to shock the copy editor. I have received no letters from readers offended by *im*plicit amatory liaisons, though many have requested increased *ex*plicitness and frequency.

Unfortunately, most category romance books prior to Dell's Candlelight Ecstasy Romances only hinted at physical relationships. If the hero was a strong, ruggedly vital man and no description of his sexual potency was forthcoming, I often found the story disappointing. Why stop at a crucial part of a loving relationship? I could use my imagination, which is fine if one enjoys filling in the blanks. It seemed ridiculous that mainstream novels could hit the reader with explicit, often crude sexuality, yet category romances couldn't entice the reader with implicit erotica when they were guaranteed the enjoyment of a happy ending with a monogamous interrelationship.

Tender or tough, physically stimulating scenes are an important part of my fictional characters' total personality, and reasons to indulge their desires can be as varied as the plots—maybe not to each reader's liking, though it does add depth for any inclined to enjoy sensual books. Public reaction, winning the "Pearl Award" at the Romantic Book Lovers' Conference in 1982, flattering fan mail, plus the rapidly increasing popularity of Candlelight Ectasy Romances and the newer, similar lines, prove to me stories of my type are vastly marketable.

Expressing diverse, loving lifestyles can help create or assist in heightening an intense state of mind, as each battles with his or her sexuality until total understanding is reached at the end of the book. How far an author should go in writing sensuous love scenes seems dependent on the number of euphemisms used in order to avoid a too clinical or graphic description, and your editor's guidelines, which often vary drastically from publishing company to publishing company.

I always try to have a range of contrasting erotic moods throughout my books, fluctuating from sex for the pure fun of it to adoring reverence, with the hero down on his knees in worship of the heroine.

In *Masquerade of Love,* heightened excitement was expressed:

Brad's mouth took hers again, the urgency of his desire communicated beneath her palms as she stroked his shoulders. His kisses were driving her into a frenzy of need when he lifted her out of the water, his hands surrounding her rib cage as his mouth trailed downward before burrowing into the deep valley between her breasts. "Oh, God, you're absolutely beautiful . . ."

As he held Brandy above him he lay back with his head resting on the edge. Bracing her slight weight easily, he moved her over him so his mouth had access to the enticing peaks of her full breasts. He took the nipples into his mouth and moaned at the pleasure of feeling them harden against his tongue. He sucked each erect tip in turn before trailing a sensuous path around her breasts. He nibbled on the satin-smooth burgeoning underside, then circled back eagerly to the rosy tips.

In *The Sands of Malibu,* anger was the paramount mood:

"Do you always stare at your customers as they undress, or does your price include stripping them too?" Nick asked cruelly. The weight of his body lowering on hers pushed her deep into the soft mattress. Senses inflamed by her touch, he growled, "Tell me how you want it first, witch.

Me on top . . . you on top . . . sideways . . . Come on, damn you, if you know so much, then teach me! I should get more than one for the price you charge!''

Carlyn lay passively, overpowered by his weight, the scent of his heated skin, his abrasive hair-covered chest. Her eyes were dark, her lips parted sensually.

Nick, wary of her silence and the glimmer of pain deep in her eyes, hesitated briefly before reaching for her bra. ''Pretty convenient having the fastener in the front, isn't it?'' He unhooked it deftly, his eyes smoldering at the sight of her flawless breasts, her pink nipples making him shake with the desire to plunder them with his mouth. But the sight of her tear-stained face and quivering lips stirred a twinge of tenderness in him that was impossible to quell. As he cupped her face his lips took hers with surprising gentleness.

In *Impetuous Surrogate*, oral sex was practiced:

De-Ann arched her body upward, instinctively pushing sideways to get under his hips. She moved restlessly, each touch more arousing than the one before.

Derek eased her onto her back again, his mouth leaving her breasts long enough to command, ''Lie still! I'm not finished loving you this way yet.'' His voice was ragged, barely recognizable, from his tormented need for relief.

He gave her throbbing breasts a lingering flick across the nipples before moving down, intent on probing each tantalizing portion of her satin smooth anatomy. His hands were gentle as they parted her thighs, then moved upward to caress her body's most sensitive area until she arched to meet the pressure of his hand, seeking satisfaction. Unbidden murmurs of intense pleasure came from her throat, tiny whimpering pleas for release from his stimulating touch.

So expert was Derek's tutoring, De-Ann made no protest when his mouth lowered across her abdomen. Her heart hammered expectantly, body arching and pliant beneath him as he placed kisses along the length of each trembling leg. Outer thigh to back of knee and down to the smooth soles of her feet, before returning a different path along the inner leg. Ever upward his lips caressed her, to the top of her velvety limbs until she lay trembling beneath his searching, restless tongue as wave after wave of sexual pleasure seared the apex of her sensitive femininity. Eager, she squirmed, arching so they could cleave as one.

In *Deception for Desire,* French kissing was described:

Brett let his eyes rove over the flushed beauty of Honey's face. Passion flowed between them like a magnetic force. His mouth took hers, deeply hungering for further contact. She felt his tongue extend inward, probing gently. He moved it slowly until he felt her tentative touch. She became bolder, excited by the havoc his stimulating kiss was raising to her senses. She inhaled, drawing his tongue deeper, instinctively sucking it until he shuddered.

In *Branded Heart,* the heroine asks to make love to her hero:

"Let me love you, Jake?" Joy whispered, her gentle fingers giving him succor from the constant pain in his injured back. "Lie back, my darling, and let me bring you a hint of the satisfaction you gave me earlier." Her hands lazily stroked the hair-roughened skin of his limbs until they reached his rapidly taunted manhood. Encouraged by his sudden moans of excitement, passion flowed from her fingertips, guiding her intuitively when he quivered within her grip. Her face lowered, allowing her luxuriant chestnut hair to cover his hips in a silken swathe that hid the perfection of her profile. Her mouth touched him boldly, without embarrassment, eager to show her love in the ultimate intimacy. At last, she was able to fulfill her most erotic fantasy.

She felt his broad palms cup her head gently, his fingers twining through her hair in reaction to the unexpected pleasure of the warm, surging moistness of her mouth. A mouth he knew to be the most exquisitely precious he'd ever tasted in his life. Words of love spilled forth unbidden, torn from his throat over and over. His mind was filled with disbelief that she would do that for him . . . and, that she was doing it so expertly.

In *Deception for Desire,* the hero was filled with reverence as he worshiped her body:

Brett knelt before her, clasping her naked form in his strong arms. His hands clutched her rounded bottom, holding her still while he buried his face into the creamy flesh of her abdomen.

Honey shook, her knees threatening to buckle. Clasping his solid shoulders, she looked down at his glistening ebony hair, moaning when he probed her navel with his tongue before descending to press fevered kisses where his fingers had wrought such erotic delight. The thought that touching her could bring him to his knees was overpowering. She knew instinctively that no other woman had been the recipient of such worship.

In *Masquerade of Love,* moments of tenderness were communicated:

Brandy flung herself into Brad's arms, her words muffled against his broad chest as her years of anguish spilled forth. "Oh darling, it was so awful not being able to talk to anyone."

He lay on his back, cradling her face to him, his arms rubbing her body in slow languorous strokes. Brad kissed her scented hair, understanding her youthful dilemma.

"I'm glad we both had plenty of sleep last night." A roaring flame ignited inside his body, his hands touching each satin smooth breast before descending over her quivering abdomen, lowering still as she arched upward. Sliding, probing, stroking to bring her satisfaction.

"Er—why?" she purred, seductively. "Hmm, that feels good." She was trailing her hand over his steel-hard biceps, gripping them when he moved.

"Because when I mentioned we would make long, slow love the second time, I meant the whole night through." Brad bent down, his breath hot against her navel, his tongue circling in ever-widening circles, touching where his hands had been.

In *Impetuous Surrogate,* despair turned to the need to find reassurance through the act of love:

With a sense of urgency Derek cupped De-Ann's supple body beneath him, moans of desire escaping his throat before his mouth clung to the sweetness of her parted lips. Terror filled him at the faint taste of salty ocean spray that still clung to her skin. Fervent words were whispered against her lips between deep hungering kisses.

Cradling his head, she felt blood roar through her veins as he plundered the side of her neck with fervent caresses.

He tasted each delectable inch of skin. Her body trembled convulsively, arching upward as he reached the taut curves of her breasts, tips stirred to erectness. The warmth of his mouth surging against her sensitive nipples caused her to cry out with desire.

Moving beneath his aroused body, she parted her thighs from the hardness of his entwined limbs. As her fingers clung to the solid muscles of his broad shoulders, her hips raised instinctively, seeking the sensual satisfaction he had taught her to crave. Out of breath, eyes luminous with desire, she beseeched him to take her, her soft body a pale contrast to his hard bronze torso.

In *Masquerade of Love*, the hero cries out his frustrations explicitly:

With his broad palms on her back he lingered, his fingers stroking the swell of her outer breasts. She could feel a deep trembling start in the pit of her stomach—a trembling of desire uncontrolled.

"You're quivering, little one. You feel it, don't you, Brandy? You want me as much as I want you."

"Don't. Please, don't say any more," she begged.

Heedless of her plea, his husky voice hissed against her ear as he leaned forward. "I want you. I want my hands over all of you—not just the parts exposed to everyone else's eyes. I want to touch your breasts, feel the nipples harden beneath my fingers. I want to rub my palms across your stomach and the smooth skin of your buttocks—let my fingers caress your inner thighs and upward."

In *Sands of Malibu*, shyness was overcome by the hero's insistence:

Patient, knowing how to give her pleasure, he slid his long fingers gently along her inner thigh to part her legs.

Carlyn's legs clenched in sudden embarrassment to stop the intimacy of his hands. "No, Nick . . ."

"Yes . . . everywhere!" he commanded in a husky voice.

She grasped his hand as it rested possessively on her feminine hair, a sudden feeling of sensual inadequacy making her body tense.

"Don't stop me, mia cara. Let me show you how beautiful touching can be. How exquisite it feels."

With each unhurried stroke he explored the hidden recesses of her virtuous body. The motion of his restless hand as he intimately caressed her, along with the torture of his wandering mouth as it descended to seek its final pleasure, brought a poignant cry from deep in her throat.

"Oh, Nick darling . . . not there!"

"Especially there."

In *Branded Heart,* the hero shows his desire to please the heroine:

"Oh, Jake, my darling husband. I've never experienced a man's passion before. I'm overwhelmed to learn how devouring it can be, how enjoyable . . ." she broke off, disturbed by her sudden yearning to feel him deep within her body.

Raining kisses on her neck and throat, Jake murmured he understood. "Knowing what should arouse a woman can be gained clinically. Learning to satisfy your lover, to give her pleasure and release, takes experience. Tonight, wife, will be my first lesson in pleasing you!"

"Texas cowboy style, no doubt?" Joy responded fervently to his experienced tutoring, unable to stop her mischievous taunt.

"Is there any other way, wife?" he retorted, his mouth silencing any further words by covering hers in a series of hungry, mind-drugging kisses. "Now hug, woman," Jake groaned, his voice thick with desire. "Lie back, enjoy and let me show you what loving's all about."

If I have the ability to write emotionally stirring romances, it is not just my yearning for a sensual fantasy, but simply a tribute to the loving reality of an exceptional husband.

> Maryland Avenue
> Royal Oak, Michigan
>
> February 1

Dear Kathryn,

Donna's and Alice's essays certainly loosened me up a lot. I was trying so hard to write the sexual scenes explicitly without realizing the finer "evocative" points of the art. I'm also reading books on releasing <u>my</u> sexual fantasies, plus some outright "porn." And Paul is cooperating nobly.

I just bought silk sheets and gardenia bubble bath.

Sensually yours,
La Roseanne

From the Desk of Kathryn Falk

February 14

Dear La Roseanne!

Keep up the good work. You make me feel like a proud teacher.

Are you using the active voice? That's a stumbling block sometimes. For example: Rhett kissed Scarlet [Good.]. She was kissed [Bad]. Jenny ironed the ruffled blouse [Good]. The blouse was ironed [Bad].

Copy editor Donna Ryan is a stickler on clarity, and I'm sending you her tips plus her wonderfully funny explanation, titled "Beware of the Pillaging Mouth."

Now that you're understanding the TORTE system and the formula, it's time to polish up your techniques even more by concentrating on the preciseness of language and the common mistakes of new writers. Our book reviewer, Renée Rubin, has made a fair sampling of what *not* to do in your first book.

Happy Valentine's Day,
Kathryn

Style and Usage

Beware of the Pillaging Mouth

BY DONNA RYAN

freelance copy editor

The kids are in bed, Frank is watching television, and tomorrow is Saturday. The reader relaxes in her favorite chair, opens the romance novel to the dogeared page, and picks up where she left off before dinner:

> Nostrils flaring, chest heaving, teeth flashing, Pierre seized Esmeralda and crushed her to him. His arms were like steel bands that threatened to crush her soft body. She ran her tiny hands over his broad, hairy chest.

Ah, the reader says to herself, *here we go. Good stuff.* She settles back to enjoy reading a sensuous love scene. Then, very suddenly, something goes wrong with the prose. Pierre disappears from sight, and things in general just get out of hand:

> Esmeralda was kissed, fondled, caressed. Her lips were ravished, her skin was stroked, her swanlike throat nuzzled.

The reader frowns. "By whom?" she says aloud, causing Frank to shrug and then mutter absentmindedly, "Damned if I know."

The reader gives him a withering glance and returns to the page. Determined to find out who did all these wonderful things to Esmeralda, she reads on:

> Esmerald's fingers were licked, one by one. Her nose was tweaked playfully. Her passion-swollen lips were ravished by the pillaging mouth.

"Aha!" the reader cries. "The Pillaging Mouth strikes again!"

"Second time this week," Frank murmurs distractedly.

The reader, a veteran romance enthusiast, had run into the Pillaging Mouth many times before in by-whom sentences that she'd found tucked away in dozens of otherwise sensible novels:

> Their lunch was eaten quickly.

> Annette's tiny hand was kissed.

> Their wine was sipped slowly.

> Jennifer's mouth was plundered.

> A mouthful of potato salad was devoured.

> Dorothea's creamy neck was kissed.

By whom? The reader, because she is experienced in the romance field, knows full well by whom the lunch was eaten, the neck kissed, the potato salad devoured. 'Twas . . . the Pillaging Mouth, a mysterious creature who has a way of appearing suddenly during love scenes and rudely snatching the girl away from the hero.

As a romance author you would do well to fight this villain off. Readers want the hero to have a chance to do things for himself. They would prefer sentences like these:

> Samantha and Garth ate their lunch quickly.

Zach tenderly kissed her hand.

Naomi and Jed sipped their wine slowly.

The trick, you see, is to write as you speak, *in the active voice,* letting your characters perform all actions. Which of these sentences is better?

Nanette caught her breath as her arm was kissed.

Nanette caught her breath as Yuri ran his lips along her arm.

The answer is the second sentence, because it is in the active voice. It is stronger and more interesting because it allows a flesh-and-blood human being to perform the action of kissing the girl's arm. The first sentence is dull and vague, as is most passive-voice prose. We learn that the heroine's arm "was kissed," but the author does not tell us who performed this action. The Pillaging Mouth has once again pushed the hero out of the scene.

Try never to use the passive voice in your novel unless you have a specific reason for doing so, and even then, use it very sparingly. What are some reasons for going passive? One is the author's wish to keep information from the reader for the sake of suspense. Perhaps you want to keep certain information a secret until the end of the novel. If so, you can slip into the passive: "When Amanda returned home, she discovered that her apartment had been searched." Few readers will argue with your use of the passive voice in this instance, although some purists will insist that you should have written "she discovered that someone had searched her apartment."

Another reason for using the passive voice is that in some instances no one knows for sure who did a certain thing. To wit:

Jean's brother was hit by a car.

Mr. Johanson was mugged.

Janet was fired from her job.

In such sentences you need the passive voice to avoid such silliness as: "A car hit Jean's brother"; "A mugger mugged Mr. Johansen." Better passivity than absurdity.

Even though the passive voice has its uses, you should try never to use it in a love scene. The instant you allow your style to go passive, you put distance between the reader and the characters. In a love scene, distance is the last thing you want. In such scenes, you must draw the reader in as close as possible to the action so that she identifies strongly with the heroine. Draw the reader in by staying in the active voice. Let the hero do things to the heroine. Let her do things to him. Never, *never* let the Pillaging Mouth take over the action.

Examine every sentence of your manuscript before you send it to an agent or editor. If you find a passive-voice sentence such as "She was kissed passionately," change it to "Sean kissed her passionately." Keep doing this until you have banished the Pillaging Mouth from every scene in your book.

The pursuit of the Pillaging Mouth is wearying, and you could end up doing a good deal of revising to get your prose into the active voice. The labor will result in a stronger, clearer book, however, and your readers will appreciate your efforts.

Tips from a Copy Editor

BY DONNA RYAN

On its way to publication, your Romance novel will go over the desks of several editors, each of whom will probably make, or at least suggest, certain changes. The last person to work on your manuscript is usually the copy editor. In some publishing houses she is known as a line editor; in journalism she is a copy reader. Don't let the titles confuse you. All three designate the person who passes judgment on your punctuation, grammar, usage, spelling, and syntax and who checks your work for consistency and accuracy.

A good copy editor can improve your book enormously; cooperate with her. A bad copy editor, however, can introduce embarrassing errors. Stand up in your own defense, but be absolutely certain that you are correct. The best way to avoid the stab of the copy editor's pencil is to hand in a manuscript as nearly free of errors as possible.

Here are some points to remember:

• Most publishing houses use *Webster's New Collegiate Dictionary,* 8th ed. (Springfield, Mass.: Merriam, 1981). Nobody likes it, but everybody uses it, so you might as well grit your teeth and go along with the pack. Consult the dictionary frequently. Even a world-class speller makes an occasional mistake.

• Check the spelling of all proper names (Pikes Peak, for example, not Pike's Peak).

• Get your facts straight. Before you allow your heroine to go shopping in Macy's and Altman's on a Sunday afternoon in Manhattan, make sure that both stores are open on Sunday (Macy's is; Altman's is not).

• Be consistent. If your hero has brown eyes in the first chapter, he cannot have gray eyes in the last chapter. A character who drives a Volkswagen in the beginning of the book cannot suddenly appear in a Renault without explanation.

• Sparingly use full caps (LIKE THIS). There are a mark of the amateur, and they make the writer sound wild-eyed and fanatical.

• Avoid exclamation points when you can, and never use more than one at a time.

This is bad!!!
THIS is even WORSE!!!

• Put the comma and period inside the quotation marks.

"This is correct American usage."
"This is wrong".

• Underscore for emphasis only when absolutely necessary. The compositor will set underscored words in italic print. Avoid using too much emphasis, especially in dialogue; it makes the speaker sound gushy.

• Use quotation marks, commas, and dashes only when you have a valid reason for doing so. Too much punctuation clutters up your style and draws the reader's attention away from the story, but if clarity depends on it, by all means be lavish.

• Use capital letters only if you have a reason to do so.

[Good] She regarded herself as a virtuous woman.
[Bad] She regarded herself as a Virtuous Woman.
[Awful] She regarded herself as a VIRTUOUS WOMAN!!!

• Write in the active voice.

[Good] They ate their lunch hurriedly.
[Bad] Their lunch was eaten hurriedly.

• Keep corrections to a minimum, and make them in pencil.
• Use a fresh black typewriter ribbon.

One final word: A plain, straight-out style will get you into less trouble than will a coy, mannered, studiedly fancy style. Fancy talk is likely to make your reader laugh. It is certain to give your copy editor the vapors.

Caveats and Don'ts

BY RENÉE RUBIN

book review editor, Romantic Times

Ideally, (1) authors who have heeded good advice would produce flawless novels and (2) bad novels would be shunned by discerning readers. Ours is not an ideal world. Some bad novels get published, and some of them are very popular. Does it follow, then, that standards are unnecessary? No. That there are no discriminating or fussy readers? Impossible. Should the crotchery reviewer give up? Never. And what *is* a bad novel anyway?

A bad novel is one that merely plods along on the journey of the imagination, meandering, making detours and local stops, and arriving nowhere. Or, to put it another way, the story is to the storyteller what the dance is to the dancer. Too many clumsy steps and the audience goes home. Anything that slows the action, distracts the reader, or leaves the reader unsatisfied spoils the illusion. True, many good novelists transcend minor errors. Some readers are indifferent to things like silly plots and lack of motivation. But no writer is consciously careless. All, I am sure, would prefer to be as perfect as possible.

So here is a list of what *not* to do in order to ensure that the beauty of the original concept is never veiled. Examples are taken from actual novels, although some are composites.

Please Don't:

I. Be inaccurate. The written language is the author's only tool. Doubts and double takes are distracting.

A. Sometimes a word or phrase may *sound* right but *be* wrong. The meaning of "there were fraught moments" is clear, but the author obviously meant "moments fraught *with tension*." Look up *fraught*.

B. A word or phrase may be grammatically correct but not quite right. "Her breasts heaved tauntingly." Try it. I think the author meant that the hero was taunted by her heaving breasts.

C. Many historical novelists are careful about facts but let anachronisms creep into the dialogue. It is doubtful that an eighteenth-century girl would have referred to the furniture as "functional" or that a pagan Roman girl would speak of Paradise.

D. Slang and clumsiness are dangerous. A phrase such as "flabbergasted by his gall" may irritate sensitive readers.

II. Pad/plump out.

A. Avoid florid writing ("Nightfall was the last resort in nature's bid to blot out her own splendor") and/or detailed descriptions of food, clothing, furniture, etc. It may be necessary to indicate a character's social standing and wealth by describing clothes and jewels, *but not every time the outfit* (or meal or room) *is changed*. Many readers feel that repeated descriptions and menus are too much and skip them anyway. And how many readers, I wonder, are still awed by designers' names and elegant department stores? Something like "He looked at his watch, a handsome piece of black enamel from Cartier" is ostentatious. The hero who is described as one of the richest men in the United States may be *presumed* to have a nice watch.

B. Dialogue is good, but chitchat (it's not possible to give an example out of context) slows the action. Small talk—dialogue that does not further the plot, or reveal motivation and relationships—should go, as should any talk that does not further the work dialogue is designed to do.

C. Do not merely sprinkle famous names in order to establish historical authenticity. Dialogue like " 'Who wrote that song?' 'A young composer named Ludwig van Beethoven,' " in a story having nothing to do with Beethoven or music, is not convincing. If the character doesn't have a reason to associate with somebody famous, don't just send him to a party attended by Byron, Wordsworth, Shelley, and Coleridge. This diverts the reader's attention.

III. Overload the plot.

A. Many a novel starts off well but soon rides off in all directions. Each change of locale introduces new characters (mostly villainous, and some with incomprehensible names yet!) who are difficult to tell apart. Confusion destroys the feeling of reality.

B. Family sagas are especially vulnerable to plot overloading. Just as the reader begins to identify with one generation, he or she is shifted to a new set with new problems. Without a unified plot, the saga becomes a string of short stories.

C. Repetition (danger, rescue, danger, rescue, or fight, reconciliation, fight, reconciliation) and teasing (the *almost* resolution of a misunderstanding, for example, repeated until the final explanation ends the novel) are good devices frequently overused. The reader may get bored and skip around for the sexy parts—or skip, period.

IV. Strain credibility.

A. The reader's will to believe is the author's most precious possession and should be treated with care. Holes in the plot—sudden reversals, impossible coincidences, mistaken identities, and illogical behavior—need not be eliminated, but should be accounted for. Otherwise, questions may arise in the reader's mind: "How come he's marching across the desert when he broke his leg the week before?" "How come she agreed to meet in the crypt at midnight when she knows there's a murderer at large?" No matter what the original premise may be, once it is stated, everything should follow logically.

B. Characters who come alive only when they are sexually aroused and are wooden otherwise, characters who behave stupidly (such as the heroine who falls into the villain's clutches not once, but many times), and characters who witness or perform atrocious acts with the blandest of reactions cannot command the reader's sympathy.

V. Lose sight of the point.

Now we come to the ending, both of this list of complaints and of the romance novel itself.

Too many novels have no proper ending. In the course of the novel readers want to imagine the ideal lover, and sex under conditions that everyday life seldom provides. They want the emotional stimulation that comes from identifying with the heroine. They want to satisfy their curiosity about other times and places, and about life among the rich and powerful. They want to triumph (someday I'll show them) over their rivals.

And they want a "happy" ending. It's not enough to have the hero and heroine in each other's arms on the last page, after having undergone terrible trials, unless their experiences have some meaning. Beyond the pleasure of vicarious experience is the glow of satisfaction that comes when evil is vanquished and virtue triumphs. I hesitate to use the word, but readers want a moral. As an example, take one of the most famous endings in film history. In *Casablanca*, Ingrid Bergman leaves the man she loves, Humphrey Bogart, and goes back with her noble husband, Paul Henreid. The ending is not "happy," but it *is* spiritually uplifting. Readers are social beings who feel good when the social order is observed. They may not always practice or experience noble action, but they still like to read about altruism, duty, self-sacrifice, etc. Virtue has an aesthetic beauty. Romance novels should end with virtue triumphant.

From the Desk of Kathryn Falk

March 10

Dear Rosie,

Are you bogged down? I haven't heard from you lately? Maybe this news will raise your spirits. Shirley Bennett Tallman (a.k.a. Erin Ross) just sold her first novel and sent me this "birth announcement." Hope this helps any "labor pains" you're experiencing.

I'll be gone for a while . . . going to Europe to plan the International Romantic Book Lovers' Conference.

À bientôt,
Kathryn

The Aches and Pains of Writing Your First Romance Novel

BY ERIN ROSS

author of one category romance

I have just given birth. My new offspring is 9¼ inches long and weighs an even 4 ounces. It has no gender, although I tend to think of it as feminine, and it does not require a two o'clock feeding. But make no mistake, between conception and delivery were long months of often torturous, always valuable, development and growth.

I have created, of course, that enigmatic, frequently misunderstood genus of literature, the romantic novel!

In all honesty, I must admit that writing a romance novel was not always my literary goal. My first book, a humorous satire on women, appeared in hardcover a year before, and I had high hopes for a three-act play that was attracting some favorable notice. If all else failed, I thought philosophically, I could always fall back on my weekly newspaper column, which had been wending its way into more than one hundred thousand homes for the past three years.

Fortunately, my agent had more far-reaching ideas.

"Write a romance," he threw at me with monotonous regularity.

"Never" was my equally tiresome reply. "They're nice little books, but not for me."

So much, of course, for famous last words. It slowly dawned on me that the romance market was where the action was in today's literary world, so maybe my agent was right. Perhaps that was where I should be, too.

Armed with stacks of those "nice little books," I slunk home, locked my bedroom door, and delved into that never-never land where men were men, women were glad of it, and happy endings were still offered with a money-back guarantee. When I finally emerged, blurry-eyed, satiated, and numb, I had changed. No longer was I the self-possessed, unwavering woman so confident of her own future. In that short time I had developed a rapacious, probably incurable disease—the same malady that is spreading in epidemic proportions throughout the rest of the United States. I had been bitten by the love bug!

The die was cast. It was here I would make my mark, and, I hoped, contribute to the support of my family. But how to start? Unfortunately, making the decision was only the first step. How did one go about breaking into this redoubtable business?

Systematically, I sorted my stock of books into neat little groupings. It seemed logical that my first decision should be which sort of stories I wanted to write. I had found there really *was* a difference between the romance houses. To add to the confusion, the individual lines *within* the houses also differed.

Actually, the decision turned out to be relatively simple: I would write the type of story I most enjoyed reading. Since I found myself far more absorbed in the "steamier" novels, I would start there. I would write a Silhouette Desire.

Burying the few niggling doubts that nibbled at my confidence, I sent for some tip sheets, those publishers' bibles outlining the do's and don'ts of the business. Armed with a healthy supply of these to my right, the dictionary to my left, and the blank screen of my word processor directly ahead, I was ready to begin. But being what? I seemed to be missing one very necessary ingredient: I had no story line in mind.

Having faced this particular hurdle before, I switched off my computer and pulled out old-fashioned paper and pen. It was back to square one, I thought with resignation, for without the initial idea, a writer is nowhere. So where to begin?

Why not start with a place, I thought reasonably. Where had I been in my life besides my kitchen and laundry room?

Halfway around the world, I remembered suddenly. Before my marriage, I had been an airline hostess. My regular routes had been the Orient and the South Pacific. What better place to begin?

Instantly, my mind conjured up wistful memories of two large craggy islands near the southwestern rim of the Pacific Ocean. I could almost smell again the salty sea breeze and feel the warm white sand filtering between my toes. I had found a place to begin. My book would take place in New Zealand.

From there the story seemed to leap to life. I remembered the Henderson Valley, and the long rows of grape vines stretched out as far as the eye could see. Years ago I had driven through this lovely north island retreat and wondered what it would be like to live there, to actually own one of those fertile, rolling vineyards. My imagination took off. What would happen if a young woman *did* find herself the unexpected owner of such a vineyard? How would she react? What would she feel?

And so *Second Harvest* was launched. To provide a little spice for my heroine, I added one handsome, hard-driving hero to the mixture, and stirred the two briskly with several spectacular evenings beneath a tropical sky. It was now up to nature to take its course. Which it did, much too quickly.

"Wait a moment," I scolded my errant protagonists. "There must be some problems for you to solve before you fall into each other's arms."

For of course it's the underlying difference between the hero and the heroine that keeps a love story simmering. No controversy = no interest; no interest = no reader! And naturally, once I had pulled the two apart it was necessary to find ways to nudge them back together again. Was there no end to it all?

Ultimately they did discover their love, and suddenly I was faced with the trickiest dilemma of all—the love scenes. How, I asked myself in distraction, do you put *that* kind of thing on paper, for heaven's sake?

Once again I withdrew behind closed doors, away from prying eyes and overactive adolescent curiosity, and faced up to the job. Here I was with two characters passionately ready to consummate their love, and my timid fingers simply could not find the right keys to help them toward their goal. Good grief! What had domesticity done to me?

Patiently I persevered, and finally the words began to trickle, slowly at first, then faster as the characters took on life in the scene.

> . . . his lips left her mouth to trail a path of burning kisses down to the hollow of her throat. Smoothly, his fingers found the back zipper of her dress and slowly eased it down to below the waist. With greater insistency now, he brushed aside the cool cotton until all that protected her was the flimsy material of her lacy bra.

Whew! Now I had them primed, but could I carry it through? The next few paragraphs were sheer misery. Again and again I rephrased the words, changed their positions, tried a different approach. My poor characters! Surely no couple in the history of literature have thrashed about for so long in this unseemly struggle for fulfillment.

Then, at long last, they were joined, the word flowed, they reached the zenith.

> . . . with a magnetism as old as time, they were drawn together, joined in a searing, consuming fire of longing. She strained upward beneath his thrusting body, as passions too long dormant awakened to his expert touch. With perfectly choreographed harmony, they melded together, his strong, hard form against her soft, yielding flesh, until, with an uncontrolled cry of passion, they were engulfed in a cataclysmic explosion of fulfillment.

It was done. My patient characters were finally released. It had taken two days, but the act was complete.

Weakly, I unlocked my door and tottered unsteadily from the room. Surely it would get easier after this, I thought wearily. From now on the rest of the gestation *had* to be uphill.

Four weeks later *Second Harvest* was finished, but my labor was not complete. Although the book was now in my publisher's care, my unborn offspring still had to endure weeks of editing, scheduling, typesetting, and jacket design before it could make its debut. Stalwartly, we both endured the last agonizing months of wait. The labor was interminable, delivery torturous.

Then, suddenly, almost anticlimactically, it was over. Drained but content, I was at last able to hold my small creation in my hands, to fondle and admire all its parts.

At long last I was the proud parent of a romance. I had weathered the pregnancy and my "child" was whole. Gently I handed my firstborn over to the custody of its readers. It was time to relinquish it. It was time to relax.

Nonsense, I chuckled, heading stoutheartedly back to the locked door. It was time to beget again!

Questions to Ask While Plotting

BY SERITA STEVENS

author of two romances

1. Hero

Is he lovable?
What flaws does he have?
Is he a perfect, handsome 10 or not?
What has made him the way he is?
How vulnerable is he? (Can he cry?)
What is his age?
Can you fall in love with him?
Does his name stand out?

2. Heroine

What are her strengths and weaknesses?
Is she career-oriented? If so, what career? (Some careers have been overused.)
How does she usually go about meeting men?
How would you rate her on looks? (Readers must identify with her, so don't create perfection.)
How sexually aware is she? How experienced?
What is her age?
Do you want to be the heroine?
Do you cry when she cries? Moan when she moans?
Is her age plausible for her career?
Does her name stand out?
Do you know her as well as your best friend or better?

3. Situation

Is the situation plausible? Is it something you can expect to happen as an everyday occurrence?
Is the situation original?

Is the situation contrived?
Does the situation present enough natural obstacles on its own so you won't have to fabricate some?

4. Locale

Considering both their careers, is this locale a likely spot for the lovers?
Have you done research on the locale so you can describe it effectively and accurately?
Can you transport readers to that locale by your description?
Is the locale an element essential to the plot? (This must be the *only* locale for your situation and meeting.)

5. First Love Scene

Are you convinced that the lovers are in love when they tumble into bed?
Is the love scene too sensible? (He must be *perfection* in bed!)
How long is this love scene? (Lots of foreplay, lots of afterplay.)
What are they doing to avoid (as they must, to continue book) a commitment?
Is he the only one for her?
How does she show that she loves him? What was the turning point in her feelings?
How does he know that she loves him? What was the turning point in his feelings?
Are you writing with all your senses? (Sight, smell, touch, etc.)

6. Separation

What drives the lovers apart?
How long do they stay apart?
Is what's driving the lovers apart realistic? Or is it a big assumption on the hero or heroine's part?
Will the readers believe that the hero or heroine seriously believes this assumption? (Mistaken identities or gross misunderstandings seldom work.)

7. Other Woman, Other Man

Have you created a convincing other woman? (The cold bitch is out. The other woman can be a family member, ex-girlfriend, ex-wife, but these roles should be downplayed.)

Have you created a convincing other man? (The other man can be confidant or hero's friend, her old boyfriend, her ex-husband.)

Have you established that neither of these people should be the ultimate reason for the lovers' separation?

8. Obstacles: Second Round

Have you decided on what other obstacles can possibly drive the lovers apart? (Check back with the original situation. Then drive them apart *again* . . . for a plausible reason.)

9. Second Love Scene

Can obstacles be momentarily dropped for his or her passion, which can lead to the second love scene? (Editors like two or three sensual scenes in a story.)

How much foreplay and afterplay?

Have they yet admitted their love to each other? (This is a good time to admit their love to each other. You're about halfway to the end, but neither is yet sure of actual commitment.)

10. More Obstacles Within Separation

Can they make a life together? (This is usually the heroine's doubt.)

Can she fit into his lifestyle? He into hers?

Will she have to give up her career for him? (Usually not.)

11. Resolution of Problems

Are you certain there are no dangling ends? (All obstacles should be resolved now.)

Have you brought the lovers together for a third love scene?

12. Awareness of Commitment

Are you convinced that the lovers really like each other and can make a go at a happy life together?
Do they end with a marriage commitment?

Testing Your Story

The most effective method of testing your novel for "rightness" (rhythm, meaning, clarity, plot movement, plausibility) is reading each word out loud. You might do this at the end of every chapter.

You will also find it helpful to read chapters to friends or family members. Not only will they give you feedback, you'll be self-conscious hearing your voice reading your work, and you will find little errors that you did not detect before.

I also suggest that you put your chapters away for a week or ten days, and then take them out for a second reading. At this point you should be objective, as if you're a reader, not the writer. This second look should give you additional insights. To double-check, again find a good audience, and listen for additional errors you didn't catch the first time.

The ear is always your best test, particularly when you're reading to someone else.

The more you "practice" your story aloud, the smoother it becomes. At this point you should not be changing your story drastically. (If that happens, you will find yourself with a ruined manuscript and plot.)

Try not to let your confidence waver at this stage, but press on. Plan and prepare properly and follow the basic rules of the romance genre. You are headed in the right direction.

Harrow, Ontario, Canada

March 2

Dear Ms. Falk,

I'm a friend of Rosie and I'm interested in writing a category romance with an ethnic heroine. (I'm a West Indian, married to a man of Spanish extraction.) Is there a publisher who would be

interested in heroines other than Anglo-Saxon? I see ethnic characters
in historical romances but rarely in the categories.

Sincerely,
Maria Hernandez

From the Desk of Kathryn Falk

March 1

Dear Maria,

I'm so glad you wrote to me. Yes, there will be a market for
ethnic romances, and perhaps you can get in on the ground floor.
Enclosed is some material and a list of publishers to contact.

Romance novels now account for about 40 percent of the paperback
sales at bookstores. And we know that ethnic readers buy them.
However, what's needed is a black Janet Dailey or a chicano
Rosemary Rogers or a Spanish Danielle Steel to come along and write
good stories and write prolifically to establish a name.

Let me know if I can be of any more help.

Best wishes,
Kathryn Falk

Writing Ethnic Romances

Booksellers continually report that there are growing numbers of
black readers of category romances. "But there hasn't been
much change in publishing circles," complains Classic Bookstore manager Charles Young. "The majority of my romance
customers are black, and yet they can't buy romances about their
own ethnic group. The same goes for my Spanish and Oriental
readers as well."

Some publishing pundits predict that "ethnics" will be a wave
of romance publishing's future. Others disagree, citing lack of
interest from white readers and a lower book-buying percentage
among ethnic readers.

Candlelight Ecstasy, then under the direction of Vivian Stephens,
a black woman, brought out a handful of ethnic romances in
1981 (black, Hispanic, and Cherokee), written by ethnic writers,
but according to the publisher, the sales were too weak to
continue publishing more. Ms. Stephens feels that they should
have been allowed to develop and eventually more popular recog-

ition and approval would have made them catch on. In her editorial position at Harlequin American Romances, Ms. Stephens published one of the line's first romances with black characters (*A Strong and Tender Thread*). "The author of our first black romance was white, and usually I never consider ethnics unless they are written by the person of the same ethnic background, but this writer was so outstanding that I made an exception."

Veronica Mixon, a black editor at Doubleday's Starlight Romances, a hardcover series that goes primarily to libraries, has published one Cherokee romance by Jean Hager, and has plans to publish several black romances in the future. She is looking at ethnic manuscripts, and prefers they be written by writers of the same ethnic background.

Teen romance may be still another "door opener" to romance fiction. Silhouette First Love introduced its initial black romance for the nine-to-fourteen crowd in 1982. Written by black author Tracy West, it opened the way for more black teen romances to appear.

What could happen to make publishers bring out more books for the waiting numbers of ethnic readers? A good ethnic writer. A black Janet Dailey or Danielle Steel, or a Chicano Rosemary Rogers, would probably be the answer. A strong and talented writer is needed to not only write sensational and compelling romances but to break through the publishers' color line.

An active editor for developing ethnic talent is Valerie Fluornoy, the third black romance editor in the genre, at Second Chance at Love. She is working with a group of black Hispanic, Oriental, and Jewish writers who have never written a romance before. If her 1983 and 1984 black romances for Second Chance at Love are successful, she will be given the go-ahead for a separate line.

Here are some of her tips for ethnic writers:

1. No slang that will stereotype the main characters.
2. A subsidiary character *may* use slang.
3. Political statements or social commentaries can be stated as long as they are handled with subtlety and are positively resolved at the end of the book.
4. Show how an ethnic person lives in two worlds; usually, their working world is with white people and their home and social life revolves around their own ethnic group.

5. At the moment, no interracial couples.
6. The ultimate goal is still the basic love story.
7. Length is approximately 60,000 words.

Published Ethnic Romances

Black

Entwined Destinies by Rosalind Welles (Elsie Washington)
Candlelight Romance, 1981

Lesson in Love by Tracy West (Chassie West)
Silhouette First Love, 1982

A Strong and Tender Thread by Jackie Weger
Harlequin American Romance, 1983

The Tender Meaning by Lia Sanders (Angela and Sandra Jackson)
Candlelight Ecstasy, 1982

American Indian

Portrait of Love by Jean Hager
Candlelight Romance, 1981

Yellow Flower Moon by Jean Hager
Doubleday Starlight Romance, 1981

Web of Desire by Jean Hager
Candlelight Ecstasy, 1981

Hispanic

Golden Fire, Silver Ice by Marisa de Zavala
Candlelight Ecstasy, 1981

From the Desk of Kathryn Falk

London
Grosvenor House

March 26

Dear Rosie,
    I asked Anne Gisonny, Candlelight Ecstasy editor (who writes our "Romantic Type" column), to forward you our mini-course on

ategory romance writing. This should be the icing on the cake. The
est is up to you.

Remember: Be precise _and_ have fun. Then you'll be on your way
o getting published.

> Still scouting castles for the conference,
> Kathryn

6

Category Romance Mini-Course

BY ANNE GISONNY

executive editor of Candlelight Ecstasy
(*Anne Gisonny writes a column for* Romantic Times *titled* "Romantic Type." *These articles are taken from that series.*)

Preparing for Your First Romance Novel

You love romantic novels; you must have read hundreds of them. But how many times have you tossed a book aside saying to yourself, "Why, even I could write a better book than that!" Surprisingly enough, this very thought launched the careers of such well-known authors as Jude Deveraux, Jayne Castle, Marion Chesney, and Rochelle Larkin. In fact, prior to the acceptance of a first novel, many romantic fiction writers had not had as much as an article or short story published. They describe themselves as women who read romances for years and were suddenly curious to see if they too could make the stories they imagined come alive for others.

If you think you're the romantic type, we dare you to come out from behind the covers. Change places for just a little while with your favorite authors. And don't be surprised if you discover that writing a romantic novel is ten times more fun than reading one.

When formulating your story ideas, it's imporant to choose a genre you're most familiar with—category, historical, longer-lenth contemporary. Then *stick to it*. No matter how well written a manuscript is, a pastiche plot that tries to cover *all* bases means an automatic rejection slip. Few authors, if any, work from inspiration alone. Taking an hour or two to think out those flashes of creativity will really pay off in the long run. A well-crafted novel requires careful planning.

Look over your favorite books, paying extra attention to the way each story unfolds, Remember this time you're not simply a reader, but one author observing another at work. If you try to briefly summarize a few plots, in most cases you'll see that the story line is relatively simple. Novels with a larger scope may intertwine a romance in a more complex structure of subplots and counterplots (whew!). But the standard romantic novel never really gets sidetracked. For, at the very heart of every romance, there's only one plot: the story of two people who fall in love.

Although there are several stock plot devices that you may already be familiar with, the most successful authors seem to put their energy into depicting an exciting, believable relationship between the hero and heroine. No matter how many times the reader has seen the basic plot structure before, the author can weave a story around it that is fresh, inventive, and captivating. Mulling over some story ideas? Maybe there has been some scintillating encounter in your past that would provide the perfect framework for your first romantic novel.

After you have laid a sturdy foundation, the next step is choosing the characters that live in your pages. And I don't use the word *live* loosely. Your characters must come alive for the readers; you must make your audience care enough about the lives of your characters to want to know what happens next. Of course, when it comes to category romantic novels, there is no such thing as a surprise ending. Every last page seems to close with the hero and heroine locked in a blissful embrace. But characters with personality, warmth, and charm will make your audience become emotionally in tune with the story. Your readers may know the ending, but they'll be compelled to find out *exactly* how it all comes out.

Again, you might want to turn to some favorite books and some characters that truly come alive for you. Scarlett O'Hara is probably the all-time empress of heroines and certainly an excellent model of character delineation. In addition to newly published titles, you might also look at novels like *Jane Eyre, Pride and Prejudice*, or *Far from the Madding Crowd*.

Since most publishers request that the story be told from the heroine's point of view (in the third person), her personality is revealed not only through her actions and conversation, but through her innermost thoughts, her memories, hopes, and desires. As the Dell Candlelight style sheet suggests, a category romance is "the celebration of the senses," and the reader sees, hears, tastes, and touches only through your heroine. Her consciousness is the filter of your entire novel, and by using her perspective to your full advantage, you can create a story that is powerful and affecting.

Though I may appear to be stressing the heroine as the figure of primary importance, that's hardly the case. The development of the hero is equally important, though, as I've already hinted, he serves a distinctly separate function. In the standard category romance the reader usually does not have direct access to the hero's thoughts and feelings. His personality must be skillfully revealed from his actions, expressions, and dialogue. He is always held at a certain distance from us. Yet that's not to imply that he should be some aloof, reticent figure who is occasionally invited on the scene to strike up a roaring argument with the heroine, or sweep her into the classic passionate embrace. If anything, the hero is the very star of the show—the book's most dashing and dynamic presence. Your readers should fall in love with the hero of your novel. A difficult goal to achieve? Not if you pick the right man for the job. Doubtless, we all have our favorite heros. (Maybe you're lucky enough to live with one.) But a bit of thoughtful research in this area should prove quite enjoyable.

The Romance Formula

Make them laugh, make them cry, make them wait.
CHARLES DICKENS

The quote cited above was Dickens's secret formula for success—a formula to which he attributed his tremendous popularity with an audience that cut across all segments of Victorian society. For the purposes of this book, I would like to interpret his words in this way: The power of a story is in the telling of it, in the ability of the author to engage a reader's emotions and to convincingly portray a full spectrum of the human experience.

Doesn't sound very easy, does it?

With romance fiction, particularly category or "formula" romance, the novelist faces an even greater challenge. A writer of formula romance must first contend with the limitations of plot, length, and characterization intrinsic to the genre. Unfortunately, the limitations sometimes win out and the resulting text is simply an exercise in convention—a book peopled with bloodless characters, mouthing dialogue that we have not only heard before, but have already committed to heart. The author has failed to interpret the formula and make a conventional plot one's own by telling it in one's own personal voice.

However, to see a novelist wrestle down the strictures of formula and *win* is a delightful and often startling sight—something like watching an acrobat attired in a straitjacket perform a very fluid, graceful handspring. A reader wants to stand up and cheer.

"There's nothing wrong with formula," the very popular Ecstasy author Anne Reisser points out, "as long as you allow the characters to behave in a way that is consistent with their individual personalities." When the internal or psychological design of a characterization is forced to conform to some external convention or set pattern of behavior, the illusion of reality an author has worked so hard to achieve begins to unravel and a story may lose credibility. Anne speaks of her method of using "decision points" in a novel, points where a character must make some choice. Take five different heroines, each placed at the same decision point in the same plot, and according to their separate and distinct personalities, they will all make different choices. And each of these characters would move the story line in a different direction.

In essence, formula or plot convention should mean the barest of outlines, a thin tracing that the author must fill in with broad brushstrokes of vibrant color. With the present boom in the popularity of romance fiction, publishing houses are flooded with submissions. The field has traditionally been accessible to new writers, and probably will remain so. However, a writer must be sure that a manuscript stands out and offers something more than a simple paraphrase of thousands of other novels. How many times have we read about "a man too rugged to ever be called handsome"? Or "luminous violet-blue eyes, a viselike grip, the perfection of her heart-shaped face," and so on and so on and so on . . . Such pat phrases may keep a work afloat for a time, but if the author offers nothing more, the reader's interest will certainly be overwhelmed by the burden of such tedium. Yes, the romance audience wants—is *addicted* to—all the sights and sounds and sensations that are the hardware of any good love affair. But they want to experience it as if they were reading it all for the first time. Here freshness, originality, and an energy that will push your imagination to reach for something are called into play.

Of course, the next question is how far can an author depart from the formula and yet produce a salable manuscript. One can only say that editorial standards differ from publisher to publisher. Very often the question of publishing a book that departs greatly from the "standard" depends upon the author's ability to create convincing, appealing characters who act in a believable way, even when placed in unbelievable circumstances. Another consideration is the quality of the story. A strong, moving love story that literally sweeps the reader away will usually win out every time, no matter what the editorial guidelines dictate. After all, editors want what the readers want.

The Romance Plot

The fox has many tricks, the hedgehog only one. But it's a good one.

HORACE

Who was it that said there are only seven basic plots in all of literature? Or is it five? Well, be that as it may, at the heart of every romantic novel there's only one: the story of two people who fall in love. Distilled to the bare essentials we find (1) the initial meeting and attraction, (2) some obstacle to the complete realization of their love, and finally (3) a resolution to the problem and a pledge of total commitment. As a rule, complications or subplots should be kept to a minimum, and the same general rule applies to populating your book with extra characters. Steer clear of plots that allow a mystery or adventure subplot to overpower the love story. Presenting scenes of the heroine's life prior to her meeting with the hero is nonessential, too.

Novels of a larger scope may focus on a single character and depict the various stages of her maturing process or "search for identity." But it's important to keep in mind that even though the heroine's maturing process may be *implied* in the narrative of a romantic novel, the novel is not the story of her personal growth. Any background information about her past should be presented indirectly, through memory and flashback, or through dialogue. Yes, she's a "young woman on her own who must make decisions for herself," but it's a good idea not to kill off her entire family in one paragraph—a string of tragic car accidents and cardiac arrests that would rival the finale of any opera. By all means be inventive. Maybe her parents are marine biologists, and because they've always had to travel she has had her lessons in independence.

Whether the novel is set in St. Tropez or a ranch in west Texas, the author's unflinching focus must be on the unfolding relationship of the hero and heroine. One could almost say that the story line is merely a subplot of this type of novel, since its primary function is to support and illuminate the central action—the romance. The developing love affair is the very framework of your novel, and any story line must be carefully and completely interwoven with the various stages of this relationship.

But how shall these two people meet and come to know each other? What event or situation will intertwine their lives and make a chemical reaction between them unavoidable? In answering that question, you should hit upon the single, directing idea of your novel. This guiding idea will supply both a backdrop for romance and a special kind of energy that will move events along. A successful plot must be composed of a carefully planned series of events—events that flow logically and organically from each other and always contribute in some way to the romance.

The lack of a directing idea can be identified as a common failing in many manuscripts. The book as a whole seems a collection of chance meetings, a sequence of illogical or petty misunderstandings, arguments, and embraces. As one editor remarked, "If they bumped fenders on page one and in every scene after that she's falling over her own feet (only to be resolved by Mr. Right), the book is *still* missing a plot." Though characterization and certain dramatic scenes may be well written, when the hero and heroine finally decide to marry we're not at all sure how this all came about. The haphazard series of events has been unconvincing, and unless the novel possesses some other saving grace, we probably don't care much about the outcome.

Lack of focus can plague a novel in many ways. The first and worst offense, which I've just pointed out above, is the lack of any controlling idea. The remedy is obvious—*total* revision. But many times a novel seems to follow along convincingly enough until the author presents the relationship's major obstacle, or the reason why these two love-struck individuals must wait until Chapter 12 to declare themselves.

Let's look at one classic scene as an example. The heroine overhears the hero's conversation with another woman, probably some tall, dark temptress who wears a lot of nail polish. (We've seen *her* before.) Naturally, our heroine "misunderstands" the whole situation, and after reflecting on the fact that she's been used and abused by the hero, she makes a decision to have nothing more to do with him. Nine times out of ten she will make this crucial decision while "soaking in a steaming-hot bath."

Typical, but a weak hinge on which to fix the turning point of an entire novel, especially if the author has done a good job of creating a warm and realistic understanding between the hero and heroine. Too often this type of plot obstacle (overheard conversations, or a villainess lying about her relationship to the hero) seems contrived and unconvincing. Most editors seem to feel that the major conflict between the hero and heroine should not be dependent on a third party, or on some bizarre misunderstanding.

This all-important tension between the main characters should be generated from the very start of the book. If you're staking everything on the heroine's misapprehension of the hero, the reason behind her blindness to his true worth has to be convincing. For example, she has certain proof that he's trying to swindle her father, but finds that she has fallen in love with him in spite of her family loyalty.

One possible way to generate this kind of tension is to formulate a plot that gives one character the upper hand from the start and consequently allows him or her to manipulate events.

Whatever the source of tension between them, the seeds of this obstacle should be sown early. Plan your story line in a single paragraph that capsulizes the book's directing idea, an idea that in some way contains this dramatic tension. Then, in a chapter-by-chapter outline, work out each major event: the first meeting, romantic evening out, love scenes or some danger/rescue scene, and the event that brings the plot full circle. Above all the causal links between these events should be thought out to your satisfaction. The scheme of your novel should finally be a tightly integrated series of scenes set in motion by some directing idea—something like a line of dominoes, falling one into the next.

Is it necessary to present every single bit of information that links one event to the next? No, not at all. We're not asking for tedium, just logic. Incomplete knowledge is a fact of life, and in a novel motivation or certain bits of information may be intentionally withheld from the reader. In a romantic novel this effect is sometimes unavoidable, especially with respect to the hero, since so much of his motivation remains unknown to us. However, whether explicit or implicit, the logical links of cause and effect must be there.

When formulating a plot idea, one major consideration should be the proximity of the hero and heroine. Will the story line force them to live under one roof, or to meet daily in a side-by-side work setting? Great! You're halfway there. The best plots seem to throw the hero and heroine into a situation where almost *constant* interaction is unavoidable. A second important consideration is time span. Sure, this is love at first sight—whether they realize it or not. But if you're out to depict a convincing and realistic relationship, give your characters a little time to get to know each other. In the lucid and succinct words of the Dell Candlelight guideline, "Two days is *not* long enough."

The Romance Heroine

Imaginaion rules the world.
NAPOLEON

I've sometimes wondered what the outcome would be if a vote were taken to establish romance literature's top ten best-loved heroines. Frankly, I would have to split my vote two ways (between Hardy's Bathsheba Everdine and Hester Prynne of *The Scarlet Letter*). No, maybe three ways—how could I be heartless enough to forget Jane Eyre? or Elizabeth Bennet? And I haven't even gotten to anything written in the twentieth century.

In fact, I don't think I would be able to vote at all. I would have to abstain. How could I choose between such dear old friends?

The point here is, of course, when creating a character the author hopes that the presentation will be as lively, vivid and appealing as, well . . . a real person. Creating a strong, fully developed heroine is perhaps doubly important for the author of a romance novel. The heroine's personality and outlook are literally the foundation of the love story. Since most romance novels (and nearly all of category length) are told from the heroine's point of view, she is not only at the center of the action but is a filter for the reader, in terms of her impressions of other characters and events. She must possess a kind of flesh-and-blood presence. As readers, we seem to admire traits in fictitious personalities that we admire in real people: humor, intelligence, compassion, and insight into the feelings of others. We admire a woman who can keep herself together in a tight situation, or can hold her own in a relationship.

One fault of the novice romance novelist is the temptation to make the heroine an image of perfection, so perfect in fact that it is impossible for the average reader to identify with her. For example, the story opens, as far too many do, with our heroine getting ready for a workday. In all of three pages we learn that she is a cross between Farrah Fawcett and Catherine Deneuve in looks, has an IQ that would rival Einstein's, eats only the most nutritious of foods, and rises at five o'clock each morning for a three-mile run. Oh, yes, I nearly forgot, she also plays the piano and would have undoubtedly been a concert pianist of world renown by now (she's twenty-four) if she hadn't been forced to quit music school and support her younger sister after the "tragic death" of their parents. This is *not* a woman I could identify with. In fact, she sounds suspiciously like that certain someone we all knew and despised in high school—you know, the girl who got straight A's, never had a blemish or frizzled-out hair, and had a locker that was neater than an operating room.

When you are setting a scene that will introduce your audience to your heroine, draw upon your own experiences and feelings. Most people's mornings begin with gulping down coffee, putting a run in their last pair of panty hose, and burning the toast, which invariably sets off the smoke alarm and causes them to miss their train. Granted, most women are reading these books to escape from such mundane details of everyday life. But what if, among the coffee mugs and jam pot, our hero (a devastatingly handsome neighbor) comes charging through a smoke-filled kitchen ready to save her from a charred English muffin or worse? She of course is discovered in a semi-ravishing, absolutely charming state of dishabille.

Ah, now we're talking. That is where fantasy enters the realm of believability. Here's a woman anyone can sympathize with, and look what just happened—the most gorgeous man burst into her apartment by mistake while she was dressing for work. Sure beats listening to the traffic report on all-news radio.

A "Real" Heroine

Of course, there is more to humanizing a character than showing her at the mercy of everyday life. Before you can even begin to tell the story of how this woman meets the love of her life, you should feel as if you know her completely, as well as you know yourself. She should be conceptualized as a distinct personality, one with bad habits as well as good, favorite foods, and special fantasies. Her secret ambition has always been to travel in a hot-air balloon. You know that she has a terrible singing voice and is a disaster in the kitchen. You also know that she enjoys puttering around the house with minor repairs and is a whiz at plumbing. Since your story is told through her perspective, through her thoughts and sensations, the narrative is filtered through her personality, and for better or worse, her outlook and sensitivities will establish the tone of your book.

The best way to acquaint your heroine and your reader is through scenes of action and dialogue, not through lengthy pages of internal monologues. The presentation of the heroine's character should be simultaneous with the developing story line, which should be set in motion from page one. Your reader should not have to wade through a chapter or two reading about your heroine's past before the love story begins. After all, your aim is not to show her personal growth, though that may in fact be part of your story. Your object is to show how this woman falls in love.

Memory is another important dimension of your heroine's personality. She is the person she is because of influences in her past life. The *selective* use of memory can be highly effective in fleshing out a character and can serve to clarify motivation, to make her actions and reactions more convincing, more real. The danger is bogging your narrative down with her reminiscences and neglecting your story line. Since your story line is your first concern, you will want to be sure that any lengthy flashbacks serve an integral function in your plot, either to further the action or to explain a situation or motivation.

Naturally, as your story progresses your heroine will be pressed to expose a great deal of her inner self and should be shown demonstrating a wide range of emotions and responses. Don't rob your heroine of her full potential or dimension. Remember, she thinks and feels and acts on a variety of levels, just as you do. She may say one thing and be feeling and thinking another. When you make your reader aware of this disparity, it is as if your heroine has taken the reader into her confidence.

Above all, your heroine should be an attractive, warm, appealing person. The reader should be able to understand why the hero has fallen madly in love with her. Though this may sound like a terribly obvious point, it's amazing to see how many characters are presented as unattractive, because they are depressed, weak, and timid, or simply so bland—boring, actually. As the professional woman begins to emerge on the romance scene (bravo!) characterizations are in danger of another serious flaw. The new breed of female vice-presidents, lawyers, and brain surgeons are often portrayed as overly serious, solemn, and pompous individuals. This kind of dehumanized or one-dimensional characterization is just as unappealing as the classic female of romance fiction—mindless, naïve, and always in need of a rescuer. She has to sparkle, and her personality should be strong and fully developed.

The Romance Hero

What *do* women want? As an author of romantic fiction it is your duty—nay, your *quest*—to at least scratch the surface of this mystery of mysteries. Particularly in regard to the qualities women want most in a man. For in writing a romance, your aim is not merely to make your heroine fall in love with your hero—heck, that's the easy part—but to make your *reader* fall in love with him.

But what kind of man will have your reader sighing on page 15 and swooning on page 70? A recent survey published in *Mademoiselle* magazine attempted to shed some light on this utterly fascinating subject. The method? Thoroughly analytical.

The results? Remarkably inconclusive! Forty-four percent of the women polled replied that they were "turned on by a tall and muscular" build. However, rivalling that figure, an equally impressive 39 percent reported that they preferred a man of "average build." "Average?" I ask "average" according to whom? Does that mean a 38 regular suit?

And speaking of suits, 41 percent found the three-piece-pin-striped look a tonic to the libido, while an equal share, 41 percent again, said their tastes ran toward men in slim fitting, worn out denim. ". . . worn Lee jeans. Adidas sneakers and a Harris tweed," was one respondent's vision of ecstasy.

Well, what can I say? "In matters of taste there can be no argument . . ." Which brings me to my next point. Does anatomy—or for that matter, the lack of it—determine destiny for your hero? Though certainly a physical appeal is an important part of characterizing your hero, your description of him should not read like catalogue copy for this season's tall-dark-and-devastatingly-handsome model. The general accepted notion of "handsomeness" is, believe it or not, somewhat beside the point. Plenty of men can strike your heroine as "hand-some"—even poor Ralph or Charles, the junior accountant she gently discards in Chapter Four, is usually "handsome." We're talking about something beyond handsome here—your perspective is that of a woman in love and the man she loves is not just another pretty face. He's a man illuminated by some mystical aura. To watch him eat a ham and cheese sandwich for heaven's sake is a beautiful, nearly spiritual experience for her:

> The breeze lifted a strand of Jord's pale gold hair. Her irritation with his remark melted away and she let the marvelous sensation she couldn't identify melt over her. What was it? . . . Was it contentment? It was more than contentment, really. It was a deep sense of belonging, of being one with everything around her, the blue sky, the panorama of the fields and cattle . . . It was Jord, casually resting his elbows on the table now that he was finished with his sandwich that made her feel complete. It was the strength of those muscled arms exposed by the rolled sleeves of his shirt, the sight of his hair blowing attractively around his head, the hard line of his jaw and throat that somehow gave her life meaning.

Dear God, that was impossible. Jord didn't belong here. And he didn't belong to her.

Surrender to the Night,
Shirley Hart, Candlelight Ecstasy

Right from the start his physiological description has to be filtered through her thoughts, and sensations, told in terms of what his looks do to this particular woman. Your reader not only wants to visualize an attractive man, she wants to experience, along with the heroine, the sensation of being attracted to and falling in love with a man who is appealing in a very unique and finally, unexplainable way. And it's this kind of specificity, the very mysterious chemical reaction which goes on between two people, which you are hoping to depict.

Beyond brawny biceps and piercing blue eyes, your aim should be to portray a man whose personality would not fail to make even the chilliest soul catch fire. "I really shoot for the fantasy man," says Elaine Raco Chase, in trying to describe how she creates her male characters. "The sensitive, helpful, passionate man women always dream about. One who doesn't mind washing dishes or folding laundry. A man who'll jump into a bubble bath—who's secure in his masculinity."

"Of course," Elaine hastens to add, "he's also a man who can only be pushed so far. Yes, he's self-assured, confident and strong in a myriad of ways, but violent behavior in the opinion of most writers and editors is not part of the personality make-up in this fantasy ideal."

Elaine's pronouncement that "The strong, silent type gives me indigestion" seems to be the general consensus. With the changing image of women in romantic fiction—active, assertive, mature and independent—the image of their ideal match has necessarily undergone some major alterations. The brooding Byronic hero has seen his day and a man's appeal is no longer contingent upon his austere demeanor, his unattainability, his role as an authority figure. Rather, in a love story designed to strike the heartstrings of today's woman, a man should be vital, warm, verbal about his feelings and sensitive about the feelings of the woman he loves. He should be able to admit when he's wrong and to admit that his feelings for the heroine often leave him vulnerable and just as open to being hurt as she has traditionally been portrayed. In one of the most touching love scenes I've read recently a very strong male character readily admits to the woman he loves that he's really putty in her hands. (A major breakthrough in my opinion.)

Yes, I think that most avid fans of romance fiction still harbor that favorite scenario of Rhett Butler, sweeping Scarlett up in his arms and taking the stairway two steps at a time. Of course, my kind of heroine would *still* prefer to mount the stairs under her own power. Let Rhett conserve his energy for the main event. But far be it from me to rob American womanhood of this much cherished fantasy. Yet, if he must sweep her up the staircase on Monday night, what if she sweeps him off to a secluded cove on Tuesday night? Carrying him off on her tawny gold stallion, bareback naturally.

The dynamics of a relationship between a man and a woman are tricky, to say the least. In order to portray a believable, effective vision of two people in love it's important not to oversimplify, or assign stereotyped role behavior: *Always* assigning your male character the dominant position in a relationship, and *always* placing your heroine in a passive victimized role is fallacious and totally unrealistic—a picture which certainly slights both male and female. There is vulnerability and also, a certain measure of clout that each partner exercises over the other. Wouldn't life be dull without this kind of table turning?

Maryland Avenue
Royal Oak, Michigan

April 15

Dear Kathryn,

I got everything—now all you need send me is a graduate diploma in category romance.

I made some revisions in my manuscript and sent it off to Anne Gisonny. She's interested in it! Thrill, thrill.

By the way, I'm flying to New York for the Romantic Book Lovers' Conference, and Paul is coming along. He wants to be one of Love's Leading Husbands.

Regards—and oodles of thanks,
Rosie

From the Desk of Kathryn Falk

April 21

Dear Rosie,

We'll finally meet! I'll introduce you to Barbara Cartland and Janet Dailey, and about two hundred other authors you've been reading. Rest up before you arrive—the conference will be exhilarating!

And congratulations on getting your manuscript sold—Annie just told me!

Affectionately,
Kathryn

PART TWO

— 7 —

How to Write a Historical Romance

Historical Romance Novels Before 1950

To understand the development of historical romance novels, and to read some of the classic writers to improve your own skill in this genre, here is a brief survey of the best novels of their time:

Early nineteenth century—English	Jane Porter *Scottish Chiefs*—hard to read today but extremely popular
Late nineteenth century—English	Richard D. Blackmore *Lorna Doone*—still quite popular, set in 1670–80s *Maid of Sher*—not known in U.S. but quite good
Mid- and late nineteenth century—English	Charles Kingsley *Westward Ho!*—Elizabethan times *Hereward the Wake*—unusual telling of last Saxon to resist William the Conqueror
Late nineteenth and twentieth centuries—English	Arthur Conan Doyle *Micah Clarke*—Cavaliers versus Roundheads

Late nineteenth and twentieth centuries—English	*Fortune of Nigel* and *White Company*—fourteenth-century English versus French in Hundred Years' War (ACD thought more of these than of Holmes!)
Early–mid–late nineteenth century—French	Victor Hugo *Quatre Vingt Treize*—stunning portrayal of Paris and Western France in Reign of Terror *Hunchback of Notre Dame* *L'Homme Quit Rit (The Man Who Laughs)*
Early–mid–late nineteenth century—U.S.	James Fenimore Cooper *The Spy, Leather Stocking Tales (The Deerslayer, The Last of the Mohicans, The Pathfinder, The Pioneers,* and *The Prairie), The Pilot*
Early–mid–late nineteenth century—English	Edward Bulwer-Lytton *Last Days of Pompeii, Rienzi, Last of the Saxon Kings, Last of the Roman Tribunes, Warwick, Last of the Barons*
Late nineteenth century—English	Robert Louis Stevenson *Kidnapped, David Balfour, Black Arrow* (a mistake to think he wrote just boys' books; good picture of England)
Late nineteenth century—U.S.	Mark Twain *The Prince and the Pauper*
Late nineteenth century—U.S.	Lew Wallace *Ben-Hur*—plodding but moving portrayal in post-Augustus era *The Fair God*—Aztec Mexico and coming of Cortez *Prince of India*

Late nineteenth century—Polish	Henryk Sinkiewicz *Quo Vadis, Fire and Sound, Knights of the White Cross* (Poland, Lithuania, and German states in fifteenth century)
Late nineteenth and early twentieth centuries—U.S.	G. A. Henty *With Lee in Virginia*—U.S. Civil War *By Pike and Dike*—Dutch revolt in Spain *Young Carthaginian*—with Hannibal *With Clive in India*—late eighteenth century (He always wrote the same plot—poor boy rescues noble and/or wealthy girl, etc. But descriptions of wars, battles, sieges, etc., are outstanding and very accurate. His "layouts" of military campaigns were used as history texts.)
Very late nineteenth century—U.S.	Maurice Thompson *Alice of Old Vincennes*—American Revolution
Very late nineteenth century—U.S.	Helen Hunt Jackson *Ramona*—Indian and Mexican life in old California
Mid- and very late nineteenth century—English	Louise de la Ramee (called "Quida") *Under Two Flags*—North Africa in Mid-nineteenth century. Tremendous picture of life in legion with Arabs.
Late nineteenth century and early twentieth—English	Rider Haggard *Cleopatra, The Brethern, Red Eve, Eric Brigheyes, Margaret, Balshazzar, Morning*

Late nineteenth century and early twentieth—English	*Star, Montezuma's Daughter, Pearl Maiden* (He wrote many romances set in nineteenth-century Africa. Some are really just adventure, very good and exciting. Some contain quite a portrayal of Dutch, English, and native life.)
Late nineteenth century and early twentieth—English	Stanley Weyman *Under the Red Robe, Gentleman of France, My Lady Rotha, The Long Night* (He wrote of the times of Henry of Navarre [Henry IV], Louis XIII, and Richelieu.)
Very late nineteenth and early twentieth centuries—U.S.	Mary Johnson *To Have and To Hold*—Jamestown in early 1600s
Late nineteenth and early twentieth centuries—U.S.	S. Weir Mitchell *Hugh Wynne, Free Quaker*
Early twentieth century—U.S.	James Oliver Curwood *The Black Hunter*
Early twentieth century—English	Jeffrey Farnol (He created the so-called Regency novel, of which Georgette Heyer and Barbara Cartland wrote so much. His novels are harder to read than theirs; he used so much of the language of 1780–1830 England.)
Mid-twentieth century—English	Georgette Heyer *Cotillion, Royal Escape, My Lord John* (Most works are Regency novels, though a few deal with certain historical events.)

Late nineteenth and twentieth centuries—English	Anthony Hope (Hawkins) *Prisoner of Zenda, Rupert of Hentzan, Simon Dale*—Time of Charles II
Late nineteenth and early twentieth centuries—U.S.	Winston Churchill *The Crisis, The Crossing, Richard Carvel* (This is the U.S. novelist, not the English statesman. Little read today.)
Early twentieth century—English	Baroness Orczy *Scarlett Pimpernel*
Early twentieth century—U.S.	George B. McCutchen *Truxton King, Graustark, Beverly of Graustark, Prince of Graustark*
Late nineteenth and early twentieth centuries—U.S.	Charles Major *When Knighthood was in Flower* (Early part of Henry VIII's reign) *Dorothy Vernon of Hadden Hall* (During Elizabethan reign)
Late nineteenth and early twentieth centuries—U.S.	P. C. Wren *Beau Geste, Beau Ideal, Beau Sabreur* (Foreign Legion tales)
Late nineteenth and early twentieth centuries—U.S.	Sigrid Undset *Kristin Lavransdatter* (Writes in various periods of Swedish history, with outstanding portrayals of people and their lives)
Early twentieth century—U.S.	Frederic Isham *Under the Rose*—1540s Francis I versus Charles V of Spain *The Strollers*—theatrical troupe and life in New York and New Orleans

Early twentieth century—English	Rafael Sabatini *Scaramouche, Captain Blood, Sea Hawk*
Mid-twentieth century—English	C. S. Forester Captain Horatio Hornblower series

Historical Romances 1940–71

[*Of his method of composition:*] *I simply seem to remember, to recall completely as if it had actually happened, what I write about. When I can't "recall" it, I can't write. It is a kind of imaginative reporting. I work slowly, a few paragraphs a day.*

HERVEY ALLEN
AUTHOR OF *Anthony Adverse* (1933;
3 MILLION COPIES WERE SOLD)

Anthony Adverse (1933), a picaresque novel by Hervey Allen, was the best-selling and most-discussed novel of its generation in the historical romance field, until *Gone With the Wind* appeared as its rival in length and popularity.

It was tiny Margaret Mitchell, who wrote just one book—*Gone With the Wind*—who set the hearts of readers aflame for more historical novels. The quiet was over; a new group of writers arose in the 1940s to fill the demand.

Many authors emerged during this period. (Some wrote until the 1950s and '60s; Frank Yerby, for one, is still writing his adventurous romps.) Readers of that 1940 era still recall the excitement when Kathleen Winsor created her historical *Forever Amber*, which offered fresh titillation. It went on to sell an amazing 2 million copies, and more than 20 million people saw the film.

Many movies of the '40s and '50s were based on historical romances. Yerby's *Foxes of Harrow* became a big hit; Anya Seton's *Dragonwyck* curled viewers' toes; du Maurier's near classic, *Rebecca*, was made into a major movie starring Joan Fontaine. And Edna Ferber's *Show Boat* became a Broadway musical.

The best-selling books of 1953 included *The Robe* (Lloyd C. Douglas), *The Silver Chalice* (Thomas B. Costain), *Desiree* (Annemarie Selinko), and *Lord Vanity* (Samuel Shellabarger).

This was also the first year that movie editions of popular books began to make a serious dent in the market.

The 1960s saw the perennial best-seller authors continuing to write books (Yerby, Seton)—and new names arose, such as Sergeanne Golon (*Angelique*), Jan Westcott, Gwen Bristow, Mary Stewart, and Victoria Holt.

But brewing passions in new writers, unbeknownst to the publishers and public, were coming to a boiling-over point. Passion on paper was about to explode over one little literary topic that no one had bothered to exploit: the opening of the bedroom door on sex scenes. So far, sex had been taboo in historical romance novels. Sex belonged to the "pulps," called "naughties," which were soft-core pornography, so "they" said.

Everything changed in the early 1970s. The turning point occurred in the office of Avon Books. The editor responsible for starting the "bodice rippers," also called "erotic historicals," took home from the office one of the many unsolicited manuscripts (known as the "slush pile") submitted to all publishing companies. It was huge, about 600 pages long, the biggest in the pile; titled *The Flame and the Flower* (1972), it was written by unknown Kathleen Woodiwiss. This novel seethed with passion unfurled, and hot and languishing sensuality flowed like cream between the hero and the heroine.

Avon Books decided to go all out on the novel, and the female readers of the country bought it. This book didn't just "have legs," it had "wings," and by word of mouth it flew out of the stores, and still sells over a decade later. Kathleen Woodiwiss became an instant millionairess. However, Woodiwiss's theme of one man and one woman's deep and continual sensual love was not to remain a lone example of new sexual freedom in historical romance fiction. As news of this unique best seller continued to reach the public's ear, a divorced California secretary who had been scribbling at her kitchen table for relaxation at the end of the day suddenly rose to challenge the "Woodiwiss priority."

Rosemary Rogers's teenager daughter had read *The Flame*. She suggested her mother send in her manuscript to Avon. The rest is history, for yet another type of the historical romance came on the scene. Not just an erotic historical romance between one man and one woman, *Sweet Savage Love* (1974) was that and more: It took readers to the other end of the emotional spectrum. Rogers's characters explored sexuality and partners with a voracious appetite. Readers were stunned by this new historical release and flocked to buy her book, too.

By 1974 the woman's market had two historical romance

varieties, and soon their imitators arrived to flood the market with bodice rippers. Other publishers matched Avon with names such as Jennifer Wilde, Jennifer Blake, and Patricia Matthews. The tame, old-fashioned historicals, with no graphic sex, along with once glorious gothics, fell by the wayside unsold.

Since those days, very few new historical authors have found a niche at the top. The stars of the '70s still dominate the field.

Why? Some critics of doom blame the glut of bad historicals that appeared later on, disappointing readers and turning them off. (Another contributing factor may be the price, usually $3.50 and up to $8.) Because of this, historical romance readers seem to stay with the tried and true, and don't always risk their money on an unknown author.

The new Tapestry Romance series has overcome some of the readers' prejudices and proves that the historical romance is a viable genre once again for new writers. The length is short (similar to the category romance length—85,000 words), the authors are quality, the price is low ($2.00), and the editor is Beverly Lewis. She's finding strong storytellers who understand the genre.

All editors still dream of a *Thorn Birds, Woman of Independent Means, Far Pavilions,* or *Tai-Pan* crossing their desk. A book like these would be a guaranteed best-seller, and that's what every paperback publisher is looking for. The problem is, where is the storyteller of the next blockbuster? The publishers are not looking for a run-of-the-mill historical; the readers won't buy that anymore. Money is becoming too precious.

Historical Romance Paperback Publishers and Senior Editors

Avon
  Page Cuddy
Ballantine
  Pamela Stricker
Bantam
  Linda Price
Berkley/Jove
  Nancy Coffey
Dell
  Judith Riven
Fawcett (Ballantine)
  Leona Nevler

NAL
  Hilary Ross
  Maureen Baron
Pocket
  Beverly Lewis
Warner
  Fredda Isaacson
Zebra
  Carin Cohen

Producers of Series
Book Creations
  Lyle Kenyon Engel

Recommendations for Beginning Writers

BY FREDDA ISAACSON

historical romance editor, Warner

As Warner does not have a category romance series such as Harlequin or Silhouette, we have never found the need for a "tip sheet." We do, however, publish at least one romantic historical each month, and usually in a lead position. In this megacategory, I do have some recommendations for the beginner.

Read as many books as you can in the genre, find the ones you like best, and try to outline the plots in your mind or on paper. For example, this is one major plot: Hero meets heroine. They are drawn together from the start. Circumstances or villain forbid their meeting again. Each goes off on his own to honor-testing adventures. Despite temptations, she is always faithful to him. Although he succumbs to sexual enticement, he keeps his love burning strong. When she is at the point of greatest risk, about to be married to someone else or in danger of losing her life, the hero dashes in and saves her. *Warning:* Do not have her involved sexually with too many men. This destroys the innocence and fidelity necessary in a heroine. If her virtue is sullied by anyone other than the hero, she should at least be married to the sullier.

The other very successful plot is based on the compilation of misunderstandings. Hero and heroine meet in the beginning of the novel. She feels he has insulted her or her family or has killed or wounded someone she holds dear. He, of course, has not done any of this to hurt her. It's all a misunderstanding. Every time that fate brings them together, another misunderstanding develops. Then at the end of the book, they are together in clear-cut circumstances. He saves her life or her honor, and all the misunderstandings are cleared up. *Warning:* Do not make the misunderstandings or quarrels so ugly that the reader hates the principals.

Reducing the novel to its bare bones this way may make it sound hackneyed, but a good writer can keep the reader enthralled and hoping right to the end. And before you can depart from the formula, you must have conquered it. You must be able to handle it so skillfully that the reader is unaware she is tuned in to the same game. In general guidance for either formula, here are a few tips:

1. Do your homework. Know your period thoroughly. Research well before you start, and look up anything you are uncertain of while you are writing. There's nothing like an anachronism to make the whole story sound silly. Be careful of slang that may make reference to present-day technology. For example: "My heart's beating like a triphammer" in a seventeenth-century novel; a triphammer is a power tool.

2. Avoid using the first-person narrative. A first novelist can run into nightmarish complications when a fact is necessary for the story and the narrator has no way of knowing it. Also, there is nothing so nauseating as having the heroine perpetually stopping before mirrors to describe her costume and herself. It makes her sound conceited. She's got to be confident and worthwhile, but not conceited.

3. Do not lapse into long descriptions to establish historical detail. Your readers want romance first and foremost, history only as atmosphere. I know you'd like to let everyone know how much you've dug up about the customs and the era, but restrain yourself. A little history goes a long way.

4. Build up to sex scenes romantically. The coming together of hero and heroine should not merely be

conjugation, it should be consummation—something yearned for by both the heroine and the reader. When you have a choice, use the delicate word—the euphemism —and for heaven's sake, after you're done writing, check back and make sure you haven't used the *same* words every time. The people involved may be the same; the act may essentially be the same; but not the words that describe it.

5. Forecast but don't tell too much. Even though you know what's going to happen at the end and the reader passionately desires the ending, keep some surprises and make the reward worth reading 600 pages.

Last but not least, after you've had some successes and your name has become familiar to the readers and you can begin to experiment a little with the formula, don't stray too far. A genre is a genre is a genre—and people buy books in a genre because they like it. And if no one buys your book, no one can enjoy it.

Improving Your Historical Romance Plot

BY KAY MEIERBACHTOL
former editor, Harlequin

We all know a good book when we read one. It has that certain something that makes it almost impossible to put down. Some personal favorites have been historical romances, and it's one of the pluses of my work as an editor to be able to help bring some of these books to life. Watching history unfold through characters who become as real to you as if you knew them personally is the essence of these books' universal appeal.

An editor receives a manuscript from a writer hopeful of publication contracts, fame and fortune. In the case of historicals, it's usually a mountainously thick pile of typescript that represents months, sometimes years, of work. What is it that makes me want to buy one manuscript and not another? What elements do I look for; what sways my opinion?

First, the period novel has to have the ring of authenticity. If disbelief must be suspended too many times because research has been thin and facts are obviously wrong, the reader's interest in the story will wane. Then one has to balance the seesaw of too much and not enough. Too many historical facts unconnected to the plot will slow the pace. Not enough detail and the background of the tapestry will be too thin to support the main characters.

Almost any period in history will provide a rich, colorful background. If you are writing a costume drama, historical events will play a secondary role and characters will live out their lives in a parallel line that only occasionally collides with the happenings of the times. If, on the other hand, you are writing a historical romance, the major characters may be historical personages or may be fictional, but in either case history will intrude meaningfully into their lives. Decide what type of story you want to tell, what best suits your style and capabilities, and write on!

The key to a successful sotry, however, lies not only in observing technical parameters, but in allowing yourself as the writer to become immersed in the lives of the characters. Conflicts, power struggles, dilemmas, moral and emotional growth, romance—these are the hooks a good writer uses to ensnare the reader in the web of narrative. The ability to make the reader care about what happens, to make the characters live and walk through the pages of history, is the essential magic. Without this glamour, or enchantment, the best-researched novel is unlikely to see print.

I have found that the novels that stick in my mind, the classics of the historical genre, are the ones in which I, as a reader, have identified with one of the protagonists. For instance, who, having once met Angelique (of the best-selling series Angelique),

n ever forget her? And what is most satisfying about this kind
identification is not just the vicarious living or escape, but the
perience of learning something new about life. People read
oks for many reasons, but one of the most important is to gain
new window on the world, to find new solutions to the
niversal problems life presents to us. Any manuscript that offers
fresh point of view embodied in charming, vibrant characters is
re to get the editorial stamp of approval.

Getting Organized

BY MIRIAM PACE

author of two historical romances

'ou're going to write a historical novel. You've done enough
esearch to fill several notebooks. You've started the first chapter
when you realize you need a particular piece of information. You
ook at all those notebooks filled with all the intriguing facts
ou've unearthed about your chosen historical period. But which
notebook contains the exact fact you need? What page is it on?

What good are all those notebooks if the notes themselves are
mpossible to retrieve? It's time to start getting organized!

I never use notebooks. I find it far simpler to use lined
ive-by-seven index cards (three-by-five are too small). I use
different colors for different projects so that I can easily spot
when cards are out of order. I have a card file and a filing

system. The filing system is the most important part of getti
organized. It takes little time, since I work directly on the ind
cards and file them when they are filled. And in it will be eve
little bit of information that might have a bearing on the stor
from the food eaten at breakfast to the historical events th
would have shaped the lives of the characters.

I usually have much more material than I would ever use, a
I never use anything that doesn't have a direct bearing on t
story, no matter how interesting the fact is. But as a writer,
would rather have and not need, than need and not have.

Bibliography

This is the most basic and important part of the filir
system. Listed is every book, magazine, and article pertaining
the historical period being researched. Included with each tit
and author is the library from which the material was obtaine
and the card catalogue number. If ever I need to check the boc
out again, I can go directly to it, bypassing the library catalogu
I also give each book a code number and mark any informatic
obtained from that book with the same code number, in case
have to go back to the source to verify it.

Chronology

Under this section is a listing of all the historical events ar
their dates that would affect the characters in the novel. In m
first book, *New Orleans,* several of the male characters fight i
the Civil War. Since each character was in a different regiment,
needed to know where those regiments fought during the war an
what battles they were in. Also under chronology, I keep a tim
line of the story. Since *New Orleans* and its sequel, *Del*
Desire, encompass a span of ten years, I kept ten cards (one fc
each year) and listed all the events that happened in New Orlear
during that time. I also keep a time line for each characte
showing what events happened to that character and the date
(such as birthday, marriage, children born, death). This is invalu
able in making certain I don't say a character is twenty-three i
one chapter and twenty-eight in the next.

Character

I can't start a story or novel without knowing who the majo
characters will be. This includes their names, vital statistics

ccupations, likes, dislikes, character traits, and any other bits of
formation that help me understand who each character is and
hy he would act in a particular manner. Each description is
ighly detailed, for major and minor characters.

Outline

By the time I reach this part I've already written the first few
hapters. This is where I stop writing and take a look at my story
o see where it's going and what's happening. I do an outline to
rganize my thoughts and to put down on paper where I think the
ovel is going, what is going to happen, and any twists and turns
n the plot that will help advance the story. The outline is usually
few short paragraphs on the plot line and on the major characters.
: is from this outline that I work out an expanded outline to send
o my publisher with the first few chapters. Writing an outline
oes not automatically lock me into it. I need to know exactly
vhat is going to happen, but I need to be open to the unexpected.
'requently my characters seem to know exactly what they are
oing. It's only a matter of time before they tell me. In *New
Orleans* and *Delta Desire*, the original character sketch for Fleur
le Champlain was quite different from the way she actually
urned out.

Plot Development

This is where I keep track of the twists and turns in the story
ine, all the problems the characters are facing, and any ideas
nd situation I might use later in the story. (For *New Orleans*, I
ead a graphic description of a cotton field on fire. I liked the
ound of it, but never did use the material.) When I start getting
o the end of a story, I go back to this file to make certain I'm
esolving all the problems faced by the characters. I dislike unfin-
shed business and try to make certain nothing is left unresolved.

Miscellaneous

This is the file that contains all the random notes that don't
seem to fit anywhere else. For *New Orleans*, this file kept a
lescription of a steamboat disaster, how plantations were run, and
:ven the population of the South broken down into slave owners
ind nonslave owners. I also included a description of what every-

day life was like for a family in New Orleans and for a famil
on a plantation. I even researched the types of medicinal herb
that were frequently used—information I later used in *Delta Desir*

As I am setting up the files, I'm also writing my first draft.
usually do three drafts, the first in longhand, the second on th
typewriter (triple-spaced), and the third as I type final copy. I
the first draft I do the conversations and set up conflicts. In th
second draft I add description. In the first draft I will simply sa
the action is taking place in a certain location. I describe th
location in the second draft. My third draft is a final polishing o
words and checking the flow of the story.

The way I write is what suits me. It doesn't necessarily follow
that it will work for other writers. But this method can b
adapted and expanded to fit individual needs and habits.

The historical novel offers a unique glimpse into history
There is no excuse for doing a poor job when there is a multitud
of material available to the writer.

Good luck and happy writing!

Researching History

BY ROBERTA GELLIS

author of seventeen historical romances

There are three main types of historical fiction, but all shadings
between these types also exist. The three most easily defined are:

1) the historical costume drama, in which historical events play no part at all or are barely mentioned and no real effort is made to depict cultural and emotional attitudes accurately; (2) the historical romance, in which historical events are a loose framework around fictional characters who live their own lives and have adventures that may or may not pertain to history; (3) the historical novel, in which the characters were real people, the plot and action of the book are fixed on the historical events, and the cultural and emotional attitudes and mores are shown with all the accuracy possible, considering the lapse of time and lack of information.

My own work falls between the second and third groups; Mary Renault's *Alexander* novels are probably as close to the third as you can get and still write a gripping novel rather than a bad textbook. In order to do research for historical fiction, you must first decide which type you wish to write. However, I must emphasize that whether you plan to write a costume drama or a serious historical novel, accuracy is essential. Readers who concentrate on historical fiction soon pick up a surprising fund of information. When such readers find a gross mistake, it jolts them and they have what is called "the suspension of disbelief": that is, they can no longer accept the fictional world in which you are trying to involve them. And this is as true for the costume drama as for the other types.

No major research is needed to avoid gross errors of this kind. Many desk dictionaries have the dates of birth and death of important individuals, and any encyclopedia would surely have such information. Some dictionaries, *Webster's Collegiate,* for example, also have a section on forms of address, as has the *Information Please Almanac,* so that an author dealing with the nobility or the clergy can use the proper title for such characters. For a costume drama the two sources mentioned—a good dictionary and a good encyclopedia—are probably sufficient, if they are consulted with intelligence.

Recently, however, there have been indications that costume dramas are not as popular as they have been in the past. Publishers seem to be growing more selective in the historical fiction they accept. Thus, it may be necessary for authors to delve a little more deeply into actual historical events and personalities. The research need not be onerous; in fact, it may be quite enjoyable.

Finding Reference Material

Now I ask those already experienced in research to be patient while I address those who are novices. Let me recommend that for a first attempt at a researched historical work you choose a limited period of time that contains one or two great climactic events—a great battle with far-reaching results is a convenient device. Such a choice simplifies the research, gives adequate scope for individual adventures for the heroine or the hero, and limits the amount of historical explanation needed. If the battle has a name (and most have), you are immediately provided with a specific word to look up in encyclopedias and the indexes of historical texts and biographies to pinpoint which books will be useful for your purposes.

It may seem more romantic to sweep from country to country around the world, but to provide "verisimilitude to an otherwise bald and unconvincing narrative" means maps, antique guidebooks, and complicated calculations on travel times by horse, cart, on foot, on land; and by sail or oar-driven vessels by sea. However, if sweep you must, there are books to help you, from atlases with maps and descriptions for every time period to books on daily life of people in weird and wonderful places at all eras of history.

Since reference books are expensive, research is best conducted through a library, where, as an additional advantage, the assistance of a librarian is available. There are even many books to help you use a library efficiently, such as Cook's *The New Library Key*, Morse's *Concise Guide to Library Research*, and Cordasco's and Gatner's *Research and Report Writing*. Such books list a wide variety of sources, classified by subject, that will help you find the books you need.

Even if the library in your area is small, it may be able to supply the books you want through an interloan system. If there is a college or university in your area, be sure to inquire whether nonstudents are permitted to use its resources. Very often this is possible, although sometimes a fee or deposit is required. However, even relatively small libraries are likely to have primary-level sources, and it is with these that you must begin, unless you are already knowledgeable in the period.

The place to start is with a relatively simple book on world history or a general history of the country in which you wish to set your novel. It is not necessary to read the whole book; you only need to cover a period of about fifty to a hundred years, which might be one or a few chapters. This is not really part of the research; the only purpose of this initial reading is to discover the names of the most important people of the period. It is with these people that true research begins.

A brief check can be made in any good encyclopedia, such as *The Encyclopaedia Britannica* (for biographical and historical articles, the eleventh edition is best), *The Encyclopedia Americana*, or *Collier's Encyclopedia*—but if your library has them, *The Dictionary of National Biography* (for British people) or *The Dictionary of American Biography* (for Americans) is better. Now you can choose one or two people who had the longest and most interesting lives (preferably a king or queen or a government official) and obtain scholarly biographies.

Study Biographies

Reading a biography provides a multitude of types of information. Not only will you get the history of the period, but you will find information on the manners and mores of the time, descriptions of clothing, of the places in which the people lived, the meals they ate, the methods by which they traveled. Often there will be quotations from letters or diaries, perhaps expense accounts. (Yes, people had expense accounts at all times in history; not the kind we have now, in the sense that some company was paying their bills, but lists to submit to get the bills paid; thus, they kept notes on what they spent for food, jewels, furniture, and clothing and how much they gave to charity.)

When I say that I read biographies as the first serious step in researching a novel, I do not mean to imply that I intend to write a novel about the person whose biography I read. Within the framework provided, "typical" people can be invented upon whose actions there are fewer restrictions, so that an author can be free without taking liberties.

At this point the hopeful novelist may feel that enough is known for the purposes of the type of book to be written, but there is another stage of depth to research on a historical novel, at least for my books. A scholarly biography has much more to offer than the accurate account of events. At the end of such a book will be a bibliography, which will list the source material on which the biography was built. Much of this source material will be beyond the reach or the patience of a novelist, but much will be of value, particularly references to published letters and diaries.

A final step necessary to provide realism in historical fiction is an accurate depiction of the customs of the times, the clothes people wore, the food they ate, and the level of technology in their society. By technology I do not mean television and computers, of course, but whether or not, for example, they had scissors or saddles or carriages rather than springless carts. There are myriad books on these subjects, but among the most useful and most direct are the Everyday Life series published by B. T. Batsford, Ltd., London, by a variety of authors. These books cover every period from prehistoric times to the nineteenth century and such varied cultures as those of ancient Egypt, Rome, Greece, Byzantium, the Aztecs, Vikings, and English. They discuss every aspect of life from food and clothing to common customs. Many more-detailed books are available, far too many to be listed here; a selection will be given in the bibliography.

Beyond such materials are more esoteric sources, such as contemporary chronicles, periodicals, and newspapers and collections of published and unpublished scholarly dissertations, legal, diplomatic, and testamentary documents. Most of these are more suited to scholarly biography than to even very serious historical novels, so I will go no further here.

The research is done, all the little bits and pieces are collected. You have notes and copies piled sky high and a head stuffed with the most fascinating details, both historical and social. Lovely, but now comes the hard part. All of this must be woven together so that you can build living characters that move and function in a "real" landscape of time and place; in other words, create a book that will hold a reader's attention and make that reader want to read everything you write.

First and foremost, do not try to give the reader everything you have learned. Some of the material will have to be mentioned directly. Readers like to be given a date, for example, so that they can orient to the time in which a novel is placed, and battles can be named. However, almost all your precious research must be concealed very cleverly. A great deal of mine goes into building the characters, both truly historical ones and fictional ones. Very rarely, you may need to summarize certain facts of history in order to move your characters from place to place or time to time, but historical summaries should be avoided

like the plague. There are far better ways to impart history to
your readers.

Let me offer an example. I want: (1) to describe a medieval
custom—in this case, the bathing of a guest by a hostess, which
will also inform the reader that medieval people, at least the
nobility, *did* bathe—describe the clothing worn by knights, and
give a picture of part of a medieval keep; (2) to relate certain
events that took place before the beginning of the book—the
taking of a castle and the signing of a peace treaty; (3) to
introduce the characters of King John, a cruel man but a competent ruler, and his queen, Isabella. This material, minus the
personal thoughts of the hero and heroine, covers about three
printed pages, from which I will excerpt only the pertinent
sections:

> The afternoon light flooded the antechamber with brightness,
> but the inner wall chamber was dim. Ian hesitated, and
> Alinor tugged at his hand, leading him safely around the
> large wooden tub that sat before the hearth. To the side was
> a low stool. Alinor pushed Ian toward it, grasping the tails
> of his hauberk as he passed her and lifting them so he
> would not sit on them. She unbelted his sword before he
> had even reached toward it, slipped off his surcoat, and laid
> it carefully on a chest at the side of the room. Ian gave up
> trying to be helpful and abandoned himself to Alinor's
> practiced ministrations, docilely doing as he was told and
> no more.
>
> In a single skillful motion, Alinor pulled the hauberk
> over his head, turned it this way and that to see whether it
> needed the attention of the castle armorer, and laid it on the
> chest with the sword. Then she came around in front of him
> and unlaced his tunic and shirt. These were stiff with sweat
> and dirt, and she threw them on the floor. Next, she knelt
> to unfasten his shoes and cross garters, drew them off,
> untied his chausses, and bid him stand. Again Ian hesitated.
> Alinor thought how tired he was and was about to assure
> him he would feel better after he had bathed, but he stood
> before she could speak. Still kneeling, she pulled the chausses
> down and slipped them off his feet. When she raised her
> eyes to tell him to step into the tub, she saw the reason for
> his hesitation.
>
> There could be no doubt now that Simon had been right.

Ian was a fine, young stallion, and he was displaying the fact with startling effect. Alinor's first impulse was to laugh and make a bawdy jest. A flickering glance at Ian's face checked her. He was certainly well aware of the condition he was in, but he did not think it was funny. . . .

"Get in."

Had Ian been in any condition to notice, Alinor's voice would have given her away. . . . [Her eyes] rested briefly on the strong column of his neck, dropped to his broad shoulders.

"Ian! Holy Mother Mary, what befell you?"

Right across his shoulder blades, a large section of skin looked as if patches had been torn away. . . . Ian twisted his head, saw where her eyes were fixed, and laughed.

"Oh, that. A barrel of burning pitch blew apart. I was like to be a torch. My men doused me with water, but when it came to taking off my clothes, some of me went with them." His voice was normal, light, laughing at a stupid mishap. "I was ill enough pleased at it because we had taken the keep the day before, and I had not a mark on me from all the fighting."

"But that was in August," Alinor exclaimed, also completely back to normal. "You idiot! Did you not have anyone look to you?"

"There were no physicians. The leeches treated me—for all the good they did. To whom should I have gone?" Ian snapped irritably. "To Queen Isabella?"

Alinor made a contemptuous noise. "At least she is not so bad as the first queen. Isabella might refuse to soil her hands on such a common slave as a mere baron, but Isobel of Gloucester would have rubbed poison into your hurts. Oh, never mind, I will attend to that later. A warm soaking will do the sores good. . . ."

[Ian] slid down . . . and tipped his head back. He could hear the maids laying out fresh clothing and gathering up his soiled garments. Alinor reached over him to scoop up a ladleful of water, poured it over his head, and began to soap his hair.

"Tell me something pleasant," she said.

"Well, we took Montauban," Ian responded a little doubtfully, but at a loss for anything to say that Alinor would consider pleasant. "And a truce between Philip and John is being arranged."

"What is pleasant about that?" Alinor asked disgustedly. "It means the king will return here. Oh, curse all the Angevins. Richard loved England too little, and John—" She gave Ian's hair a rough toweling so it would not drip in his face. "Sit up and lean forward."

"Yes, Alinor, but John *does* love England." Ian elevated his knees, crossed his arms on them, and rested his forehead on his arms.

"Most assuredly. Like a wolf loves little children. He could eat three a day."

"That is his nature. Like a wolf, he is dangerous only when running loose."

"And who will cage him?"

There was a long pause . . . and then he said, "I have much to say about that, but not here and now. To speak the truth, Alinor, I am tired and sore, and that is no condition for me to match words with you."

If you examine this brief section, which appears near the beginning of *Alinor*, you will see that I have not only accomplished the purposes stated but included many other small details of medieval life. The reader can see that there was no separate room for bathing and the type of tub used is described. The presence of the maids Ian hears indicates the lack of privacy in which these people lived. The fact that Alinor undressed Ian (or it might have been a maid for a less important visitor) and intended to treat his wounds not only demonstrates the frankness with which medieval people regarded the body but points out the type of service expected of a woman. The wounds I described served several purposes (aside from the plot purpose, which was to relieve the tension between Alinor and Ian temporarily). Mention of them permitted me to inform the reader—naturally, and without giving any separate description—of one of the devices used in war: that is, barrels of burning pitch were dropped on or thrown at enemies. In addition, I was able to mention the two types of doctors available in those times and to imply that neither was as adequate as a well-trained medieval housewife.

The point is that the bits and pieces of information that come from my research are inserted in very small doses—mentioned as part of the action or in conversation. As far as possible, the major events of history around which my plot revolves are treated in the same way; that is, if I want to discuss the events of a war, one of my characters usually takes part in it.

One final example may clarify my meaning: When the Magna Carta was being negotiated in 1215, King John was at Windsor and the rebel barons were at London, about thirty miles apart. There was no communication system, just word of mouth or courier. Thus, messengers had to be employed to carry the

---

Researcher's Bibliography

BY ROBERTA GELLIS

For those who would like to establish a very basic library of their own for historical research, I would suggest the following books as essential:

Reference Books: A Brief Guide, published by Enoch Pratt Free Library, 400 Cathedral St., Baltimore, Md. 21201

Webster's New International Dictionary, Unabridged, 2nd ed.

Webster's Biographical Dictionary (any edition).

The Encyclopaedia Britannica (or *Americana*). These may be obtained at little expense, since the older the better for historical novels; older encyclopedias give more space to biography and less to science. One often sees sets of encyclopedias at book fairs for $5–$25.

Muir's Historical Atlas: Ancient, Medieval, and Modern. This might be more expensive than desirable, and substitutes, such as *The Penguin Atlas of Ancient History* and *The Penguin Atlas of Medieval History,* might be obtained. Maps are very useful for keeping one's feet out of one's mouth.

Costume Through the Ages by James Laver. (There is a softcover version of this that is inexpensive.) There are many costume books. My own favorite is *European Costume* by Doreen Yarwood.

Everyday Life series of books published by B. T. Batsford. Various authors. Check the list of books available and choose country and period best suited to your own work.

drafts of the document back and forth between Windsor and London. No violence is done to history if my hero is named as one of those messengers, and the reader is thus given a firsthand, personal view of the document and the feelings of the people involved, without a cold, historical description by the author.

Casting the Part of Your Reader in Historical Romance Novels

BY JOAN DIAL

author of eleven historical and contemporary novels

Part of my apprenticeship as budding novelist was baby-sitting for my younger sister and her friends on long gloomy afternoons in my native northern England. My father was a radio buff and had hooked up an amateur intercom system, broadcasting over a microphone in the sitting room that played on the living-room "wireless." I used to deposit Sis and company in the living room and tell them stories over the radio to "keep them good."

At intervals I would break off, race into the hall, and peer through a crack in the door to see if my young charges were sitting listening, enraptured, or demolishing the antimacassars on the couch. I thereby learned the golden rule, which I still write by: Thou shalt not bore thy audience!

It was quickly evident that the way to bore listeners, or readers, was to "tell" them a story, rather than letting them experience it for themselves. The first thing a reader looks for is a character with whom to identify. Through whose eyes am I going to see this story? Who am I—what do I look like—what do I wear—what are my dominant character traits? Am I brave, resourceful, pretty or plain?

When writing contemporary romances, most aspiring writers have little difficulty keeping this in mind, but many a promising historical romance has faltered because the author was unable to accomplish her primary task—that of getting readers to identify with the characters.

Of course, this is more difficult in a historical novel. Characters from long ago speak and dress differently, have different customs, manners, mores. People of even ten or twenty years ago were different from today's people.

The first step is to remind yourself that while the above is true, it is also true that human emotions haven't changed since the beginning of time. Love, hate, fear, envy, jealousy, compassion—this is what your story is all about.

You must be concerned with *what you have in common with your reader,* the shared knowledge and experiences that enable her to be a participant in your novel, rather than merely a spectator. Don't worry unduly about making your historical characters sound "absolutely authentic." (Very few people know anything about how people really talked a couple of hundred years before humankind had the ability to record sound, for instance. Early books aren't much help either, since written and spoken speech have always been dissimilar.) Be more concerned with preserving your reader's sense of reality.

This is not to say we should have our historical characters speak in modern slang. Far from it. Nor should they emulate real-life dialogue. Real people wander from the point, repeat themselves endlessly, and commit all sorts of speech atrocities. If we wrote "realistic" dialogue, in either a contemporary or a historical romance, our readers would soon lose interest.

Keep in mind that you are creating a make-believe world and your partner in the creation is your reader—who will fill in all the details you must, of necessity, leave out. Your reader will have a certain expectation—a preconceived idea of what people of a certain time and place should look and sound like. It is more important to avoid breaking the bond between writer and reader than it is to reconstruct exactly the speech patterns of the period.

Aspiring writers often plead, "But that's what really happened," or "But that's what he really said." Maybe so, but that's not always what your reader *expects* to have happen, or expects to hear.

In discussing the World War II period with a would-be novelist (I had done reams of research and talked to participants for my *Roses in Winter* and the sequel, *Lilies in the Spring*), I gently pointed out that his European partisans sounded more American than European. He rejoined, "But they *did* use American slang—they'd been brought up on American movies of the thirties." Since he was old enough to have lived through the period, he was presumably right. However, the American idioms in the mouths of Resistance fighters jarred the reader, and *anything* that brings the reader up short, reminds her that she is reading a story rather than living it, has to go. Better to write short, rather precise English phrases—to indicate the characters are actually speaking in a foreign language.

But World War II is history within living memory. What of history centuries ago, or even biblical or prehistoric times? When in doubt, simple English devoid of slang is best. Beware of using words and phrases not yet invented, but remember that then, as now, people expressed rage or frustration, often with colorful and descriptive words and phrases that need no explanation for modern readers.

When the pirate captain exclaims in exasperation, "God's blood, woman, but you try my patience—" (*Dreamtide*, Katherine Kent), we have no way of knowing if this was something an actual pirate captain might have said (since they didn't leave instructions for us on re-creating their speech), but it sounds right to the modern reader—and that's what we're after. The test for all dialogue, be it modern or historical is: Can it be read aloud?

We do know, of course, that our ancestors were prone to use *thee* and *thou* and various other archaic words. The writer of historicals can certainly insert an occasional *thee* and *thou* to enhance the historical flavor of the story, but they should be used sparingly, like exotic spices, serving merely to remind the reader that the events are taking place in a different time. If caught up in an exciting plot, the reader won't notice that characters say both *thou* and *you*.

Strive to create in the reader's mind an atmosphere conducive to the growth of certain reactions. Every word of narrative, every line of dialogue, should play on the reader's emotions. She should constantly be hoping for wonderful things to happen to the characters she cares about, while worrying that perhaps they will not. You are eliciting responses from your reader—who in turn is helping you create the illusion of reality.

But is fiction an illusion? No more so, I believe, than a wonderful symphony, or an exquisite oil painting. If you can make your reader laugh and weep and cheer for your characters— even characters who purportedly lived centuries ago—then those characters are alive, because your reader is experiencing real emotions.

So keep your reader identifying with your characters, feeling what they feel, thinking what they think . . . especially in the love scenes, whether your gentlewoman is both thrilled and frightened by the unexpected ardor of her knight, or your Victorian heroine is reminding herself that "nice" women do not feel sensual yearnings, or some lost waif from the dawn of time is fleeing in terror from a barbarian chief. Your character's emotions, in the reader's mind, must exist in the here and now—even if the here and now is centuries ago.

Your readers do not want to hear the author's voice, telling about the characters. Readers become Scarlett O'Hara in *Gone With the Wind*—they were never Margaret Mitchell.

In a long complex romantic saga, such as *Roses in Winter* and *Lilies in the Spring,* it is necessary to switch viewpoints in order to paint the historical drama on a broader canvas. The rule for multiple viewpoints is simple: It is preferable not to switch viewpoint in midscene. Make the switch after a hiatus, or in a new chapter.

In the most spellbinding tales, the reader is always identifying with one character or another. The magic of the novel is that for a little while we can be someone else.

Channeling Feelings into History

BY JULIA FITZGERALD

author of twenty-six historical romances

The major rule for writing successful historical novels is: Step right inside your heroine's skin, feel her heart beating as yours, breathe the same air that she breathes. Her heritage must be your heritage while you are writing about her; likewise her beliefs, religious and temporal. It is no good having a heroine born into the Spanish royal family at the time of the Inquisition who has the beliefs of a modern woman and declares that she does not believe in witches (as did one eminent author). In her day, she would have been burned for heresy. If you want characters to be original, controversial thinkers in the late Middle Ages, for example, then by all means let them declare that they believe the earth is round, not flat, but again, do not forget that men were burned for saying this.

Piety was the apogee of female virtue until quite recently. This cannot be ignored when writing seriously about women in history, fictional or otherwise. Religion dominated their lives one way or another. More than one of my heroines is pious, but that does not preclude a passionate nature, as some might think. However, too much sexuality and insufficient humility breed lust. Heroines do not lust!

Your character's every ache, fear, doubt, longing, and yearning must be disclosed. Anything less is superficial, and means that you are not inside her skin, wearing her shoes, and thinking her thoughts.

Actors are aware of this necessity, for they frequently become the character that they are playing, both on and off the stage or screen. You must be like them while you are getting your story on paper.

It can take some time to learn how to channel all your feeling into writing, but it must be done, heart, soul, and spirit. This channeling is what makes a book a warm and living, unforgettable experience for the reader. So do sincerity and the absolute belief in your product.

Love stories are an enormous power for good. While so many are writing and reading them, their thoughts centered on the most important blessing in life, a terrific counterbalance to all things evil and destructive occurs. Be aware of this as you create your characters and story. I do not mean create a do-good heroine with a grand cause, but she—and you—must be aware of the immense and transforming power of love. Frequently the hero takes a little longer to convince, but that is all part of the story line tension.

Last, create the mood of the times you are writing about. Play the music of that era, and not only while you are actually writing. Read the poetry and prose of the period, for this will give you insight into the most sensitive and creative people of that time.

While writing *Firebird* (Troubadour, 1983), set in eighteenth-century Spain, I played Spanish guitar music constantly, read the Spanish poets from the late Middle Ages onward, and did my usual in-depth research. Playing the music of the country (and of the period) is programming yourself in the most pleasant way to switch on to the creativity that is required for one's writing.

There is a fine dividing line between wholesome, erotic love scenes and soft pornography. To my mind, the latter involves a subjugated and humiliated heroine who is powerless to resist the brutal advances of a far from powerless male aggressor. Perhaps in actual fact there was a place for such a subjugated and brutalized heroine, but not in historical love stories. Yes, there can be brutal and ruthless men who attempt to treat the heroine badly or to crush her spirit, but they must *always* fail, and it must never be a regular occurrence. She must resist in whatever way is open to her at the time, and this must be a genuine part of the plot and not slotted in for effect.

If your heroine is spirited and fiery, if she fights back, asserting her own personality and needs, then giving in is not soft pornography. But if she is at the mercy of every obnoxious male in the book, then it is pornography, and *that* is sickening.

Tenderness, depth of feeling, spirituality, passion, ardor, and joy all have their place in the wholesome love scene. Humor, too. Intimate detail can be employed if it is tastefully done. Clinical details and phrases are not a good idea. The hero must of course have terrific sexual powers and be indefatigable, the ideal man in fact! But it is the interaction between hero and heroine, the tender yet searing feeling that they share for each other, that makes their love story special.

The heroine always has a passion to equal that of her lover. Both will be, to coin a phrase, naked and unashamed. Heroines can even be prostitutes or courtesans, as in my *Scarlet Woman*, if they have integrity, their hearts are loving and sincere, and they truly love the hero. Also, they must have been driven to their immoral existence through no fault of their own. Further promiscuity by choice is not allowed. Fidelity to the hero is obligatory once he has entered the heroine's life, although the villain or villains may do their utmost to change this. Even if they succeed, the heroine's heart remains with the hero. The hero, being a male, may be stubborn or reluctant to realize that the heroine is the only woman for him, but that too is part of the story line tension.

Passion that transcends the centuries is an eternally fresh theme and one that I use in *Venus Rising* (Troubadour, 1982). Personally, I believe that such a thing is perfectly possible. Even the ancient Greeks believed in reincarnation, calling it metempsychosis.

There is no necessity to enter into the intricacies of birth control in times past, unless it is part of the story line. It is unrealistic to have a sexually active heroine who fails to become pregnant. That has always happened to women, and does so today. However, it is unreal to have heroines who always sail through pregnancy and childbirth. Ignorance was so great, even until this century, that there were often problems all along the way. No vitamin shots, no blood transfusions, severe lack of knowledge about hygiene, so that puerperal fever was considered normal—these are realistic facts in a historical, while a healthy pain- and trauma-free birth is not. Some of the lighter historicals never touch on disease, plague, lack of drainage, difficult childbirth, and so on, and indeed, some readers like an idealistic picture when they relax with a book. But to ignore all this is to ignore the consequences of passion in ages before our own, consequences that were always borne by the woman.

While your heroine would know of the risks and terrors, she is so spirited and fearless, so wildly in love with her hero, that she casts caution to the winds and loves recklessly and wholeheartedly. He will reciprocate, for passion will rule them, but it will be a loving passion that unites them closely. It is history's love stories that we remember: Heloise and Abelard, Antony and Cleopatra, Elizabeth and Leicester, legendary Guinevere and Lancelot. Some have a happy ending, some do not, but in the romantic genre, modern or historical, the happy ending is obligatory. Unhappiness, discontent, divorce are the sad endings for us ourselves to experience, as we must. In fiction we want a happy ending to remove us from all this.

Writing the Erotic Love Scene, or Sex Sells!

BY BERTRICE SMALL

author of six historical romances

Writing about the sexual act is not really simple. A lot more than just a description of the copulation is necessary. I break sex scenes down into four major types: Seduction, True Love, Sweet, Savage Passion, and Rape, arbitrary as this may seem.

Seduction

This category has two minor parts, the Seduction of the Virgin by the Hero and the Seduction of the Virgin by the Cad. Nonvirgins are seldom seduced. My theory is based upon the idea that "losing something" can be done only once. It really seems a shame that a woman cannot lose her virginity twice! (Usually the first time in real life isn't the stuff romance novels are all about.)

In *Skye O'Malley*, I had my heroine lose her memory, and among the things she couldn't remember was making love. What fun! It allowed her a second chance at being seduced by a man she loved (although the first time for Skye wasn't so bad either). One reason this book stayed on the best-seller list was that it described the ultimate fantasy.

Two of the gentlest first encounters I have ever done were in *The Kadin* and *Unconquered*. In *The Kadin*, Prince Selim, an imperial Ottoman prince, tenderly deflowered the somewhat frightened fourteen-year-old girl who had been given to him as his slave. Selim took the time to reassure the beautiful Cyra, and thus won her love forever. His nineteenth-century counterpart, Jared Dunham, was equally patient and caring of his seventeen-and-a-half-year-old bride. Heroes should be caring men.

The Seduction of the Virgin by the Cad is usually a very poignant thing. Everyone except the besotted heroine realizes that he is a bounder. Nonetheless, she is coerced one way or another, and only afterward does she know her seducer for the rotter he is. I personally don't use this type of seduction. It's unpleasant, and it sets the heroine up as not being particularly bright. There are also enough seductions of virgins by cads in real life to strike an unpleasant chord in the heart of many a reader, and we are, after all, here to entertain them, not to make them feel renewed guilt by association.

True Love

Ah, true love! This is where you can let out all the sexy stops, but don't be overconfident. It's not as easy as it sounds, for fictionalized true love should never run smooth—except in bed!

The first rule of thumb when exercising your sexual imagination is: *Don't be in a hurry!*

If you've got any hang-ups with regard to sex, try to keep them out of your books. Remember that passion is "in" these days. You are, after all, painting a glorious word picture of total sensuality, and you want your readers to feel as wonderfully ravished as your heroine and her lover as they drop off into an exhausted sleep after their delightful bout with Eros.

On a more amusing note, be sure that hands, feet, and everything else involved are where they should be. This calls for plotting the sex act very carefully, going over it several times. It's easy to get carried away by enthusiasm, and not move the parties involved from one spot to another. Did you really mean to have your heroine making love on her tea table, or did you intend to get her over, and onto, her bed?

With True Love, you can also concentrate very heavily on genuine feeling between the man and the woman, and that kind of love—even in bed—doesn't always involve simply fiery passion. People in love enjoy thinking about each other as they give each other pleasure with their bodies. People enjoy talking in bed, and the talk can be serious, tender, angry, even humorous. Interjecting such moments in the midst of passion makes your characters far more interesting and real than they would be in just an automatic sex act.

When dealing with any sexual situation, use research books on sex. Even an expert on sensuality doesn't know it all. (The *Kamasutra* is not complete, either.) I keep books in my research library that have lots of pictures that help me to check out positions, or whether something I think unusual is within the realm of the possible. I realize that my readers often think I spend as much time in lovemaking as my ladies, but if I did I couldn't meet my obligations to Ballantine Books!

There is a *lot* to lovemaking. There is kissing, which can be described in great detail. There is touching, an incredible stimulant, which can also be described in great and salacious detail. Become the heroine during these moments of creation. Conjure up the hero; imagine what it's like to have this marvelous man making love to you. Feel his strong arms, the strength and pressure of his muscled thighs against your quivering thighs. Feel yourself turning to jelly as his mouth takes yours. Are your breasts growing taut with desire, the nipples hardening as you feel his big, warm hand cupping you? If it can be good for you, it will be even better for your readers!

Sweet, Savage Passion

This is a category unto itself. It can involve the women of your book with either the hero or the scoundrel. In any event, the ladies are overcome by delightful, delicious lust for the gentlemen involved, and although their minds may say "no-no," their luscious, flawless bodies say "yes-yes!" Again, there are subcategories. Some heroines succumb because for a brief wild moment they simply can't resist.

For example, there is the beautiful Countess of Glenkirk, Cat Leslie, heroine of *Love Wild and Fair*. She mentally resists her king's hold on her and is nonetheless forced to serve his baser needs in bed. The same thing happens to the lovely Queen of Palmyra, Zenobia, the heroine of *Beloved*. Zenobia finds herself forced into a highly charged sexual situation with the Roman emperor, Aurelian.

Mental resistance is most important when a lady is involved with a gentleman she doesn't particularly fancy emotionally. It keeps her moral, and heroines can be moral without being prudes. Heroines forced into a sexual encounter usually are reduced to yielding by threats of harm to their loved ones.

Sweet, Savage Passion is also illustrated in *Unconquered* when the heroine, Miranda Dunham, is rescued from a brutal and terrifying captivity by a wonderfully romantic prince. Miranda allows the prince to make love to her on several occasions before being reunited with her beloved husband. Miranda has been badly abused, but her spirit is unconquered. She reaffirms her own self, her womanhood, in the arms of a sensational and thoughtful man.

Sweet, Savage Passion can also occur between a woman and the man she loves, but this kind of emotion usually comes about because the people involved have been estranged for one reason or another. They use their bodies as weapons against each other to forward their own aims. Sometimes this isn't a very admirable trait, but it certainly can move a plot along. Other times it begins as Sweet, Savage Passion only to end with a reconciliation of True Love.

The hero of a novel can also involve himself in a Sweet, Savage Passion with a villainess. It's usually done because the man is unhappy, having been rejected by the heroine, thinking he has lost the heroine, facing some trauma he is unable to cope with. Even the gentlemen, bless them, are marvelously vulnerable.

Bad girls aren't always low-class whores, either. Very often they are high-born whores, as witness the socially unredeemable Lady Gillian Abbott is *Unconquered*. Gillian not only uses her body to gain her own way, she spies for Napoleon against her native England for money! Horrors! Our hero, Jared Dunham, has a torrid experience of Sweet, Savage Passion with the wicked Gillian in a garden house during a rather tony ball. He does it, of course, for his country's honor. Jared, fortunately, has a very patriotic wife!

Rape

This is the last category in my sexual encounter group. It is not a form I like, because there is nothing romantic about rape. For the romance novel it is a plot device, and although I try to avoid it, I am not always successful. I therefore attempt to avoid cruelty and violence in such a scene.

In *Love Wild and Fair,* the heroine's faithful young maid is raped by three officers from a pirate ship when she and her mistress are abducted. The three men are very matter-of-fact about what they want from the girl, but they don't abuse her. Learning that she is a virgin, they take care in deflowering her. They are not cruel men, just simply desirous of having a woman. Afterward they offer her water to wash with, and even food. It's not an offensive scene; in fact, there is even a little matter-of-factness on her part as the spunky girl gives the three men hell for ruining her only garment.

In *Adora* the heroine is raped by the man who eventually becomes her third husband. Murad is, and has been, the great love of Adora's life. His rape of the woman is the harsh act of a desperate man afraid of losing the woman he cares for, and lose her he does for a time before they are reunited in their happily-ever-after.

Rape is a crime against women, and it should never be shown as fun. In *Love Wild and Fair,* the heroine is raped by her first husband and then, with her husband's permission, by the king. The Earl of Glenkirk had been portrayed as a hero up to this point, and many readers were shocked by his actions, as I intended they should be. The Earl misunderstands his wife's situation with the king, and thinking the worst, he doesn't stop to ask for an explanation but in his pain seeks to avenge himself. His wife leaves him, falls in love with another man, and is lost to him forever. Crime doesn't pay, even in the sensual world of historic romance.

In the end, writing the erotic love scene boils down to having a knack for it. It's like doing the samba. Either you can or you can't. Still, with a lot of hard work it is a skill that can be acquired if the author keeps at it. Again, I repeat, take your time. Work on a scene until it moves you, because if you can make yourself end up squirming in your typing chair, then you will certainly make the readers feel the same way, and even more so.

As you struggle with your creative effort, just think of those lovely royalty checks to cash, and remember the two famous and oft-quoted words attributed to this particular Love's Leading Lady. "Sex sells!" Done right, it sure does!

Ten Tips for Getting in the Mood for Writing Love Scenes
BY SHIRLEE BUSBEE
Historical Novelist

1. *Unplug the phone.*
2. *Open the wine.*
3. *Play classical music.*
4. *Take a bubble bath, dry with scented talc, and slip into your most provocative nightwear.*
5. *Make love to your mate.*
6. *Picture Tom Selleck.*
7. *Picture yourself with Tom Selleck.*
8. *Smell a rose over and over and over.*
9. *Apply all of the above to the writing formula of your choice.*
10. *If you're stuck, make love again.*

Building a Novel

BY PATRICIA MATTHEWS

When I first began to write, twenty-five years ago, there were two major things I had great difficulty with. One was dialogue. I could write fair exposition, set a good scene, get my characters to do their roles, but I could not make them talk. They didn't sound natural, and every time they opened their mouths all the color faded.

The other big problem was plotting. It had been my experience that beginning authors often stumble here, as they seldom understand what plotting is, and I was no exception. Learning to understand how to plot—and what plotting is all about—seemed to me like succeeding with est, or feeling the click when the mystery of working algebra suddenly became crystal clear.

I knew I could handle them—with considerable care and imagination. I realized that my requirements as a novelist were to construct a believable and interesting structure (plot), rather like a house, provide it with furniture, people, and true-to-life sounds (dialogue), and take it from there.

As a case in point, let's take a look at the novel I've just finished, my fourth for Bantam, and my fifteenth historical romance. Although I had never done a sequel, I decided in this case to let the plot grow out of my first historical, *Love's Avenging Heart*. The lead character had had a daughter named Michelle, who was a baby when the book ended. The child's coloring, etc., had already been described, as had the seeds of her personality. Now I could add on details that would logically follow. I knew something of her disposition; I knew she was going to be bright, ambitious, and strong. And it seemed fitting for her to have such a love of dancing that she would automatically shy away from the time-consuming prospect of having a serious relationship with a man. She is aware that women can end up with unfulfilled careers, with only husband, children, and housekeeping to console them, except for secondhand adventures and excitement gleaned from the husband's activities. To Michelle, then, love is a trap. This immediately establishes the conflict when she meets the hero.

In the first book, one of the main characters was Andre, the effeminate Frenchman who became Hannah's dancing master, mentor, and friend. Why not bring Andre back and have him instruct Michelle in the art of the dance, the ballet? She could then go to Paris to study. Since my early years, when I studied ballet, I have been fascinated by this subject, and I was eager for the fun of researching.

That takes care of the general story line for Michelle, but what of Hannah? Well, Hannah is still young—she had Michelle at seventeen—and still beautiful, but it would be difficult to work up much conflict or love interest there. After all, she has been married for about twenty years.

Well, let's say her husband, Michael, is recently dead, thrown by his beloved horse, Black Star. To add a little mystery, let's say that he died under somewhat mysterious circumstances; after all, he was an excellent horseman, and he and Black Star operated as one. So now we have a bit of conflict set up, but we need much more.

Okay, how about Malvern, the plantation that Hannah loved so well? What if she is about to lose Malvern? Of course, there must be a reason. Let's say that Michael, for some reason unknown to Hannah, borrowed money on Malvern shortly before his death. She finds this out when she receives a letter from an unknown man, Courtney Wayne, asking for payment on the loan. Now we have her in real difficulty.

Of course, there must be a love interest for Hannah as well as for Michelle. Let's make it Wayne for Hannah, so that there is an opportunity for her to hate or dislike him, giving a legitimate reason for conflict between them, despite a strong mutual attraction. Good. You can't let the hero and heroine get on too well too soon, or you have no suspense, no tension; and I hate the stories that contrive this by artificial means, making the lead players look like idiots, kept apart only by their stupidity.

Now we'll put in another male character for contrast, and to further plot complications. Let's make him an overseer, for Hannah will find that she cannot manage Malvern entirely alone, and she has already given permission for Michelle and Andre to go to Paris so Michelle can develop her art. The overseer has an eye for Hannah, and his other eye on the main chance; and although he is fascinating and handsome, he is not entirely trustworthy.

And we must have a villain for real conflict, in this case Jules Dade, an unscrupulous moneylender, who wants to own Malvern for the prestige and acceptance it will bring him, and who lends Hannah the money to pay off Courtney Wayne. Dade intends to see that Hannah is unable to pay off the loan, and then Malvern will be his.

Now back to Paris and Michelle and Andre. Andre of course is very happy to be returning to France. *Love's Avenging Heart* established the fact that he had fled from Paris some twenty years earlier, under a cloud that was never explained. So let's say that Andre left because he got into trouble for having the wrong lover. He is the only dancing teacher Michelle has had, and as she needs to be good enough to be accepted by a ballet company in France, let's say that in his youth in Paris he was a premier danseur, one of the best. Also let's say that he kept up his connections in France and has important friends who will help Michelle in her career.

Now for Michelle's love interest. On the ship, while sailing for Paris, she can meet someone. As I had just been in Scotland, it occurred to me to introduce a young Scottish laird, incognito for the moment, doing some traveling before settling down to manage his family estate. Michelle will be attracted to young Ian MacDonald, but he rushes her too fast and frightens her, and they part on bad terms.

Once in Paris, settled in with a friend of Andre's, Madame Dubois, Michelle will be exposed to all the glamour of the French social life of the eighteenth century. It is the reign of Louis XV, not too long before the Revolution, and the life of the aristocracy has grown a bit overblown and overripe. Lots of local color. Needs another love interest. Should it be a male dancer, or perhaps an older man, the ballet master, Arnaut Danpierre, fascinating, charismatic? Arnaut by all means. More conflict. He is her mother's age, and doesn't like to fool around with his dancers. Despite her intention not to fall in love, Michelle will become enamored of him.

Conflict in the dance troupe, too. Michelle is not exactly made welcome by the other dancers, who are interested in their own careers and are not anxious for competition. Michelle will finally make some friends and win her place in the troupe, but not without effort.

There is real conflict between Michelle and one of the other female dancers, Denise de Coussy, a determined and cold young woman who would do anything to get ahead. She and her friend Roland, a male dancer, consider themselves Michelle's enemies, for Michelle is Denise's only real competition.

Color again. Michelle will be called to perform at Fontaineblue, the king's country château, thus giving the opportunity to show court life and something of King Louis himself.

This can also be the place for the reentrance of Ian MacDonald, who in his position as a Scottish laird often attends the court of France. This time love will blossom. Ian will ask Michelle to go with him to his castle in Scotland, but at the last moment she will tell him no. The chance has come for her to dance in a starring role.

Well, the plot is coming along pretty well. Just needs a little more flesh on the bones. Hannah is in love with Courtney Wayne, and he with her, but Hannah has now received a letter that accuses Courtney of being Blackbeard's illegitimate son, and in addition suggests that he is the murderer of Hannah's husband. Well, you can imagine what this does to the romance. Also; there is Dade lurking in the background, and the lascivious overseer.

And in Paris? Well, Michelle, despite her feelings for Ian MacDonald, is ready to dance the lead role in Arnaut Danpierre's "Beauty and the Beast," and to take her place as the première danseuse, not knowing that Madame de Coussy and her daughter Denise are plotting against her, and that she is in very real danger.

Of course, this is not the end, and I won't tell you that, because it would spoil the story for you who will be reading the book; but perhaps it is enough so you can see what I mean by plot, and so that you have some idea of how I go about making the outlines for my books.

Sometimes I think it is a bit like doing a piece of sculpture. I start out with an idea, then a slender framework, and I add to this framework until it begins to come alive and grow.

At this point, each thing I add seems to create more and more ideas, until the story at last takes shape under my fingers. It is a fascinating process, and a pleasurable one. As far as I am concerned, there is no greater thrill than the thrill of creation.

Well, maybe there is—when my readers write to me and tell they have enjoyed my books, and thank me for the pleasure I have given them.

How to Write Like Rosemary Rogers

BY ROSEANNE KOHAKE

author of two historical romances

Rosemary Rogers is often described as the romance writer who first flung open the bedroom door. While it's true that her novels are packed with explicit love scenes from beginning to end, her undisputed innovation in the field is her ability to produce unforgettable characters who embody a titillating blend of violence and sensuality.

If you want to capture the electricity of a Rogers novel, then you must begin with impassioned, tempestuous characters. Your heroine ought to be a fiery but innocent temptress (at least in the first few chapters) who has deep roots in society and money. She must have sparkling eyes and a lush, curvaceous body that would drive any man to distraction.

Your hero will be a James Bond type, who slashes (sometimes literally) his way into the heroine's heart. He will be a terribly independent character born to wealth and status, who has turned his back on a life of ease to walk the dangerous tightrope of international intrigue. He thrives on challenge and danger, he constantly courts death, and he naturally employs violence as an effective tool in achieving his ends.

By nature he is a fighter, an excellent shot, and a cunning liar. Though he has many, many women, both before and after the heroine, she is the only one who manages to marry him, and the only one who has any real hold on his heart. The hero will be an extremely passionate lover, and his passion will be tinged with brute force.

The heroine will also tend to be wild and fierce in her lovemaking, with the instincts and wiles of a courtesan. Yet no matter how many men she takes to her bed, she will somehow maintain the aura of sensual innocence that drives the hero crazy. So crazy, in fact, that he will kidnap her, if necessary, and hold her against her will just to have her to himself. The only thing he will not do is admit that he is in love with her.

Minor characters must include several rich, desirable, and experienced women who take up all-out competition with your heroine for her man; a middle-aged, poker-faced old friend of the hero's who nudges him into assignments leading to the brink of death; and various other men who try their darndest to win the heroine's heart (some through upright and some through underhanded methods).

Your heroine's father will be a huffed-up, slightly-less-than-honest gentleman who doesn't get along particularly well with his daughter's true love. (Could be he's jealous.) The heroine's mother has long since passed on, and if her father remarries, it will be to a much younger woman with eyes for the hero.

Hero and heroine are not the type to talk out their problems, and the result is a definite lack of communication. Much of your dialogue will be eruptions of their mutual distrust and hurt, not unexpected in a love-hate relationship such as this. Most of their arguments will end in a cross between lovemaking and ravishment, with the problems temporarily laid to rest along with the hero and heroine. Nothing is ever actually resolved between them, and though your book will end with the lovers locked in a blissful embrace, you will always leave an opening for a sequel.

If you have chosen to write a historical, you must make your history come to life (even if it means doing a little surgery here and there). Your characters will always take precedent over history, however, and will always be center stage. All historic events must flow through them; they must be totally involved with whatever is going on. Both your hero and heroine will be admired and welcomed into the inner circles of royalty, and their actions will always have international ramifications.

If you choose to write a contemporary, your characters' influence will not be quite so broad. It will only extend into areas such as the movie industry, the Mafia, and the CIA.

Be prepared to sweep through at least two continents, no matter which time period you have chosen.

Now you're ready to begin. Just find the underscore button on your typewriter and let your imagination fly. Keep that plot moving! Let your heroine indulge in a full range of sexual fantasies while your hero poises himself precariously between life and death. Ah, now you have it—a sweeping, sweet/savage Rogers's romance of passion, suspense, and intrigue. (With a combination like that, how can you miss?)

Jottings from My "Castles in the Air" Notebook Journals

BY PATRICIA GALLAGHER

author of twelve historical romances

I don't write from outlines, but I do keep journals on work in progress. These notebooks are filled with every kind of information that I might possibly need in the writing of a particular novel, and some are very thick. Things are not listed in precise order, however. Ideas don't come to me catalogued on certain dates. Thus, my notes are jotted down when they occur, whether day or night, wherever I may be at the time—in the kitchen, bedroom, car, on the patio, even at someone else's home. I try to incorporate the gist of the idea as briefly as possible, and often use my own shorthand. I may just scribble a few words to remind me to write a certain love scene, describe a character, gown, event, etc.

Here are a few entries from the immense journals kept on *Castles in the Air*. They are not dated or in sequence. There was much, much more I could have included, but I tried to touch on the highlights, the entries I considered most important at the time, those most inspiring or significant in developing the plot and characters.

I took only a few lines or sentences from some of the crowded pages, which may have inspired an entire chapter or more. Notations from other entries are much longer and clearer.

NOTE: *Castles in the Air* is about a lady would-be journalist in late-nineteenth-century New York—her trials, tribulations, and triumphs—all inspired by a chance grain of idea that struck me as interesting when I read a magazine article.

Clip and save Barbara Walters's article relating her difficulties and frustrations in trying to get more serious assignments when she first came on the *Today* show. Possible idea for a new novel. Contemporary? No, should have a broad scope, say something significant to women . . . and men. Historical probably, offers wide tapestry. Romance, of course, but more than that.

Theme: If a brilliant female journalist has troubles like that today, what was it like for aspirants to the profession a century ago? Could be interesting, informative, entertaining plot. Combined with strong romantic angle, sympathetic characters, and historical aspects of the era. Begin research . . .

Women's Movement most active immediately after Civil War. Read biographies of Anthony, Stanton, Mott, Woodhull —all excellent journalists. Also Horace Greeley's Kate Field, *New York World's* Jenny June. Lincoln's favorite lady reporter, Grace Greenwood. Others in Washington, Philadelphia, Boston, New York.

Heroine must be more than beautiful, passionate, charming, feminine; must be intelligent, ambitious in admirable way, determined about career in journalism but not bullheaded.

Hero must be more than handsome, virile, masterful. Not a womanizer, but obviously unhappy in his personal life when he meets and is immediately attracted to heroine. Attraction mutual. Perhaps he's married, not getting along with wife.

Make list of possible names for these three principals.

Restless night, trying to decide on names. Finally! Devon Marshall for heroine. Keith Curtis, hero. His wife, Esther.

Plot firmly established. Creation of principal characters next. Describe them in detail. Physical appearance, mannerisms, mentalities, personalities.

Introduce Devon in first chapter, Keith in second.

Conflicts. Geographical, Virginia and New York. Personality, Rebel and Yankee. Economic, poverty and wealth. Moral and social, his marital status, her strict Southern rearing. Male-female conflict—her desire for career, to be self-sufficient and self-supporting, his disapproval of her goals, ambitions.

Story opens in postwar Richmond, one year after suicide of Devon's father. She's destitute, living as companion and maid to an elderly widow also impoverished by the war. Devon's only worldly possession, the ruined property where stood the razed newspaper building and home when Union Army enters the surrendered Confederate capital. Keith Curtis arrives in town in elegant private railroad car—Wall Street banker seeking real estate investments in the destroyed city.

Should make for an interesting, provocative meeting!

Three weeks later, five chapters completed. Revised several times. Seem okay now. Actually quite good. Got the narrative hook in early—first page! Anxious to continue, eager to know what'll happen next . . .

Five months later. Writing and researching at hectic pace. Muses kind to me. Inventing new characters, situations, episodes with comparative ease. Polishing as I go along. Esther Curtis is a bitch, but a fascinating bitch. She could get out of control, try to monopolize and dominate the story. Can't let that happen. Must reveal more of her shady past . . . make her the villainess . . .

Mesmerized by social, political, economic history of this period. Must make separate list of books used in research, with library call numbers, for future reference. New York and Washington history particularly interesting and helpful. Fabulous real people involved in spectacular historical events. Must incorporate and coordinate data and people into novel— especially the foremost feminists, female journalists, socialites, writers. Wall Street financiers and their mistresses— fantastic—especially flamboyant Jim Fiske and his gorgeous, extravagant Josie Mansfield. Politicians incredible, none more so than Boss Tweed. Notorious Madame Restell, friend of Tammany Hall and abortionist for the wealthy. Use her somehow.

Read more on Cornelius Vanderbilt, Greeley, James Gordon Bennett, Barnum, Henry Ward Beecher, Mrs. Grant, Kate Chase Sprague—all bonanzas for possible scenes. Use Vanderbilt's superstitions and sexual involvement with Victoria Woodhull and her sister, Tennie Claflin. Let Devon be invited by her new friend, Kate Field of the *Tribune*, to attend a séance on the Commodore's yacht to try to contact the spirit of Margaret Fuller, considered by also superstitious Greeley to be the finest feminist journalist of her day, and drowned in shipwreck off coast of Fire Island.

Devon and Keith's love for each other intense and paramount throughout book, but marred by many separations. Opportunities here for terrific love scenes in reunions! Many battling scenes between Keith and his beautiful, faithless wife. Grand balls and other entertainments, describe in detail. Ditto clothes, mansions, society in New York and Washington. Fashion leaders and their publications, especially Madame Demorest. Feminists working for their causes. Good scenes possible in all these . . .

One year later—where did the time go? Things are rolling along smoothly, gathering more and more momentum, whirling like a cyclone now—all sorts of angles, subplots, episodes to explore. More fascinating people and events to include.

Devon becomes pregnant on a yachting trip with Keith. In desperation, considers consulting Madame Restell. Keith, furious, promises to get divorce and marry her, no matter what. Buys beautiful hideaway on the Hudson River. She lives there with servants, works on a novel while waiting for baby's birth . . .

I'm writing 12–14 hours a day now, researching at night. Filling notebooks with important information. Becoming a recluse, leaving home only to shop and run to library. Answering phone only during certain times, so family can contact me.

Devon's child, a boy, is born. Keith desperate for a divorce, begs his wife, promising anything. Esther agrees, provided he takes her to Europe first, to visit Lourdes for a possible cure for her "paralysis." She experiences the "miracle" but changes her mind about granting the divorce. Fireworks on their return!

Brokenhearted, Devon takes steamboat trip to Manhattan, meets influential Tammany politician, Peter Sweeney, on boat. In conversation with him, Devon confides her journalistic ambitions. Many newspaper publishers beholden to Tammany Hall for favors. Sweeney gets an interview for her with one who can't possibly turn her down. Keith insists that she quit, Devon refuses. He's forced to grin and bear her new career. Devon covers important social and fashion events in New York. Finally gets her big break— the ultimate assignment for a female reporter of that day: covering social affairs in the White House of President and Mrs. Grant . . .

At Grant's inaugural ball Devon meets a tall, macho Texan; he and his father formerly wealthy ranchers, now ruined and operating a small newspaper . . .

New twist for plot. Rewrite several previous chapters to lead into this. Keith and Esther can attend the ball! Marvelous opportunities for scenes between Devon and Keith, when his jealousy is aroused . . . And between Keith and Esther when he demands a divorce at any cost . . .

Can't wait to research and write this part!

Patricia Gallagher has been honored far and wide for Castles in the Air. *It is considered a classic of the genre and is studied along with* Gone With the Wind *in university courses on popular literature.*

How I Create My Heroes and Heroines

BY CYNTHIA WRIGHT

author of five historical romances

It's a tremendous challenge to transform characters made of ink and paper into *people* capable of drawing laughter and tears from unknown readers. The creation of the hero and heroine in a romance can be fraught with unique problems. And as the number of romance novels multiplies daily, writers are challenged anew to breathe life and individuality into these two people, who have often been labeled cardboard stereotypes by critics.

Most romance authors are women, and many who are new to the genre worry about creating believable male characters.

We all know the hero. Margaret Mitchell's Rhett Butler, Barbara Cartland's standard "Wicked Marquis," and Kathleen Woodiwiss's Brandon Birmingham could be cousins. All three are lean, hard, deeply tanned, and tall, with broad shoulders that taper to narrow hips. They have black hair, features that are chiseled and handsomely arrogant, flashing white grins, and one eyebrow that arches ironically to remind the reader of the hero's dry wit and cynical view of life. They are over thirty, with dashing, independent lifestyles, and have striking mistresses who realize that these special men are not "the marrying kind." It's enough to glory in the expert touch of their sun-darkened fingers and . . . Well, we know what else. (The occasional mistress who *does* want marriage invariably becomes a villainess.) Usually the hero has been hardened by life during his twenties—via a war, world travel, or a love affair that taught him not to trust women.

It is natural for a romance author to want her hero to be even more irresistible to the reader than those in other books. Like proud parents, we want to create the perfect man. That's the trap. The challenge is to find a way, amid the flashing grins and arching brows and sardonic quips, to allow this man to become an individual that the reader hasn't met.

How?

First, think long and hard about his appearance until you can picture each detail in your own mind. A woman in Kentucky writes to me after she finishes each new book of mine, and she invariably begins, "I *loved* Alec [Lion, André, Damon]! What a HUNK!" I always laugh, but that term is important. In our quest for individuality for this man, we cannot tamper with his "hunk" attributes. Readers are used to nothing less than rakish perfection. I wrote my first book, *Caroline,* when I was just twenty-two, and the hero, Alexandre Beauvisage, was the ideal man from page 1. Another "cousin" to Brandon Birmingham and the Wicked Marquis! By *Touch the Sun,* I was catching on. This time the hero, Lion Hampshire, not only had burnished-gold hair, but also an interesting character flaw. *Spring Fires* features Nicholai Beauvisage, brother to Alec in *Caroline,* who has wonderful "sun-washed" chestnut hair and emerald eyes. He's at least as much of a hunk as any standard raven-haired hero! There are lots of other touches that can make these men physically unique: a creatively located scar, a certain attractive scent, a beard or mustache, a strange piece of jewelry or clothing, etc. (Such as the golden armband in Shirlee Busbee's *Gypsy Lady.*) Take a personal quirk and make it attractive—for example, a habit of rubbing the back of his neck when tense, or a fondness for some exotic food. In fact, I have an excellent new editor who encourages me to explore new ways for my men to express themselves through body language. She wants to find substitutes for many of those ironically arching eyebrows, twisting corners of mouths, and (substitute your favorite) jewel eyes—well worth considering in the interest of richer characters. Attention to details, even superficial ones, can make your book stand out from the masses.

Now that you are familiar with every physical inch of your hero, get inside his skin. Think back to Rhett Butler. He was the ultimate romantic hero—dark, strong, knowing, and ready with a witty-sardonic rejoinder, even when Atlanta was burning down around him. Yet Margaret Mitchell shaded Rhett so skillfully that the reader was fully aware of the emotions beneath his careless exterior. Scarlett was too self-absorbed to tune in, but *we* did! Rhett Butler remains one of a kind.

The rest of us strive. Fantasize conversations between your hero and heroine or other characters in your book. Imagine his reactions to various words and events. Hear his voice, laughter, and angry shouts until they are familiar. Then don't *tell* your readers that this man is fun-loving or brooding—demonstrate! Dialogue in romance is great fun to write, and if done well can be an effective tool to bring not only the reader but also the author in closer touch with the characters.

What about a character flaw for the hero? Usually this is an inability to love, caused by some event in his past, but personally, I think this approach is becoming a bore. It's difficult to develop a relationship if the man is too hardhearted to let down his guard. I know. I tried it in *Silver Storm,* and what bothers me about this approach is that the heroine is always having to back down and give in to the uncommunicative hero. Why not try something new? In *Touch the Sun,* Lion's problem was ambition. He set a goal of becoming a senator (1789) and, in order to cleanse a less-than-spotless reputation, decided to make an advantageous marriage. After the betrothal, he fell in love with Meagan, his fiancée's maid (actually a wealthy girl on the run), and his ambition and stubbornness—complicated by Meagan's pride—are the obstacles that must be overcome. Personally, I am fascinated by relationships and I love developing them over the course of my books. I fell in love with my husband thirteen years ago, when we were sixteen, and perhaps it is my appreciation for the constantly changing, textured relationship we have built that colors my books. In romance novels, the people and situations are obviously ideal, but they can still be human. That's what readers relate to.

Many of the hero's guidelines apply to the creation of a heroine, but frankly, I feel there is more leeway in her case. I have a theory (not particularly original) that readers like to vicariously fall in love with the man in romance novels and that they emphathize with the woman. Contrary to what Phil Donahue thinks, passiveness is definitely one trait no romantic heroine of today needs. In real life, some of us may have trouble telling macho, superior-acting men where to stuff it, but not our heroines—no matter what their time period! I hope that readers of my books have as much fun reading these scenes as I have writing them. It does seem that spirit and intelligence are required qualities for every romantic heroine, as cynicism and wit seem to be for the hero.

Physically, there is more room for each girl's individuality to shine through. Unlike a "hunk," she can be almost any height so long as it doesn't exceed his. Some heroines have lush curves, while others are small-breasted and slim-hipped (a body type preferred by Rosemary Rogers). Hair and eyes can be any color, and her complexion can range from creamy-white to lightly tanned. Search for a combination that makes the woman in your book as individual as possible, and again, pay attention to the details that add so much spice to a character.

Your heroine can also have any number of personality problems. In *Shanna*, Kathleen Woodiwiss confronted us with a heroine who was selfish and spoiled—and an incredible hero who loved her anyway. It was an excellent twist of the standard scenario. Shanna, of course, matured into a woman during the course of her relationship with Ruark Beauchamp. In my book *Spring Fires*, Lisette Hahn is a 1793 version of today's liberated woman. The women's movement has certainly changed me, and I wanted to attempt to translate what I've learned and feel into the context of a romantic novel. It was a tremendous challenge. After her father dies, Lisette becomes sole proprietor of a coffeehouse in Philadelphia; she is a supremely self-sufficient woman, devoted to her work. At twenty-one, she is the oldest and most physically beautiful of all my heroines—and the most difficult for any man to get close to. Nicholai, who has escaped the French Revolution, has problems of his own, yet the two are inexorably drawn together. One scene that I enjoyed writing took place after their first night of lovemaking. Nicholai confronts Lisette, who had left his bed before dawn, in the keeping room of the coffeehouse while she is busy working. He reassures her, saying that he respects her and she shouldn't feel guilty. Lisette replies that nothing could be further from the truth. Women have needs too, and she was using *him!* Of course, the reader knows that Lisette does care, which poses a threat to her safe, disciplined existence. It's a long, eventful road to the book's end, when Nicholai and Lisette find a way to share all aspects of their lives as equals.

Since *Spring Fires* will probably be my last book in the

1780–95 time period, I thought it would be interesting to create. subplots (at different points in the story) for the heroes and heroines in three of my previous books. They have been married for periods of four to twelve years, and I found it especially enjoyable to reveal them as human beings who hadn't necessarily lived happily ever after. The love endures, which enables each couple to work out the problems that arise. As a writer, I was delighted to discover that I still viewed each character as a human being. They are my old friends, and judging from my mail, readers feel the same way.

In 1980 Richard Gallen Books published *Crimson Intrigue*, set in Washington, D.C., during the War of 1812, which I wrote under the pen name ''Devon Lindsay.'' The heroine, Courtney Ashton, is different because she is the pursuer—and engaged to another man. Having tumbled headlong into love at her first glimpse of Damon Sheffield (we know *his* type!), Courtney throws caution to the wind—even though people whisper that Damon is a British spy.

It's a pleasure to be able to write about women who reflect various aspects of my own views on life. I love originality and often remind my nine-year-old daughter that life would be boring if all people looked and acted the same. This certainly applies to romance novels, too. The days of the demure, innocent heroine seem over, but perhaps we'll return to her after exhausting all the possibilities for women of spirit.

As difficult as it is to invent story lines, I feel that the challenge to create fresh, distinctive characters is an even harder task. In the end, each author can compete only with herself. Try to make the characters in one book come alive in a certain way, then try a new or better approach in your next. I am now at work on my sixth book, *Golden Magic*, set in France during the reign of François I, in 1526. I traveled through France for a month in 1980 and realized that I *had* to do a book around François. I am aiming for gaiety; no message except that universal one of the importance of love. After the stubborn independence of Lisette in *Spring Fires*, this is great fun. It's important to vary characters so that you don't become bored. Aimée de Fleurance, the heroine of *Golden Magic*, is headstrong, intelligent, and brimming with sensations she hasn't explored. The hero, Thomas St. Briac, is based on Tom Selleck's *Magnum* character—can't you see him in a doublet with slashed sleeves, tights, and a neatly trimmed beard? St. Briac is forever being drawn into Aimée's escapades against his will.

Tom Selleck brings me to another point I want to make. Don't be afraid to use real people as the basis for your characters. I first did this in *Touch the Sun*, when a certain blond man I had studied at length (professional research, of course!) became my inspiration for Lion Hampshire. This is a trick that can help if you are having trouble getting a handle on male charisma. Steal some from a live man that you've been attracted to. Analyze his qualities, the source of his magnetism. You can do this with secondary characters, too. Study people to discover whether they have qualities that you could affix to a character. James Stringfellow, the barman in *Spring Fires*, is a bartender I met at the Market Bar in New York's World Trade Center. I took his name, appearance, background, accent, and manner of speaking, and transported him back to Lisette's Coffee-House in 1793. I got the idea for Lisette herself from my best friend, who not only looks like Lisette but has had similar problems with opening up to men. Of course, Lisette quickly emerged as an individual, but real people can often produce the seeds of colorful fictional creations.

Finally, I want to remind every new writer to keep the faith with the "people" you create. Don't allow them to go against *any* of the shapes and aspects you have given them for the sake of a plot twist. A good author will discover a way to credibly wed characters and plot.

If all else fails, bring out your sense of humor. Every romance needs laughter!

Writing the Sensual Novel

BY TOM E. HUFF (A.K.A. JENNIFER WILDE)

author of four historical romances

Sensuous novels? Me? There must be some mistake. I got into the business of writing historical romances purely by accident—I had written a number of mysteries and contemporary novels when a former editor phoned my agent and asked if I'd like to try a historical. I agreed and *Love's Tender Fury* was born—and I've certainly never considered myself a "sensual" writer. However, readers and Kathryn Falk assure me that I *am*, so perhaps we'd better discuss sensuality and clarify things.

Sensuality has to do with the *senses*—taste, touch, sight, smell, etc.—and in all my books—mysteries, contemporaries, historicals, whatever—I have tried to make my readers *feel* what is going on. If the characters are dining, I want readers to taste the chateaubriand, see the bubbles dancing in the golden wine, smell the aroma, hear the music tinkling softly in the background. If they are walking by the river, I want readers to hear the water washing gently over the pebbles, hear the leaves rustling in the wind, smell the mud and moss, and see the strands of moonlight shimmering like silver threads on the water. This is all extremely sensual, and it has nothing to do with sex—well, almost nothing.

One of my very favorite writers is the great French novelist Colette. I have read her complete works many times, in the original and in translation, and she is unquestionably the most sensuous writer of all time. Colette has a marvelous, magical sense of immediacy—the reader is *there,* the reader feels every subtle nuance of emotion because Colette has so skillfully prepared the senses. We feel the texture of old velvet and rough wood, we smell the stale face powder and sweat, we see the faded wallpaper and shabby Aubusson carpet, we hear the rustle of bedsheets and the short gasps of breath. This is all very sexy, true, and Colette earned an undeserved reputation for writing racy, quite scandalous novels—to the contrary, the majority of her writing is autobiographical, much of it about her childhood and her incredible mother, Sido. No sex there—but exquisite sensuality in every line.

All right, enough about the senses. What about sex? When people tell me I write exceedingly sexy novels—invariably rated X by the Doubleday Book Club—I am amazed. There's really not that much sex there. You don't believe me? Go back and look. There is an aura of sex, yes, and a certain sexual tension tends to crackle quite a lot, but the act itself occurs far less frequently than it does in the books of most of my colleagues. The books *seem* sexier than they are, and there's a very good reason for that.

When the heroine is laid every few pages or so—as oft happens in a number of books in the genre—I, for one, find it a bit tedious. Quantity is interesting only to Dr. Kinsey. It's the quality that counts for most readers. Although I'm certainly no authority and am writing this only under duress, my belief is that a very few scenes that have been carefully set up are far more effective than a profusion of "sex scenes."

I will use an example from my most recent Jennifer Wilde novel, *Love Me, Marietta,* which I am told "simply exudes sex." There are precisely four sex scenes in the 600-page novel, although a great many more are implied, as Marietta is living with Derek Hawke at the beginning of the book and becomes the unwilling mistress of a notorious pirate in the next section. Most of the book concerns Marietta's "love affair" with dashing Jeremy Bond—and poor Jeremy only has her one time under the Texas stars.

When Marietta first meets Jeremy in New Orleans, most readers know immediately that they were destined for each other. When, in the moonlit gardens, with the fountain splashing softly and purple bougainvillea perfuming the air, Jeremy asks Marietta to love him, the reader expects, anticipates, hopes she will give in. She doesn't. If she had, there would have been no suspense —I'm talking about sexual suspense here. We know that Marietta would *like* to, and as the book progresses she is tempted on more than one occasion, but Marietta is engaged to Derek and faithful to him (in her fashion), and readers would find her unsympathetic if she casually hopped into the hay with the first handsome scoundrel who came along.

When, believing that Derek is dead and after Jeremy has rescued her from pirates, saved her from drowning, protected her from savage cannibal Indians and such, Marietta finally succumbs to his charms, the reader has been waiting and waiting and waiting—and the scene seems much more erotic than it is. There have been 400 pages of buildup, and if you read carefully you will note that most of the description has to do with the sky, the stars, the scent of hay, the soft rustle of pale blue silk as it slides to the ground.

If I have a theory at all, it is that atmosphere and anticipation are the most important ingredients of a "sensuous" novel. To be truly effective, a love scene must be carefully, painstakingly prepared, and then it must truly be experienced through all the senses. If not, you might just as well describe your heroine brushing her teeth.

The Tapestry of Historical Romance

BY MAURA SEGER

author of two historical romances

On top of all the challenges faced by the romance writer, those working in historical settings confront a special problem: how to give the reader the information she needs in order to visualize the setting without smothering her in extraneous detail.

In writing for the Tapestry series of historical romances, I've discovered some guidelines that may help.

How to Start

1. Know your period well. Be able to close your eyes and visualize what it was like to live in fifteenth-century Paris, seventeenth-century England, or whenever.
2. Resolve that only the smallest part of this information has a place in your story. You aren't writing about a period so much as a group of characters. Your reader doesn't want a history lesson; she wants a romance.

How to Build a Set

Any writer, whether working in contemporary or historical fiction, has to create a world the reader will believe in and care about. If you were writing a contemporary romance, you'd slip in natural details of life in this world through dialogue and action. Do the same in your historical.

For example:

FOOD

Don't write a menu; create a scene.

> Heedless of her nudity, Verony scampered from the bed. On a cloth-covered tray were joints of roasted meat, cheeses, breads, and a small bowl of custard dusted with precious cinnamon. An ewer of wine and another of water stood nearby beside two goblets.
>
> Gleefully, she turned to tell Curran of the bounty only to discover he had left the bed and was happily submerged in the mineral spring. Propped up against the natural rock formation that had been left in place when the bower was built, he grinned at her lewdly. "Bring my supper over here, wench. And be quick about it!"
>
> *[Rebellious Love]*

Here the details the reader needs are a natural part of the setting. The reader can absorb them without feeling she's momentarily lost the story.

CLOTHING

I like to put this in love scenes. Clothes are most fun to write about when they're being taken off. Consider the following:

> Slender, white hands were making quick work of the lacing of his surcoat before Curran recovered enough to speak. "That gown . . ." he muttered thickly, "I don't remember seeing it before."
>
> "It is new," Verony informed him simply, continuing the pleasant task of removing his tunic.
>
> Docile as a child, though his body already gave ample proof that he was anything but, he allowed himself to be stripped of his chausses. When nothing remained but his straining loincloth, Verony turned away from him. A devilish smile curved her lips as she scrupulously folded each article of clothing and put it neatly away.
>
> *[Rebellious Love]*

Now isn't that better than saying "noblemen of thirteenth-century England wore surcoats over tunics, with chausses covering their legs and boots on their feet, their undergarments consisting most often of a loincloth''?

Housing

By all means talk about building materials, architectural details, fabrics, and frequently overlooked details such as: was the housing comfortable or do your characters freeze in winter and fry in summer; how were specific household tasks, such as cooking, washing, and cleaning accomplished; was there safety, privacy, luxury? And so on.

In Tapestry's *Defiant Love* (set in pre-Conquest England), I faced the particular problem of describing a way of life about which very little has been written. Readers may be well acquainted with life in a Norman castle, but chances are they don't know much at all about what went on in an Anglo-Saxon hall. That problem was solved with such passages as:

> The arches fascinated Brenna. She could not quite understand what held the wedge-shaped stones in place. Each time she walked under one, she glanced up as though expecting it to collapse.
> Noticing her concern, Matilda laughed. "They're quite safe, you know. The architects insist they'll last forever. In fact, I've even heard that these arches may eventually make it possible to roof buildings in stone."
> That would certainly be a vast improvement, Brenna thought. Timbered roofs meant the constant danger of fire. Great keeps that were built entirely of timber, such as Earl Harold's at Winchester, customarily suffered major fires every few years. Edythe had lost count of the number of times portions of her home had to be rebuilt. That was why separate bowers set some distance from the main hall housed the family, chief retainers, and honored guests, as well as most household goods.
>
> [*Defiant Love*]

Social Details

There are times when you may have to explain the tricky subject of class distinctions, which often had so much influence on the events of an era. Try doing it within an action scene, such as:

Someone snorted doubtfully. Hard hands moved over the mare, seeking clues. Hearing frightened whinnies, Brenna dared to peer round the tree trunk. What she saw fulfilled her worst fears. Half a dozen men stood in a circle around the chestnut. In the bright moonlight she could clearly make out their dress. Tattered tunics matched oddly with well-cared-for weapons.

Landless thegns, Brenna thought in terror. Men who through some failure of honor had been disbarred from service to their sworn lord. Left to roam without position or purpose, most had no choice but to leave England in search of some place where they might serve again.

It was likely the group before her was planning to take ship from London or one of the ports further south. Along the way, these embittered, violent men wouldn't hesitate to take full advantage of anyone too weak to defend against them.

[*Defiant Love*]

POLITICAL INTRIGUE

You may be fascinated by the subtle plots and counterplots of your period, but they can confuse the reader and detract from the essential romance. To avoid this, try explaining the necessary details through dialogue:

"Are you saying you mean to rebel against the king?" Verony asked in a voice little more than a whisper.

Seeing her white face and strained manner, Curran longed to reassure his wife. But he could not lie. "We hope it will not come to that. If all the barons join with us, John will have no choice but to give in. But if it comes to armed conflict, we will not retreat."

"But your oaths of fealty . . ." Verony began, only to break off as Lady Emelie insisted: "The King's utter disregard for his own responsibilities has made these oaths void. How can honorable men be expected to follow a weakling knave who had brought only shame to the crown from the day he first claimed it?"

[*Rebellious Love*]

Keep in mind that human nature hasn't changed all that much from one historical period to another. Your readers will have no trouble following your story if you create believable characters, dialogue, conflicts, and resolutions.

Most importantly, never lose sight of the fact that the romance—which is timeless anyway—is every bit as important to the tale as the history. And happy writing!

How I Outlined Highland Velvet

BY JUDE DEVERAUX

author of seven historical romances

It's been my experience that when the word *outline* is mentioned to beginning authors, they usually exclaim, "But an outline will kill my creativity! If I know what happens next I won't have any *fun!*"

It took me three years and several novels—and parts of novels—before I could rid myself of that notion. I'd have a great idea for the beginning of a book and spend months researching everything in the time period, and finally I'd get to sit down and write. For the first 150 pages I'd write fast and furiously; then would come, what happens next? I'd almost always end up adding a new, and often superfluous character or having my hero and heroine travel to someplace, and that would mean returning to the research books for a few weeks.

Money was the incentive that made me start outlining. My editor wanted an outline of my next book so I wrote her one, a dreadful thing that sounded like a very bad Charlton Heston movie, and she turned it down. It was then I decided to teach myself how to write a good, usable outline, to prevent turndowns.

To illustrate my points, I'll tell you how I outlined my fifth historical romance, *Highland Velvet*. The idea behind the story was to show that medieval women could be used in settling disputes. I had the first pages in my head: Bronwyn, laird of a Scottish clan, is to wed her enemy, an Englishman; being sensible, she is willing to give him a chance to prove himself. But Stephen personally insults her by being late for their wedding. While Bronwyn waits, she comes to know Roger Chatworth and logically decides he's better for her clan. When Stephen comes, he has to fight Roger. The rest of the novel I planned to be a tug of war between Stephen and Bronwyn until in the end they learned to compromise.

This is all I started with, a basic idea, and from this one paragraph I had to create a novel.

Before I begin even my major outline, I like to know my characters. It isn't enough to write that the heroine is brave and courageous; you must show it. I had Bronwyn risk her life over the side of a cliff to save one of her clansmen, and to me this showed not only her courage but also her love of her clan. I try to come up with at least one scene per character to show what he or she is like.

Once I have an idea of my characters, I tackle the major outline, dividing it into small sections and creating illustrating scenes for each section. For example, I wanted to compare and contrast Roger Chatworth and Stephen, so I took both men through the same scene—a horse race and a picnic. Stephen's actions and reactions further deepened the conflict between him and Bronwyn.

Next I outlined the time in Scotland. I made Roman numeral headings and wrote the ideas I wanted to show: "I. Stephen refuses to even consider the Scots' ways. II. Stephen begins to consider the Scots' ways. III. Bronwyn will not believe Stephen can be trusted. IV. Something makes Bronwyn see that she can trust Stephen."

I spent days, and pages, writing ideas for scenes to show these basic story concepts. I created Stephen's friend Chris, who had to be killed to make Stephen realize that perhaps his English ways were wrong. I felt that Bronwyn would have to be taken away from her protective clansmen if she was ever to learn to rely on Stephen, and so I created Kirsty and Donald. I went through the entire novel like this, making major headings and listing scenes under each concept.

When this part is complete, I put the outline into a notebook, don't look at it, and write the whole story from memory. This usually types out to about fifty or sixty pages, and from this I do my research, knowing exactly where my characters go and what will be included in the novel.

The first time I started to write from an outline I was afraid I'd be bored, but I found that when I didn't have to worry about what happened next I could concentrate on my first love: dialogue. And, too, many surprising things happened. I had planned to show Bronwyn's courage by lowering her down a cliffside, but Stephen surprised me by being at the top when she was pulled up.

My objective with an outline is to make every scene have a purpose and not just to write a book that has a heroine tossed from one bed or sea captain to another. My second book, which I never wrote, was to have started in New Mexico, gone to an Army fort in Arizona, to the docks in San Francisco, to a harem in Tangiers, to Paris, to London, and ended in Gilded Age New York. I wrote about 150 pages of the book, then stopped because everything seemed to be happening *to* the hero and heroine and mostly they seemed to be getting in and out of coaches.

If you have, as I have, several unfinished novels sitting about, it might be because they aren't really novels but a series of unrelated scenes. Your conflict between the hero and heroine has to have a concrete basis, and it can't just be that she hates him because he "acts as if he owns the world." Perhaps they're on opposite sides of a war or he loves someone else. State your problem, deepen it, and then begin trying to resolve it using scenes and dialogue.

Perhaps all this sounds like a lot of extra work to you, and maybe it is, because I know many romance authors who don't outline a word, and they write great stories. You have to find what works best for you. Since I had my first novel published I have been given more orders, criticism, and advice than you can imagine. I have been told I must have my hero sleep with other women to prove his virility, that it's permissible to have my heroine raped and/or bedded by other men, that they need to travel to exotic places to sustain interest. I've cried a lot, raged a great deal, written my friends long letters about my anger and frustration, but through it all I've stuck to what I believed. I've listened to everyone, used what I could, tried to be polite, but in the end I wrote the kind of books I like to read.

My advice to beginning authors is to believe in yourself, don't try to imitate other authors, and work to find your own style. Years ago I was told to read so and so's work and write like her, and now I hear some new authors are being told to write stories like mine. Write your own stories, put all you've got into every manuscript, and you'll make it!

The Magic Touch

BY CELESTE DE BLASIS

author of two historical romances

Kathryn Falk said she'd noted an element of sadness in the leading characters of my novels that make them seem more real than those in other books, and she asked if I could explain how I create these characters.

My first answer was and is that it is magic.

Sometimes it begins with a specific historical event or period that interests me; sometimes it is a particular human condition, tragedy or triumph. But I can't explain why one of these takes precedence over all others for long enough to become a book. That's part of the inexplicable alchemy and a good reason why many writers worry so about where the next book will come from—the process is so elusive, you are never sure it will happen again.

However, full development of a character involves a great deal of practical work once the first image is realized. My fact sheets are so thorough that the police could use them in tracking down suspects. When was the character born? What was his/her family like? How many of the family are still living and how much influence do they have on him/her? Who are the friends, the enemies? What circumstances of history would bear directly and indirectly on daily existence? And the report gets much more detailed than that. Physical characteristics: appearance, mannerisms, preferences in dress, etc., grace or lack of it, etc. Mental and spiritual attributes: education or lack of it, interests, likes and dislikes, self-image, strengths, weaknesses, world view or lack thereof, religion or the absence of it, etc. How do all of the characters fit together, how do they view each other—with love, with hate, with jealousy, compassion, fear, humor, etc.? And the most basic question of all—what are the major events or attitudes in the character's life that have made him or her react to life in specific ways?

Every aspect of one's personality is not determined wholly by environment; if that were so, humans could be bred and raised as alike as Mendel's peas. But certainly environment, specific life events, and how we react to them has a great deal to do with what sort of people we become. For instance, people who were cherished and made to feel secure when they were children usually seem to carry that accepting love throughout their lives, as if they have a talisman against complete despair, no matter how the external world falls apart. And the opposite is also valid—children deprived of emotional support so often grow to be adults who fail to feel secure, even when it would seem by all outward signs that they never need worry again.

I apply the same connections to my fictional characters, because they are wholly real to me. If they do not seem so, I know I'm doing something wrong or blocking the natural filling out of the character sketch.

The best way I can illustrate the way the blend of characters and events have become books for me is to use the specific cases of my novels. *The Night Child* grew out of seemingly disparate interests. I had visited Maine several times and had been interested from the first by the people there and by their ties to the sea. Also, I was struck by the historical records that indicated that Maine, despite her allegiance to the Union, had also done much trade with the South and had experienced profound changes along with the South when war so radically altered its fortunes.

Then I began to think about the enormous differences that had existed between life in San Francisco and life on the East Coast, the former being quite Elizabethan while the latter was Victorian. I was intrigued by the idea of a young woman trying to go from the freedom of San Francisco to the restrictive atmosphere of the East. Thus Brandy Claybourne was created, and with her came Grey King, a seemingly proper product of New England who is in fact every bit the renegade that she is. Where Brandy had been cherished in her childhood, Grey had had to accept too much responsibility too soon and had been betrayed by people he loved. His greatest tragedy is his daughter Missy, who has not communicated since she witnessed the death of her mother by fire, and who seems terrified of her father. Though they would not have named it so then, Missy suffers from secondary autism, and she grew out of yet another interest.

A friend of mine spent some years working with autistic children, and her stories of the immense brightness and incredible control of some of these children fascinated and haunted me. Twisted though the result is, few of us would have the discipline to shut out the world as these children do. With Missy I dealt specifically with secondary autism, meaning the case of a child who has developed in completely normal ways up to a certain point and then shuts down. My grandmother knew a family who had an intelligent and loving three-year-old son who never spoke or behaved naturally again after one night with a new babysitter. The sitter was never found; what had been done to the child was never discovered. His chances would probably be better for recovery now, but how much less they would have been a hundred years ago! So Maine, Brandy, Grey, Missy and the other characters came together in sorrow and joy to be *The Night Child*.

Suffer a Sea Change came also from various currents converging—a trip to Bermuda, where I observed a troubled social consciousness under the pastel beauty of the land, plus the unease moving through the marriages of some of my fellow travelers. There was, in addition, another matter entirely. There were large signs at the airport and warnings elsewhere about the strict enforcement of all antidrug laws. I checked on the reason for this when I got home and found, on interviewing a DEA agent, that that part of the Atlantic is afloat with fortunes in cocaine and other prohibited substances.

Out of all of this emerged Jess Banbridge, still mourning the death of her family in a sailing accident, but also strong with the love she had been given while they lived. She meets Winston St. James, who seems to be one thing when in fact he is something quite different, but always bearing the burden of having been betrayed by the wife he adored. Jess believes absolutely in the power of loving; Win has no faith in it at all. Conflict and change are inevitable because neither can deny the fascination each has for the other.

The Proud Breed came from "What if one had been born as a Californio before the Gold Rush, what would it have been like to see the Yankees come in such numbers and change life forever?"

As soon as I became interested in that question, I met Tessa and then Gavin, the Californio and the Yankee. And then I discovered how very little I knew about the history of my own state. Thus began seemingly endless hours of research, punctuated by the delight of discovering historical events and personages that would weave through the book. And always, the characters remained the essential reason for the book.

Tessa is a child and then a woman of heart, capable of making mistakes but always essentially just because she is constantly conscious of how others feel. She is also a woman of great strength and purpose, very centered, very focused on the matter at hand—all factors that make her a one-man woman. She lets Gavin into her life so completely, there is never again room for another on the same level. Gavin, on the other hand, has never considered love for one woman as the central point of his life. His childhood was bleak, and he is accustomed to fending for himself, taking risks, and moving on. In a very real sense, his experience of love is even more profound than Tessa's, because it is so unexpected. He is also more vulnerable than she, something Tessa comes to realize and accept, though she is at first afraid of the knowledge that her strong man is not invincible.

The novel in progress (to be published in 1985) is also growing from various threads. Part comes from family legends told to me by my grandmother—tales of the woman strong enough to have emigrated to America, bringing ten family members with her; and tales of the smugglers who earned enough from their illicit trade to also come to America and continue in prosperity with the breeding of fine horses. I've visited the sites they inhabited in both England and the United States, and I can see them clearly now and hear them talking, and their lives and the lives of their children and friends are unfolding day by day.

All of it is intertwined, the characters and their time. And yet each character must be so fully realized that I would recognize him or her were we to meet in the real world. Perhaps the most pronounced feature of this is the way they speak. If characters are fully born, they have individual speech patterns, ways of thought and expression just as distinctive as those heard in daily life. If I don't hear those differences in the voices, I know something has gone sadly awry in the writing.

The central characters, male and female, of my novels possess the attributes I would like to have and admire in other people. They take responsibility for their actions, and they do take action—they are not passive people. They are aware of themselves, of the people and the world around them. They are compassionate, capable of seeing the other person's side of things, even if it does take a while to admit the other view. They are capable of being jealous, angry, etc., but they are not petty in mind or spirit. They have strength and courage, but they are not invincible; the only truly invincible people I ever met were dull and insensitive rather than possessed of any virtue. Because they are involved in life and other people, they are vulnerable to hurt from both and to misunderstandings. They know or learn in the course of the novel that love in all its variety—love for one's mate, love for children, for friends, for principles, for ideas, for the earth—is the steady light against the darkness. The bittersweet edge to the characters is honed by that other character, Death, the inevitable darkness.

Death is in all the novels on various levels—in the memory of loss, in the immediate threat of life ending, and in the certainty that it will end. It is not always an enemy, but it is a constant reminder of how sweet and small in time life as we know it is. The most overt use of it as a character is in *The Tiger's Woman*. Rio is a gun for hire; he is Death walking, compelling in his beauty and danger. It's been interesting for me to learn how many readers have been attracted to the character of Rio, as if they understand that he is by his very nature the contrast that throws the joy of being alive into high relief.

It's an eternal irony that human nature often needs sorrow to recognize joy, needs the knowledge of death to recognize life. And the characters in my novels would be of no use to me or to the reader if they did not share these bonds.

I feel compelled to end this with an apology. For all my attempts to explain the creation of characters, I think "magic" remains the best answer.

How to Write Like Kathleen Woodiwiss

BY ROSANNE KOHAKE

author of two historical romances

The Woodiwiss romance novel is based almost entirely on a skillfully sketched hero and heroine involved in a plot that concentrates on their attraction to each other. It is a story neatly colored with both comedy and drama, framed in a wonderful, elegant style. Because so many elements of Kathleen's writing are developed to perfection, she is one of the very best sources of study for the beginning romance writer.

Woodiwiss does a great many things well, but perhaps her single unique attribute is her flowery, ultradescriptive, easy-to-read style: "His mouth eagerly took hers and their bodies strained together hungrily, Brandon's nearly famished for the full draught of love, Heather's just beginning to taste it. She moaned softly under his exploring hands, his fierce, fevered kisses, and clung to him as she gave herself wholly to his passion."

If you want to copy this style, which is closely akin to poetic free verse, you must first work to build and employ an extensive vocabulary, including many picturesque, slightly archaic words not stumbled upon in daily conversation. (Dated, nostalgic words just seem more romantic.)

Your words must flow easily. Each sentence must have both clarity and balance. There is a smoothness to Kathleen's writing that can be easily detected when passages are read aloud. This is the result of a careful choice of words and good, varied sentence structure.

While Kathleen's books are quite lengthy, her plots are relatively simple. Most readers prefer a romance that sticks to the conflict between the hero and heroine rather than drifting into numerous subplots that add lots of pages and little excitement. A great deal of this author's popularity comes from her ability to maintain a heightened sensuality chapter after chapter after chapter, and this is possible because of the originality and credibility of her characters. No two Woodiwiss heroines or heroes are exactly alike. Though certain qualities—namely beauty, brains, and gumption—are cornerstones of every Woodiwiss heroine, and each of her heroes is handsome, courageous, and possessed of deep convictions, each personality is fresh, new, and above all real to the reader. Characters become real to the reader only through consistent, viable portrayal in scene after scene. Woodiwiss also reinforces and explains character traits in other ways—by basing them on the shaping, molding experiences of childhood and by developing the deep bonding relationships between her characters and their parents, friends, and associates. In *The Wolf and the Dove,* for example, Wulfgar's reluctance to commit himself to Aislinn is a direct result of the rejection he suffered as a child. Yet his faithfulness and loyalty to his lord, his generosity to his father, and his honest dealings with his subjects all bear out of the fact that he is a man of honor, and worthy of her love.

Another way the reader becomes better acquainted with the hero and heroine is through vivid descriptions of what they feel, and subsequent vocal and facial expressions of those feelings. Nothing brings a character to life quite like a dramatic burst of emotional dialogue, and the Woodiwiss romance abounds with clever exchanges of conversation.

While you must take seriously the development of characterization and style, you must also pack your novel with amusing details and many scenes that contain elements of comic relief. The thread of levity that embroiders the more serious plot is an important factor in the movement of that plot. During those breaks in the suspenseful buildup, when very little else is happening, your reader will be held firm by humor.

No Woodiwiss romance would be complete without a generous helping of wonderfully sensuous love scenes. Nothing can compare with that magical moment when hero and heroine finally blend in a swirling, gushing tidal wave of emotion. And that is precisely the key: *emotions* behind the characters, their motivations, their feelings, their sensations, their individuality—all are brought to the fore in that miraculous joining of man and woman. It is the volatile, explosive burst of emotion coupled with the beautiful, lyrical flow of words that packs power into every love scene.

A writer must tie many facets of good writing together to emulate the successful impact of a Woodiwiss romance. Be prepared to face repeated editing in a struggle to achieve her smooth, elegant style; to put the special effort into developing fresh, credible characters; work to add strategic incidents of comic relief; and finally, pull all these elements together with strong, poignant love scenes. (Is it any wonder that it takes her over two years to do all that?)

Historical Series and Sagas

The key word for writing the saga is planning. *More than any other type of fiction, it is critical that the author be well prepared before he or she actually starts to write. First of all, a saga usually spans several generations in the lineage of a single family, so the story inevitably begins in the past. In fact, history is a crucial element in this kind of novel, and it provides more than just a convenient setting for your story. Both the historical context and the ebb and flow of dramatic events actually influence the actions and change the characters' lives. This is also true of historical novels; however, the conflicts in a historical are usually resolved in one book, while those in a family saga continue through many volumes. Because of this, the author's strategy in planning a saga must necessarily be different.*

Planning a Multivolume Saga

BY KATHRYN DAVIS

author of The Dakotas *series*

In a multivolume saga, the author is given the opportunity to *use* history to enhance the plot; therefore, periods of turmoil and violent change are particularly appropriate. These periods in history give rise to the sweeping drama that often characterize such novels. For example, a family determined to conquer a wilderness or to fight for freedom and survival in a hostile world offers endless possibilities. The lawless, uncivilized Badlands of North Dakota, where my family saga, The Dakotas, is set, drew only a certain breed of men—madmen, dreamers, outlaws, and heroes—who were larger than life. I needed only to record what they had done. Thus, the setting influences the kind of conflict that arise in the story.

Extensive research is very important, not only in helping an author choose a story in the first place, but also in authenticating the events he or she decides to portray. Essays by other authors in this book have covered the subject of research thoroughly.

I *have* heard it said that, when working with historical figures too much information can actually be a handicap. I encountered this problem in *At the Wind's Edge*, the first volume of The Dakotas. The Badlands activities of my hero, the Marquis of Mores, were so well documented that I felt obliged to use every scrap of information. I soon became bogged down in the voluminous facts and lost the drama of my story. Eventually I had to rewrite the entire section, retaining only those facts and incidents that were most compelling. Just keep in mind that the author is telling a dramatic story, not writing a scholarly history. The skillful novelist can learn to cull the unnecessary facts and to combine history and drama in such a way that readers are not even aware of the writer's craft. The idea is to keep readers so entertained that they will keep reading as fast as they can.

Once you have chosen a historical period and conceived a basic plot, you should spend some more time considering the unique problems which a multivolume work presents. In other words, learn how to plan for the long run. It helps to have a notebook divided into sections. Choose a section for each volume you intend to write, then jot down ideas as they come to you, so you don't forget them later. My notebook includes character sketches, brief encapsulations of scenes, plot developments, and snatches of dialogue. Often I find myself recording whole scenes that occur to me completely out of context. Needless to say, this work becomes invaluable later. By the time I actually begin writing, I have several lists, a full outline, reams of notes, and very little of the difficult work left to do. At that point I can let my characters take over my imagination; the novel seems to write itself.

When you *do* finally begin your book, it is wise to plan to
ork on the project until all the volumes are completed. Readers
:come frustrated and sales drop off when the publication of
bsequent volumes is delayed. The sooner you finish, the sooner
e publisher can schedule your novels for release.

Unlike contemporary romance novels, multivolume sagas are
:opled with many characters, all of whom are somehow impor-
nt to the novel as a whole. In fact, in some cases it is even
fficult to decide who the major hero and heroine are and who
e the more minor characters. This is because the author, in
lling the story of an entire family through several generations,
ust necessarily make the minor characters plentiful and well
ounded. For example, in *At the Wind's Edge*, Phillipe Beau-
ont is a minor character whom we see first as a bitter, hostile
oy who seeks revenge against the Marquis. However, as the
ory progresses Phillipe matures into a sensitive young man who
aware of his faults. At this point, the reader has been prepared
or Phillipe to emerge as the wise, compassionate man who will
e the hero of Book II.

Just as there must be well-rounded minor characters in a
amily saga, so must there be well-developed subplots that help
advance the strong central story. In Book I of The Dakotas,
e story of the Marquis's attempt to build an empire in the
adlands is complicated by several critical subplots, including
e destructive behavior of the half-breed, Mianne Goodall, the
roblems within the Pendleton family itself, and Phillipe's rela-
onship with Katherine Pendleton. All of these subplots in Book
become pivotal forces in the events that follow in Book II.

It is important to recognize that the saga has a broader scope,
ot only in historical terms, but also with regard to the growth
nd maturation of its characters. Thus, the story should not be so
imple that when the major conflict is resolved the reader feels
he novel should come to an end. Complexity is critical in such a
multivolume work. Your novel should encompass the trials and
ribulations of a family that struggles, not only against their own
wayward emotions, but also against their environment and the
orces of history that threaten to destroy them. It is precisely
because their conflicts can never be truly and completely re-
olved that a saga can continue through several volumes.

Finally, you must plan each novel's conclusion with great
:are. The author of the family saga has the difficult task of
simultaneously satisfying the reader's curiosity about the strug-

gles in the current volume and leaving them anxiously anticipatin
the events that are to come in future volumes. To leave the majo
conflicts in any one volume unresolved has the same effect as endin
a murder mystery without revealing the killer's identity. Remember
these novels are usually released at least six months apart. Woul
you want to wait six months to find out who done it? The write
should always be conscious of the fine line between suspense an
pure frustration.

In Book I of The Dakotas, I attempted to deal with thi
problem by bringing most of the plots to completion and hintin

---

Tips for Series and Saga Writers
BY SUZAN EVANS

series and saga book reviewer of Romantic Times

1. *Provide a family tree at the beginning of every volume.*
2. *Stay away from making characters the same nationality (for example, a Russian princess swept away by an American hero has built-in conflicts that create excitement and interest).*
3. *Make readers feel the love between the hero and heroine by simple showing, not telling.*
4. *Don't spoil a good story by using the same setting in too many volumes.*
5. *Don't get lazy and become predictable to the point of stereotyping.*
6. *Don't skimp on adventure.*

Recommended Series and Sagas for Study

The Novel of New York
Bruce Nicolaysen, Avon

The Borodins
Leslie Arlen, Jove

The Australians
William Stewart Long, Dell

The O'Hara Dynasty
Mary Canon, Worldwide Library

The Rakehell Dynasty
Michael William Scott, Warner

The Saga of the Steeles
Joseph Csida, Pocket

Kanata
Dennis Adair and Janet Rosenstock, Avon

Angelique
Sergeanne Golon, Bantam

Roselynde Chronicles
Roberta Gellis, Playboy

at future events that would change the characters' lives in Book II. The central story, that of the Marquis's unstable business empire and the wife he nearly lost, was concluded; it was clear which direction his relationship with his wife, as well as his business dealings, would take in the future. But to keep the reader intrigued, I hinted that although Phillipe and his family were leaving the Badlands for the moment, his relationships with both Mianne Goodall and Katherine Pendleton were by no means finished. But, more than anything else, it was the Marquis's final warning to his greatest enemy that portended future trouble in the Badlands: "I'm not the kind of man who gives up, regardless of the odds. We'll be back, Pendleton. I promise you that!"

All of the techniques I have discussed are important to remember when you begin to plan a family saga, but most important of all is to keep in mind the realization that your characters, plot, and theme must remain compelling and convincing beyond just one volume. Your careful preparations can help make your characters live throughout the sprawling generations that will give your novel its breadth and power.

The O'Hara Dynasty

BY MARY CANON

author of four historical romances

Originally, The O'Hara Dynasty was conceived as a single book. In tracing my husband's Irish heritage, I fell in love with the wonderful real-life characters who existed in the seventeenth century, and commented to Jack, a writer of contemporary international thrillers, that this particular era would make a fascinating topic for a novel. He agreed. He then promptly challenged me to help write the novel. Never one to turn down a dare, I dove right in.

In the course of presenting the idea to the publisher, the question was raised: Why should we stop at the seventeenth century? Why not continue the saga of this Irish family and bring them all the way to present-day America? As you might imagine, the idea of expanding this tale four hundred years seemed overwhelming at first, particularly to a first-time novelist. But in my elation at selling *anything,* I decided to try it.

Several problems unique to a historical saga became quickly apparent: (1) the staggering amount of research necessary to become versed in the life and times of each period; (2) conceiving a mythical family that would span four hundred years; and (3) weaving the real and fictitious characters into actual events in a way that would capture the reader's imagination, with emphasis on both romance and high adventure.

I didn't want us to write a history book; I wanted history to come alive through the characters, so that the reader would feel almost transported back in time, with all the sights, sounds, smells, etc., of each era.

To begin the research, I spent many months scouring libraries and used-bookstores for any information regarding the lifestyle of the times. This data was catalogued in a file (it's now on a word-processing disk), so that I could draw on the information as I needed it. Although the research has been formidable, I think it's added immeasurably in capturing the flavor of each period.

I also collected as much actual correspondence between the famous personages as I could, believing that we reveal ourselves in our letters, and in this way I could give real flesh-and-blood personalities to characters from history. And some of them were indeed *characters*—almost leaping from the pages of history and demanding to be put in The O'Hara Dynasty. For example, in researching *The Defiant,* I came across one Grace O'Malley— the Pirate Queen of Connaught. This somewhat-less-than-genteel but high-spirited lady wreaked havoc on English shipping during the latter part of the sixteenth century; so much so that Queen Elizabeth I, in an attempt to win the irascible pirate over to her side, offered Grace the title of Countess. To which the lady replied, "Why, madame, should I deign to such a lowly title . . . when I am *Queen* in my own land?"

Now, how could I *not* include her in the story!

And so it has been with each of the books in The O'Hara Dynasty; Cardinal Richelieu in *The Survivors*, Oliver Cromwell in *The Renegades*, Patrick Sarsfield in *The Exiled*, and the Irish spy for the Patriot cause, John Honeyman, in *The Kinsmen*—extraordinary individuals all—who help bring history to life, in *human* terms.

It has been a joy to take those real characters and interweave them with the mythical O'Haras. Beginning with the very first two progenitors, Elizabeth Hatton and Rory O'Donnell, the O'Hara family tree is now on a chart that covers one entire wall of my office. If I don't finish the series soon, I'll have to move!

The secret to solving the third problem probably applies to all authors, regardless of genre: Let the *characters* tell the story. All the author can do is create them, given them "soul," and then let them take over the novel. When I learned that lesson, the writing process became infinitely easier, and I honestly think the books became a more exciting, fulfilling read.

Now if I can just survive the rest of the series . . .

Writing Series and Sagas for Book Creations, Inc.

BY LYLE KENYON ENGEL

producer of Kent Family Chronicles, Roselynde Chronicles, Rakehell Dynasty, Windhaven, The Australian *series*, White Indian *series*, Wagons West, The Centurions, etc.

What I look for from an author is great writing. By great writing

I mean that you can really see what is being described. You care about the characters and feel what they are feeling. I like the kind of writing that is so good you don't want to put the book down, or at least you can't wait to pick it up again. It is writing that is clear, that says things in a straightforward way. The writing must look easy. If one word can say it, why use two or three, or why use words the reader might not understand? After all, we *are* writing for readers, not college professors, not judges of book contests (though our books have won plenty of contests and awards, too). But always it's the reader that you have to think about.

Who is the reader? He or she could be anyone: a subway rider, a secretary, a retired lieutenant colonel, a housewife, a farmer, a bookstore owner. We get letters from hundreds of readers with many backgrounds, but their comments are always the same: Keep those books coming! We love having a good read!

What gives me the greatest pleasure in the world is knowing the book that I and my staff at Book Creations put out is going to make readers happy, is going to give them pleasure. The pleasure of reading is one of the most special things we have in life. Reading is something that will never be duplicated or replaced by television or movies or video cassettes. Reading is unique. It offers a person the enormous pleasure of being in his chair, his bed, a bus—anywhere in the world, for that matter—and being able to create a world of his own. The reader becomes the producer, the director, the actor when he reads a book. He alone casts his characters the way he wants them. This is something you can't do when you watch a movie or television. A book is *your* own wonderful world.

The process starts at Book Creations in Canaan, New York, where I am the largest independent producer of paperback fiction in the United States. I look for a writer who has had books published by a major publisher but is dissatisfied with the way the books have been edited, designed, promoted, and distributed. The writer is eager to work for Book Creations because BCI has the know-how and the ability to create a major mass-market book and to see that it has a chance to become a best-seller. I read the books, and if I'm able to say "This is great writing," I contact the author and explain the extent of our interest. I may have an existing project in mind to assign to that author, or I may develop an entirely new project based upon a manuscript the author is working on. Whatever the case, our projects carry excellent advances, and the author is delighted to sign up with us.

The existing projects that I may assign to new authors are ideas I've developed for books I feel people want to read, with characters people want to get to know. They are almost always envisioned in terms of at least a four-book series, because the story and characters are too wonderful just to be told about in one volume. The books I want to do take place all over the world in all different times, and about all different people. These books can be romance, historical, western, and especially family sagas taking place in America.

These stories are just waiting for the right author. This doesn't mean that a big romance sega I have in mind has to go to a romance writer. Rather, I see from the books the author has already written those qualities that will work for my new project. Is the author good at describing characters' feelings, motivations, likes and dislikes? Does the author write well about women and what they think and what they do? As an example, John Jakes's books prior to the Kent Family Chronicles were science fiction, and he also wrote several historical novels under the pseudonym Jay Scotland. I saw he had the ability to write about characters living during an important historical period without letting too much history get in the way of the story values. Jakes, I knew, could describe real characters who lived and loved the way real people do. The only difference was that I wanted to see these characters on an epic scale, living during the American War for Independence. But it doesn't matter what period in history writers are dealing with: *People* come first, and in every era—from ancient Rome to the present day—people have fears, desires, dreams, and joys. These *must* be present in any great book.

I mean, if a character in a book receives a letter from his sweetheart and we're told he reads the letter three times, we must be so involved with the people and the story that *we* want to read the letter three times, too.

As I work with writers on a project, I tell them these things. We speak on the phone or else I write them letters explaining what the book needs. I also like to get to know the writer, for I feel a writer's background, interests, and attitude say a lot about the kind of book he or she can write. Then we come up with an outline, which must be filled with the exciting and passionate incidents that make up people's lives. When the outline is just right, the author goes to work on the book.

My staff also works closely with our writers. The editors at Book Creations follow the authors' progress, helping them with characterization and plotting, using our in-house library to help authors research their material. Book Creations also has its own in-house librarian. Our editors prepare the manuscripts, copy editing and proofreading them, so that when they are submitted to the publishers they're ready to be set into type. That's what it means to be a book producer. When the publisher gets one of our books (and these publishers are the biggest in the industry), they know they're not going to have to do major rewrites and editing, as they might if they were working directly with an author. The publisher knows they are going to get a good, solid manuscript from Book Creations, virtually ready to be sent to the typesetter.

The publisher and the bookseller also know Book Creations' books *sell*. We have the lowest average return rate in the book business. We do a great deal to promote our books. We have our own in-house publicity-promotion department. We have built a selected mailing list over the years consisting of 4,500 radio-television stations, daily newspapers, wholesalers, distributors, and B. Dalton, Walden, and Crown bookstores, as well as some independents. From its inception in 1973 until the end of 1982, Book Creations produced 261 books in thirty-two series for eighteen publishers with more than 65 million copies of these titles in print, plus sales in fifteen foreign languages. The appeal of our books is universal and phenomenal.

I read every manuscript that we send to a publisher. I will not send it out unless I am perfectly satisfied it's a good book, one that I can be proud of. As I said before, a good book gives people incredible pleasure, enjoyment that can't be duplicated by anything else. And it gives me great pleasure to know I've produced books that give people joy.

A Sampler from Lyle Kenyon Engel

- *Show, don't tell.*
- *Keep it simple.*
- *Know your subject.*
- *To write about people, you must know and like people.*
- *Animals are important in a story. Animals make people human.*
- *If a character in a book receives a letter from his sweetheart and we're told he reads the letter three times, we must be so involved with the characters and the story that we want to read the letter three times, too.*
- *A good book, like a good writer, is made, not born.*

*An English Historical Novelist's
Writing Views*

INTERVIEW WITH MALCOLM MACDONALD

author of six historical novels

Did you outline your great historical series, The Stevenson?

I've always distrusted detailed, written outlines. They become such a tyranny, they take all the fun out of writing. Writing for me is such a stultifying activity, anyway. You can talk at this speed, but—you—can—only—write—at—this—speed. Which is why a lot of writers make poor public speakers: They *think* at a different speed.

And so, to keep the interest up, you almost have to fool yourself into thinking that you don't really know what's going to happen and you're discovering it along with the reader. But at a much slower pace, at the writing pace. I've found that writing any detailed outline is a recipe for disaster for me.

How do you see the story? Do you just have the germ of an idea and an opening?

You have to have the opening, and it must be riveting, and set the scene and grab the two characters. And state the central drama of the book fairly quickly to capture the reader. There must be a drama from the beginning.

Do you put a detailed plot together before writing?

You must know fairly clearly where your characters are going. You must know the destination, and you must know where they start from. But in between it must be an adventure, as much for the writer as for the reader. If the writer is merely following down railway lines he built in the beginning in an outline, it's going to be pretty boring.

When telling a story, how do you keep a strong storytelling voice?

It comes by long practice. You have to fit the voice to the characters you've got. And the narrative has to fit around the dialogue. You'd have different kind of narrative if you were talking about two housewives meeting, as opposed to two oilmen.

You have to both be *in* your writing, be excited, thrilled by it, and *apart* from it, coldly watching it and yet critical of it. That's the hardest thing to get. I still haven't got it.

Do you have any tips about sentence structure?

Beginning writers should try to keep the ideas and sentences simple. Avoid masses of subsidiary clauses. Think, "What is the main thing I want in this sentence?" and then state it. Subsidiary clauses with lots of "which's" and "who's" and "what's" and "when's" and so on all add more information that slows up the moment when you get to the main point. In fiction writing, what people want is not information, but a story that zips along.

Can you give us some points on character description?

You have to pick out two or three salient things that make the reader say "I *know* that woman," "I've *seen* that man." You're trying to get the reader to bring out of his own portfolio pictures to fill in this blank you've created. You have to find just those two or three words that will do it. What usually happens is that you draw from the great common literary stock of the Western world: "fat people are jolly," "people with narrow eyes are mean," "blondes have more fun." These are clichés of character. To establish something quickly, you can lean on them and use them. But if you do it too much, then *your* writing is one big cliché.

Do you visualize your characters when writing?

I write down what a character looks like, and I keep referring to this while I'm writing. I have a picture of a character at any given moment, but that picture isn't constant. During the writing, something unexpected will happen, something that changes the original plot outline, and that character suddenly becomes important. He's suddenly involved in the plot, so you give him more characteristics. So a character can build up beyond, or away from, your original perception of him.

What about descriptions of settings?

You have to be a worrier about the exact meaning of words, even to the point of being considered finicky. But a description of a room is a recipe for slowing down the action. The things in a room must be there because they help the story along. You should only describe things that have some meaning in the plot, or could suggest a mood. The reader knows there are ceilings and walls, you don't have to describe them. Fit what you're writing into why you're writing it.

If I had to write about the desert, I'd do research to get a physical description of it. I wouldn't go there, but I'd read books on it. From these books I'd pick out the features that would give the reader a feeling for the atmosphere.

Can you tell us more about your views about outlines?

I really think the enthusiasm, love, and hate for the characters are really what should carry them through, rather than saying "Now I've got to have him meet her in Chapter 7." That's mechanical. If you feel happier having a fixed outline, yes, by all means write it. But never let it become your master. If you're going to be a writer, writing should come as naturally as speaking. If you can't enjoy it, you should try something else. If you haven't filled a blank sheet in half an hour, then you ought to be doing something else. Writing came naturally for me from the very beginning. I've always written, first nonfiction, then fiction. Journalism can be a good training ground for fiction writers, as it teaches you to be parsimonious with words.

Tell us about the actual process of your writing.

I write paragraph by paragraph, and polish each one after

writing it. I'm constantly polishing and rereading paragraphs. I love cutting words from a paragraph. That's easy to do, as I work on a word processor, one of the most liberating devices for a writer.

Should new writers try to emulate the styles of established authors?

Only as a means to an end. A new writer should emulate his favorite author's writing, unashamedly. This is a way of becoming tutored. There's nothing wrong with your first ten efforts being pure pastiche. Once you learn a hero author's style, you can branch out to others.

Do you have any ideas on structuring chapters?

I have no system for figuring out how many chapters will be in a book. But you get to pace yourself over time. The usual thing is that I think, "This is going on a bit, isn't it? I've really got to think about shortening," or "I've got to have a good reason for making it longer."

If I've got a good reason, then I'll go on. Ending each chapter properly is as important as having a good ending to a book. It's no good getting the story right over three chapters if at the end of each chapter you haven't reached a kind of mini-climax that makes the reader say, "I've got to know what happens next." My natural book length is about 120,000 words. I think it may be genetic. Something in me likes that length. I prefer reading long novels, as well.

What books have influenced you?

I've read more science fiction than anything. I've also read a lot of straight novels. My favorite novelist is Joyce Carey, who I think is one of the most underrated writers of this century, as D. H. Lawrence is one of the most overrated.

PART THREE

8

Introduction to the Other Romance Genres

Sigh, Spy, Cry, Sci-Fi

In Regency novels, the heroine and her "abigail" sigh a lot. In romantic suspense and gothics, the heroine spies or is spied on a lot. In the contemporary novel, the reader cries a lot. And in the new science fiction and fantasy romances, all reality is defied a lot!

Although the category romance and historicals dominate publishing in the 1980s, there's still a loyal and demanding readership for traditional ones, such as the gothics and the Regencies.

Regency

Since Jeffrey Farnol created the form, and Georgette Heyer immortalized it, the Regency novel has had an enthusiastic following among men as well as women. Either very short or mainstream length; the trend now is toward the 55,000-to-75,000 word romance.

Tone: Light.

Milieu: England during the Napoleonic Wars, a stable, upper-class society.

Moral: Hinges on proper social behavior.

Unique feature: Humor and satire made evident by witty dialogue and literary style à la Jane Austen.

Sexuality: Nothing explicit; emphasis is on love made in heaven and destined for marriage.

The Regency heroine is usually not encumbered by relatives, which leaves her free to form new attachments. (Recall Jane Austen's Miss Bennet and her problems with her mother, which became the plot!) There usually isn't enough space in the average-length Regency to dwell long on extraneous characters. As in category romances, minor characters serve the purpose of revealing information about the hero and heroine that they can't directly relate themselves, and the more humorous or amusing they are, the better the Regency.

A similarity to the gothic is that the heroine's world is always small, a small upper-class society in London or Bath.

Other periods of history are appearing in small-book form. Some publishers call them Georgian, Victorian, or Edwardian romances. Like Regency romances, these stories are colorful and descriptive of the social history of the times.

Barbara Cartland, who has written her more than three hundred little romances in the Regency and other periods leading up to Victorian times, is the consummate weaver of her brand of romance. Each heroine is a virgin and receives nothing more titillating than a chaste kiss on approximately page 152. A Cartland story gives the reader beauty, love, and a happy ending with a wonderful marriage partner—a Cinderella story in period costume.

Romantic Suspense and Gothic

The first gothic was Mrs. Radcliffe's *Mystery of Udolpho*. The spooky elements originated here, the creaking doors and evil. Then came Fannie Burney's suspense novel *Evelina*, a tremendous success, also a society novel (foreshadowing the Regency tone) with mystery.

But the classics that are still widely read and discussed today, and have influenced the modern gothic novel, are Charlotte Brontë's *Jane Eyre*, Daphne du Maurier's *Rebecca*, and Emily Brontë's *Wuthering Heights*, the classic story of star-crossed lovers with elements of the supernatural and mystery.

The plot formula of a gothic still works today (although publishers are ignoring this type of romance at the moment in favor of other types). It is put to use by the small handful of authors who still manage to get published—Victoria Holt, Barbara Michaels (a.k.a. Elizabeth Peters), Virginia Coffman, Daoma Winston, Jane Aiken Hodge, Phyllis A. Whitney, and others.

Whereas the old-time gothic novels depended on instantaneous sensations of surprise, fear, and bewilderment in an innocent world, the modern gothic novel has these elements:

Tone: Menacing mood, an entertaining *frisson* of terror.
Milieu: An isolated old house, usually on the northern coast of England or the moors.
Mystery: She is being menaced because of an error in her judgment (someone thinks she saw or heard something).
Unique feature: Master of the house, or the hero, appears to be evil in the beginning but turns out otherwise. When two men are presented, one is the villain.
Sexuality: As mystery unfolds, romance unfolds; heroine is a virgin; no sex.

The enduring popularity of the gothic tale may very well be the result of its similarity to the Cinderella legend. When the heroine has no family attachments she can leave childhood behind, go through her "rites of passage," and form her own relationships. Therefore, a writer should always avoid giving her any family, friends, or sorority sisters to cling to, so she can be very vulnerable, isolated, and alone. (As in Henry James's *The Turn of the Screw*.)

It is important to remember that the heroine's error in judgment (she is *never* just an innocent party) leads her into trouble. She's thinking that the good guy is the bad one (class distinction may cloud her logic). In any case, she doesn't know what is happening. The reader and the hero *do* know.

When the mystery is solved and the sometimes silly heroine realizes that the bad guy is the good one, she is happier and wiser than before, and on her way to the altar.

Contemporary

This type of romantic novel does not follow any formula or set plot points, unlike the previously discussed romances. The contemporary has unlimited page length and a broad range, with the plot depending only on the characters' problems and, of course, a modern setting.

Usually the heroine's troubles are caused by circumstances regarding her job, family, lovers, or status. (Remember, she's not being attacked by Indians.) Readers of this form include those who think they've been ill used, put upon by their job, family, lovers, or status.

The late Helen Van Slyke endeared herself to the general feminine reading public because her heroines always triumphed by nimbly jumping from abject poverty to social standing or career success, almost overnight, attracting men effortlessly, like moths to a flame. She gave readers a vicarious pleasure, in her soap opera-style nine novels, when the heroine married the editor and made an easy jump to power. Van Slyke also wrote a kind of reverse snobbery, as does Danielle Steel, a lower-middle-class idea of the upper class.

The subject matter of a contemporary romance novel can range from erotic fantasy to the presentation of modern problems. The most distinguishing character is the author. The personality of the writer determines the success of these novels, and the best usually give good psychological insights. Those writers succeed who can achieve even a glimmer of what Jane Austen possessed in her writing—independent point of view, astute observations about people and their behavior, the ability to depict people accurately. Writers who master these qualities are most likely to get published. Austen's great talent gave her the ability to listen and hear people talk. It is a matter of listening. An author can write one line and bring out the character.

An offshoot of the contemporary novel is the roman à clef, a story with thinly veiled well-known people and celebrities. They are also called the gossip column novels. *Valley of the Dolls* was the mother of the current flock. Now readers expect to recognize Gloria Vanderbilt, Prince Charles, or an American president in a story. In some cases the books are "factions"—part fact and part fiction—that makes even more deliciously satisfying reading. June Flaum Singer's excellent novel *The Debutantes* not only has the real Gloria Vanderbilt in the plot, but she is a main character; there are other celebrities galore, the likes of Oona O'Neil, etc.

Esther Sager, sometimes described as writing long Harlequins, always presents the heroine as good, and it's her inability to hurt others that is her problem and controls the plot.

In the contemporary romance novel, there's a growing interest in having the heroine be a "bird in a gilded cage," surrounded by the very rich and famous. Usually the heroine starts out poor, marries well the first time around, is widowed, and then meets her great love. Virgins are out in contemporary romances. These stories don't have a "first love" theme.

Today's contemporary novel reflects our times, just as the forerunners did theirs. When Richardson wrote *Pamela* in 1739, he became the first writer to portray the working girl. (This book caught on because two prerequisites for popular fiction occurred—the ability of the masses to read and cheap mass production of books.) Eventually these women's novels became known as "dime novels"; in England, "penny dreadfuls." Late-nineteenth-century factory-worker readers sighed over Bertha M. Clay and novels such as *Birth of the Sewing Machine Girl.* A few decades later, Ethel Dell thrilled women around the world with *The Sheik,* one of the best fantasies in category romances, and still well known. One of Dell's contemporaries, Rhoda Boughton, also enthralled romantics with such titles as *Not Wisely But Too Well.*

The next generation of contemporary romance writers included Viña Delmar, author of *Bad Girl,* and the two highest-paid fiction writers of the Depression, Faith Baldwin and Kathleen Norris. They wrote about what their working-girl readers were actually doing—mainly office jobs and menial labor—and their stories illustrated every shopgirl's dream: to marry the boss's son or become a famous singer. A favorite plot was the manicurist who wants to marry for money and who instead meets a man who *also* wants to marry for money. They fall in love, and love overcomes greedy ambition.

Today, all that has changed. Secretaries and governesses, manicurists and lowly clerks have disappeared from the plots. Like the readers, the heroines want successful careers and to be prosperous. Virgins are out, but so are vulgar, cheap characters such as Susann portrayed in *Valley of the Dolls.* Class and manners are found most frequently, as is the struggle to get or keep the accomplishments.

Contemporary novels will always depend on a persona. A writer who can express herself or himself and be intuitive about what the reader wants (usually it's mirrored in popular movies) will find no holds barred in this type of writing. If there's one new trend in the contemporary romance novel of the '80s, it would be toward glamour and "glitz" settings and people.

Science Fiction and Fantasy

With the exception of Anne McCaffrey, no SF writer has attracted the usual romance reader. Romantic novelist Carole Nelson Douglas is bringing more romance to her science fiction and fantasy readers. Jean Auel has captured a lot of reader interest with her prehistorical settings for *Clan of the Cave Bear* and *The Valley of Horses*.

Only time will tell if SF jargon will creep into the standard romances. It is doubtful that the regular romance readers are ready to give up a Hawaiian resort or a Mexican paradise to don a spacesuit over planet Jupiter. Perhaps more romantic settings in space travel will be one key. Any space traveler should be able to win a lady's heart and put his galactic boots under her bed if he's devastatingly handsome and romantic and they're truly star-crossed lovers.

Defining Sci-Fi and Fantasy

Science fiction is a tale of the possible, though not necessarily probable, and is based on scientific knowledge. Fantasy is a tale of the impossible, and is based on the supernatural or magic.

Today's SF and fantasy novels overlap and use elements of both. Both create other words—SF in a universe that can be understood, fantasy in a universe created by each author.

A distinction is found between high and low fantasy. Low fantasy is a tale of happenings that occur but are not explained according to nature's laws. High fantasy is a setting where laws are created by supernatural creatures such as elves, fairies, and gods with magical powers, where even the flora and fauna are magical.

Science fiction and fantasy fiction overlap because both deal with another world, and another time and place.

Science fiction writing is governed by scientific knowledge, however tenuously described. Fantasy fiction deals with the impossible, being based on magic or the supernatural.

There are distinctions made in the fantasy types. Low fantasy belongs with a world governed by nature's laws; high fantasy is peopled with supernatural beings such as gods, elves, fairies with magical powers.

Classic authors include Ann McCaffrey with her Dragonworld series; Mary Stewart, author of The Crystal Cave, The Hollow Hills, The Last Enchantment; *T. H. White,* The Sword in the Stone; *and Carole Nelson Douglas,* Six of Swords.

Classic Romance Authors of the Sigh, Spy, Cry, and Fi Genres

Regency

Joan Aiken
Paula Allardyce
Audrey Blanshard
Barbara Cartland
Gail Clark
Clare Darcy
Vanessa Gray
Georgette Heyer
Fiona Hill
Jane Aiken Hodge
Elsie Lee
Maggie MacKeever
Mary Linn Roby
Joan Smith
Mira Stables
Sheila Walsh

Romantic-Suspense

Joan Aiken
Evelyn Anthony
Gwendoline Butler
Laura Conway
Mignon Eberhart
Dorothy Eden
Catherine Gaskin
Jane Aiken Hodge
Isabelle Holland
Victoria Holt
Velda Johnston
Norah Lofts
Ann Mayberry
Barbara Michaels (a.k.a. Elizabeth Peters)

Mary Stewart
Phyllis A. Whitney

"Sweet" Romance Authors of the Past

Ruby Ayres
Faith Baldwin
Ursula Bloom
Ethel Dell
Grave Livingston
Emily Loring
Kathleen Norris
Denise Robbins

and of Today

Taylor Caldwell
Catherine Cookson (a.k.a. Catherine Marchant)
Alice Dwyer-Joyce
Dorothy Eden
Catherine Gaskin
Norah Lofts
Rosamunde Pilcher
Helen Van Slyke

Gothic

Joan Aiken
Juliet Astley (a.k.a. Norah Lofts)
Evelyn Berckman
Charlotte Brontë, *Jane Eyre*
Emily Brontë, *Wuthering Heights*

Philippa Carr (a.k.a. Victoria Holt)
Virginia Coffman
Dorothy Daniels
Daphne du Maurier, *Rebecca*
Dorothy Eden
Georgette Heyer, *Cousin Kate*
Pamela Hill
Jane Aiken Hodge
Isabelle Holland
Victoria Holt
Susan Howatch
Margaret James
Velda Johnston
Phyllis Leonard
May Mackintosh
Anne Maybury
Barbara Michaels
Andre Norton
Caroline Stafford
Mary Stewart
Jill Tattersall
Phyllis A. Whitney

Romance Genre Publishers

Regency
Avon
Bantam
Fawcett (Ballantine)
NAL/Signet
St. Martin's Press
Walker and Co.

Romantic Suspense
Avon
Berkley/Jove
Fawcett (Ballantine)
Harlequin
Silhouette
Zebra

Contemporary
Every paperback company

Science Fiction and Fantasy
Ballantine
Pinnacle

Confessions of a Regency Romantic

BY MEGAN DANIEL

author of four Regency romances

My interest in the Regency is a natural outgrowth of my theater experience. I was once asked to design a production of *Pride and Prejudice*. It was love at first reading. I loved the book. I loved the play. Mostly, I loved the clothes and the society and style of life and gentility they mirrored.

I started reading every Regency romance I could find, both good ones and bad (and some were truly awful). I tried to discover why I liked some and hated others. I felt especially drawn to the wit and clever dialogue, the sense of playing with the language used by such writers as Clare Darcy (especially in *Allegra* and *Gwendolen*), Joan Smith (*Imprudent Lady*), and Elsie Lee (*The Nabob's Widow*).

I read everything by Georgette Heyer, of course. My favorites, such as *Frederika*, *Cotillion*, *Black Sheep*, and *Friday's Child*, I read again. And again. To this day, I never start a book of my own without rereading at least one Georgette Heyer and one Jane Austen (usually *Pride and Prejudice* or *Northanger Abbey*).

I also started doing library research, a vital step in any historical writing, but particularly important in Regencies, I think, because our readers are voracious. They know a great deal about London during the Regency. They know that an earl's daughter is a ''Lady'' but a baron's daughter is just a ''Miss.'' They know a pelisse from a spencer, and they know that ''shot the cat'' means dead drunk. Accuracy is doubly important when you readers are so knowledgeable.

I once read (or *started* to read) a Regency that was, on the whole, nicely written. There were one or two small inaccuracies that were annoying, but I kept reading. Until, that is, the heroine hurried down London's Pall Mall toward Windsor Castle. Now, even the most casual traveler or anglophile knows that Windsor Castle is *miles* from London. I clapped the book shut in disgust, unable to care anymore what happened to the heroine on her way to that castle in the wrong location.

Such sloppiness of research is inexcusable. Your readers will *not* excuse it, or simply let it go. Nor will they continue to buy your books.

After reading a few general histories of the period and more specialized books, such as *Dandies of the Regency, The Annals of Almack's,* and a biography of Beau Brummell, I concentrated mainly on newspapers and magazines of the period, as well as diaries, journals, and collections of letters. These are excellent ways to learn the telling details of the period and pick up patterns of speech and thought. I also studied old guides to London and tacked an 1816 map of the city over my desk for easy reference.

I am extremely fortunate to be married to a man whose endless string of ideas constantly amazes me. In plotting my first book, *Amelia*, Roy and I established a working pattern that has stood me in good stead ever since.

Once I have the germ of an idea for a plot—and it is usually a very small germ indeed—we sit down with a pot of coffee and a notebook and play ''What if?'' It's a freewheeling brainstorming session in which no idea is thought too outlandish to be mentioned. Plot possibilities come pouring out: What if the hero pulls the heroine from the Thames only to fall in love with her wet hair? But what if he's always hated redheads and she's a carrot-top? What if they are marooned together at a country inn? What if he hates her father? What if she loathes his mother? What if . . . ? Well, you get the idea. The important thing is to throw out any and every idea that comes to mind, no matter how crazy it seems. The right ones will float to the surface soon enough.

Often, even the original idea will get lost along the way, replaced with something better or expanded out of all recognition. The plotting for my third book, *The Unlikely Rivals,* began with just two words: "scavenger hunt." The idea disappeared entirely early on, but the central notion of some kind of question remained and became the basis for the book as it finally came out.

Once the bare bones of the plot and characters are decided on, I begin to flesh them out. When I have an outline of from fifteen to twenty pages, I send it off to my editor for her okay.

At the end of each day I spend some time thinking through the next day's work. I usually do this lying in bed at night, letting the scene play itself out in my tired but fully relaxed brain. The next morning I needn't agonize over "What happened next?"

When the whole story is told, I go back to the beginning and start rewriting. I check the accuracy of every historical fact. I make sure I haven't changed the color of the hero's eyes halfway through. I clean up murky writing and sloppy syntax, pare, trim, expand, or contract as necessary.

And then it's done! I take a vacation until the next story starts trying to kick its way out of my brain.

I enjoyed my years in theater, but I haven't missed them even once since I set pen to paper to begin *Amelia*. The work's not always easy. Sometimes it's like pulling teeth to get down one page. Some days I wonder what horrid crime I could have committed, unknowingly, to have earned such punishment.

But mostly I glory in my good fortune. I've had a chance to journey to another time and place and to get to know some intriguing characters, to ride in elegant carriages and waltz the night away in the arms of a handsome Marquis.

A Lighthearted Plot

BY MARION CHESNEY
author of eighteen Regency romances

One of the first things to grasp is that the Regency romance is fun. It is a frivolity with a lighthearted plot. It is a comedy of modes and manners. It does not need to contain any particularly dramatic action, unlike, say, a gothic.

It is essential to know the history of the period thoroughly—more so than in any other category of book I know. It is necessary to know not only the outline of history, but also the actual *feel* of the time: how they spoke, what they wore, what they ate, *how* they ate. The look of the streets, the lighting, the types of carriages. And above all, it is essential to know all the intricate social taboos that were imposed on a young debutante of that period.

A Regency romance is an escape from a harsh world where macho seems all, and courtesy, style, and good manners sometimes seem to have been forgotten. The hero is handsome, well-dressed, and above all *polite*. The heroine may be intelligent and have a mind of her own, but she must be extremely feminine. Speech is important. Dialogue between the hero and heroine should be light and witty. It is important to avoid modern words and phrases. It is not necessary to be *too* accurate. For example, although Britain was at war with France, the atmosphere was different than it was in the First and Second World Wars, when everything German was heartily detested.

French modes and manners were slavishly copied. The debutantes interlarded their conversation with a lot of French words and phrases, often not very accurately used. Some of the Regency debutantes would sound to us a bit like Miss Piggy. It is a personal choice, but I mostly avoid the use of French phrases, since it is likely to irritate any reader who does not understand French.

Then, much as you love the dashing lord you are writing about, you must not start feeling guilty about him because he is an aristocrat and start making him found orphanages or soup kitchens. An aristocrat was in many ways a farm manager. Now, if you were writing about, say, a modern-day company director on Wall Street, you would surely not feel obliged to make him run along the Bowery saving souls to justify his wealth. They were very rich, but not all of them were idle. If they took no interest in their estates or the welfare of their tenants and tenant farmers, then they were apt to lose money and eventually their lands.

You sometimes have to discard some history because it is going to spoil the escapist fun of the romance. Some historians even do this. Sir Arthur Bryant's splendid history of the period, *The Age of Elegance,* is packed full of fascinating detail, yet he chooses to give us a picture of a happy, buccolic countryside full of jolly people dancing around the maypole and rather glosses over the terrible harvests and the fact that workers were dropping dead in the fields from starvation.

Captain Gronow, who fought in the Peninsular Wars with the Duke of Wellington and who made his London debut at Almack's, wrote his recollections of the Regency period in 1862.

Remembering the dandies, he writes:

> How unspeakably odious—with a few brilliant exceptions, such as Alvancy and others—were the dandies of forty years ago. They were a motley crew, with nothing remarkable about them but their insolence. They were generally not high born, nor rich, nor very good-looking, nor clever, nor agreeable; and why they arrogated to themselves the right of setting up their own fancied superiority on a self-raised pedestal, and despising their betters, Heaven only knows. They were generally middle-aged, some even elderly men, had large appetites and weak digestions, gambled freely, and had no luck. They hated everybody, and abused everybody, and would sit together in White's bay window. . . . They swore a good deal, never laughed, had their own particular slang, and looked hazy after dinner,

and had most of them been patronised at one time or another by Brummell and the Prince Regent. . . .

Thank Heaven, that miserable race of used-up dandies has long been extinct! May England never look upon their like again!

So there you have it. An authentic Regency voice telling you what they were really like. But for me the dandies in the bay window of White's club in St. James's will forever be dashing and elegant, broaching their sixth bottle of port and eyeing the world through long quizzing glasses.

P. G. Wodehouse's famous character Bertie Wooster says that he always wanted to be one of those Regency bucks, one of those chappies who slayed the girls with a look from beneath his smiling eyelids while he flicked an infinitesimal piece of dust from the impeccable Mechlin lace of his cravat.

There's a bit of Regency romance in all of us. We all want the hero to be forever witty, forever bantering, forever rich.

The true Regency romance should supply women with an amusing hour or so's escape without insulting their intelligence.

An Explanation of the Regency

BY ELIZABETH MANSFIELD

author of fourteen Regency romances

My family is quite literary. We read Tolstoy and Byron and Gide and Sophocles and Bellow and Donald Barthelme. So it isn't as if I don't know what literature is. I've taught English lit on the high school and college level for years. No one has to tell me that Regencies aren't high on the list of "serious" literature.

But they aren't meant to be. Regencies are written to be entertainments—diversions. However, if entertainments are to be really diverting, they must be good. Otherwise they *are* a waste of time, because poor ones don't, in the end, really entertain.

But if Regencies aren't "serious" reading, you can take my word for it that they're serious writing. A good Regency must be stylish, witty, original, historically accurate, sophisticatedly peopled, and ingeniously plotted. One must be a good writer to write a good book. One must create, one must research, one must care.

I write Regencies for fun and profit. I used to love to read them, and now I love to write them. I write them with full respect for my readers—they are people like me. They are people who like to read; therefore, they have better vocabularies than the average, they can spot an overly contrived plot, a phony character, or a line of dialogue that couldn't ever be uttered by a living human being in *any* historical period.

So, listen . . . I ain't Tolstoy . . . but then, nobody else but Tolstoy is Tolstoy, either.

To be completely honest, I'll admit here and now that I'm proud of every one of my dozen or so Regencies. Despite what that journalist said above, they exhibit "real" writing. And they haven't kept me from writing plays, articles, etc.

Regencies are not a waste of time to read for those people who are entertained by them, any more than a movie one enjoys is a waste of time or a tennis game is a waste of time.

The trouble with the Regency as a type is that the vast majority of readers and book buyers don't know what it is. They don't know that a Regency is something special. And to explain it takes a lot of effort.

Why? Just what is a Regency? What's so special about a thirty-year period of English history that gave it a special fictional category all its own?

I think Regency writers and readers know the answer: Jane Austen and Georgette Heyer. It's their period. For some readers, those two writers are the only ones whose romances are worth reading.

Jane Austen and Georgette Heyer did for the Regency what Charlotte Brontë and Daphne du Maurier did for the gothic romance. The first created it and the second popularized it. And they left their readers hungry for more. That's where we come in. We try to fill the empty space the originators left behind.

They say the popularity of the Regency is declining. I'm not surprised. Publishers have overproduced them, thinking they'd sell like the sexy historicals. (They won't. Sorry.) In their eagerness to outproduce each other, they've encouraged writers to try them who were not suited to the genre. The publishers believe that anyone, given the right formula, can write Regencies. That is not true. Even though many Regencies are category fiction, they can't be written by formula. Remember that Regency readers are admirers of Jane Austen, and consequently far from fools.

The people who buy the sex-fantasy historicals are probably not the same ones who buy Regencies. One of the reasons has to do with attitudes toward sex. Some people believe that love and sex are the same; they probably don't read. Some people believe that sex acts lead to love; they probably are male. Some people believe that love leads to the sex act; they will probably like Regencies.

Sex existed during the Regency. It was even discussed. When Lydia Bennet ran off with a roué in Austen's *Pride and Prejudice,* every one of her neighbors knew exactly why the girl had to be married once it became known that they'd been gone overnight. But the attitudes toward sex—and toward talking about it—were different from ours, and therefore have to be handled differently in a Regency. A proper Regency heroine would never indulge in a sex act with a stranger (as one did in a Regency I recently came across) just to see what intercourse was all about. The behavior of the characters must be appropriate to the time. Characters, like real human beings, are prisoners of their times, even if they are also unique and idiosyncratic.

Every book, however, has something of the author in it . . . and the author's attitudes are shaped by his time. Therefore, none of my heroes are anti-Semitic, even though anti-Semitism was prevalent among the aristocracy of Regency England. Nor are my heroines namby-pamby slaves to men, although the laws and attitudes of the period were decidedly male-favoring. A writer can, with discretion and some semblance of verisimilitude, create the world in her own way. We writers must be permitted *some* revisionism.

The answers to most problems in writing Regencies, as in writing any fiction, must be, in the end, personal. I, for example, don't like what I call overactive plotting—stories in which there are very villainous villains, artificially contrived obstacles to the happy ending, violent confrontations with blood and gore. I prefer the conflicts to come from the characters' flaws or from small domestic misunderstandings that might have arisen in real life. Georgette Heyer is a model of the active-plot school, while Jane Austen's plots move slowly and center about minor upheavals of domestic life. Austen is my mentor in regard to plotting, but not everyone likes her sort of story. Each writer must find her own story and her own way of telling it.

There are hundreds of other questions of Regency style and content that bear discussing. But after all the talk, in the last analysis each of us must answer them for herself, in the solitude of the workroom in front of the blank sheet in the typewriter.

For me, despite the above examples of the lack of respect I sometimes suffer, the writing of Regencies has been sheer delight. I spend wonderful waking hours in a world that, within the bounds of historical reality, is shaped in its particular details by my imagination and peopled by creations of my own. The work, like virtue, is very much its own reward. It's a lovely bonus to be paid for it.

How to Write Today's Gothic

BY VIRGINIA COFFMAN
author of twenty-four romances

There is always an eerie feeling about a true gothic novel. The laws of nature seem about to be bent, twisted. The unbelievable and terrifying threatens the protagonist, but if it is a gothic romance, then a scene of someone vomiting pea soup is definitely going to hurt the romantic aspect.

If you are drawn to reading gothic romances, chances are you already have an active imagination. It's pretty obvious that you allow it free rein, or you would throw the book away the minute the heroine wanders off to an attic or cellar unattended. But it is possible to do everything the masters warn you not to do if you try for that eerie note built in from the very beginning, plus a levelheaded lead—heroine, hero, or even a salty companion—who puts down such "nonsense" at every turn. But make your false dangers amusing, not absurd and boring red herrings.

I wrote *Moura* in the 1950s and my publisher said, "Don't call it a gothic. No one today ever heard of the word." But I had deliberately written it as a kind of tour de force. The great nineteenth-century *Uncle Silas* by Sheridan Le Fanu had the classic ingredients: a Wicked Uncle, an Endangered Niece, a Cruel Housekeeper, and an ancient house that was falling apart. I made the Wicked Uncle my hero, Edmond Moura. The sweet, endangered sixteen-year-old niece became the Monster, and the Cruel Housekeeper was my heroine, Anne Wicklow.

Anthony Boucher of the *New York Times* said I had revived the nineteenth-century gothic. Ironically, the success of the book cancelled out what I originally intended, to turn the elements of the gothic upside down. So I wouldn't advise you to put your heart into writing an exposé of the gothic romance, because these always turn into genuine gothics with a little humor, not an exposé at all. And if it fails, no one will care.

You can be just as wildly romantic and spooky as you like, so long as you pave the way, especially with a little humor that laughs at the absurdity just before the absurd danger becomes all too real.

It seems to me that the main difference between gothic romances and suspense romances is the degree of the unnatural found in gothics, meaning, in this case, those elements that seem to be against the laws of nature.

Suppose your heroine has her picture taken outside a pub in Belfast. An IRA terrorist is accidentally photographed behind her, though his alibi for a bombing puts him somewhere else. Heroine is pursued for four hundred pages without knowing why. Chances are, the danger here is "suspense," not "gothic." It deals with natural elements, logical action.

The gothic scene can still be classic. Two or three years ago a friend who worked in the management of the Paris Opera House took me backstage through that magnificent baroque series of halls, passages, rehearsal rooms, lifts, etc., from the cellar to the little dusty stage just under the highest green roof. When I wrote *Lombard Heiress* I used these settings for an eerie adventure of my heroine. You will say it was easy to make gothic atmosphere out of strange mimes, all white-faced, crowding the lift with you in silence, or the ease with which you could lose your companions and find yourself alone, hearing the wind moan through that rehearsal room under the roof. After all, this was the haunt of the Phantom of the Opera.

Maybe it was easy. On the other hand, anything can adapt itself to the gothic. Recently I leased an apartment used as a "model" to induce people to buy that type of apartment. The owner hasn't yet completed escrow, so he put me into a larger (empty) apartment. I have stored all my furnishings and possessions except my Smith-Corona until the escrow is complete, so I am living in a large, empty, rather luxurious apartment on the sixteenth floor with a couch, a fold-up chair, four TV trays, a typewriter table, and plastic (not tin) dinner plates saved from TV dinners. Most of the apartment hasn't a stick of furniture. I lie on the floor when answering the telephone.

True, we are used to overfurnished gothic romances. But there is something eerie about living high above Reno with its bright city lights, and the exquisite fall colors along the river, while all around me is a vast, echoing emptiness. In a twenty-three-story high rise, fifteen years old, people have certainly died. Who died in this apartment? Is there anything remaining here of them? Even the atmosphere?

Of course, I haven't considered the romantic hero part of this condo classic. That could be my landlord, for instance, an attractive Latin type, or even one of two deputy sheriffs my sister and her husband and I met recently when the car vapor-locked. They found us a motel in a town famous for only one thing, the biggest brothel in Nevada. They parked and waited to see if the clerk would take us in (to the motel, not the brothel) with our eight-pound Shih-Tzu. Then they waved to us and drove away. True heroes, both!

Gothic romances can occur anywhere, even in empty, modern high rise apartments. And maybe we missed a bet. How about that brothel sitting out there in the sagebrush, surrounded by the moaning wind and mysterious dark figures trudging over the path to its door in the dead of night?

Like Alfred Hitchcock, gothic novelists in the 1980s often find there can be more suspense and "cauld grue" in a Midwest cornfield at noon than in a dank cellar at midnight. Aside from actually caring what happens to your heroine (hero?), the trick is to build up the atmosphere, interspersed with a realistic note (often humor) as the false fear subsides, and then sock it to 'em! The reader wants to feel that she/he is heading into spine-chilling or at least titillating danger. But today's gothics don't rule out humor, used as a denial of danger. In *North by Northwest,* everyone, including Cary Grant's mother, laughs when he claims in a crowded elevator that two men behind him intend to kill him. We may laugh, but we feel that primordial childhood fear that "no one will believe me."

In fact, if you want to use a haunted house, it's not impossible, providing you have the strong inner vision of it. You can make fun of the spookiness, show the house as dimensional, real, then bring on the big guns of terror. There can be several absurd moments that end in laughs before the real danger comes along. False danger ending in a laugh of relief is a wonderful way to point up the terror the reader fears is about to arrive—and does.

In the movie *Uninvited* (from a marvelous ghost novel), we expect the evil ghost to appear at any minute. The whole audience screams when the double doors blow open. Then we laugh, realizing nobody is there. Seconds later the hero starts to close the door, and the ghost is waiting for him, above him, on the staircase. The thrill of terror and shock is twice as great because we had let down our guard and laughed at ourselves a moment before.

In *The Old Dark House,* an early talkie, they discuss the terrifying, hideous creature in the attic. When he sneaks out, creeping down the stairs, we all roar. What a pathetic little fellow! We pity him after the horror buildup. Later, when he is revealed with all his horrible propensities, he is twice as terrifying because of that unexpected element.

Staircases are great for gothic novels. Someone once said Mrs. Danvers dominated the play made from *Rebecca* even though she only appears in four scenes. In every scene she is placed above the leads, on a balcony or staircase. She never seems to *arrive* on scene. She is simply there, all in black, a horrible basilisk.

Generally, the staircase figure dominates from a position above, but in Henry James's classic *Turn of the Screw* the malign ghost, Peter Quint, actually stands at the bottom of the staircase looking up at the governess. He has cut off her escape. He provides greater horror because we have formerly seen him only outside and at a distance.

These eerie creatures who give gothic novels their chill of terror need not be ghosts. Mrs. Danvers was real enough. So was Mr. Rochester's wife in *Jane Eyre,* though a rather one-dimensional horror. But then, the romance outweighed the terror in that classic.

The thing is to make the reader wonder uneasily if the "thing" *is* a ghost, and to have a good, realistic explanation after.

Mirrors are as good in a gothic of the '80s as they were a hundred years ago in *Uncle Silas*. There is a great moment in which the heroine sits at a French dresser, having seen that Uncle Silas (whom we suspect is a monster) is lying apparently ill and asleep in his four-poster bed across the room. She looks down an instant, and suddenly, when she looks up, she sees him in the mirror only inches behind her, silvery hair, silvery eyes, and smiling, moist lips. The shock of his sudden appearance is another screamer. Even if he were innocent it would scare us.

Haven't you gotten a shiver sometimes when you thought you were alone in a room and suddenly saw someone else close behind you, even a loved one?

Of course, my agent, Jay Garon, gave me sound advice when he said, "Give your protagonists dimensions. Make them real, with a past and a present." But do they have a future? That's a gothic dread.

The First Gay Gothic: Gaywyck

The cover tells you immediately that it's a gothic. There's the palatial house on the estate in the background, the threatening sky, the shadowy, sinister garden. In the foreground, a restless sea beats on the rocks, splashing two figures—a tall dark man in a black cape resting his hand on the shoulder of a fragile-looking blond.

But there's a catch. The blond is male too.

"He was innocent . . . until he fell captive to the brooding master and sinister secrets of *Gaywyck*," the cover copy reads, and at that point it's obvious that what looked so familiar is something different after all. It's *Gaywyck* (Avon, 1980), the first gay gothic. Author Vincent Virga has followed all the rules for the gothics—but one.

The novel is a "serious gothic," says the author, "a true gothic. That is, it isn't camp, or a spoof on popular gothic novels; its roots are firmly set in the Brontës, Mrs. Radcliffe, and Horace Walpole." *Gaywyck* doesn't make fun of the gothic traditions; it unashamedly uses and borrows them for its own purposes.

Many of the "borrowings" are little homages to classic gothics like *Jane Eyre* ("Reader, I was dumbfounded") and *Rebecca* ("Last night I dreamed I climbed again that columbine-covered stairwell. In my dreams, its walls were aflame."). Astute readers will find references to Agnes Grey, *The Mysteries of Udolpho,* and even James M. Barrie and Eugene O'Neill. The only thing borrowed from Anya Seton's American classic gothic *Dragonwyck* is the title.

The plot and conventions of Virga's novel are all from the standard gothic mold; the house with a dark secret, the madwoman in the attic, incest (several kinds here), secret rooms, and closets with trapdoors. The characters here are a young man, Robert Wyte, who is hired by the brooding, fabulously wealthy Donough Gaylord to catalogue the 75,000-volume library in Gaylord's mansion on Long Island's south shore. There is the usual assortment of minor characters—loyal friends, intriguing servants, devious house attendants, faithful and faithless family retainers—all gay, of course. Any parallels with prim governesses and craggy-faced masters harboring terrible secrets are cheerfully accepted!

Virga claims to have borrowed some lines from movies, too. "I was blocked in my writing one day and idly turned on the television to hear Charles Boyer (in *Back Street*) saying, 'I'll fill every corner of my life with your love.' It was just the line I needed. I went right back to the typewriter."

His greatest problem was finding a publisher. "My agent set up an auction and no one came," recalls Virga with a bemused smile. Finally, Avon books bought the novel for paperback publication. (They have a successful series of gay books.) The gamble paid off. The first printing of 45,000 books sold out, and a second printing was done.

The mass-readership response was quite positive. The book

has been used in some writing courses, which discussed its literary value and power to evoke the turn of the century. (Virga's detailed research is quite thorough and exemplary.)

The author painstakingly tackled the period in which *Gaywyck* takes place, even having two lawyers in the book working on real court cases of that time. "And when I knew I'd be talking about gardens," he says, "I went back to gardening columns in old newspapers."

Working in this manner, Virga unearthed a number of surprising facts. "I discovered that the wristwatch was around back then—something I then used to figure prominently in the plot. Just by thumbing through old catalogues, you discover a lot of interesting things."

Why is he a stickler for historical accuracy? "If the era is not believable," observes Virga, "it's hard making the characters inhabiting that time credible to the reader."

But this careful research is in service to a higher goal. "What I've tried to do in my writing," Virga says, "is break old role patterns. Women don't want to be thought of just as 'ladies,' and I don't think men want to be locked into tight, narrow categories, either."

Thus, love in *Gaywyck* means never having to say you're sorry for not being straight!

The Contemporary Romance Novel: The Woman Who Breaks Readers' Hearts

The top-selling female author in the world is Danielle Steel, with her 25 million readers anxiously awaiting the next tearjerker. Picasso once said that to know an artwork, you must know the man behind it and how he did it. For a complete understanding of Steel's success, a look behind the scenes is imperative. She is a hardworking professional who knows how to organize her time and talent.

While her San Francisco mansion was being remodeled, Danielle Steel worked away in a laundry room, typing over one hundred words per minute on a 1948 Olympia manual, eighteen hours a day for twelve days, to complete her novel *Crossings*.

After writing twelve published novels, which have sold more than 25 million copies and have been published in eighteen languages, Steel has evolved a loose but efficient work schedule.

Having an infinite patience for details, Steel has acquired a sixth sense of cutting tasks down to size. Once her contract is negotiated, for at least two books, Steel blocks out her work schedule for the coming months.

"I sit down with the contract and set up the whole year. I schedule vacation and time off. I calculate my vacation and time off. I calculate my time to the hour. Then I prepare an outline.

"I present it to the publisher several times. There's lots of honing, lots of rewriting. I have no ego about rewriting the way they tell me to. I'm in the business for the pleasure, but I'm in it just as much for the business," she says.

Steel works on other things while the publishers "gnaw on the outline," she explains. Once the outline is approved, the first drafts goes quickly. "It's very intense. I usually work twenty hours a day, sleeping two to four hours. This goes on seven days a week for six weeks." The household is trained to expect these virtual disappearances by Steel, who prefers to write on her old-fashioned manual typewriter. "I've spent more money keeping it repaired than if I'd bought a sophisticated new model," she says.

Danielle is very sentimental. "Readers tell me how much they cried reading my stories." She sighs. "I tell them I know, I cried when I was writing them, sometimes on the eleventh draft at six o'clock in the morning. People say they can't put the books down when they're reading them, but neither can I when I'm writing them."

Writing her first novels was a far cry from her life today. She first holed up for three months in a San Francisco hotel, decked out in her habitual writing uniform of flannel nightgown, with perhaps a sweat shirt for warmth, forgoing baths and shampoos when the writing fever was upon her. To her amazement, she finished the book, *Going Home,* and sold it to Pocket Books. Her next three efforts were turned down by several publishers for almost five years. She was about to give up and try to become more active in her religion (Christian Science) when her seventh book hit the mark, in 1977. Dell published *Passion's Promise,* followed by *Now and Forever* (which was filmed with Cheryl Ladd in Australia), *The Promise* (which became a feature film), and more. A few titles later, Dell published *Palomino* as a trade paperback in 1981; then Delacorte brought out *The Ring, Remembrance,* and *Crossings* in hardcover.

In the immediate future Steel intends to devote more time to her four children, husband, and new San Francisco mansion. It is here that Steel will eventually settle down, with her old Olympia, a head full of ideas, and her well-honed work habits.

Steel's new second-floor office, considerably larger than the old laundry room, holds no mementos or special appeal, but the ceiling is painted with nebulous clouds like a whipped-cream heaven.

"I'd like to work another fifty years and write another seventy-five books," she says. "I really enjoy spinning the yarns."

How to Write Like Danielle Steel

BY ROSANNE KOHAKE

author of two historical romances

Danielle Steel has been a phenomenally successful writer of long contemporary romances, and certainly a beginning romance writer can learn from her work. Her books are very much like soap operas, similar in characterization and plot, with melodrama and pathos enough to make the average reader hear violin music in the background.

The winning Steel formula begins with a lovely, cultured heroine, inherently artistic in nature, raised with all the advantages of wealth, yet totally unspoiled by money, beauty, and talent. She must wear elegant, stylish, ultraexpensive clothing, which will be described in detail down to the last button, but the most important things in her life will have nothing to do with clothing. She will attend parties with terribly interesting and important people (ambassadors, presidents, business magnates, etc.) and will decorate her home in a wonderful, tasteful blend of priceless antiques, plush Asian carpets, and expensive but functionally comfortable pillows, chairs, and sofas. Furnishings are very important in Steel novels. They provide a setting of wealth and luxury that few romance readers will ever experience personally.

Yet you must make it ever so clear that all that money doesn't bring happiness, so that your readers won't feel too bad as they curl up on a plaid Herculon sofa to read the next chapter.

As far as the story line goes, there are two basic Steel plots to choose from. Plot number one begins with a heroine who has an unusually close relationship with her father, and is attracted to an older, sophisticated, wealthy man as a sort of replacement father figure. This older man provides the heroine with her first love affair. He is a vital, attractive, slightly graying man who still plays tennis every day and keeps up with men half his age. The May-December attraction culminates in a temporarily successful marriage, until the December half of the partnership becomes too old, too sick, or too tired to fulfill the heroine's needs. A Steel heroine thus abandoned never goes out looking for love, however. She encounters it by chance. The new hero is a handsome younger man who wants nothing more than to love and protect the heroine. Their instant, undeniable attraction, which strikes like a bolt of lightning, causes the heroine no end of pain and guilt. She cannot fall out of love with this younger man, who makes her feel alive and has brought her a sudden, piercing awareness of her own needs. Neither can she be unfaithful to the husband she once loved so deeply, and still loves as a friend. Round and round she goes, feeling terrible aching loneliness when she does the "right" thing, and terrible aching guilt when she succumbs to her humanness and does the "wrong" thing. About this time, the wise old husband becomes aware of his wife's problem, and would willingly free her to pursue the younger man, in gratitude for the wonderful years she has given him. But she's far too noble to allow that, knowing that he will face the rest of his life alone. She'd rather suffer through a few more chapters than live with the fact that she abandoned him in his need.

Finally, when the reader can stand it not a moment longer, the heroine's husband does everyone a favor and dies. By this time, though, the heroine is so fraught with emotions of loss and guilt that she cannot run happily to her sweetheart's patient, loving arms. She stoically suffers through a few more pages before fate or a well-meaning friend finally resolves her love life, and gives the reader a happy ending.

Plot number two involves a heroine who initially chooses a man her own age, usually a terribly handsome and talented hunk pursued by every woman within a hundred-mile radius. Together, they build a perfect life, a dreamy happiness that is envied by everyone. But the dream ends abruptly in one way or another. Her "perfect" husband is unfaithful to her, or suffers an untimely death, and she is left to pick up the pieces of her life and find love again. The second time around, of course, the path of love is anything but smooth. Sometimes this woman goes through three or four heartbreaking relationships before she finds "Mr. Right," and in the end she has suffered just as much as the heroine in plot number one.

No matter which of these plots you choose for your novel, your hero must be a handsome, sensitive man who has been through an ugly divorce recently, or is stuck in a loveless marriage for the sake of his children. The deep scars he carries from this earlier relationship gone awry make him appreciate the honest, affectionate nature of the heroine.

Your hero and heroine must adore children. They must be perfect, understanding parents, and they must never lose their tempers with their own kids or anyone else's. If the heroine has a baby during the book, she must be prepared to rush to the hospital with a lollipop in one hand and a bottle of lotion in the other, so that she can deliver by the Lamaze method of natural childbirth. Her only other option is enduring a terribly painful, traumatic delivery that will affect both her and her child for the rest of their lives.

If circumstances prevent your heroine from having children of her own, she must somehow manage to take someone else's misunderstood darling under her loving wing.

Your Steel novel will not be complete without a hard-as-nails, scratch-your-way-to-the-top bitch who uses a lot of foul language and makes life difficult for everyone. The hero of the story can match this villainess word for word if he puts his mind to it, but your heroine never trades insults with anyone. She may use an off-color word now and then, but mostly she spends her time suffering and feeling guilty.

Perhaps the most entertaining and lively portions of your story will be the dialogue. Initial exchanges between hero and heroine ought to bounce with levity and yet carry an undercurrent of serious romantic attraction. Later on, their words must gush with sensitivity and understanding for each other. The bitchy villainess must scream incessant insults at everyone, and use expressions like "For Chrissake!" and "What in the hell . . .?" and "goddamn bastard!" And your heroine ought to have a sympathetic friend (male or female) who listens and feels ever so sorry for her.

The most important key to writing a successful Steel novel, however, is to write a first chapter that gets the reader firmly on the hook. The prose ought to be polished and flow smoothly. Later on, your book may become an English teacher's nightmare, with as many run-on sentences, fragments, and repetitious statements as you'd care to insert. Just be sure you use plenty of phrases like "felt it in her gut," "felt it deep in her soul," "felt completely torn apart," and "felt a stab of agony deep in her heart." These are Steel's most effective tools. Use enough of them and your readers are sure to feel so sorry for the heroine that they forget grammar altogether, and just want to get on with the story to give the poor girl a break.

Advice on the Contemporary Romance Novel

INTERVIEW WITH PAMELA STRICKLER
editor, Ballantine

Ballantine Book's innovative Love and Life series was the first short modern romance line of its type when it appeared in 1982. A mini-mainstream problem novel for today's woman, it offers a new writer exciting opportunities to develop into a major contemporary novelist. At first, guidelines were available, but eventually, as the line developed, the only editorial advice was length—50,000 to 60,000 words; heroines—American, ages twenty-five to fifty; and setting—American.

"I want every book to be different," says Strickler, who is also the editor of Ballantine's historical romance novels.

"I look for writers with a very special unique voice, with a lot of ideas and very intriguing plots. At present, I'm interested in problem novels, women's interior novels, for Love and Life.

This means the heroine goes through interior thinking and looking through the problem to solve things in her life.''

What advice does she have for new writers? "They should just sit down and write. They must have a story inside them, otherwise they don't have anything to write. I also think they should write the story in scenes, rather than narration. Scenes with description and dialogue.''

What is the most common fault with the manuscripts she rejects for this series? "A lot of them are perfectly adequate, solid stories, but in my opinion the writers don't have that special voice, that really intriguing plot. They're just not fresh and different. And some don't realize that our books are 'problem' contemporary novels.''

To give an example of Love and Life's problem novels, Strickler explains: "One of our titles, *Searching*, was about a woman who is asked to marry the man she has been with for several years, but she has to go into her past (she had given up a child for adoption ten years before) and she has to work through her conflicts (this was both a problem *and* an interior story) to satisfy herself before she can start a new life and family.

"Another title, *Tomorrow*, has the premise that if a woman is given a chance to have a new life because of a fluke, she takes that opportunity to make herself strong, and then she goes back and faces her old life.''

The audience for Love and Life is not necessarily the one that reads Harlequins regularly. "We don't consider ourselves category romances, even though we have the same length,'' explains Strickler. "But we are getting some of the other romance readers who are over forty and enjoy our modern romances.''

Romance is not the primary focus, but problems and quality writing are. One problem that cannot beset a Love and Life heroine is cancer. "Fighting cancer is a genre of its own,'' the editor says. "That's the only taboo at the moment for a writer in my Love and Life series.''

What does she think of the trend toward "glitz" novels in the contemporary field? "I like them, but I object to writers who name drop and throw in labels when they should be describing these things. I will publish some 'glitz' books, but I'll also bring out at the same time the story of a waitress in the middle of the dessert. Our line strives to give as much variety as possible.

"I'm very fond of 'rich' books. A book that has a lot of great atmosphere and description, even a lyrical writing style, appeals to me. As long as writers really have the story *inside* and really want to tell it, they have the best chance of being published at Ballantine. So far, our Love and Life books are written in the third person, but they are not confined to one viewpoint. I think the first-person viewpoint is tough to make work.''

> Love and live is now out of print and the authors developed for this experimental new series are now writing the longer contemporary novels.

Romance in Science Fiction and Fantasy

Is there room for a free spirit with literary leanings in the world of romance fiction? Can an author who writes historical romances or contemporary romances find a niche for romance writing in the science fiction and fantasy field?

The answer to the above is: Yes, and very nicely, thank you.

It goes without saying that a writer who wants to combine the genres must be well read in both. The Queen of sci-fi romance, Anne McCaffrey, nourished herself by reading authors such as Andre Norton, Edmund Hamilton, Avram Davidson, Damon Knight, Frederick Pohl, Leigh Brackett, and Zenna Henderson.

McCaffrey is an accomplished romantic novelist, having written gothics, and is now an even more accomplished science-fiction writer. It was when she combined the two genres that she caught a larger reading public than most science-fiction writers ever experience.

What is her advice for new writers? ''I can only describe what I do. I'm a storyteller, and I'm telling the story to myself as much as to the reader. So I generally start from a situation, a conflict between personalities, or between people and their society, or a 'society' that I create in science fiction. That's a good way to emphasize a modern-day problem—remove it by a couple of centuries and cultures, and take another look. I've noticed that if a situation is valid in terms of human interactions, the plot will grow from the conflict. Some books have written themselves, others have taken a lot of work. For instance, I had written 370 pages of the second version of *Dragonquest* and could not get the book to write itself further. Betty Ballantine, my editor, suggested that I come up to her place for the weekend and we would 'do' the book together. Examining scenes, word by word, can be a rather harrowing experience, even for an experienced author. Betty zeroed in on the problem. I was telling the story from the wrong character viewpoint. The moment she suggested that *Dagonquest* was F'nor's story rather than F'lar's and Less's, the rest of the novel slotted into focus.''

Another SF influenced author, Karen Juneman, who writes as ''Flanne Devlin,'' gave readers one of the first UFO romances, in a nice little book, *Alien Encounter* (1981). The man and woman fall in love during a UFO incident in their town.

Carole Nelson Douglas, a romance author, made a successful entrée when she wrote *Six of Swords* for Ballantine's fiction and fantasy series. Soon after its appearance in 1982, it made the SF-fantasy best-seller lists in such ''unromantic'' company as *E.T., Star Trek II,* and *Bladerunner*. She may well have opened the door for another outlet for romance writers.

My First Si-Fi Fantasy

BY CAROLE NELSON DOUGLAS

author of Six of Swords

The cover copy from *Six of Swords* evokes the romance formula: Boy meets girl, they strike sparks, etc. The novel is anything but that, yet a fantasy is a quest story, too, simply with more universal applications than the mating game. Readers of *Six of*

Swords get romance in its purest literary form—adventure, wonder, self-discovery, and the finding of common cause with another—romance as it was when the word was coined from the French to describe the *Song of Roland* and other chivalrous sagas.

Women did not play major roles in such tales. Perhaps that's why romance fiction evolved, to make women heroines in our own books when we could only be noble mothers, evil seductresses, and pedestaled ladies in men's stories. Women's fiction became intensely concerned with relationships between men and women characters, specifically. And characters and how they dovetail form the joints of all my fiction—and of romance in its largest sense.

Irissa and Kendric in *Six of Swords* have opposite attributes that make it difficult to trust each other: She is the intuitive seeress, he the blunt man of action. Yet they need each other, and that need, if not uncomplicated, touches on deeper societal needs.

When Irissa wants to elude Geronfrey, a sorcerer who has revealed that the first man to share her bed will share her powers, she is so resolved that he will not use her that *she* uses another. She appears at Kendric's bedside in the night:

> "Is there something the matter?"
>
> Her attention focused on Kendric, a Kendric who looked puzzled and rumpled and totally innocent of guile. It was not the question she needed, but she searched herself for a reply. Her sensations centered finally, not on her need to defraud Geronfrey of his desires, but, oddly enough, on her bare feet growing icy beneath the rich, remote drapings that masked them.
>
> "My feet are cold," she finally complained, like a child roused in the night by some inescapable physical need.
>
> Kendric considered the statement dumbfoundedly. Then comprehension lit his features more brightly than the shining hilt, and he reached out and drew her into the bed, the gown dragging behind her until he pulled once on the bulky golden orb that anchored it and all that swathing black slipped into a puddle onto the floor.
>
> There were, Irissa thought as dark enveloped them, occasionally more satisfactory ways of dealing with things than sorcery.

In enlarging on the romantic theme, it's helpful to draw on the common mythology rooted in the reader's subconscious. I often refer to fairy tales in my fiction, especially the Cinderella story, which pinpoints the moment when a young woman confronts her wish to attract a man and dreams that this alone will solve her problems. It is as she confronts the female "role" of achieving through romantic upward mobility that she is most vulnerable in her new-found vanity. The Cinderella transformation scene and her lost slipper, with images right out of Disney, symbolically lace my books, historical and modern. Irissa traverses most of *Six of Swords* wearing unisex trousers, tunic, and boots; the black velvet gown that she is "latched" into by a gold fastening in the above scene is a gift from Geronfrey and a temptation to her vanity. She is barefoot because she wisely chose not to wear his offered shoes, a symbol of confinement.

So, do my books end with "And they lived happily ever after"? In my novels, it's never quite so obvious. Realism will always have its day in court, the better for readers to believe the happy ending they envisioned lurking just around the turn of the last page.

9

Can a Man Write Romance?

Maryland Avenue
Royal Oak, Michigan

July 2

Dear Ms. Falk,

I'm Paul Reynolds, Rosie's husband. I feel a little embarrassed writing to you. After all the kindness you showed my wife, the last thing I wanted to do was trouble you further.

But I've a pressing problem and I don't know who else to turn to. Ms. Falk, do you think a man can write a romance novel?

Rosie is having the time of her life getting published. She's on her way, and I'm still helping her in every way I can. However, now I have the urge to write one too.

I have a story in mind, but I won't bore you with it. However, I do want to know what the pitfalls are—or is it impossible for a man to write these women's books?

Sincerely yours,
Paul Reynolds

From the Desk of Kathryn Falk

July 16

Dear Paul,

I most certainly do think a man can write romance. My friend Tom E. Huff has been wowing readers as Jennifer Wilde since he wrote his first historical romance, <u>Love's Tender Fury</u>.

Since his debut, many men have become romance writers. Publishers

314

have found that women readers prefer to see a romantic-sounding female name on a romance cover, but they don't object to a male author revealing himself _after_ he has established himself with a few titles.

The difficulty a man faces writing a romance is: Can he think and feel like a woman? Many men make the mistake of not learning a woman's feelings during the sexual moments, and instead describe what the hero is feeling. The hero's inner dialogue is not in a category romance; because of the limited point of view, only the woman's feelings are expressed through inner dialogue.

Men have a tendency to use harsh words, such as _flank_ or _inviting mound,_ and verbs of _pushing, pulling, tugging._ That's okay for a Mickey Spillane novel but not a romance. The words, the feelings, the evocation of sensuality are always pretty, sensuous, and gentle.

Editors claim they know when a man has written a romance, not only because of the strong vocabulary and the focus on the man's feelings during the sexual act, but because of the degrees of intimacy. Heather Jeeves, a Mills & Boon editor, believes, "Men cannot easily describe what it's like to be made love to as a woman. They write too voyeuristically, as though they're watching through a window, not experiencing it directly."

Colette's novels are a big inspiration to male writers, because Colette is so successful at moving the reader's emotions by shades of meaning and observations. A romance reader wants to recreate the act of lovemaking in her own imagination, and doesn't want everything spelled out or described in graphic, explicit, nonpretty terms. You should light the fires of the imagination and fan the flames for your reader, and allow her to savor the intimate moments at her own pace. (Much different than male fiction.)

I've asked Vanessa Royall and Jenny Wilde to pass on some advice to you. They send regards and wish you luck!

You will not only have to write and get published, but you may soon be thinking of a proper pen name, as they did. Some authors with pseudonyms always look for their last name to begin in the middle of the alphabet, somewhere around _G._ The reason being that it's best to not be an _A_ or a _Z,_ because of a cover's placement on the bookshelves. Fact? Perhaps. But Kathleen Woodiwiss isn't suffering because she's a _W,_ and neither is Jennifer Wilde.

A helpful book would be Nancy Friday's _My Secret Garden._ Women's sexual fantasies figure strongly in romances. Along with the generally acknowledged sexual fantasies, the Cinderella concept of being found, loved, and cherished should always be at the base of your plot, in some form.

Follow the formula, study the genre, tap into women's feelings and fantasies, and write sensuous, pretty prose, and you'll be on your way, Paul.

Best wishes,
Kathryn

My Secret Life: How I Became Vanessa Royall
BY MIKE HINKEMEYER
author of five historical romances

"May I speak to Vanessa Royall, please?"

"So that's who I'm going to be!" I replied.

It was my agent on the phone. I had been waiting for his call with a combination of trepidation and curiosity. My first historical romance, Flames of Desire, *was soon to be published, and while I knew a pen name would be used, I had no idea what sort of* nom de plume *Dell would invent. My own suggestion, "Melissa Harte," was considered too bland, and some of the possibilities bandied about—"Jessica Wilder," "Katherine Morsavage," "Tammy Tenacious"—did not move me close to the thrill threshold.*

"Well, what do you think of the name?" my agent asked.

"Not bad at all," I said, after momentary reflection. "It has the elegance of a British actress and the richness of an ice-cream sundae."

Is that the best of both worlds? Perhaps. My relationship with Vanessa is now five years old—not bad, as modern relationships go—and we have developed quite an affection for each other. Since I write suspense novels under my own name, I sometimes tend to be cryptic and secretive. Vanessa is open and trusting. I often dwell upon her darker side of human nature. She is filled with hope. My sentences are sparse and cutting. Hers are lush with the beauty of women, the power of men, the richness of the landscapes across which her heroines grow.

I guess you could say we complement each other. I'm interested in romance, too, like any other prototypical red-blooded American man, and Vanessa goes for just that kind of guy.

My friends and neighbors—even my relatives—have accepted my secret life with surprising equanimity, although at first they seemed a little startled to discover that the former professor they had known was possessed of the lyrical sentiment found in romantic novels. "That's just Vanessa helping me," I explained. "I'm really as remote and scholarly as ever."

But they don't believe, not anymore. Certainly not after I sent out season's greetings with a card proclaiming:

Diffidence in the defense of romance is no virtue;
Zeal in the pursuit of love is no vice.

Vanessa told me to say that.

How Can a Man Write Romance Novels?

BY MIKE HINKEMEYER (A.K.A. VANESSA ROYALL)

I never gave it much thought.

I mean, until the preparation of this piece for Kathryn posed the somewhat chauvinistic question "How Can a *Man* Write Romance Novels?" I had happily believed that my keen perception of the female psyche was responsible for my (that is, for Vanessa Royall's) success.

Several keenly perceptive women of my acquaintance, however, including my wife, suggested that I might account for my skill along different lines.

I guess they meant that there is more to writing romance than simply possessing the kind of intensely romantic nature women appreciate. After all, I gave a girl an original love poem once, ("How do I love thee? Let me count the ways . . ."), I sent flowers at least twice to the same woman, and I have never *ever* failed to "touch her hair when I pass her chair," so I've obviously mastered the basics, all right.

Little things mean a lot.

But romance, in all its glory and sorrow, is no little thing, and I suspect we all have the memories to prove it. I know I do. These recollections illustrate a paradox that has long puzzled me, but that is tremendously informative in the analysis of the contemporary romantic novel: We remember best—and enjoy most?—those wildly passionate affairs, with their moments of soaring enchantment, that in retrospect seem patently irrational. Yet this heightened sense of awareness is seldom sustained, so if we are lucky, it is the comfort and succor of long-lasting love that we eventually come to treasure.

Which of the heroines of my novels would I want desperately to take to bed?

Selena, of *Flames of Desire,* fiery, clever, loyal, and transcendingly resilient? Definitely.

Maria, of *Come Faith, Come Fire,* intelligent, patient, passionate, and determined? Absolutely.

Dey-Lor-Gyva, of *Firebrand's Woman,* with the beauty of her heritage of mixed blood, and the tenderness of her spirit? Yes again.

Kristin, of *Wild Wind Westward,* the most gorgeous of them all, and in some ways the most cunning? Sure.

Or Elizabeth, in *Seize the Dawn,* who has the strength to persevere when it seems that everything is lost, the wisdom to know that dawn will come again, and the patience to wait? Of course.

So I would gladly take *all* of them to bed (assuming they would have me!), but which of them can I see myself staying with for a long time, perhaps even marrying?

Gyva and Elizabeth.

Why?

Because, with their very natures, they encompass the paradox I mentioned above, and render it meaningless. They are mature enough to see beyond the "happy ending." With either Gyva or Elizabeth, I could have *both* the passionate affair and the long-lasting love. And countless happy endings.

Ah, fiction. It is so sweet.

I cannot speak for mankind, or even for men, but I *can* write romantic novels because I was sufficiently fortunate, both in cloistered study and in real life, to divine the sine qua nons of the genre, without which a credible tale would not be possible. What, indeed, must a man possess if he intends to write romance?

He must *appreciate* the complexity of the female nature, even though he does not understand it. What does woman *want?* asked Freud pathetically. Folly! Mysteries need not be understood to be cherished.

He must have a *sense of history*, of the real history behind dry "research." I mean by this that the prospective author of historical romances must be aware of the psychological ramifications behind the sweep of human events. If you think that you can simply "look up the facts," forget it. A writer must *feel* the hot dampness beneath those raintrees, be able to *weep* for Napoleon at Waterloo, and *thrill* with exultation when John Paul Jones says, "I have not yet begun to fight!"

Next, the writer must be able, without inhibition but with good taste, to *describe accurately* the joys of human sensual encounter, and to do this truly and well I think a person must enjoy sensuality himself (or, of course, herself). "How can you *write* about making love?" a woman once asked me at a party. "I could just *never* do that." (Probably not the only thing she can't do.)

Last, and most important, he who writes romance must have the enthusiasm and the technical ability to develop a *good strong story*. All great novels are good stories first. And that means plot, story line, scenes, characters, language, style, surprises, exuberance, and—in the case of romances—a happy ending. I still get letters because on the last page of *Flames of Desire* Selena was separated from her true love, Royce Campbell.

So we return to our paradox, do we not? I have stated that I would want a woman who would stay with me beyond the "happy ending," and yet now I am rejecting just that sort of ending. But this is merely an apparent conflict, and one that is easily resolved: Writer and reader are always in cahoots from the start. We give *each other* a happy ending. And then, with the luck of time and chance, we go on to a lasting love.

What does woman want?

Elizabeth, in *Seize the Dawn*, says it all:

"I was yours before you found me, you were mine before I found you. There would have been an emptiness in both of us if we had never met. But then we would have met in heaven. . . ."

To which her betrothed replies: "Darling, I thought we did." Poor old Freud.

The End

P.S. For those readers who still wonder just what became of Selena MacPherson and Royce Campbell in *Flames of Desire,* let me offer this: Selena escaped the British in New York, followed Royce to France, endured the French Revolution with him, and finally, with him, returned to Coldstream Castle in Scotland, in which she had grown up and which she loved as much as life. Royce and Selena lived happily ever after.

The Man Who Breaks Their Hearts: Tom E. Huff

The most successful male author of romances is Tom Huff, a.k.a. Jennifer Wilde. He thinks it's easier to write about women than when women write about them, because "I've observed them carefully for many years and I see them accurately," he says, rather smugly.

Millions of readers must agree. He's signing million-dollar contracts for his books, and his books always sell in the millions.

When Mr. Huff came out of the closet and revealed his identity (actually, People magazine revealed it, and he admitted it in Romantic Times as a headline story: "Jennifer Wilde Reveals Himself."), his publishers were a little aghast, but his sales were never affected. However, he recommends that male authors not reveal themselves until they're established with the readers, because many women do object to men writing their fantasies.

His fans agree that he has an acute sensuality that few women authors possess. He has been a professional writer for years, going back to his days as a journalist. Under his male name he has written several critically acclaimed contemporary novels (Marabelle being the most acclaimed).

But it is as Jennifer Wilde that he makes the best-seller lists, which is how he pays for his swimming pool and "security in my golden years." He has a wry and caustic wit, Jenny does.

Tom writes long novels, historical romances, and he works many months on each. One book may take a year or more, and his daily writing schedule is grueling: sometimes ten straight hours in his attic writing cell.

Many authors don't have the patience or the skill to polish and repolish like Jennifer Wilde. But he writes and rewrites until each and every sentence flows and captures the reader's imagination.

His greatest technique is sensual buildup, and he brings great credibility to the genre because of his skill. Colette is his muse.

When he's not writing, he relaxes by watching trashy movies on his TV video recorder (he adores Jayne Mansfield, so he says), eats raw cabbage and health foods—he's constantly on a diet—and acts as the telephonic confidant of spirited historical romance authors Rosemary Rogers and Shirlee Busbee. He's the friend who told me to keep this book "light and bright."

When the going gets tough, I always call Huff.

Male Pseudonyms in the Romance World

FEMALE TEAM

Felicia Andrews	Charles L. Grant
Megan Barker	Roger Longrigg
Monica Barrie	David Wind
Stephanie Blake	Jack Pearl
Rae Butler	Raymond Butler
Riva Carles	Irving Greenfield
Jenifer Dalton	David Wind
Gena Dalton	David Wind
Maggie Gladstone	Arthur Gladstone
Victoria Gordon	(An anonymous Harlequin male author)
Alicia Grace	Irving Greenfield
Louise Granville	Daniel Streib
Anne Griffin	Arthur Griffin
Jessica Howard	Monroe Schere

Rebecca James	James Elward
Robin Joseph	Robert Joseph
Jill Kearny	Ron Goulart
Fortune Kent	John Toombs
Willa Lambert	Bill Lambert
Petra Leigh	Peter Ling
Lisa Lenore	Craig Howard Broude
Rochelle Leslie	Graham Diamond
Samantha Lester	Lester Roper
Debrah Lewis	Charles L. Grant
Leila Lyons	James Conaway
Cissie Miller	Stanlee Coy
Paula Minton	Paul Little
Aurora Moore	Arthur Moore
Colleen Moore	Jon Messman
Leigh Nichols	Dean Koontz
Claudette Nicole	Jon Messman
Elisabet Norcross	Arthur Gladstone
Diana Randall	Dan Ross
Barbara Reife	Alan Reife
Clarissa Ross	Dan Ross
Vanessa Royall	Mike Hinkemeyer
Stephanie St. Clair	Donald Maas
Margaret Sebastian	Arthur Gladstone
Alana Smith	Bruce Smith
Jennifer Wilde	Tom E. Huff
Jocelyn Wide	John Toombs

MALE TEAM

Kerry Newcomb and Frank Schaeffer (a.k.a. Peter Gentry) also write as Shana Carol and Christina Savage.

10

Teaming Up to Write Romances

From the Desk of Kathryn Falk

August 1

Dear Paul,

I was out of town when your message came in. I'm sorry you are finding it lonely going. However, a collaborator may be your answer. Since Rosie is occupied with her own work, you might look around for someone among your friends, or at a writing class.

I asked several of the writing teams to give you some tips. I hope it's all helpful. Who knows, now that you're buying flowers for Rosie, you might meet up with a writing partner in the flower shop and call yourself "Ivy Vine"!

For Rosie's sake, I suggest that your collaborator not be a six-foot gorgeous blonde!

Cordially,
Kathryn

Half the Headache, Double the Fun

Some people find writing easier when they work with someone else. In today's romance writing world there are endless varieties of teams—husband and wife, mother and daughter, sister and sister, friend and friend, even triplets and quadruplets (three and four friends together).

However, the perfect collaborator does not grow on trees. Certain areas of skills must be established before getting down to the business of team writing.

The most important essential is proximity. Collaborations succeed best when the two parties live in the same neighborhood. Later on, when one member must move a distance, as recently happened to three teams, this can be dealt with, but starting out, distance hampers the project.

From the beginning, each member of the writing team must decide what each does better. Perhaps one excels at dialogue and will do most of the actual writing of it, while the other creates the basic plot, is the innovator, the one who directs the characters as if in a stage play.

Successful writing teams are aware that they worked out their compatibility and have learned to think together, to create as an ensemble. Some teams will break down the story, each working on different chapters, and then exchange them until both are satisfied.

A writing team will have to spend a lot of time together, preferably in person or on the phone, going over scenes and ideas. The team should like each other or else—like a marriage—they will not survive. Trust and respect are important ingredients here. Each must believe that the other partner is pulling her share of the workload and has enough talent to help the other.

The most famous writing teams in the romance world today started out with very humble beginnings.

In the friend-joins-friend situation, through sheer desperation the duo of Fern Michaels (Roberta Anderson and Mary Kuczkir) entered the field of romantic novels. After exploring other money-making schemes together, with little success (handing out product samples in supermarkets, painting yellow lines down their neighborhood streets, and fixing lunch in the school cafeteria), they decided to bone up on the market for romances—which filled up their local stores' book racks. When they felt they had surveyed the field, they wrote a pornographic novel, to try out not only their ideas but release their inhibitions as well. (They also came up with a pen name borrowed from the husband and son of one, and a plastic fern in the other's living room.) The Fernies, as they're called, can't explain how they write. "We were great friends and it comes easy, working together," they claim, and it appears they're closer in spirit than sisters. Their work schedule combines getting together, with Roberta at the typewriter and Mary at her elbow, and discussing the plot endless hours on the telephone.

Husband and wife team Clayton and Patricia Matthews (with

over 15 million books bearing their names) follow the formula of many professional writers, and write during the day in their respective offices and then show their output to the other. Now that they have a word processor, they may even speed up their work and double up on efficiency. They write novels as a team and separately, and their historical romances usually follow the classic formula of a struggling young woman meeting two men, choosing the first for a while, and eventually ending up with the second when he shows redeeming qualities.

Teams of three and four writers cropping up now are from the new word-processor-orientated group. This machine has made it easier for two or more writers to collaborate and polish. Usually these teams have some kind of work system, handing over the most recent revisions "en masse" after the initial story line is established.

Additional Tips

From Lynda Trent (Dan and Lynda Trent): "By each of us writing what we like best—Lynda is stronger at characterizations and descriptions and Dan is better at plotting and story development—and by keeping personalities out of our discussions, we not only write better together, but have a lot of fun doing it."

From Margaret Summerville (sisters Barbara and Pam Wilson): "We have a lot of the same interests and the same humor. We have to know exactly where the book is going, with some minor changes along the way, and then the flow of our contributions is smooth."

From Lynda Erickson (Molly Swanton and Carla Peltonen): "Together we brainstorm, make up story lines, scribble notes, do research, etc. Then we work on a list of characters and create the outline. When it comes to actual writing, we generally alternate chapters, then reread and rewrite each other's work. We feel we are the yin and yang, but we are also amazed to find that our thinking (while we work) has become very much alike."

From Lillian Shelley (Lillian and Shelley Koppel) a mother-daughter team): "My mother is very organized and paints the picture, really. She makes the set," explains Shelley. "I usually work on the first draft after we've come to a decision about the flow of the story. I do a blueprint, a first draft that is almost a screenplay. In my case, my first draft is almost all dialogue as I get the story down. When that's done, I know what is going to happen. The first chapter is usually the hardest to write, because you're trying to set the mood. Sometimes it's easier to write the first chapter after you know how the story develops.''

How We Write Together

BY JUNE HAYDEN

one half of the writing team of Rosalind Foxx and Sara Logan

We start with a germ of an idea. Then we work by the ''what if?'' theory, not any different from writing a romance novel on one's own. ''What if there is this gorgeous redhead, of marriage-able age, who is on her way home to her family, but she's kidnapped by the chieftain of a neighboring clan and . . .'' We work hard on that plot outline, trying to foresee any problems we may have invented for ourselves.

After we plot and plot and plot, my collaborator Judy Simpson writes the first draft. As she writes, I read and suggest how to weave in the next part, what foreshadowing needs to be done, and whatever else I can devise to make the book go. If Judy hits a snag, or has not finished research on the book, she simply puts in a note for me to do ''the scene between the villains,'' for instance. After the first draft is finished, we read it and get our husbands to read it and try to fix and straighten anything that doesn't work.

Then I write the second draft, and put in all or a portion of the local color and description. What we want to have at the end of the first draft is a book that has all the elements in it. Does the plot hang together? It can be a bare-bones draft, but it must all be there. Then I set about putting the flesh on the bones.

When the second draft is done, an even longer time is spent pruning and polishing and cleaning the draft. We check spelling and try to avoid "German" sentences with dangling participles and indefinite modifiers. I can spot a comma misplaced in a manuscript of Judy's and can't see a garbled paragraph in my own. Once all that is cleaned up, one of us types the final. Then we proof and proof until we have taken the book along as far as we can. After that, it goes to our agent, and we cross our fingers.

Having our helpful husbands read our first and second drafts saves us a lot of grief. They spot inconsistencies. In *Winds of Fury,* Agnes gets pregnant early in the book. We had her do this for a reason that involved the main characters. Once we had her this way we didn't need her anymore and the poor thing stayed pregnant for thirteen months. We were red-faced when that was pointed out, and we cleaned it up for the second draft. Also, later in the book, Rufenna comes down the stairs dressed in a green velvet dress she had had made in Edinburgh. Fine, except she had left Edinburgh pursued by the English and never did get to pick up her velvet dress. In fact, she fled dressed in her brother's clothing.

Some of our favorite goofs, found, thank God, before we typed the final manuscript, are:

1. "Davon took out his and pressed it against the Englishman's prickly throat." There should have been a *dagger* after *his*.

2. "Louis took out his pistol and cut the ropes that bound Margaret."

3. "Emmons, dozing in his chair, crept to Francis's side." Can you picture that? Emmons with behind firmly attached to the chair.

4. "Amanda slipped out of her bikini and returned to the counter to pay for her purchases."

5. "After her devastating encounter with Brad, Emilie knew

she must look like a person.'' Where did the adjective before *person* go?

6. ''She saw sheep dotting the steep meadow and cows.''

Judy and I work well together because we complement each other. My strengths and her strengths are different. Judy can plot faster and tighter than I could have imagined. It takes me a long time to plot a book alone. I get into blind alleys and impossible situations.

Judy can also make the leading man strong and tender. He does impossible things but the reader still likes him. I can create villains that make the flesh crawl, villains who defile the girl, violent scenes of rape and plunder. We both are good editors, each catching the flaws in the other's work.

Unhappily, Judy has moved away, so we use the telephone a lot and the United States postal service, and the Greyhound bus if we're really in a hurry. We get together rarely, but we plot three or four books in a week. Judy has recently bought a word processor and that will expedite a lot of things, such as final manuscripts. In spite of the distance and our family responsibilities, I'm confident that we'll continue to put our heads together and come up with another Rosalind Foxx novel for our readers.

Romance Writing Teams

Lee Arthur	Lee and Arthur Browning
Diana Burke	Sue Burrell and Michaela Karni
Mary Canon	Mary and Jack Canon
Joellyn Carroll	Marie Flasschoen and Marian Scheirman
Justine Cole	Claire Kiehl and Susan Phillips
Lucinda Day	Marie Flasschoen and Marian Scheirman
Lynn Erickson	Carla Peltonen and Molly Swanton
Rosalind Foxx	June Hayden and Judith Simpson
Lydia Gregory	Diane and Greg Brouder
Alyssa Howard	Ruth Glick, Louise Titchenor, Eileen Bucholtz
Nancy John	Nancy and John Sawyer
Anna James	Madeline Porter and Harper Shannon

Robin James	Sharon and Thomas Curtis
Alexis Hill Jordan	Ruth Glick and Louise Titchenor
Janet Joyce	Janet Bieber and Joyce Theis
Catherine Kay	Catherine Dees and Kay Croissant
Sara Logan	June Hayden and Judith Simpson
Jan MacLean	Anne MacLean and Sandra Field
Denise Matthews	Denise Hrivnak and Patricia Matthews
Patricia and Clayton Matthews	Patricia and Clayton Matthews
Alicia Meadowes	Linda Burak and Joan Zeig
Fern Michaels	Roberta Anderson and Mary Kuczkir
Diana Morgan	Irene Goodman and Alex Kamaroff
Jacqueline Musgrave	Jacqueline and David Musgrave
DeAnn Patrick	Dotty Corcoran and Mary Ann Slojkowski
Lia Sanders	Angela and Sandra Jackson
Elizabeth Shelley	Elizabeth Schaal and Elaine Cichanth
Lillian Shelley	Lillian and Shelley Koppel
Valerie Sherwood	Jeanne Hines and husband
Margaret Summerville	Barbara and Pamela Wilson
Day Taylor	Sharon Salvato and Cornelia Parkinson
Lynda Trent	Lynda and Dan Trent
Valerie Vayle	Janice Young Brooks and Jean Brooks-Janowiak

11

How to Write Teen Romances

Atlanta, Georgia

October 2

Dear Aunt Kathryn,

I know you get requests all the time, but I'm your niece so maybe it's different.

I have an idea. I want to write teen romances. Do you think I could? I read them all (twelve a month). Mother is not sympathetic. But then, she grew up on <u>My Friend Flicka</u> and those other horse stories. I prefer heroes to horses.

I'm like you, Aunt Kathryn. I love Love.

Help!!!

Your loving niece,
Krissy

From the Desk of Kathryn Falk

October 10

Dear Krissy,

What went wrong with my life? What did I do to deserve this? Weren't you going to become another Esther Williams or whatever you were practicing for in your swim club?

I'm sure your mother doesn't know you're writing to me on this subject. When I once told her that I gave birth to books and she gave birth to babies, she was not, I repeat not, impressed.

Aren't you suppose to be looking for a doctor to marry and live happily ever after with in the Deep South?

In the meantime, I don't want you to think I'm ag'in you. Enclosed is

, teen romance tip sheet, and a publishers' directory so you can send or the others. Since you're such an avid reader, I don't have to tell you to know the genre. However, there is less variation between the lines than in the adult romances, and the word count is from 35,000 to 60,000 words for a MS. (that means manuscript) depending on the publishers.

I've also asked some friends to help you along with their advice. Audrey Johnson you know of because she won the dinner with Prince Khedker at the first Romantic Book Lovers' Conference. It might interest you to know that Suzanne Zuckerman started writing in her twenties, not much older than you, and she has some terrific tips.

Don't write to me again until your next birthday. I can't stand too many shocks. By the way, when did you grow up? I used to send you Raggedy Ann books and you were satisfied. Now you need writers' tip sheets? <u>Meine Gott!</u>

> Your New York "Ant"
> Kathryn
> xOxO

Sample Tip Sheet

Caprice Romances (Tempo Books)
Berkley/Jove

Caprice Romances are contemporary young adult first-love novels that will express the restlessness of youth and the wonder of falling in love.

PLOT: The first meaningful romantic interlude in a young woman's life. Although she may have dated before, she believes that this romance is the real thing. The development of emotional and physical feelings toward a young man, the confusion these feelings bring on and the happiness which results when confusion gives way to caring . . . this is the world of CAPRICE.

The young people are basically good. One or the other may be selfish or vain on occasion, any number of pitfalls are allowed as long as they are acknowledged and rectified by the end of the book, and as long as both members of the relationship remain likeable to some extent.

A strong subplot is encouraged. The plots will reflect current day attitudes and themes that are of interest to teen readers. There can be family or school traumas, problems or joys, as long as the focus remains on the love aspect.

Although these books are traditional romances in that they are comparatively innocent, our young people are not unaware of sex. They experience the stirring of sexual desire but these descriptions must be sensitively handled and our characters will not follow through on their desires.

CHARACTERS. The girl is fifteen or sixteen. Her experience with dating up to this point is the author's choice but it is within this relationship that the girl's emotions blossom.

The boy is sixteen or seventeen and has had varied experience with girls. Again his prior experience is up to the author.

We strongly recommend that other characters be developed . . . a best friend, possibly an understanding adult (not a parent), an ex-girlfriend or boyfriend, etc.

POINT OF VIEW: From the girl's point of view, either first or third person.

LENGTH: 50,000 to 60,000 words. Dialogue is an important element in each of these stories.

Editor: Marilyn Poe

Publishers and Senior Editors

Caprice
Berkley/Jove
200 Madison Avenue
New York, N.Y.
(Marilyn Poe)

Sweet Dreams
Bantam
666 Fifth Avenue
New York, N.Y. 10013
(Ben Baglio of Cloverdale Press)

First Love
Silhouette
1230 Avenue of the Americas
New York, N.Y. 10020
(Nancy Jackson)

Wildfire and Wishing Star
Scholastic
50 West 44th Street
New York, N.Y. 10036
(Anne Reit)

The Teenage Formula

BY AUDREY P. JOHNSON

author of six teen romances

Teenage romances are an important part of the fast-growing
paperback romance market. Young love is luring teens into the
bookstores in unprecedented numbers. Nine million teenage readers is a conservative estimate. Girls who were reading their
mother's adult romances now have many for their age group.

If you don't like teenagers don't attempt to write for them, but
if you are concerned with the universal problems they face
today, and can write with warmth and understanding, this field
may be yours.

When anyone asks me how to write a teenage romance, I tell
them to think *love*—sweet, tender love—and carry it all through
the book. The primary interest of a teenage girl is almost always
a teenage boy, and if you intend to write a young adult romance,
keep in mind that feelings are extremely intense through the
teenage years.

Underlying the romance should be some good, solid conflicts,
such as peer pressure, personality flaws, troubles with parents,
school problems, overcoming shyness, finding one's identity,
career aspirations, etc. The novel should be written from the
viewpoint of the young heroine, and can be in either the first or
third person. You will be writing primarily for girls nine to

fourteen, and girls like to read about girls slightly older tha
themselves, so make your heroine from fifteen to sevente
years old. Usually she is a junior or senior in high school. T
boy should be about the same age or slightly older, or if you a
writing a summer romance, he could be starting his first year
college in the fall.

The plot may contain one or two boys the girl is interested i
and she may be undecided which one to choose. One may be th
"boy next door" and the other an entirely different type wh
offers excitement. The setting is familiar: a small town or city i
the United States.

Sometimes she is infatuated with an inappropriate type or sh
joins the wrong crowd at school. The story should deal with he
day-to-day problems, her uncertainties and anxieties, her fir
romantic encounters and how she handles them.

Avoid teenage slang. In a few months the words or phrase
may be obsolete and will only date your book. The same goe
with music, television, or movie personalities. They can als
date your novel, and young readers several years from no
may not have even heard of the current rock star.

Characters in your teenage romance are schoolmates, famil
members, an understanding girl friend, teachers, and, of course
the boyfriend.

How do teenage romances differ from adult romances? Vic
lence and explicit sex are taboo; so is profanity. Avoid moralizing
but the books should carry a high moral tone. The romanc
should be light, with the emphasis not on the physical expressio
of love but on the anxieties and emotions shared by teenagers i
their first romantic encounters.

In writing for teens, avoid the subplots that often mark th
adult romances. Sometimes I am given manuscripts to be rea
from a hopeful writer aiming at the teen market, and the flaw
are often the same. Instead of centering on the young heroin
and her problem, the writer branches off into subplots tha
threaten to take over most of the story. The story line mus
center on the heroine and *her* problem all through the book.

Scholastic Book Services was the first publisher to launch
line of young adult romances in 1980, entitled Wildfire Romances
but when I wrote *Don't Look Back* I was unaware of the nev
trend in teenage fiction. My novel was about Ellen, sixteen, wh
lives on an apple farm and struggles to bring the apples t
harvest with the help of an elderly hired man when her fathe

dies of a heart attack. Ellen was a strong character and the story did have a love interest all through the book. Gabe, who comes along in a van, is hired by Ellen to work the farm and complicates her life.

Scholastic editor Ann Reit was starting their Wishing Star line, with a more serious flavor than Wildfire, and added my book to their list.

How did I handle the love scenes in *Don't Look Back?* Gently, tenderly.

> "Don't laugh at me! I want you to like me." Ellen moved in Gabe's arms.
>
> "But I do like you. We can be friends," Gabe said softly.
>
> "I want to mean everything to you!" What was wrong with her? She never thouht she would beg a boy to love her. All her dreams of Gabe bobbed to the surface . . . dreams of a future together on the farm, of sharing their lives. Tears streamed down her face.
>
> "Hey, don't cry. I do care for you." His eyes were serious as he brushed a tear from her cheek and traced her lips, slowly, thoughtfully.
>
> She found herself responding to his gentleness, his tenderness. She reached her hand to his face and held it against his cheek, feeling it grow warm under his touch. There was comfort and caring in their first kisses.

In my second book, *Sisters,* also bought by Scholastic, tension between two sisters adds to the conflict. Rae is beautiful but slightly handicapped, while Robin, who is rather plain, is outgoing and popular. Robin feels guilty because she has boyfriends and good times while Rae is withdrawn and rather bitter. Then they both fall in love with the same boy and their problems increase. As in the former book, romance played an important part, but sibling rivalry was strong too.

> Rae was seated by the window writing a letter when Chris and I came in, tracking snow on the floor. Rae's shining hair fell across her shoulders like an advertisement for shampoo and I found myself wishing for the thousandth time I had inherited, too, the blond good looks of my father's side of the family.

The setting for a romance should be an easy one for the

readers to identify with—school, a beach, vacation spots, a small town, or a city neighborhood. In *I'll Tell Him Tomorrow,* my third romance sold to Scholastic, the setting was Cape Cod, where Shannon was spending her summer baby-sitting for an affluent family. She meets a wealthy boy on the beach, and to impress him she tells him she is a guest of the family, instead of their baby-sitter. When she realizes she is falling in love with the boy she wonders what he will think when he discovers her lie.

Originally I had planned on her lie being discovered in the second chapter, but editor Ann Reit advised me to carry Shannon's deception through the entire book. She was right. It made a far better story as the lie snowballed and got Shannon deeper and deeper into trouble.

In spite of my protests, Blake led me across the room to where his parents were admiring a painting over the mantle. Even if they had been wearing warm-up suits you would have known they were wealthy socialites.

"Mother and Dad, I would like you to meet Shannon McCabe."

Blake's mother was a tall, regal blonde in a blue gown with a sapphire pendant at her throat, and Mr. Harrison looked distinguished with graying sideburns and a deep tan he probably acquired sailing on his yacht.

"So you are the young lady who is visiting the Beaumonts this summer?" Mrs. Harrison smiled.

I stood there like a robot trying to smile and you know how hard it is for robots to smile. I must have looked ghastly.

In this specialized field, write with young girls' dreams in mind—popularity, a steady boyfriend, fantasies of a great career, a great figure, the leading role in the school play, a champion skier or tennis player.

Remember when blotchy skin or the wrong haircut was a complete disaster, or a look from a certain boy made your day? "Does he like me a lot? Or a little? Is he going to ask me out?"

Writing for teenagers is a satisfying experience. It will keep you in touch with the youth of today and will keep you young.

A happy ending is not always essential, but the story should have a satisfactory solution and the reader should be left with the feeling the heroine has learned something of value from her experience.

Turning Teenage Fantasies into Fiction

BY SUZANNE ZUCKERMAN

author of four teenage romances

As a teen romance writer I can explore all the youthful missed experiences and might-have-beens that I never knew as a teenager. In my first novel, *Two of a Kind*, I gave my main character, Carol Clark, the lead in her school play, something I had dreamed of but never achieved. In my second book, which has not yet been titled, Jenifer Roberts has an older brother who brings her into the "in" crowd, a fantasy that only a time machine could give to me, the oldest of three siblings. And in my third, *Montauk Summer*, Laura Wilson dates a handsome, wealthy young man who introduces her to the sophisticated world of the arts that I had to learn through classes and books.

Of course, as an adult I can recognize and point out the negative aspects of these experiences, which I had no possibility of realizing as a young girl longing for them. The star of the school play suffers from stage fright and the other girls' envy; the "in" crowd requires strict conformity to peer pressure; and the "perfect man" must spend so much time on his image that he has none left for relating to other people.

Although detailed descriptions of clothing and homes are vital to all romance writing, in teen romance the settings are limited to the mundane world of high school, summer camp, and the local hangout. It is the main character's developing sense of self-worth that fills in for the palm trees and palaces of adult romances. She learns that no one dies from failing a vocabulary test or tripping in her first pair of high-heeled shoes. The girl comes to understand that having a boyfriend may be wonderful, but she is a whole person on her own, with achievements, responsibilities and relationships.

In developing abilities for my girl characters to explore, I try to offer my readers information about activities they may not have experienced. Carol Clark learns about the technical aspect of theater; Jenifer Roberts develops skill in basic electric repair; Laura Wilson works at a marina. Sometimes I find myself learning only one step ahead of my characters. In the book I am just beginning to develop, the girl will have a part-time job in a historic building, working with colonial antiques.

Perhaps one of the most important differences between adult and teen romances is the use of humor. While an adult reader will delight in the characters, plot, and setting, teenagers, and preteens caught in the giddy period of life called adolescence, experience silliness as part of daily living. Holding their interest requires the fast dialogue and complex situations with almost predictable results of a television comedy. In *Two of a Kind,* I created a first kiss of such incredible clumsiness that my typist giggled while pounding the keys.

The real challenge is finding amusing similes and metaphors that express both the event and the feelings of the participants: "Rolling her eyes skyward, Nancy dropped the telephone like a bad test grade." "Lenore Carrol's hands, with their bobbing, brightly colored nails, flitted at Jen's like fish lures."

Occasionally, while searching for a funny line or an awkward situation for my heroine to suffer through, I find it necessary to do research. If I were writing adult romance I would visit Paris, Hong Kong, or Tahiti; but, unfortunately, the disadvantage of teen romance is that I can find an overabundance of local color and appropriate detail right here at home in Brooklyn. I selected the rock groups mentioned in *Two of a Kind* by interviewing students in a local high school cafeteria. My clothing descriptions are often based on individuals I notice in the stampede that disrupts my block at 2:35 on schooldays. And some of my favorite lines are germinated while eavesdropping on the chatter in my neighborhood record shop or stationery story.

In spite of the disadvantage of being able to write without

visiting a single exotic locale, I adore working on teen romances. My girls are the friends I would have liked to have grown up with and the aspects of myself that I was never able to develop. My career as a romance writer has probably saved me a fortune in therapy fees by freeing me to relive all the worst moments of my youth . . . only this time I think I know all the right answers!

Tips from Audrey and Suzanne

1. *Teen romances are written primarily for girls nine to fourteen years old.*

2. *Write from the viewpoint of the young heroine, who is ideally fifteen to seventeen years old. She must have an interest other than boys, such as a hobby or skill through which she develops her personality and overcomes her feelings of inadequacy.*

3. *The young hero can be the same age or slightly older.*

4. *No explicit sex or profanity. Stay away from sexual situations.*

5. *Avoid waning slang, flash-in-the-pan show business personalities, short-lived fads, and fading fashions. It will only date your book.*

6. *Stay away from religious and ethnic references.*

7. *The setting for your story should be familiar to the reader—home, school, vacation spots, etc.*

8. *Manuscripts should run 35,000 to 50,000 words.*

9. *The stories are about the average middle-class American girl with typical adolescent problems. Foreign backgrounds are seldom used.*

10. *Check the tip sheets from the various publishing houses before submitting your manuscript. Some will look only at complete manuscripts, while others will accept three chapters and a four- or five-page synopsis for consideration.*

PART FOUR

12

Love's Literary Labors

From the Desk of Kathryn Falk

November 3

My dear sister,

Are you really calling yourself the mother of Atlanta's answer to Janet Dailey, Jr.?

What do you mean, how do you type a manuscript and get it published? You aren't going to do that, are you? You will have to remove your strawberry artificial nails for the occasion, in case you haven't figured that out.

I'm sending along my complete collection of manuscript-preparation notes. I also asked Hilary Guerin, a publisher's reader, to fill you in on some publishing knowledge. My artist friend, Iggy, designed a game for me, a bit like Monopoly only it does show you what will happen to Krissy's manuscript if it is accepted. Should I offer it to Parker Brothers?

As an afterthought, I'm including information on editors and agents, since I do think blood is thicker than ink, and Krissy does have promise.

Hope this answers all your questions. And watch out for those nails.

Ta soeur,
Kathryn

Manuscript Preparation

BY MARIANNE LOPRIORE
aspiring romance author

Query Letters

These are a must for all new novelists, the first of many musts, even if you and an editor or agent have talked the book

340

over; the concrete idea, with cogent information, must be put
down in letter form. This will tell your recipient a lot about your
writing skill and style prior to the actual reading of a manuscript.
It will also provide her with a record, so that she won't have to
rely on memory.

Not only does she have a record, but if the query letter is
persuasive and well-enough constructed, an agent can use it to
show to an editor.

Your letter summarizes your novel in one page, three paragraphs,
if possible (single spacing for text, double spacing between
paragraphs).

This is one element of writing that baffles many authors. It is
very difficult to compress a text of 95,000 words into such a
short format.

Think positively! Tell your story to a friend, or use a tape
recorder first, and then condense your thoughts. You have to
stress only the essentials of your story.

Form

Use the usual business heading.

TEXT

FIRST PARAGRAPH. State the type of romance you have
written (category, historical, etc.), length of manuscript, time
frame, and setting. Describe in one or two sentences the hero
and heroine. (For a historical novel, describe other important
characters.) Explain the first half of your plot, in one sentence.
(Example: deals with open marriage, marriage to consolidate a
business, reuniting of former lovers, etc.)

SECOND PARAGRAPH. This explains the middle of your novel,
what happens when all your characters are in place, the conflicts
that tear them apart.

THIRD PARAGRAPH. The resolution of your novel. How the
loose ends are tied up, the conflict is resolved, and the ending
worked out.

SUMMARY PARAGRAPH. Inquire as to the proper way to
present the whole manuscript for consideration, but do so tactfully.
Don't make this paragraph appear to be the only one of real
interest to you in the query letter—i.e., will you read it or won't

you? (For heaven't sake, never say something abrupt, such as "When do you want to look at my book? How much money will you give me?")

Outlining

The academic outline you learned in your English classes isn't what an agent or publisher needs when they ask for an outline of your manuscript.

If the publisher wants a chapter-by-chapter outline, you are expected to supply several short, pointed sentences about each chapter.

If a general outline is asked for, you proceed as with the query letter, dividing your novel into the three major parts (beginning, middle, and end). Use one page to describe each section. Then reread and begin to whittle it down, discarding extra descriptions that the reader will discover when reading the work. Remember, you want to tempt the reader to consider the whole manuscript, so keep a few details for the imagination.

BEGINNING

Tell the essentials of your two major characters. Say what motivates the hero and heroine's actions with each other. What is the first interaction between the two major characters, and what is the result?

MIDDLE

Try not to be wordy. Avoid useless details. Stick to the story. Mainly stress the hero and heroine's interaction.

END

Don't tell everything; allude to the reasons for the happy ending, but make the reader want to read the whole story to discover all the details that come about.

Counting Words

On page 8 are exact instructions for casting off manuscript length, as publishers' production departments call word count. If you use this method instead of the customary approximate count, be sure to say so (in parenthesis) in an appropriate place on the title page. All concerned will be grateful and impressed.

If you use an approximate word count (easier) remember that an elite typeface (the smaller letters) for the total words per page will be more than the pica typeface. The number of words per page with elite type will be about 300; with pica type about 250 to 275 words. A 60,000-word manuscript equals about 200 pages.

Typing

Type everything you intend to send to a publisher. Use either pica or elite type *only*. (Always type double-spaced and allow for wide margins.)

If you can't type well, inquire at your local high school for a student who would be willing to type for you, or put an ad in the newspaper.

Never send your original copy to an agent or publisher. Use regular 8½-by-11-inch white bond paper (preferably not the kind coated with a special chemical so errors can be corrected with a pencil eraser). Then copy your work. Be sure these copies are clear, clean, and black type on white paper.

TEXT

Number pages consecutively. Type the number in the right-hand corner of the page, three double spaces from the top of the page. Don't use a period after the number. However, it is helpful to the editor to add your last name on the same line; accidents *do* happen, and you don't want your page 20 to get mixed up with Jane Doe's manuscript! And if your last name is Doe (or Smith), include your first name as well.

Make margins 1½ inches to the left; 1 inch from the top, bottom, and righthand side.

Pages that begin a chapter should be numbered in the same manner, except for Chapter 1, which *may* be numbered at the bottom. It's up to you.

Text begins two double spaces after the page number, indent 5 spaces going left to right.

Type the entire text double-spaced throughout.

Have someone read your text for grammar, spelling, and typing errors. It is very easy to transpose letters such as "iwth" and not catch it, but someone else usually will.

You want to present the agent or editor with the best-looking, readable manuscript possible. The wrappings *do* impress!

Editor Etiquette

Mail your manuscript in a large manila envelope, using a typed address label (include a self-addressed stamped envelope with sufficient postage for possible return of manuscript). If you send it certified mail you can request a return receipt to verify its arrival. Some publishers will send you an acknowledgment postcard, but many won't, so don't expect it.

How long should you wait for an answer? Six to eight weeks is the average time for notification.

What should you do after five or six weeks, when you are sitting on the edge of your seat waiting to hear? There are two major suggestions. One is to write a letter inquiring if your manuscript has been read and considered; the other is to telephone. This is tricky, as the editor or publisher probably has a very busy schedule and you might be calling at a bad time. Apologize for interrupting her/him and ask about your manuscript. Most editors are very nice and will spend a few minutes with you, but everyone has bad days, so if you call and things aren't going well and the editor sounds annoyed, hang up gracefully.

Avoid being a pest. You don't want to get that reputation. You want to be thought of as a considerate person as well as a talented one. Keep your calls short, sweet, and nonbelligerent.

Sample Title Page

TITLE

By

Your name

Your legal name
Street address
City, State, Zip Code
Area code/Phone number
approx 000 words 00 pages

Query letters should be brief but complete and persuasive and—if possible—charming. Keep it short. This is just to introduce you and your manuscript.

Miss Romance
Love Lane
Heartland, USA

Dear Editor (name if possible),

   *The first section should state that your book is a category,
historical, Regency, romantic suspense, or contemporary
romance. Give the approximate number of words in the manuscript (55,000 or 60,000 or whatever, rounded up to the
nearest thousand). State the manuscript's title and explain
very briefly the meaning of the title, if an explanation is
needed.*
   *In the second section, describe in approximately a hundred
words the general story line of the book. Think of this as a
selling blurb that might appear on a book cover.*
   In the third section, give quick sketches of your characters.
   *In the final section, include details of your writing experi-
ence and specialized expertise that qualify you for writing
on this subject. Is the heroine's work milieu something you've
experienced? Is the setting or historical period the result of
special research or travel?*
   The final, final paragraph should be:

If you are interested in seeing the book, I can send the complete
manuscript or a synopsis and sample chapters, whichever you
prefer. I enclose a stamped, self-addressed envelope for your reply.

                              Signature

                              (Don't give pen name if you've
                              never been published)

Tips on Query Letters

Like a press release or anything else that comes in piles regularly over someone's desk, you should try to make your offering stand out.

Neatness, clarity of thought, and evidence of writing talent are what count in a query letter, along with your ability to persuade the editor to look at your manuscript.

Some writers include the extent of their reading of romance. Editors do appreciate knowing that you are well read in this field.

Making a query letter funny or amusing, as long as all the essential facts are there, can catch the eye of an editor.

One new writer who had written a romance about a woman veterinarian who meets a rodeo rider (love blossoms at his horse-breeding ranch in Texas) ended her query letter by saying, "If you would like to lasso this story, just holler."

It goes without saying that your letter should be checked over by someone who acts as your copy editor, to find glaring grammatical and spelling errors. A beautifully typed letter, with proper margins, means a lot to the editor's eye.

Synopsizing a Novel

BY MARION CHESNEY

author of Maude

The Scottish Earl of Crammarth has two daughters, Marigold and Maude. Marigold is extremely beautiful and Maude is accounted small and plain. The Earl is in financial trouble and hopes to repair his losses by marrying Marigold off to some rich lord. He arranges for Marigold to have a London "season." Maude is to go as well, but more as a sort of companion than anything else. No one expects Maude to marry.

Maude is in fact not all that plain, and perhaps might be noticed if she were not perpetually overshadowed by the dazzling beauty of her sister. Both girls make their coming-out—and then the incredible happens. London's most notorious and wildest rake, the Marquess of Dunster, proposes to Maude. Wild he may be, rake he may be, but the Marquess is also handsome and extremely rich. Marigold has hysterics from jealousy and then sets about to try to stop Maude from marrying the wild Marquess. "Once a rake, always a rake," says Marigold.

Quiet Maude replies gently that he will change once he is married, and Marigold sneers spitefully. Marigold is still sneering when her little sister marries the Marquess with full ceremony at St. George's, Hanover Square.

Then Maude finds herself more of an object of pity than ever before. For the Marquess shows no sign of stopping his wild nights, his gambling—or of getting rid of his mistresses.

Maude asks him why he married her, and the Marquess laughs and says he had to get married and produce an heir and any woman would do and he was sorry for her. With that crashing insult, he takes himself off for another hectic night on the town.

For the first time in her life, Maude wants revenge. With great skill and cunning, she begins to frighten away her husband's mistresses one by one. Then she proceeds to emulate her husband to see how *he* likes it. She trains herself to become a wit, dressing extremely fashionably and sets up as many flirtations as she can.

But Maude is still an innocent, and underneath her new clothes and new manner, she does not think much of herself. And so she flirts outrageously with one of the town's most sinister lechers, Lord David Devizes; has a young poet, Jeffrey Burr, so much in love with her he nearly commits suicide; and enamors a Captain of the Hussars to such a point that he challenges the surprised Marquess to a duel.

Then the wicked Marquess finds he has an even wickeder wife on his hands, and his days and nights are spent rescuing her from one scrape after another.

And so at last, surprised society and infuriated Marigold find that little Maude has succeeded and the wild Marquess is tamed at last.

The Outline Hurdle

BY BONNIE GOLIGHTLY

author of ten contemporary novels

Back when it was at least possible to get a first novel accepted on the basis of three chapters and an outline, nearly everybody who could write could manage one. Sometimes the outline was just a gimmick to show the editor, never to be adhered to after the contract was signed, and sometimes it was a real working outline, to be followed faithfully.

Now, almost *no* editor is willing to part with his publisher's money for anything less than the whole book *plus* a genuine outline, professionally constructed. (This may be due in part to editorial indolence: he/she can read the outline and then decide if the book is worth reading. A little cheaty, but sensible.)

The problem with the present situation is that though the author may be Margaret Mitchell, Jr., sired by Frank Yerby, in the outline department she may be as ignorant and awkward as a boulder. What to do? Again, go back to the beginning and relearn—or learn—what an outline is, what it should stand for, and how to make one that will dazzle and tame the editor into submission.

The fine craft of outline making seems to have met the same fate as sentence diagramming (parsing), spelling and punctuating correctly, knowing the parts of speech, good grammar, and so forth. But while these important aspects of writing may now be considered negligible by many, outlining has risen to the top of the list as a *must*. If an author has been able to complete a manuscript that she considers very worthy of publication, it has to be accompanied by an outline of equal worth: again, stunning and professional. This, by the way, has nothing to do necessarily with the private outline she makes for herself—that can be as amorphous as a free-form sculpture, so long as it serves her purpose.

So what constitutes the good, able outline, and how does a writer go about building it? First, an outline always goes from the general to the specific, such as:

I. Twenty-four-year-old PDQ, an orphan and a tested IQ genius who was raised in an institution in Iowa, applies for a teaching job at the small university where she graduated with honors by working her way through school with a modest scholarship. Her would-be boss rejects her, as he hates orphans, having been one himself.

    A. We see XYZ, the boss, feeling violently guilty for his actions, deliberately picking a quarrel with his secretary.

    B. The secretary tearfully relates this to her best girl friend.

C. The girl friend knows the secretary is in love with the boss, and also knows that she is too, but can still maintain some objectivity.

II. PDQ decides to go over the head of XYZ and sees the college president, who was always appreciative of her abilities . . .

And thus it goes, chapter by chapter. Very often, in addition to the initial subheadings (A), (B), (C), etc., the author will need subheadings, such as 1., 2., 3., and even after that, a., b., c. But further details will eventually bog down the outline, and the editor will either put the whole thing down or decide to idly glance at the manuscript itself.

Being *precise* and very thrifty with words means everything in an outline. All the salient information must be included, but with an economy far stricter than that used in actual writing of the novel. Overloading is also a danger; spiders spin intricate webs, but outliners should not. *If in doubt, leave out* should be the byword. After all, it is presumed that the manuscript itself will be read, so save the small surprises. Just include enough information and detail to give that tired editor an idea of what you're writing about and where the story will go and how it will finally end.

Since writing a proper outline can be the making or breaking of a book these days, the more time and care spent on it, the better. If the actual structure of drawing up an outline remains hazy, consult a handbook of English comp to get "how-to" firmly at your command.

What Happens to Your Manuscript When It Arrives at a Publishing House

BY HILARY V. GUERIN
free-lance reader

As a reader for a mass-market paperback company, my job is to read and critique books or manuscripts that the editors do not have time to read themselves. When a publishing house receives a romance novel, it is assigned to the editor who specializes in romantic fiction. If you do not have an agent, your submission may languish for days in the slush pile. The slush pile contains all the unsolicited mail sent to the editorial department. Many New York publishing houses do not accept unsolicited novels. However, if you are lucky, an editor just might read your novel. After all, Kathleen Woodiwiss was discovered in the slush pile!

Once an editor receives a submission from an agent, she (or he) assigns it to a reader, if she is unable to read it herself. After reading a novel, I write a detailed plot synopsis and review of the book. When an editor reads my synopsis she learns if the novel's plot is original, entertaining, and engrossing. The critique is an objective discussion of the submission's strengths and weaknesses. In short, the critique tells the editor the following:

1. If the book is worth reading.

2. What revisions are required.

3. If the book is a marketable property—i.e., will it sell?

If I reject a book outright, it will not be read by anyone on the editorial staff. When I recommend a submission, someone on the staff will read it.

Having read hundreds of submissions, I have discovered a few talented authors. The books written by these novelists all have noticeable similarities. The novels are original; the plot lines are dramatic, innovative, romantic, sexy, carefully researched, and occasionally suspenseful. The protagonists (the hero and heroine) are always multidimensional people, who are intelligent, sensual, adventurous, and courageous. Often, the hero and heroine are kept apart by seemingly insurmountable obstacles. Yet by the novel's conclusion they conquer all! This technique may seem melodramatic, but an exciting action-filled plot does improve a historical romance. *Jemma* by Beverly Byrne is an excellent example of a complex plot that works. Set in Europe and the United States during the American Civil War, *Jemma* is laced with subplots depicting political and romantic intrigues. The book also is colorful, erotic, and deliciously passionate. Both protagonists are glamorous adventurers who dare all; thus, *Jemma* is an exciting read.

A good novel must engage and *maintain* the reader's attention. A slow-moving, sloppy, clumsily constructed, contrived novel is boring. Every so often seemingly unsuitable plot devices do work in a romance novel. *Lady of Fire* by Valerie Vayle is brimming with humorous episodes. This amusing, outrageous romp abounds with dastardly plots, funny surprises, and, of course, passionate, sensual romance. Vayle also inserts interesting period detail into her novels.

Having read so many novels, I know that inferior books have trite plots, stereotyped protagonists, excessive brutality, and no genuine romantic flavor. When writing your novel, try to create characters who *differ* from the usual stereotypes. In other words, make your protagonists human. As Muriel Bradley aptly demonstrates in *Tanya,* even villains can have genuine emotions and realistic motivations. Furthermore, Tanya and her lover, Alexi, possess believable, sensitive, intuitive qualities. Thus, the standard romance is transformed into a first-rate novel.

Once I recommend a novel, the editorial department reads and evaluates it. Thus, your book may have a good chance of being published. Of course, other variables are considered by the editorial staff. For instance, if revisions are needed and an author refuses to make these changes, the book might not be published. Publishing *is* a business, and publishers are required to earn a profit. However, nothing excites a reader and the editorial staff more than discovering a talented new author. An entertaining, well-written novel has an excellent chance of being published. Yes, most publishing houses do have exacting standards, but if you truly have talent, your work will eventually be published. Who knows, one day your book may appear on the *New York Times* best-seller list!

Hints from Hilary

On Dialogue

1. Be sure to clearly identify the speaker.

2. Do not use dialect unless you really understand and know the language you are reproducing. Incorrectly presented dialect can be offensive or inadvertently comical.

3. Avoid aimless conversation. Be sure the dialogue has a specific point.

4. Do not use twentieth-century expressions in period novels. Eliminate slang and jargon.

In General

1. Know your audience before writing a historical novel, to discover (a) what books are successful and (b) why these books work. Then tailor your work to fit within these guidelines.

2. Do not use sensationalistic devices. Do not insert a gruesome scene into a romance for shock value. This cheapens your work.

3. Be original—try to create protagonists who are not stereotypes. This is not easily accomplished, but protagonists possessing individuality and unusual characteristics are more interesting.

4. Do not be afraid to use humor—the use of comic devices can improve the book. However, use humor only if the plot line is suitable.

5. Have fun! Writing often is a tedious, hard job, but it also can be enjoyable, rewarding, and productive. So try to relax and enjoy yourself.

The active voice is more direct and concise than the passive. The active voice ensures a more emphatic, dramatic, and lively writing style.

Passive: A walk is being taken by Ed. (This awkward clumsy construction produces a dull sentence.)
Active: Ed is taking a walk. (Simple and direct statement.)
Passive: Some plants were bought by Diana.
Active: Diana bought some plants. (Precise and natural sentence.)

Avoid artificial writing and diction. Stilted language often yields pompous sentences.

Example: The edifice was consumed by fire. (This passive voice sounds phony and stilted.)
The house burned down. (This sentence in the active voice is simple and direct.)

Avoid wordiness and vagueness. Succinct, compact expression is almost always the best. Eliminate *all* unnecessary words and phrases.

Keep *The Elements of Style* by your bed.

Romance Jargon

When authors and editors get together in the romance world, they inevitably fall into considerable trade jargon. Here are some basic expressions you should recognize so you can join in any conversation that gets going.

"My *agent* got me a nice *advance* only on a *partial*, but the *points* aren't so hot. The *contract* is for 5 percent on the first 100,000 and 6 percent over that. The *earn-out* should be good if they *print* 300,000, but *categories* have such a short *shelf life*, and without a *book club*, and not much in the way of *PR*, I won't know until my *royalty statement* comes in if I've made a lot of money.

"The *editor* suggested I write a longer book, possibly for *trade* or *hardcover*. *Mass-market* books are so competitive that it's hard to stand out. I hope the salesmen are working with the *chains* and *distributors* to circulate all the books, or else they will wind up in the *warehouse* or have the covers *stripped*. My dream is to write a *lead book* someday, and get a *dump*. Thank God the stores have *romance centers* now, and the *subsidiary rights* director is getting our *line* magazine *serialization*."

agent A man or a woman who represents you with the publisher and negotiates your contract for a fee of 10 to 15 percent of your eventual earnings on said romance. He or she acts as your salesman and adviser.

advance The amount of money a publisher gives you upon acceptance of either a finished manuscript (if you're a new romance writer) or an outline and first three chapters (if you've previously sold a number of romances that did well). This money is an advance against your own earnings. Advances range from $3,000 to $6,000 for a category romance. Historical romance advances be as low as $2,000 for a first novel and up to $15,000. An agent may get you more.

blues The printer's copy of the book, a later stage than galleys. Some corrections are done at this stage, but it's costly to the publisher.

book club At the moment, only Harlequin and Silhouette have romance book clubs, but one teenage book club, Heavenly Romances, has been launched. Book clubs, such as Harlequin's, reprint and reprint their most popular titles, and an author may sell over one million of a title eventually.

categories The subgenre label for short contemporary novels written to guidelines.

chains Referring to Waldenbooks and Dalton Bookseller. It is most important that your book gets into the chains; that will bring you a distribution of over 1,000 stores. There are smaller chains, too, around the country.

clean manuscript A submitted manuscript, carefully typed, with grammatical and spelling corrections made.

contract Usually standard form, it states your advance, your royalty rate, the submission date, number of free copies, subsidiary rights, etc. The percentages and monies are negotiated by your agent or lawyer.

deadline The date your manuscript is due. You can be a little late, but don't frighten your agent and editor to death, or get a reputation for not being reliable.

distributors The guys to court. If they don't get your books to the chains and independent bookstores, no readers will find them.

dump A cardboard display case, usually paid for by publisher or in cooperation with bookstores. Only the big names and lead titles get one.

earn-out What the accumulated royalties will earn you. If you are earning 12¢ a book, and your company prints 300,000 and sells 250,000, you may possibly earn out $30,000 (but must repay your advance and pay off your agent).

edited manuscript Your editor goes over the story to suggest revisions, and when you have made such revisions, the entire work is turned over to a line editor, who may or may not make major revisions; then this version goes to the printer. Galleys are then proofread for printer's typos and last-minute changes.

editor Usually a woman; she represents your manuscript throughout its route from acquisition to publication. Editors jump around, as do most publishing personnel, so you can't count on dealing with the same one with every book. Authors who adore their editors may follow them from publisher to publisher.

filler An editor sometimes needs a certain type of romance to balance her line.

formula Category romances have a simple one (like westerns and other genres). Woman meets devastating man, motivation for their attraction is established, they are separated, torn apart (without this, there is no story), their problems are resolved, and they commit themselves to marriage.

galleys The manuscript set in type. It goes to the proofreader. Usually authors are given a set to go over.

genre A type of popular fiction. Romances are a genre, as are westerns, science fiction, spy, mystery, and adventure novels.

good cover Many books don't sell because of bad covers. The category romance lines are standard, but historical romances are not. A good cover should be pleasing, sensuous art, and the heroine should resemble the character in the book as to eye and hair color. Historical authors vie to have Harry Bennet, Tom Hall, Elaine Gignilliat, Bob McGinnis, or Elaine Duilow, etc., as their illustrators. The blurb lines on the back of the book are also specialty work.

hardcover Still printed for reference books, special fiction (but only the big names), nonfiction books, and library editions. Few romances are ever printed in this form except for the stars and in book clubs.

harlequin hero An older man, sophisticated, arrogant, rich, handsome, domineering.

lead book Every author's dream. Additional publicity, monies, preferential treatment, large space in the catalogue, plus the advantage that many distributors automatically order lead titles for their stores, sight unseen.

line The term for category romance series.

mass market The small, under-$5 paperback novels.

new author A term used to describe someone just getting started, who perhaps has sold one book but is still not recognized enough to get a contract without showing the completed manuscript.

pagination The number of pages in the finished book. Category romances range from 182 to 250.

partial Refers to the first part, or first fifty pages, or first three chapters. If an agent or editor likes this material and your complete outline, you can sell this idea for a contract and an advance, if you're already published.

PR *Public relations* is a blanket term for getting your book write-ups and special promotional campaigns. National TV advertising and magazine ads are the best publicity a publisher can provide.

print, print run, printing Refers to the number of copies of your book printed. This number, of course, affects your eventual royalties. Many authors check to learn publishers' print runs and try to write for the one with the highest average. This figure is usually not stated in your contract. Just pray!

prolific writers   Authors who can write a romance in a month or six weeks, and turn out at least four or five a year.

real estate   The amount of shelf space or rack room in a bookstore. Publishers work very hard to get their share of the available selling space—this is the secret of success.

revision   After your category romance manuscript is read by the editor, she will make suggestions for revisions, and you will not get the contract until this stage concludes satisfactorily. If you protest, the editor may ask you to go elsewhere.

romance centers   The burgeoning lines of category romances find their way each month to specially designed racks in the chain stores.

royalty rates or points   Based on the percentage you receive of the retail price of the book. If your novel retails for $2.00 and your contract royalty or points are 6 percent, you will receive approximately 12¢ on every book sold. (This money repays your advance to the publisher and *then* you get the rest of the monies.)

royalty statement   Your payment of royalties, which arrives twice a year, usually in the spring and fall. There may be "holding" money to cover any returns, but usually this is for hardcovers.

schedule   Each line must send out four to eight books to fill up its reserved space with the distributors and booksellers.

serialization   Magazines such as *Good Housekeeping* and *Family Circle* frequently print a portion of a forthcoming romance novel.

shelf life   Most category romances have just one "shot" at a store. The new titles come in at the beginning of each month, and are usually not reordered unless some unprecedented sales occur. Then the categories are replaced by the next eighty-three selections.

sizzle   Steamy sex. Could be oral, and very explicit. Jacuzzi baths, silk sheets, any sizzling activity helps the steam rise.

stripping   A practice used by booksellers to save the cost of shipping back returns of mass-market paperbacks. Some bookstores sell the stripped books for 50 percent off, meanwhile getting credit from the publisher for the returned book covers only (terrible!).

strong story   Many category romances lack this element, and authors need to strengthen their fiction skills to achieve depth of motivation and character.

subsidiary rights The publisher tries to sell reprint rights of your manuscript to magazines, which excerpt and serialize, to foreign publishers, and to movie production companies looking to option romances. Book clubs are an important subsidiary sale.

sustained sensuality From the moment a romance opens and the heroine sees the hero, they are aware of if not enthralled by each other, and the thread of their chemical attraction must continue until the end.

tip sheets The guidelines available only from the category romance lines, which give their preferences for heroes, heroines, age, sensuality, word count, etc.

Tom Selleck "hunk" The new hero, who is handsome, sexy, vulnerable, and resembles a TV personality.

trade An oversized paperback book, usually costing $5 or more. In the old days this would have been a hardcover, but now production costs are prohibitive.

typos Typing errors, such as "siad."

warehouse Where the books are stored and shipped from; where the books are returned for credit.

word count Each category romance line and historical romance publisher prints to a certain length, and authors are expected to learn how to arrange their chapters accordingly.

The Romance Novel Route

Start with square 1, send finished manuscript to your choice of publishers, and if the reader likes it, and recommends it to the editor, she will introduce it at an editorial meeting, and if everyone else agrees, you will receive a letter or a call with the news you've been waiting for—manuscript-discussion time.

If you get to the fifth square, alongside the editor's pleasant image draw in a self-portrait: you, the new aspirant to romance writing fame. (See illustration on p. 358.)

Unfortunately, the maze could end there if you haven't diligently learned the rules and have turned in an unsuitable submission. But if your novel is all it should be, and the editor is expressing real interest, then consider the ways and means of moving your picture of yourself into harmony with the editor's. Of course this means you two must be compatible. She must find you easy to work with (prime donnas move back to square 1),

the R♥MANCE route

WRITER · PUBLISHER · READER · EDITORIAL MEETING · ARTIST · BLURB WRITER · ART DIRECTOR · EDITOR · PROMOTION · SALES FORCE · EDITOR · PROOFREADER · BOOKSTORE · GALLEYS · COPY EDITOR · LINE EDITOR

alert, willing to take suggestions, reasonable, intelligent, and not in need of constant encouragement or babying. No stormy weather, either, and no personality quirks foisted off on your overworked would-be benefactor. In these harassed days of heavy competition among romance writers and publishers, a great deal of success or failure depends upon the author's attitude as well as her ability.

Be positive should be the watchword. But don't be *too* submissive or eager. In other words, be pleasant and natural. Overdoing it will stall you.

If you have revised your manuscript properly, according to the editor's suggestions, and have landed that contract, and have proved to the editor's satisfaction that you're okay and not a troublemaker, you'll move on along the line, past places 6, 7, and 8, and you'll be conferring with the editor again. Now is the time to begin being a little assertive, but not demanding. The editor is still in the commanding seat, so be tactful. If you antagonize her by temperamental behavior, she can easily shunt you into an indefinite "hold" position, and publication of your book could be delayed for months, or even eventually cancelled altogether.

Assuming that you still have a good foothold in the maze, that she still likes you and wants the best for your book, to her credit and yours, she will appreciate any discreet and enterprising notions you may be able to offer for making your title a winner. But if she finds your ideas tiresome and not all that original or in keeping with her line, don't press her. After all, she can only suggest to other key positions along the route what she thinks might enhance sales and produce a best-selling author. Publishers do just as they please, remember, but if you have come up with something fresh and eye-catching, they'll like it, even if you never get any credit for your creativity—that's *their* function, don't forget.

It doesn't hurt to make up your synopsis of the plot, with the characters' physical descriptions and the locale, to give to the editor to add to whatever she is giving to the illustrator of your book. That is one way to make certain the hair coloring will be exact.

From now on, after the artist (who thinks your painter friend's idea for a cover is dreadful), the blurb writer, the art director, the sales force, you are now almost at the end of the hurdle.

Promotion alone is left to win over before your romance is shipped to the bookstores. It is with this all-important power that you must be your most adroit, charming, clever (if you have any shrewdness in the area of marketing), and delicately attuned to what will or will not go. The promotion department is second only to the editor and sales force in the future of your career.

If you have run the maze, now is the time to proceed with all caution and strength. Reread this book for marketing tips; talk to other writers who have been highly successful in helping to promote their work with ads in a romance publication, personal notes to their readers, and friendly relations with booksellers.

Then you go on to work with your local booksellers, and commu
nicate with booksellers across the country.

The rest is up to her quixotic Ladyship—Luck!

Author/Editor Relationship

Category romances have been the hottest game in publishing
since explicit sex became acceptable. The person responsible fo
choosing the two to eight books of a line each month is the
senior editor.

She may be the only human being at a publishing house that a
new author communicates with, outside of an agent. However
authors and editors, the presidents, publicists, and other staff get
together once a year at the Romantic Book Lovers' Conference
in New York. Since many writers have contracts with more than
one publishing house, there's a lot of entanglements when they
all get together.

Today's romance editor is the most harried of all editors in
publishing. Not only is she required to do the usual editorial
work, but she must work closely with publicity, sales force, and
promotion, and appear as her line's spokeswoman on TV and at
writer's conferences. Time is of the utmost importance.

The reader's report is what makes her look at a manuscript.
She cannot read the dozens and dozens of unsolicited and agent-
offered manuscripts that reach her desk. Editors are very selective of their readers, taking them along when they change jobs,
like a personal secretary. It's essential that readers have the same
convictions as to what is good and is wanted for an editor's line.

When the editor gets a good report, then she reads the manuscript to make the final decision. If revisions are called for, a
new writer is expected to comply, without benefit of a contract.
This is the crucial stage. Many new writers won't or can't
manage to repair or enhance a story, which is why money is not
exchanged at this stage.

It's only after the revisions are made and accepted by your
editor that a contract is given to a new writer. Many category
romance houses do not have line editors, but rely on copy editors
to make the next round of suggestions.

The queen of line editors seems to be Jan de Vries, who works
out of her Pennsylvania home, mainly for Avon historical romance authors, including Kathleen Woodiwiss. She is under
contract to some companies exclusively.

Many line editors of historical romances agree that it takes two to edit: an editor who believes that a good book can be made better and a writer who is skillful with his or her prose. With a lesser writer, an editor is reduced to one part English teacher, correcting grammar, and one part rewrite expert (if she has time, and most romance editors don't).

After this stage the author next sees the galleys, the proofs from the printer, put in her hand by her editor, and if there are any changes the author must make them now.

What are the horror stories of romance publishing? Once, a publisher had a mix-up in the warehouse, and none of its six titles for the month went out. Many times the hero and heroine on the cover don't vaguely resemble the story, even down to the wrong time period and hair and eye coloring. Most confusing is when the blurb writer misunderstands the tone of the story and the reader is led to expect a completely different story from the one inside. And, horrors of horrors, a chapter is left out, as happened to Bertrice Small's historical romance classic *Kadin*. Avon went on to six printings and never replaced it.

To better understand the role of the editor, here are some of their responsibilities:

1. Honing fine details.
2. Giving a plot more "oomph."
3. Fleshing out a character.
4. Inspring writers to make the right revisions.
5. Making the final decisions.
6. Being willing to hand a book over to another editor in the house if the writer-editor relationship has deteriorated.
7. Coordinating the manuscript with art department, cover-copy writer, production, publicity and promotion, and sales.
8. Developing writers, preventing them from becoming copy machines or "burning out."
9. Guaranteeing a book is written in proper English and with proper usage.

An author will be wise to team up with one of the best editors and stay with her. Many careers have been developed because an author took the time to find out what editors had edited what writers and consequently produced the best books.

A new writer may not have this opportunity, but an established writer will eventually have the power to ask for a particular editor. Speaking to other writers and keeping up with the latest industry news is one way of learning about the editors and their authors.

An editor who goes to bat for you with the company is your best weapon. And if you ever have a financial squeeze, she can see to an emergency loan, if need be. There may not be any Maxwell Perkinses on Publishers' Row today, but there are a lot of editors with heart!

The Literary Agent and the Book Contract

Do you need an agent? Maybe yes, maybe no. Some of the leading agents in the romance field speak out here on their responsibilities and benefits to a writer.

Most editors will suggest that you deal with an agent. Companies such as Fawcett (now part of Ballantine) will not look at unsolicited manuscripts. Editors prefer to discuss contract terms with professionals who understand the business. They don't have the patience to explain it all to a writer. Also, editors put out calls, particularly in the category romance field, for new and perhaps very specific kinds of novels. An agent can help you get such assignments, and others to follow.

If you don't want to give an agent 10 to 15 percent of your earnings on each book, there are certain things you can do. (1) Hire a literary lawyer (but not any other kind) to read and negotiate your contract. Bertrice Small and several other top names retain a lawyer for all their contractual negotiations, which costs much less than paying an agent's fee. However, he does not play a part in advising a writer on her career, or acting as a critic and salesperson for the next manuscript. (2) Study some books on the subject, speak with other authors, and sign the contract yourself. The only way you might lose out is in fighting for the royalty points; however, most category romance houses aren't open to negotiation on this issue, except, perhaps, with the superstars.

In essence, most contracts are standard. You can learn to understand your royalty rates, advance money, foreign and subsidiary rights. At NAL Rapture, a standard advance to a new writer is $4,000 and 6 percent royalty. Harlequin American Romance gives a $6,000 advance and similar percentage points or royalties. (Foreign rights are 50 percent [low] to 75/25 percent, in your favor [high], depending upon publisher.)

Historical romance authors may get slightly higher advances for their first books. More time and research go into the manuscript, and the cover price is higher, so editors advance money accordingly.

A new romance writer usually has to hand in a finished manuscript to get her advance money. In other areas of book publishing, especially if you are an experienced writer, you may get an advance against a partial manuscript, or even an outline. In the old days, an advance was to cover a writer's living expenses till completion of the manuscript. Now publishers are dubious about turning over money to an inexperienced author. They have been burned in too many cases by writers getting scared and not finishing, or not fulfilling the promise of an outline or partial.

A royalty statement is based on the accumulation of money earned according to the percentage you get from each book. If a contract says 6 percent royalty and your title retails for $1.95, you will earn approximately 11 cents on each sale. The accumulation of that money must add up to cover your advance, be it $3,000 or $6,000, before you get paid any additional monies. Royalty statements and checks are sent out twice a year, usually in the fall and spring. Sometimes there is a reserve figure, which means a certain amount of books are still in stores and it isn't known if they are sold or will be returned. Royalties on these books are withheld. A writer makes money only on copies sold.

What is a bad agent? Someone who only looks over your contract, takes his cut each and every royalty period, and does nothing else for you. An agent should be like a confidant and take an interest in your career and your next manuscript, which he should read and discuss with you.

Some agents ask for an exclusive contract with a writer. Other agents work with a writer from book to book, without a personal agreement. If an agent convinces you that he/she will work for you and doesn't want you to fly the coop while he/she is working on your behalf, you can't harm yourself by signing a short-term personal agreement and seeing if the arrangement works. But if you like to be cautious, talk to some of the other clients before you sign up. Some authors have been with the same agent for decades, and will continue to be. When this sort of dual loyalty occurs, you may be sure that they have been good for each other.

As historical romance authors these days are getting a variety of advances, an agent is particularly helpful for new writers in this field. The lowest advance paid a new author is usually $1,000 by Zebra, and the highest up to $8,000 from Avon or Pocket (sometimes higher). These figures are for first-time authors, who can expect *at least* a $2,500 increase with their next contract, as that's the standard raise.

An agent will get the best deal, for he or she is an experienced bargainer. On your own, the company will offer you its standard (lowest) advance and royalty point. However, the advance is against your own money. You pay it back, remember, in your first royalty statement, of which your agent takes a percentage. The check goes to the agent, who deducts the agency fee and then sends the remainder on to the writer.

Foreign sales, subsidiary rights—these clauses are known to agents and lawyers. The percentage you get of these sales varies, but you do split them with your publisher. A hardcover publisher sells the paperback rights to your book, and splits the money with you, at a negotiated percentage.

Retaining movie rights is up to the writer. Many category romance lines already have arrangements with film production companies. Unless you're Janet Dailey, who has her own movie production company, run by her husband, what will you do with the movie rights that your publisher won't do?

A contract also includes the date the manuscript is due. Most authors are a little late, so it's not crucial if your're slightly tardy. But do try to be punctual. Editors come to rely on, and give special favor to, their dependable writers.

There are other considerations in getting a contract, but this is the basic information to think about.

How to find a literary agent? A list is printed on page 368. Also, if you have been one of the lucky ones and can sell your own manuscript, you can always ask your editor about getting an agent. She has her favorites to recommend.

The Author-Agent Relationship

BY DENISE MARCIL

romance literary agent

What does an agent do? An agent sells and markets an author's books and/or magazine articles, negotiates contracts, and develops an author's career. The agent is an author's business partner and handles the business aspects so the writer can focus on his/her job of writing. For example, the agent takes care of problems that don't even concern the manuscript, such as making sure the author receives his/her check and royalty statements. The agent is an author's link with the publishing industry and often is the only permanent person the author can rely upon. Editors often move from one publishing house to another, leaving their books and authors behind. And authors change houses as well. Finally, companies are bought out by conglomerates, often changing personnel.

A good agent gives an author guidance and develops his/her career as a writer. Most agents are not interested in one-shot deals, and as authors, you shouldn't be either. Agents help writers realize ideas and convey market trends. They often find specific ideas from editors and will link up an editor with a writer.

In today's tough marketplace, it's crucial that writers be aware of market trends—what's selling at any particular point in time.

Agents know the market, and this is one of the most important advantages agents offer their clients. We know who's buying what, what the advances are, the style of the house, individual editors and their personal tastes. We also know the capabilities of other departments in a publishing house. For example, one house might have a far superior sales force and better distribution than another house.

Authors frequently want to know how agents submit manuscripts to publishers. Relationships are developed between agents and editors. We lunch together, dine together, and are constantly on the phone with each other. So when a publisher is developing a new line of romances or needs a big book for their next list, the editor will call the agents that he/she is most friendly with or knows has the types of books needed. It's the agent's job to understand what an individual editor's personal taste is so that when a manuscript comes in to the agent, he or she can read it and automatically say "This saga would be perfect for a specific editor at a specific house."

Submissions are either single submissions, sent exclusively to one editor at a time, or multiple submissions, sent to several editors at the same time. Another submission possibility is the auction. Several manuscripts are submitted and a date is set for the closing, the final date the agent will accept offers. The agent can set rules for the auction prior to the closing. For example, he/she could stipulate that there would be only one round of offers (each publisher can make only one bid, so it should be their best offer). Auctions are usually only held on major books where an agent wants to create a sense of competition to increase the advances, improve contract terms, and increase the commitment of the publisher.

How does an author find an agent? You can begin by talking with other writers to find out about their agents. Many agents find their clients from referrals from current clients. Book editors are often helpful in locating agents for authors. If you have established some contact or rapport with an editor, or certainly if an editor has made an offer on a book, you can ask them for a list of agents that you can contact. It's usually company policy for editors to give writers the names of several agents upon request.

Magazine editors are another good source for finding an agent. If you've ever written articles or short fiction for magazines, the editors there can suggest an agent.

Reference books such as *Literary Market Place* and *The Writer's Market* can give you leads on agents. Organizations such as

Poets & Writers or the Independent Literary Agents Association and the Society for Author's Representatives all provide lists of agents.

Finally, writers can contact agents directly by writing a query letter. Always include a self-addressed stamped envelope with your letter. In one page, you should tell the agent about the book, a bit about yourself, and why you are qualified to write the book. The letter should be enticing, though not cute. Ask if the agent would be interested in reading your work. If he/she asks for sample chapters, send the first three chapters. *Never* send a few chapters or pages from different parts of the book! The first three chapters should convince the reader that he/she wants to read more. Finally, most agents prefer to see an author's work on an exclusive basis. Do not submit to more than one agent at a time. It is unfair for the agent who reads the material and would like to take on the author to discover that another agent has the material as well. If you want to be taken seriously as a professional writer, then you must act in a professional manner.

Tips from Denise Marcil: Five Steps to Writing a Successful Romantic Novel

1. *Read and study the genre in which you want to write.*
2. *Always prepare an outline before starting to write.*
3. *Prepare short characterizations. For romances, know who your heroine is and what she wants; who the hero is and what he wants.*
4. *The major dramatic question of the romance is, will they get together? All the complications in the book will relate to that question.*
5. *The crisis answers the major dramatic question, that is, do they get together or not? As soon as the couple does get together, you should* **end** *the book!*

List of Romance Literary Agents

Jay Acton
825 Third Avenue
New York, N.Y. 10022

Stephen Axelrod
Sterling Lord Agency
660 Madison Avenue,
New York, N.Y. 10021

Meredith Bernstein
33 Riverside Drive
New York, N.Y. 10023

Brandt & Brandt
1501 Broadway
New York, N.Y. 10036

Curtis Brown
575 Madison Avenue
New York, N.Y. 10022

Columbia Literary Associates
Inc.
10594 Jason Court
Columbia, Md. 21044

Jay Garon
415 Central Park West
New York, N.Y. 10025

Adele Leoni
52 Riverside Drive
#6A,
New York, N.Y. 10024

Ellen Levine
370 Lexington Avenue
New York, N.Y. 10017

Barbara Lowenstein
250 W. 57th Street
New York, N.Y. 10107

Donald MacCampbell
12 E. 41st Street
New York, N.Y. 10017

Denise Marcil
316 W. 82nd Street
New York, N.Y. 10024

Jane Rotrosen
318 E. 51st Street
New York, N.Y. 10022

Cherry Weiner
1734 Church Street
Rahway, N.J. 07065

Writers House
21 W. 26th Street
New York, N.Y. 10010

The above agents handle many of today's published romance writers. Contact them with a query letter, plus outline-proposal or outline plus sample chapters. Include a SASE.

Writing Tools

In this age of technology, Barbara Cartland is not the only author who likes the old-fashioned way and dictates. Sidney Sheldon

Electronic Pocket Typewriter

Cy Endfield, who wrote and directed the film, Zulu, has invented a pocket typewriter called the Microwriter. The slimline battery-operated electronic gadget measures 8½ inches long, 4 inches wide, and 2¼ inches deep, and weighing 24 ounces, has been hailed by one computer industry expert as "the biggest thing since man discovered the pencil."

The Microwriter is designed for use with an automatic high-speed printer and produces the text at up to ten times the speed of normal typing. It can also be attached to a television monitor, enabling the writer to see sixteen lines of text at a time; an adaptor plugs it into a domestic TV.

When Endfield began to write the novel of the sequel film, Zulu Dawn, it occurred to him that there must be a quicker way to put thoughts on paper rather than penciled notes, a regular typewriter, or dictation. He invented the prototype for Microwriter—the original model can be seen in the science museum in London.

You type on it with one hand, because it has only five keys on the board, plus a sixth control key at the side. Each letter is produced by touching a button or combination of buttons— like playing a chord on the piano. To memorize the keyboard code, special positioning of the fingers is required to simulate the shape of the character or part of it.

Microwriter produces the full Roman alphabet, upper or lower case, numbers, punctuation marks, and other normal keyboard symbols. An ordinary pocket casette recorder makes it possible to transfer the contents of the memory bank onto a microcassette.

dictates his entire manuscript, about ten pages a day, and then spends months working on it and polishing. Marie de Jourlet depends on a Stenorette.

Finding your favorite writing tool may depend on your budget. A simple electric typewriter needs only a change of ribbon. An IBM Selectric runs up a bill with the nonreusable cartridges and erasure tapes.

Each writing tool has its saving grace. Most professional writers keep two typewriters on hand for the time when one breaks down—choices are endless today for which two.

A writer just invented the electronic pocket typewriter, which can be read via a television monitor. This is "the biggest thing since man discovered the pencil."

The best typewriter, according to a poll of romance writers, is the IBM Selectric II, with the automatic erasure feature. This machine costs close to $1,500, and a service policy can be acquired at an additional charge. This service is a must if you use your typewriter daily, and the repairman usually arrives within two days.

There are more sophisticated machines, with a memory feature, but the next step in machinery these days is the word processor.

There are probably as many choices as there are writers, but here's what a survey turned up: The Wang is much admired, but to date there is some difficulty getting service in particular regions, so this point *must* be checked. Bonnie Drake is enamored of the Victor model, which seems to be an up-and-coming choice (and costs approximately $8,000). Patricia Matthews has just mastered her model, the Xerox Word Dedicator (that costs around $12,000).

There are several books on the subject, and the *Writer's Digest* (October 1982) ran a special section describing the features and particulars, but made no recommendations.

Janelle Taylor is probably the most enthusiastic writer using a word processor today. As she explains, it helped her to become a best-seller, and to keep her books coming forth with less manual work.

How to Write a Best-seller on a Dictaphone Word Processor

BY JANELLE TAYLOR

author of six historical romances

For years, the only way modern technology seemed to assist the professional writer was with the electric typewriter and its infrequent improvements. Finally, a "wonder" machine has been invented that removes the physical struggles, mental stress, and laborious time of preparing manuscripts. I'm referring to the Dictaphone Dual Display Word Processor, which I found superior to other models I tested and investigated. I have many writer friends who purchased other machines, but now drool with envy over my marvelous Dictaphone.

After three years of manuscripts requiring nearly ten months to type after the basic research was completed, I can have a manuscript ready to mail in only a few months. It constantly amazes me what this machine can do. It allows the writer greater freedom with the manuscript because entire texts can be shifted or rearranged easily and quickly. Editing is a breeze, for the machine almost corrects errors for you. The machine neatly aligns pages, and numbers them, with a single command. The machine also formats to give the appearance of a book page. You are practically refused the privilege of making an error. When you are in doubt of a command, the machine will supply it. If an erroneous command is given, the machine politely rejects it. Previous piles of paperwork are now stored on softwear disks the size of 45-rpm records: a completed book on two small disks! Each time I begin a new manuscript, I realize just how hard I used to work on the writing mechanics, which my new machine does with speed, neatness, and, most of all, simplicity.

When I wrote *Savage Ecstasy*, my first historical romance, the demanding mechanics of writing nearly ended my budding career. My typing was rusty at that time, so I hand-wrote the first draft of 600 pages. Then I proceeded to type, while editing and polishing, draft after draft on a manual typewriter. After a year of seemingly endless work, I discovered the final draft was not in the correct format. I looked at the monstrous stack of pages, cried, then asked myself if writing was worth the stress, labor, and time involved. Since I'm presently working on a contract to complete my eleventh book, my final decision is obvious.

When I began writing *Defiant Ecstasy*, my husband purchased an electric typewriter. I thought my prayers had been answered by the reduction of work. Then I misnumbered the last 300 pages of the manuscript! It was a tedious chore to correct; now, by pushing one button, I would merely tell my machine to number the pages in order. Fortunately, the Dictaphone uses English Command Language, not a technical code, making commands easy to learn and to use.

A writer sits down, turns on the machine, inserts a disk, types in the manuscript, then commands the machine to insert the format and page number. Later, when the editing task comes along, the text can be called up, worked on, then printed if ready. If a page has errors, they can be corrected with one button, then a new page is printed out; no more retyping single pages after messy corrections. Days of retyping corrections can be done within a couple of hours, simply by correcting the word on the screen, then commanding the machine to reprint that page. If the publisher asks for additions to a previously written manuscript, the text can be quickly and easily inserted anywhere in the manuscript. The succeeding pages are automatically backed up and renumbered. If a scene finds itself in the wrong place, simply tell the machine to relocate it at another chosen spot. With a single button, words can be corrected, added, or deleted. The machine can print the final draft without the writer even being in the room. Publishers find the neat copy most appealing.

At first I was intimidated by the thought of working on such a complex machine for hours each day, even though I had previously worked with Wang computers on my last job in medical research. Dictaphone solves this mental crisis by giving free classroom lessons with a genial, well-trained technician. The machine is installed by a qualified person, then more instructions at home are given. If any problem arises, Dictaphone quickly responds with repairs or advice, preventing any loss of time when you're up against a demanding deadline. Any updated disks or features are supplied. The cost of supplies decreases with the decreased need of multiple rough drafts.

While I was working on *Forbidden Ecstasy*, many of Dictaphone's marvelous features came into play. Each component has its own memory bank. While using lengthy Sioux names and vocabulary, I could simply type in the first few letters of the phrase or name. Later, I could instruct the machine to "global search" those abbreviations, and it would simultaneously replace them with the correct word or words, saving a great deal of time and preventing possible spelling errors. Another help is the "replace" feature for those words we "learned" to misspell; type in the faulty word as spelled and the machine will correct it each time it is used. If a name (character or location) needs to be changed, this same feature will automatically replace the old one with the new one in a few moments.

From what I personally viewed and learned, Dictaphone has more features and simplicity than the other models. Naturally it has the "bold," "center," and "underscore" features. No more counting spaces to properly center something; the machine does it with one button. If a chapter gets too long, the machine allows you to split and form new documents. It tells you when the ribbon is out and when you've hit a wrong key. It blatantly refuses an incorrect command. It eliminates a writer's horror of accidental erasure of text. If the erase command is given accidentally, the machine verifies this command before responding—a virtual lifesaver. Friends with other machines have accidentally erased entire texts, short stories, or portions of text, which required extra work and unnecessary tension to replace.

Many of the other models require several steps for each command and lack many of the helpful features Dictaphone has. I believe the simplicity of the commands is a big advantage.

Dictaphone also includes many other features of great use to writers. A "phrase library" feature enables the writer to store and to recall at will certain phrases used time and time again. Research material can be stored on a desk and called up for use at any time, without your having to go through pages of handwritten or typed notes. Ask for a certain research word, and the machine puts that text on the screen. There are features I do not use—footnoting, math, fielding, marked (highlighted) corrections, etc.—but others might find them useful.

If a command is used infrequently and possibly forgotten, the machine will supply the command upon request of one button, preventing loss of time caused by referring to the manual. If the phone rings, which it inevitably does while you're working, the machine can be left on; a blinking light tells you where you halted. The four-part unit is attractive and quiet. It requires little electricity to operate, as attested by the minor hike in my power bill.

These four parts include a CRT full-page screen, a keyboard similar to a typewriter, a printer, and a dual-drive module. However, I purchased two keyboards so my husband could work simultaneously with me, or on his own projects. The same disk can be used by both, but not the same document upon that disk. The machine can do several things at one time: insert text, print another text, paginate and format still another, edit another, etc. The only thing that can't be done simultaneously is work on the same text. Each chapter is a document, listed as that chapter. Therefore, any other chapter in the manuscript can be worked on by another person; or the writer can be editing one while printing another. If the writer doesn't wish to retain the text, the disk can be erased like a tape and used over and over. As for myself, I keep the final draft in a disk box with the others. I also retain research disks, as sequels are often desired, or I may write another book set in that same period. This, of course, cuts down on paper and storage space.

While working on *The Black Mist*, I saved countless hours and stress by printing out one rough draft and working from it for editing, then printed out the final copy. The screen is charcoal and the print green, colors tested and approved by the FFA for eye ease. The approximate cost of this unit is $14,000, more than the others I looked at and didn't like. As this was a one-time purchase that would be used daily, the price was not a factor. Why buy an expensive machine if it can offer little over an electric typewriter, as I felt the others did? Having just signed a new six-book contract, I felt the money was minor when compared to the benefits it supplies. What better way to spend royalties (a business deduction) than to find the stress missing as you go from doing one book every ten to fifteen months to completing one in only a couple of months? A writer should have pleasant surroundings and all possible distractions removed from her daily work schedule; the Dictaphone accomplishes these valuable services. I heartily recommend this machine over any other I'm familiar with. I'm not sure how I survived those first two years of writing without my "wonder" machine.

For certain, I couldn't do without it now. It seems to do everything but create!

P.O. Box 212
APO New York

December 18

Dear Kathryn Falk,
I must remain anonymous, but I don't know who else to write to. My wife is about to get published as a romance writer and I don't know if I can handle it. I think I'm going crazy. Do I wear the pants in the family or does she?

Fretful

From the Desk of Kathryn Falk

December 31

Dear Fretful,
I'm going out of town for the New Year and I don't want you to suffer when it's needless. I called George Small, the husband of historical novelist Bertrice Small, and I asked him to send you an inspirational message. He thinks that being one of Love's Leading Husbands is kind of fun. (If you know how to handle it.)

Best wishes,
Kathryn Falk

Advice to Husbands: Don't Bite the Hand That Writes

BY GEORGE SMALL

husband of historical romance novelist Bertrice Small

Being married to a successful lady novelist certainly presents some unique problems for men. A man who considers it normal to spend half his life absorbed in a business his wife is locked out of suddenly finds his wife absorbed in a business *he* is locked out of and, what's worse, spending hours involved with romantic situations in which he doesn't even figure. Is she merely concocting fictitious romance to sell, or is she actually writing down the romantic situations her little heart expected out of him and never got? Does she really expect him to act like the heroes in her books? If so, is it love or is she trying to bring on a heart attack?

What happened anyway? Here he had a normal existence with a sweet demure little wife, and one morning he woke up and found he was married to Ernest Hemingway. The sweet demure little girl sits curled up on the couch with an enigmatic little smile on her face and writes about things she never learned from him. How will he explain her to his friends, his mother, his shrink? What's worse, the rewards are incredible. She mails in her little stories and the tooth fairy dumps a pot of gold on the doorstep. They have a new house, a new car, six mink coats, plus a brace of Russian wolfhounds, and the cops are beginning to follow him around on the suspicion that he is peddling more than just Tupperware . . .

First let's look at a few male hang-ups that arise when hubby discovers that the little woman has suddenly turned into a literary lion.

1. Inferiority complex over not maintaining his traditional role as the breadwinner. Feeling he is losing control.
2. Resentment over being crowded out of the last traditional masculine position in a world where areas of exclusive masculine activity are shrinking daily. The girls are into everything.
3. Feeling of being left out because his wife operates in a field he is not familiar with.
4. Annoyance over wife's "overnight" success. She made it big, and for all his years of struggling he never did.
5. Conviction that to apply himself to household chores or to assume a supporting role would be demeaning.

Men feel that in handing over family support to their wives they have been beaten out by women in a role they created for themselves. Much as many men dislike the aggressive business world, they did create it, which gives them a proprietary interest they feel obligated to defend. This can lead to a number of subversive tactics (often subconscious) by which, in the guise of giving the little lady a helping hand, they are actually helping her over a cliff. This is "torpedoing," and it usually consists of giving wifey bad advice or bad management, or creating situations around her that make it difficult to write, in hopes that she will be a failure and wind up back in the kitchen. In its more virulent aspects it can extend to insulting her publisher, drinking too much at business lunches, and putting wifey down on every possible occasion.

If men handle this right they can turn the whole thing around and come out looking like heroes, even to themselves. To this end I would like to suggest the following approach:

Forget who traditionally does what. The "me" generation is out. Today it is the "us" generation, and whatever benefits the family comes first. Wifey has the potential to make a great deal of money in the next few years, which means luxury for everyone, including you. When you were working she stood behind you. Now she needs your help and support if she is to succeed. So, after some consideration, you decide to put aside your own interests for the time being, in order to back her up and support her efforts in every way possible—because she needs you, because she deserves her success, because you love her and her triumphs are your triumphs. However, she must understand that this is a temporary arrangement. You have your own destiny to fulfill, and when she is safely on her feet you intend to pursue it again.

If support involves taking over household chores, so be it! You'll do whatever is necessary, but she is to understand that you think housework stinks; you do it as a sacrifice, not as an act of submission, and you intend to dump it at the first opportunity.

Now you have turned what could be a negative submission into a positive assertion, and if you played it right you'll have managed a complete role reversal and still be wearing the pants (as well as a merit badge for chutzpa). You will also be in compliance with Small's Law, rule #1, which simply states, "Never drop the ball."

Now that you have achieved a position of stature you must maintain it, being very careful never to venture into a situation where you could wind up with egg on your face. Always play it within safe perimeters by strictly observing the following list of taboos.

1. Never, never attempt to negotiate with your wife's publisher unless you have the guile of an Arab street merchant and six degrees in contract law. Publishing is not a game for amateurs.
2. Never attempt to invest your wife's earnings unless you are very good at that sort of thing . . . nor should you attempt to set up tax shelters or other income hiding devices unless you qualify as an expert. Be safe! Follow Small's Law, rule #2: "Do not tempt God or the IRS."
3. Above all, never try to tell your wife how to write her books. If you think you can write a book, write it. Editing by well-meaning husbands has loused up a lot of otherwise good romantic fiction. Don't bite the hand that writes!

If you want to take a positive and assertive position in handling your wife's affairs, you can do so by carefully selecting and hiring a top-notch agent or a good contract lawyer, a good accountant, and a reputable broker or investment management concern. They will handle all the things you can't with vigor and expertise, and you can take all the credit. This should put you firmly in control of a situation that a short time ago you were virtually locked out of. Your wife will love you for taking care of things, and if she wants to give you a Ferrari for Christmas you won't have any trouble convincing yourself that you deserve it.

The challenge to women is the bitterly difficult problem of obtaining loving cooperation from a husband who is suffering from some or all of the hang-ups I have mentioned, and may be looming up as a major obstruction on the rocky road to success. If you go aggressive and shout him down, waving your royalty checks and your latest publicity releases, he is liable to go into a silent funk and wait for the first opportunity to torpedo you. The trick here is to rebuild his damaged ego, not tear it down.

First, you throw guilt at him by reminding him that you have been a loving and devoted wife (always serving, never complaining) and that you deserve the opportunity to do the one thing dearest to your heart (the insinuation being that only a selfish creep would deny this to his wife). This is an old "Jewish mother" trick but it still works and it will do fine for starters. The next step is to hand him back not only the pants, but a suit of shining armor and a sword and buckler as well. You explain that without his love and support you can never hope to accomplish what you want to do. More than ever, you need him by your side as a bastion of strength as you take on the publishing business in mortal combat. Remind him, "Whatever I make isn't for me, it's for us—our home, our lives, our future. If you love me, help me."

If you don't care for these particular sentiments, then write your own script, but don't vary from the plot line. Remember that what men want more than anything else is to be recognized as strong, capable, and chivalrous. Like everyone else, they need to be needed. It helps to augment this approach by asking hubby's assistance in handling some aspects of your career, such as arranging travel or riding shotgun on public appearances to handle problems and deal with unpleasant people. However, a desire to assuage hubby's resentment at being left out should never lead you to permit him to meddle with aspects of your career that he is not competent to handle. This particularly applies to contracts, copyrights, and financial management. In these crucial areas, never economize. Hire the best.

In the final analysis, every woman knows the bitter sense of unfulfillment that goes with being in a purely supporting role. That is not to say that the love and support that a wife (or in this case, a husband) gives is without value or merit. It certainly is not, and in its more selfless manifestations approaches saintliness. It is still, nevertheless, an inadequate life experience. There has to be something else, some self-expression, some contribution that gives a sense of personal achievement and personal worth over and above service to others. Ladies, remember this: Sooner or later your man is going to tire of being a supporting angel to the gods of romance fiction and concerning himself twenty-four hours a day with *your* books, *your* plots, *your* money, *your* health, *your* problems, *your* royalties, *your* contracts, *your* agent, *your* editors, *your* diet, *your* publicity, etc., etc., etc., and take a sudden interest in something entirely new that has nothing whatsoever to do with you or romance fiction. If it hurts having him withdraw some of the attention he has been kind enough to lavish on you and you feel a vicious urge to put down whatever it is he is into, take a deep breath and then *don't do it*. He isn't withdrawing support from you. He just needs an activity that is exclusively his own. For him it provides a safety valve. Take it away and the resultant explosion could blow your relationship into a cocked hat.

Men: For all the annoyance and aggravation of having to assume a supporting role to a wife who has suddenly become a literary tycoon, there are some wonderful benefits to be derived, and when you stop feeling angry or sorry for yourself you will find you can reach out and grab the brass ring without even bending over. Being dropped out of the work force is not a one-way ticket to the old elephant's graveyard. It is a golden opportunity to do something really wonderful, something maybe you wanted to do all your life and never thought you could because you were sweating blood to pay the rent. Now the monkey is off your back. You've got the time and money. Think how many poor guys out there would give their eyeteeth to have that opportunity, so don't waste it! Maybe you always wanted to start a small business restoring antiques or classic cars, or wanted to paint, or sculpt, or work on an archaeological dig, or anything else that is completely soul-satisfying, albeit unprofitable. All these wonderful dreams are possible because you now have access to the ultimate weapon—your wife's checkbook!

By the way, have you ever thought of trying your hand at writing romantic fiction? I understand it pays good money.

PART FIVE

───── 13 ─────

An Interview with
Barbara Cartland

*When I was in England recently, naturally I made
a beeline for the Queen of Love's Leading Ladies—
Barbara Cartland. Thanks to my trusty tape recorder, I got every delicious word she had to say.*

A long time ago, when I was writing my health book, *The Magic
of Honey*, I said to my secretaries and friends, "When you get to
a big paragraph, what do you do?"

"Skip it," they replied.

So I realized, which apparently no one had realized before,
that everybody I write for and you write for is always listening to
the radio and television.

What do they hear?

They hear a conversation.

So I realized that one must have short paragraphs so that it
looks like conversation.

Now my paragraphs are never more than three lines, three lines and a half at the outside, so my books are easy to read.

They read *The Magic of Honey*, in which I wrote "he said" "she said" all the way through and sold millions of copies all over the world and everybody bought honey. In fact, it emptied the shops of honey. Strangers still come up to me in Tokyo and Hong Kong and say, "I've taken my honey today!"

It is the same as my novels. They are easy to read, and once people have started they go on reading them.

In 1920, while I was writing my first book and dancing all night, I telephoned paragraphs every morning to the gossip column of the *Daily Express*. I was paid five shillings a paragraph and I thought I was rich! In those days five shillings was quite a lot of money.

I then wrote two or three rather mimsy articles—"Youth Speaks Out," "Flaming Youth," and that sort of thing. Lord Beaverbrooke sent for me, said he admired my style, and taught me how to write as a journalist.

So you see, why I'm so readable is that I write as a journalist.

Sir Arthur Bryant, who's our greatest historian, said the other day at a public meeting, "You may not like what Barbara writes, but I call her a very good writer because she never uses a superfluous word."

Now that is journalism! In journalism you stick to the point, you can't dribble on about other things.

You also write with a bang at the end, so, as with a serial, people have to read the next chapter to see what's happened.

I do it subconsciously now. I don't really think about it, it just happens.

But it is a way of writing for entertainment. When I started to write long ago, Godfrey Winn, who wrote a lot of novels and was a very well-known journalist, said to me, "When you are writing for entertainment, Barbara, always dictate. Because otherwise you write 'too good' English. You are always thinking, 'I must put this word in . . . I must add some extra adjectives . . . I must turn that sentence around.' "

He said, "Write as you talk, because it's very easy to read."

And that is why, as I write my novels for entertainment, I dictate them.* I dictate a chapter every afternoon when I'm at

---

*Barbara Cartland always lies on a couch with her dogs at her feet and her secretary sitting behind her because she finds it distracts her to see anyone while she is concentrating.

home, which is between six and seven thousand words. For me seven chapters make a book.

When I'm writing my more serious books, history, sociology, autobiographies—I've covered everything—I write them in my own fair hand.

Dictation is, I think, essential for entertainment. Otherwise one becomes too pompous.

Also, it's easy when you're sitting down with a blank piece of paper to think, "I'll just add extra words, extra adjectives, extra descriptions."

As Sir Arthur Bryant says, "Too many superfluous words."

So if anybody wants to write a romantic book, I think it's very important to get the mechanics right.

When publishers send me books to read, the first thing I look at is if they have long paragraphs.

I've just been sent a book by an English publisher which is being reissued, and it's *How to Write a Best Seller*. The first thing I found was two pages with *one* paragraph on each.

So I rang up the publisher, and I said, "Look, I don't want to find fault, but honestly, that's not the way to tell people how to write a best-seller today."

"Oh, would you like to write a book on the subject?" he asked.

"No, I've not time to do that," I replied, "but I do think it's a bad way to sell a book. The editor should make the author paragraph it. Everybody has short paragraphs nowadays."

Even in history books it's awfully boring if everything is in long, long paragraphs. It's difficult to adjust your mind to it simply because you're so used to conversation in everything you hear, and so used to reading newspapers, in which, again, you'll never find those long, long paragraphs. Journalists are not so stupid.

Then I asked her a question about how she managed to draw the reader on.

I automatically come to an exciting moment at the end of the chapter, when she's just going to fall in love with the Duke, or there's a drama. It is a very good way to end by saying, "The door opened—she looked up in astonishment and he stood there!" The reader has to turn over to see who stood there.

They think, "I must just read the beginning of the next

chapter before I go to sleep,'' and they finish the whole book.

When people start reading my novels they say they have to go on, because they have to know what happens.

They know there will be a happy ending. They know that the virgin heroine is not going to bed until she has the ring on her finger.

But they say, and I can feel it myself, it's an excitement to see how it is going to work out.

It's boy meets girl, whether he's a duke or an ordinary young man, and it's a man and woman who are attracted to each other despite themselves, and of course they are going to get married in the end.

But it's the little bits in between which matter, and it rather annoys me when people say, ''You always do the same plot,'' because they're not the same plot. I set the background in a dozen different parts of the world, five books in India, which I love, Hong Kong, Singapore, Bali, Nepal, Venice, Turkey, Morocco, and many, many more.

I read twenty to thirty history and travel books for every novel I write.

I've just been doing a book on Alsace when it was taken over by the Germans in the Franco-Prussian war. I've read a dozen books on it to get my details and dates entirely right.

I am very careful, because I am used quite a lot in schools.

The one piece of advice I can give to people who are writing books is they must write about things they know.

It's no use writing about gold-digging in Australia if you've never been to Australia. It's very difficult to write about something you haven't seen. And that's why I've been reluctant to write many books about America. I've had handsome, exciting American heroes and lovely American heroines, but only one book with wholly American background. I don't want people to say, ''That's wrong,'' because it's annoying for them as well as for me.

I want to get everything exactly right.

It's very difficult when you haven't lived in a country long enough or even seen enough of it to write about it.

With other places in the world, I really take an enormous amount of trouble.

I went to Venice for Easter, and I read a lot of books on Venice and looked at a lot of pictures. And I've got the whole feeling of that magical city and I've described the wonderful light of Venice, which I know the people who live there will appreciate because it's what they feel.

Because I've written for so long, I'll say to my sons on Tuesday, "I'm finishing my novel today. I've got to start another tomorrow and I haven't got a plot."* They say, "Don't worry, Mummy, a plot will come."

Then I say to my subconscious, "I want a plot, and don't give me two!" and it is there! It is absolutely fantastic!

I speak to my subconscious. It's like saying a prayer, or, if you like meditation, concentration, positive thinking; they are all the same. I say, "I want it, I want it." Then it appears.

I have an absolutely blank mind and suddenly the whole thing falls into place.

Or else something might happen.

I went to France with Glen, my son, on a week's holiday . . . we always go once a year to this fascinating country. He adores France . . . and we drive through from Paris to the Côte D'Azur and eat at wonderful restaurants.

This year I was thinking of doing another cookery book, but we got lost.

We went over the Vosges Mountains. We had left where we were staying in the blazing sun and then it was hailing with snow on the tops of the mountains. There was also fog, and I was disagreeable because we were late for lunch in Strasburg.

"You're so stupid," I said to Glen, "you've come the wrong way. Why didn't you look at the map?"

Then suddenly I thought, "Oh, snow, skiing," and the whole plot was there, with the Duke sitting in a woodcutter's hut, having sprained his ankle, and the girl being taken off to a convent by her wicked uncle to incarcerate her as a nun. The whole story was in my mind. I've written it now. It's a lovely, exciting tale. Quite different from what I've done before.

Do you have any tips for new writers of historicals?

In the first few pages, unless it's something dramatic, I try to describe the background.

For instance, I've just done one with the Duke coming back from the Napoleonic wars, so he hadn't been in England for some years. He had been in the Army of Occupation in France after Napoleon was defeated.

*She has been writing approximately two books a month for many years.

So I established what had happened in England . . . correctly, I may say, every word of it . . . how the farmers were suffering and a million men were coming out of the forces without any pension and the ones who were crippled had nothing to do but steal . . . I established all that before the hero reached his ancestral home, which was falling down from neglect.

Have you any methods for finding new ideas?

My subconscious writes my books. When I feel for an idea it's there. I've only got to think about it. It may be trick shooting, it may be something from outer space. I can't tell you, but that's how it happens.

So I really don't have to worry at all.

When I'm dictating, and I dictate very fast, my secretary takes it down in shorthand. She has a tape recorder. I won't have a tape recorder . . . I can't bear things twiddling about, which makes me think about them. She has one just in case she forgets a word and I go too fast. If I pause, for a word, I listen, and I can hear in my mind the word or sentence I require.

What kind of heroes are in your mind for your novels?

He's the man I've always been dying to meet.

Tall, dark, cynical, and handsome, bored with all the women he's been to bed with—and they're innumerable—until he meets the heroine. She is pure, sweet, young, feminine, soft, gentle, every man's ideal of what a woman should be.

And of course she is me when I was eighteen. That's how I felt, that's how I thought when I was young, innocent, very good and very pretty.

My hero's always the same.

He is *my* hero. The man I've always longed to meet, a rake, a roué who is reformed by the sweet little girl.

Do you agonize over your plots?

No, it has always been fairly easy for me to write.

When I wrote my first book, called *Jigsaw*, it took quite a long time because I wrote it by hand. I wrote my first four books and got a lump on my finger, which I still have.

So I then started to dictate. And the words began to flow!

My first novel was a perfectly pure little love story. The Duke kissed the girl on page 200, and my great-aunts never spoke to me again because they said it must have been an experience! Actually, at that time I didn't know a duke and I had never been kissed.

I wrote entirely by instinct. I had a very indifferent education. Because my father was in the army in France, I had governesses and went to several day schools before I went to a finishing school.

They took me at a reduced rate because I was the daughter of a serving officer. It was their contribution to the war effort. It was in fact a rather expensive school that my mother couldn't have afforded.

They had no library. You can't believe it today, when there are these wonderful free libraries for everyone. I felt starved of books to read. But I found in the holidays there were little libraries in every town. For two pence I could borrow a book for five days.

Of course, I only chose love stories. I was thrilled by these. I read Ethel M. Dell, E. M. Hull, Berthe Ruck, and Elinor Glynn. All the romantic novelists.

I never read the classics until I was grown up and my brother said to me, "You're so terribly badly educated!"

So I then read Jane Austen, Anthony Trollope, and all the others. But to start with I was completely uneducated from a literary point of view.

But I had read a lot of love stories.

To me Ethel M. Dell was frightfully exciting. She had the heroine cry on every page, but the hero was always strong, masculine—an overpowering man who saved her from all sorts of dangers and swept her off her feet in the end.

The plots have always remained in my mind.

How do you sustain tension in your novels?

Agatha Christie, who wrote wonderful crime stories, never wandered off; she always kept to the point of what was happening. I keep the tension of stories—the love which is happening, instead of crime—going all the time. It all builds up to a climax. They meet and they're not sure what's going to happen (though you may know). They may hate each other, and yet there's a vibration between them and gradually you can feel them beginning to get nearer and nearer to one another. My readers know what's going to happen in the end, but they are fascinated as to how it's going to work out. I can understand why people feel my stories are compelling and are addicted to them.

When I was in hospital having a very bad operation, so that I very nearly died, my sons brought me in my lovely Regency research books because they knew how much I enjoyed them. But because I was so ill they were difficult for me to read.

I had taken in with me a large amount of "Barbara Cartlands" for the night nurses. So I lay in bed and read my own love stories and I got well a lot quicker than the doctors expected or thought possible. Because I was so happy, so immersed in love, I lay in bed thinking not about my aches and pains but about my handsome dukes!

Mrs. Billy Graham said recently when she was in hospital and so ill, the only thing that stopped her from suffering pain was reading my books.

You become so immersed in them. And they do take one's mind off everything else. When people are ill . . . they don't want tension, ugliness, misery, or pornography. They want love and beauty. There is nothing dirty or unpleasant in my stories. You can't stand that when you are not feeling well.

You know everything is going to end happily, so you go to sleep in the arms of the hero and get well quickly!

People today all over the world suffer from a lot of tension. Of course they are worried, of course many are lonely, and a great many are financially worried and afraid they might lose their jobs. They worry whether their daughter will be raped if she goes out dancing, you worry if your mother is going to get hit on the head if she goes to collect her old age pension or your husband may be run into by some lunatic who is driving a car having taken drugs.

All those things go through women's minds!

Therefore, they say to me, "I get lost in Barbara Cartland. I'm carried to a wonderful, a fanciful land, the land I'd like to be in. I find the ideal love—the spiritual and physical ecstasy which everybody wants! It is the Romeo and Juliet, Dante and Beatrice, the love of the troubadors. It makes me so happy!"

If I can make a few people happy, that is my ambition.

My brother, who was the first member of Parliament to be killed in World War II, said to me, "You must never make a speech and not give the people who are listening to you something to take away personally." Now I think that's tremendously important.

So if you read my books carefully, you'll find when my heroine is in trouble, she prays and she always believes that she will receive help from God. This is what I believe is true.

Therefore, you will find something in every novel I write which will help you personally and will enlarge your mind.

There is a lot of teaching in my stories. I teach a belief in reincarnation and believe that you can do things yourself and most of all to have faith in God. The Lord will triumph over evil. All this spiritual teaching is in every book I write, covered up with lots of jam, but there! If I can help people in that way, and I know I do help especially young people, then I've done a good job.

Do you envision your plots?

I describe them just as I see them happening. One of the reasons they read "real" is that I live every word I dictate. It is just like a movie, with my mind rather than my eyes. I am walking up the stairs of Chatsworth or Blenheim Palace or any of those wonderful houses that I've visited, and of course my own house.

She goes into a room which I know. She sees the pictures on the wall which I've seen. So it's all real. Everything that happens in the background is real and possibly actually exists.

If I'm writing of George IV, I look up dozens of history books and check his life, his characteristics, the women he loved, the courtiers who surrounded him, the pictures, the furniture and china he kept, and his joys and sorrows.

"And then we had to leave . . ."

PART SIX

——————— 14 ———————

Keeping Fit While Writing

A Writer's Regimen

The aches and pains of writing are not just mental and psychological, but very much physical. Writing long hours at a desk takes a terrible toll on the body. Many writers have ignored some warning signals and developed stooped shoulders and weak stomaches—conditions that can lead to other health problems.

What do romance authors do? Some fight it, and some give in and suffer.

Tom Huff (Jenny Wilde) built a swimming pool in his backyard and does a workout every day (there's a bubble overhead for cool days in Forth Worth); Rosemary Rogers wakes up and goes into a yoga routine; Celeste De Blasis takes a brisk five-mile walk; Rebecca Brandewyne is a belly dancer; Jude Deveraux (who developed calcium deposits under her arms as a result of long typing sessions) has improved herself greatly by taking up iron pumping; and Bertrice Small has a private exercise class every other morning.

On the other hand, Janet Dailey suffers from sore back and neckaches but claims to hate distractions while she's working, so she continues to suffer the pains. "Bill claims he'll get me a masseur," she says with a grin toward her husband.

Danielle Steel is another intense writer. Whereas Janet Dailey stops work after the twentieth page, Danielle writes in a "fever" that lasts up to eighteen or twenty hours; in this way she completes a book in a few weeks. She, too, has aches and pains.

(These two speed writers put in almost the same hours as another writer would put in if they only worked three to four hours a day. Hitting each key on the typewriter is still the final step, whether you do it in long or short stretches.)

Some exercises will help a writer's problem with backache. The head weighs seventeen pounds, and when it is stuck out over the typewriter for several hours a misalignment occurs. Keeping the neck muscles holding up the head strong is essential. The muscles at the side of the head are what support it, so they should be hard to touch. A series of head lifts done while still lying in bed is one good way to build up this important part of a typist-writer's body.

When answering the telephone, read and obey a sign you put on the set that says, KEEP MOVING. This is the best time to jog in place, do knee bends, stand on the toes, stretch, flail, and generally exercise. By training yourself to move at the first word of a conversation, you will successfully sneak in a good exercise workout.

Swimming and brisk walks will also clear the head. Barbara Cartland starts her writing regimen by taking her dogs for a stroll outside her house.

What you eat while you're writing is another matter to consider. Tom Huff and Rosemary Rogers watch their diets carefully and stick to raw foods for easier digestion. Drinking and eating vary according to digestive systems, so analyze yours. Water mixed with lemon juice is another healthy habit; try it first thing in the morning for a wake-up tonic.

The intelligent writer should prepare a physical fitness program and follow it, just as an athlete would. Sitting all day is not healthy. Not moving is injurious to the body and horrendous for the figure. A writer who disciplines herself early to setting up an exercise program will be glad she did.

Daily Exercises

1. Start with 100 head lifts and work up to 500. Lie flat and bob head gently up and down; this can be done in bed or on a hard surface. At the beginning, put hands behind head to support the bobbing.
2. Wall press. This helps loosen up and strengthen the shoulders. Do this 25 times, and concentrate on the use of muscles in the upper region.
3. Headstand. Use a wall for a brace, but get yourself upside down for a change. A slant board will also give you this effect, and it does wonders for the skin.

4. Jump rope for a few minutes. Work up a fast heart-beat and get the oxygen circulating in your system.
5. Take a daily *brisk* walk. Give yourself an idea to work on as you walk, moving along at a good pace. Think only of this, and let your subconscious do the rest.

Posture

It's not possible to sit perfectly straight for long periods at the typewriter, but you can put up reminder signs in front of you, or on your bulletin board. Following a frequent exercise program, concentrating on posture, and pulling in your stomach when you're standing or taking a walk, plus sleeping on your stomach (on "all fours") will make a difference.

Women should always wear a bra, regardless of their breast size, to avoid sagging breasts and help to support the upper part of the body.

The Eyes of Love

Writing is a tremendous strain on the eyes. Eye exercises, frequent catnaps, proper lighting, and correct reading glasses will help. Also, cleaning the glasses frame every day cuts down on skin breakout around the nose and cheeks. Alternating between regular glasses and reading "on-the-tip-of-the-nose" glasses helps to stave off the telltale "pinch" glasses mark that writers develop.

Health and Beauty Tips

BULLETIN BOARD

Barbara Cartland's Vitamin List

Indian Ginseng
Fo Ti Teng
2 Gev-Tabs (multi-vit)
2 Vitamin B$_6$, 100 mgs each
1 Vitamin E, 1,000 IUS
3 to 4 Vitamin C, 1,000 mgs

Exercise Program

8:00–8:30 Brisk walk

12:00 3 minutes jump rope, headstand

3:00 Stretches and kicks

9:00 45 min. in front of TV

Breakfast

Water and lemon juice

Fruit, bran, egg, wheat toast

DRINK LOTS OF WATER . . .

BEAUTY CALENDAR

10–10:30

Monday	Tuesday	Wednesday	Thursday	Friday
Hair treatment	Nails	Hands and feet	Facial	Fast or semifast

Slogans of the Month—
"It's Only a Book."   "Take a Kittywink."
"Have Fun."   "Sit Up Straight."
"You are bringing love and joy to people."

KITTYWINK

Tell yourself to go to sleep for 15 minutes. Wake up refreshed.

HONEY COCKTAIL FOR FATIGUE

1 tablespoon honey and the juice of a fresh lemon

TELEPHONE

Jog up and down
Don't sit
Squeeze an old tennis ball to strengthen arm and hand muscles

WORK HABITS

Do One Thing at a time   Cut Out Nonproductive Activities
Rank Work Activites in Order of Importance   Keep Time
in Perspective   Allow Room for the Unexpected   Make Decisions Promptly

Creative Writing Tips

BY DR. LONNIE MACDONALD

psychiatrist

Creative writers are most successful when they are simply being themselves. This is the fundamental idea of writing. In order to really communicate and have impact, writers tap their own individuality and uniqueness. For this, they must believe that they are unique, special, and have something to say.

It takes time to organize the lifestyle and discipline necessary to bring forth sensitivity, awareness, and craftsmanship, but it is an achievable goal.

The process of becoming a writer requires change, and one must look upon the change as an opportunity. The most importance change is to go from *I cannot* to *I can*. This may mean getting rid of many negative attitudes and feelings.

New writers should be familiar with their vulnerable areas, such as procrastination, fighting against real fatigue, not finishing a manuscript, embarrassment about expressing real, honest feelings, showing work to someone else, and accepting criticism.

The rewards of writing will mean learning to trust oneself more and trust others more, and finding that the geunine love of self will flourish or grow.

Here are some of the tips that will promote success in writing fiction:

1. Identify the time during the day when you do your most productive writing.
2. Discipline yourself to create the environment for productive writing.
3. Reward yourself by thought and deed when productive.
4. Look for daily progress, not perfection.
5. Remind yourself to relax when feeling tense.

6. Work for your own individual vision.
7. Take risks in tapping your own unique feelings and expressing them.
8. Share your insights and changes with others for positive feedback, and practice telling your story to them.
9. Strive for fun and joy in your writing.
10. Strive for honesty, clarity, simplicity, and directness in expression of feelings.
11. Identify blocks or inhibitions to freer, easier expression of feelings, such as anger, anxiety, guilt, love.
12. In moments of confusion or doubt, stop and ask yourself, What am I talking about? Don't work against yourself.

The Demon of Writers

BY DIANA BROWN
author of five Regencies

The writing life is not, as I had supposed, an easy one. It drains all energy: not just mental, but physical energy too. And it never stops, never. It is exhausting, but I wouldn't want to do anything else.

There is one tip I should like to pass along—that is, finish everything you begin. Don't listen to that demon who comes along as you are five eighths into your book and tempts you with a better idea. Believe me, he always appears, and always the idea he imparts is so much more enticing than the one on which you are working. Finish your work, even though it may seem wanting; finish it! There is nothing sadder or more unsalable than an unfinished manuscript. Be polite to that demon, tell him you will indeed give that marvelous inspiration consideration in due time, but ask him to go away until you are quite finished. Finish, submit, and tell your editor that you have just started work on a marvelous new book that she's simply going to love. Then let the demon back in.

To Thine Own Self Be True

As difficult as it may be for some new writers to believe, your voice must be *heard* in your novel. And the better you know yourself, the better drawn your heroine will be.

To know "thyself" is the most important step to improving your writing. In order to see the heroine and predict her actions you must be able to step outside your skin and analyze what you would do. Then jump back in, if need be, and write it.

Some writers claim to stay out of their skins and observe for longer periods than others. This ability may rest entirely on a writer's acceptance and awareness of self.

Give yourself some "situation" questions ("what if") to answer, such as: "If I were eighteen, at my first dance, and was an instant wallflower, what would I do? (1) Be hurt, (2) Be assertive, (3) Be shy, (4) Shrug it off, (5) Other?"

Use your memory, if such an experience really happened to you or a close friend; or if your heroine did not have your personal reaction, be objective and think of the right one for her and put it on your filmstrip.

By choosing your own reaction or a close friend's, you *know* the person who made the decision and why it was made. In other words, you have an insight into that person's character, her "style," and every decision she makes, every action she takes, becomes predictable for you with very little variation. You know the girl who pouts because she isn't instantly popular will be a rather childish, self-centered young lady who wants her own way and has no patience. Getting a minute perception is a secret of achieving authenticity, the making of real people, not inconsistent fictional figures. This is why many writing instructors constantly hammer: "Write about what you know." And the accent should be on *you*, not the knowing.

You have the feeling when insight occurs that you freed yourself from your skin and are beyond it. Some writes call it "like getting a ticket to anywhere." Writers, as well as readers, have "exhilarating" armchair travel while they create.

However, it is easier to be a reader than a writer, as it is the author who must provide the part that makes travel possible—rather like the difference between being in the audience for a play rather than being the author or director.

PART SEVEN

——— 15 ———

How to Promote a

Romance Novel

Dear Eldest Sibling Kathryn,

<u>Merci beaucoup pour tous.</u> I brushed up on my typing skills and borrowed a Selectric (and discarded nails, per your suggestion).

Krissy has sold one manuscript to Caprice Romances, and it will be published in six months. What can we do to publicize it?

> Affectionately,
> The Mother of Krissy, the next Janet Dailey,
> of Atlanta

From the Desk of Kathryn Falk

April 1

Dear Sis,

Congratulations on Krissy's first book. Is she using the pen name "Krissy Le Vent," out of deference to Margaret Mitchell, your hometown heroine?

Enclosed is my promotion file. This should get you started. Try to come up with a key line for her. So far, none of the teen romance writers have gotten much personal publicity, so she could be the first, at least in your area. How about Love's Youngest Leading Lady or the Princess of Pink Ink?

I'm writing this at 2 a.m., my eyes are burning, so maybe sleep will help me to come up with something better. If she was older and writing for one of the steamy lines, we could call her Lust's Leading Lady.

> Goodnight,
> K.

Love Is in the Air: TV, Radio, Media Lists, and Publicity Agents

Romance authors today face fierce competition on the book shelves—which book will a reader pick out of some new seventy category romances and another thirty historicals and contemporaries? Because of this, many writers have undertaken personal publicity. This has a twofold purpose—their names become familiar to readers and the bookstores who know the authors will give preferential treatment to them.

"But should I do publicity? Isn't that the publisher's responsibility?" used to be a frequent question asked by writers. Now the authors, with a few exceptions, go out on the hustings on a tour that is either paid for by the publisher or paid to a private publicist out of the writer's pocket.

Everyone is pretty aware of what happens. Authors may have TV and radio advertisements, ads in the *New York Times, Publishers Weekly, Magazine and Bookseller, Romantic Times,* personal appearances on local news shows, and write-ups in local papers. Usually the authors go to cities in California, Texas, and Florida, the romance strongholds.

What can an author do if the publisher does not get additional publicity or ads; what can she do to bring people's attention to the book she slaved over, which now has only a three-week shelf life, maybe longer if it's a historical romance or a contemporary?

The first thing to decide is how much time you have to give to being your own publicist, or will you have a willing mother, like Rebecca Brandewyne's, or a willing husband, like Janet Dailey's and Donna Vitek's, who looks after some of this end of the book business?

Then you have to determine your budget. The cost of printing (whether to use a good typewriter or get type set), envelopes, follow-up telephone calls, photographs, postage(!) . . . all this and your time, or someone else's, adds up. Perhaps you'd better splurge on a publicist to handle all this?

If you've addressed the above questions, and still want to do it yourself, here's what you need to do:

Six to eight weeks before the publication date of your book, have a press release on the desk of the editor of the local paper, also on that of the TV and radio program director, that tells them your book is coming out on such-and-such date. They may or may not call you, but it serves as an alert from you and will give you an opportunity to let them know your name.

Send the same material to your local bookstores and libraries and to any organization you may belong to. How widely you distribute these releases depends on your budget and success in getting names and addresses of the persons in charge.

An example of a press release would include this information:

- Your name, title of your book, publisher, and release date.

- A description of the book and the audience it is to appeal to.

- Your position in the community, county, city, or state. The point being you're a local girl who's made good, and everyone loves to read or hear of good news about a local resident. (If you can make your accomplishment sound lucrative, that's all the better; everyone likes to hear of financial success, or even the potential for it.)

Write this notice sincerely, and if you can be amusing, try. Bringing a smile to the reader's face is as important as it is in your books. Use an attractive letterhead (use press type or get a professional to do it). If it can be just one page, all the better. Have an address and telephone number for a contact point to you.

Press Kit

Three to four weeks before your book is on the bookshelf, get a press kit and either a review copy of the book or at least its cover and put it in the hands of all the people who received the press release. You might find out on your own just when a particular publication wants to be informed. Three weeks may be enough leeway for a newspaper, but your state magazines should be contacted much earlier if they're monthly or bimonthly. The same applies for the editor of Sunday supplements.

Include a press release (updated since the first "alert" about you and the book) and make it complete and amusing but not corny; keep it light and bright. Include schooling, background, marital status, family information. (Remember, this is for local media outlets; you wouldn't be this detailed for a national publication, which couldn't care at all that your son played on the John Kennedy football team in Walla Walla.)

Also include your black-and-white publicity photo. Go to a professional and ask for a glamour treatment, otherwise you'll look like you paid for a mug shot with makeup. Look at Danielle Steel's photo or Rosemary Rogers's; those are glamour shots. *Backlighting, filter*—that's what you ask for. And also *touch-ups,* so your bags, deep lines, and wrinkles aren't the focus of the photo. You may not photograph well, but at least photograph attractively and softly. Wear something feminine, not a tailored suit. Use a Polaroid to test-shoot for yourself your dress, your makeup, your hair. Don't go to the photographer until you've gone through this practice session.

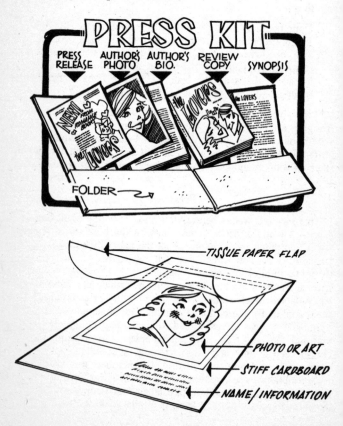

Order a pose that has you and the book in the picture, but the book shouldn't show above your neck. This way the photograph can be cropped, if need be. (A chest shot takes up a larger space in a publication, and the head shot can be cropped tightly.) Always send black-and-white publicity photos; some publications won't take the time to convert a color photograph, and it's true—a photo is worth a thousand words. Make it easy for the editors to use your story.

Also, consider having a photograph taken with your family, perhaps in front of your house; and a pose of you in your very neat office with your research books, typewriter, etc. Maggie Osborne always writes her first draft in a bubble bath with a special desk arranged by her husband, who brings her coffee. A photo of Maggie's work area got her a lot of coverage and consequently the fun title of "Colorado's Queen of Romance." But do have at least one photo—the head shot or chest shot with book always in sight. Send this with your press kit. If you are on a budget, you may save some money by not including the photo in kits to radio stations, since they aren't interested in what you look like. (Modernage Photo Service, 18 Vesey Street, New York, N.Y. 10007, has a low price for reproducing black-and-white photos in quantities of twenty-five or fifty or more.)

Your book contract can entitle you to a discount for buying your own book, if you ask for such a clause. Usually it's a 40 percent discount, which is what the stores receive. Sometimes, if you inform a publisher, and show them what you are doing by way of publicity, you will be given some free copies or be able to purchase them at a bigger discount. You should at least get book covers, if you notify them early enough that you need them. (Sending a cover costs much less in postage than sending a book, which usually requires a special mailing envelope.)

A follow-up call should be made if you don't hear from the media outlets in about two weeks. Sometimes your material can get shuffled to the wrong department. You could also call to make certain that it arrived, and while talking to the editor . . . who knows?

Speaking on Radio

Most radio spots are short, and that's why it's important to get the title of your book in early in the conversation (at least three times). The host isn't as concerned as you are with selling your book. Don't get carried away by yourself and who you are; you're there to sell a book, so work to make the book sound enticing. This isn't simple, so it's a good idea to practice at home into a tape recorder.

Always carry your book with you, and perhaps several extra copies to give out (autographed) if you think you'll be coming around to the station again. It helps to spread your name and goodwill around. Send a thank-you note after the show. Keep all the names of the personnel in a special address book.

Call-ins are the most fun of all shows. The station calls you and usually you go live over the air. Be prepared for strange calls—once an author heard a beep-beep coming over the air and the host explained that it was someone with a computerized larynx (that took some time to straighten out). But the question was answered. Have some stock answers ready for run-of-the-mill questions, but keep them amusing. Don't talk fast; a soft, warm voice, easy to understand, and sincere, gives the best impression.

Appearing on Television

Most TV spots are short, so again be holding your book (if you can; some stations won't allow it). Wear something feminine that won't hike up when you sit down. Don't wear white or black. Choose romantic colors. Ruffles and softness and a lot of well-applied makeup is the answer. Always check to see if a TV station "does makeup." Even if they do, still carry your blusher, eyelashes or mascara applicator, and a lipstick liner. Make certain white cover-up is put under the eyes to erase circles and a shadow (due only—of course—to the exhausting book tour you're on!).

Always smile, even if the camera isn't on you. Carry lozenges if you have a cold, to offset a coughing attack. Make the show fun. And chat with the host. Wear your contacts, not glasses.

Many TV shows resist having authors as guests because they aren't animated or "up" guests; many can't keep a conversation going. A new author might do well to have an audio tape available of another program (radio or TV) to show that you are a lively guest, and send it to a show that you would like to appear on.

The Lecture Circuit

Many clubs are looking for lectures. The usual situation is after a ladies' lunch. What can an author do? First of all, you're there because you did something exciting: You wrote a book. This script is a good one to examine:

Introduce yourself, talk about the romance novel industry, some of the figures, the audience, the writers; drop names they know—Cartland, Victoria Holt, etc. Explain how you got the idea to write, what it took to write, how you chose your story, and what has happened to the book since—getting published, promoted, etc. What you're going to do with your money, and what kind of writing you plan for the future. Finally, the satisfaction you've gained, education, esteem, whatever, by becoming a novelist. Have copies of your book to sell, and hand out a bookmark or some kind of promotional piece, for when they look for your books at a later time.

Does Publicity Help to Sell Books?

No one knows for sure. The books have to be in the stores, which is why some authors lug their own books around and sell them out of the trunk to the booksellers while they're in town. Big names such as Judith Krantz, Rosemary Rogers, Danielle Steel, and Pat Matthews are sent on publicity tours by their publishers and very willingly promote themselves with the distributors and warehouse personnel—whoever takes book orders for the stores. All the publicity is for nought if the books aren't there.

Some authors correspond with their fans. Janet Dailey has a newsletter orchestrated by Pocket publicist Joan Schulhafer that reaches close to 50,000 fans who love to read a little gossip and have the opportunity to order her books through the mail. This newsletter idea also works at Avon, which has a healthy little mail-order book business through their free newsletter.

Individual authors such as Janelle Taylor, Danielle Steel, Rebecca Brandewyne, and a few others send their fans occasional notices of what they're doing and a coupon for a new book. This is nice for the fans, as most like getting something free. But is it really profitable, considering the postage and printing? No one knows except those authors with mail-order businesses.

Taking co-op advertisements with your local stores is a good way to publicize the title of your book. And an ad in *Romantic Times* gets to the hard-core readers and specialty bookstores.

Paying for an ad in the *New York Times, National Enquirer, The Star,* or *Family Circle* could work too, but you're spending thousands of dollars. Plus, reservations for these orders must be placed several months in advance. Ads and timing must be worked out, even with your local papers.

Publicity should not become an obsession. Try to schedule your time so you get the most effect from what you do. Some shows may be fun, but is it worth taking taxicabs back and forth across a city for these plugs?

All the PR in the world won't give a book "wings." (This is the term used to describe the books that "walk" out of stores, due to word of mouth.) A writer's first responsibility is to be a great storyteller and entertain the readers, who will come back for more. Publicity is essential, but concentrate on what's effective, not just ego-boosting.

Appearing on shows is the best confidence booster in the world. After many lonely days behind the typewriter, it's very uplifting to get some attention. But be wary. Don't let it go to your head or become a prima donna. You prove yourself through your pages, not over the TV or radio microphones.

Sometimes the best result a publicity-minded author can get is the positive impression made on one's editor and publisher. These authors are usually eventually rewarded by their company, sometimes with an unexpected advertising budget, or by a party, and in some cases favored position in the lineup. Personal promotion has helped new writers, with only a book or two published, to get the attention of other editors at competitive companies. Publishers need all the help they can get, and if an author is doing something effective, they're appreciative.

A new phenomenon has arisen, and that's the case of the prima donna, who gets one book tour and decides that she's worth more money, more attention, more everything. She usually ends up annoying everyone and her career doesn't improve, often because of her pestering attitude. Of course a writer must know her worth, not be unduly modest, but the real success comes from writing books that captivate readers. Kathleen Woodiwiss rarely steps out her door, but her books continue to sell, with only an ad campaign and first-rate distribution.

Does extra publicity help? Well, it doesn't hurt.

Media Outlets

Here are some addresses to get you started. No names are given, because personnel changes occur frequently. You might send just a press release to see if this particular media outlet would be interested in hearing more from you. Address release to Feature Editor.

Print

Associated Press News
  Features
50 Rockefeller Plaza
New York, N.Y. 10020

Cleveland Plain Dealer
1801 Superior Avenue
Cleveland, Ohio 44114

Detroit Free Press
321 Lafayette
Detroit, Mich. 48231

Detroit News
615 W. Lafayette
Detroit, Mich. 48231

Newsday
Long Island City
New York, N.Y. 11747

People Magazine
Rockefeller Plaza
New York, N.Y. 10002

United Press International
220 E. 42nd Street
New York, N.Y. 10017

Woman's World Magazine
177 N. Dean
Englewood, N.J. 07631

Radio

"Barry Farber"
WMCA
888 Seventh Avenue
New York, N.Y. 10019

"Joel Rapp"
34 Perry Street
New York, N.Y. 10014

"Woman's World"
Ruth Williams
40 Veronica Box 100
Broadcast Center
New Brunswick, N.J. 08903

WTWN Radio
Rick Weronko
101 C Waters Building
Grand Rapids, Mich. 49503
(Conducts call-in show)

Radio Call-Ins

"Sunday Night" WDRQ radio/Lincoln Park, Mich.
"Talk Radio 14" WOC radio/Davenport. Iowa
WINZ radio/Miami, Fla.
KGB radio/San Diego, Calif.
WJR radio/Detroit, Mich.

"Morning Magazine" WOAI radio/San Antonio, Tex.
"Good Afternoon Phoenix" KSUN radio/Phoenix, Ariz.
"Joel Rappoport Show" WSJS radio/Winston-Salem, N.C.
"Midday" WFDF radio/Flint, Mich.
"Charlie Pagor Show" WMRO radio/Aurora, Ill.
CKWW radio/Windsor, Ontario, Canada
"Charlie Stevens Show" KARN radio/Little Rock, Ark.
"Hello Henry" WBT radio/Charlotte, N.C.
"Talk Back" KLYC radio/Laurel, Mont.
"Gary Tessler Show" KNUS radio/Denver, Colo.
"Bob Lee Magazine" KSL radio/Salt Lake City, Utah
"Talk Radio With Julie Gamack" WHO radio/Des Moines, Iowa
"Sandy Payton Show" WIOD radio/Miami, Fla.
KTOK radio/Oklahoma City, Okla.
"Author's Corner" WSDR radio/Sterling, Ill.
"Bob Gifford Show" WHO radio/Des Moines, Iowa
"KNUS Talk" KNUS radio/Denver, Colo.
"Features" WINZ radio/Miami, Fla.
"Warren Pierce" WJR radio/Detroit, Mich.
"Bookworld" WDST radio/Woodstock, N.Y.
"Morning Drive" WERE radio/Cleveland, Ohio
"Scott Cassidy Show" WTKN radio/Pittsburgh, Pa.
"Robb Westaby Show" WOWO radio/Fort Wayne, Ind.
"John Clemes" WPXN radio/Rochester, N.Y.
"John Kellor Show" WRKO radio/Boston, Mass.

Television

CBS-TV
524 W. 57th Street
New York, N.Y. 10019

"Chicago AM"
190 North State
Chicago, Ill. 60601

"Donahue Show"
630 McClurg Court
Chicago, Ill. 60611

"Elizabeth Richards Show"
WTSP-TV
St. Petersburg, Fla. 33733

"Good Morning America"
ABC
7 W. 66th Street
New York, N.Y. 10023

"Hour Magazine"
5800 Sunset Boulevard
Los Angeles, Calif. 90028

"I'll Take Romance—"
Kathryn Falk
Bob Stewart Cable, Inc.
200 W. 57th Street
New York, N.Y. 10019

"Jane Whitney Show"
WCAU-TV
City and Monument Avenue
Philadelphia, Pa. 19131

"Kelly and Co."
WXYZ-TV
20777 W. Ten Mile Road
Southfield, Mich. 48075

"Merv Griffin"
1541 North Vine Street
Hollywood, Calif. 90028

"Mid-Morning"
KHJ-TV
5515 Melrose Avenue
Hollywood, Calif. 90038

"Philadelphia AM"
WPVI-TV
4100 City Line Avenue
Philadelphia, Pa. 19131

"Sonja Show"
WDIV-TV
622 W. Lafayette
Detroit, Mich. 48231

"Today Show"
NBC
30 Rockefeller Plaza
New York, N.Y. 10020

"Velma Daniels"
1624 Lake Musor Drive
Winter Haven, Fla. 33880

"Weekday"
WNEC-TV
RKO General Building
Government Center
Boston, Mass. 02414

Write to the program directors of the above shows and they might respond to your press release. Let them know when you will be in their city, or would like to be. Some shows will pay part of your expenses.

A press-clipping service will send you a clipping or a copy of a clipping each time your name or book title appears in print. Most publishers subscribe to one, as do large PR firms.

The Luce Clipping Services is one of the top names. Their service costs $139 a month, and 73¢ for each clipping they mail. They will also send printed transcripts of TV and radio broadcasts, but this is costly.

> *Luce Clipping Service*
> *420 Lexington Avenue*
> *New York, N.Y. 10017*
> *(212) 889-6711*

Personal Publicists for Romance Authors

Diane Glynn Publicity and Public Relations, Inc.
200 Madison Avenue
New York, N.Y. 10016
(212) 686-6950

Chelley Kitzmiller
Love Beat, PR
2149 Tynes Drive
Placentia, Calif. 92670
(714) 524-2193

Melissa Lande Promotions, Inc.
200 Madison Avenue
New York, N.Y. 10016
(212) 689-0930

Betsy Nolan Group Incorporated
515 Madison Avenue
New York, N.Y. 10022
(212) 751-2150

Eileen Prescott Company, Inc.
733 Third Avenue
New York, N.Y. 10017
(212) 922-1270

Peggy Tagliarino
105 Fifth Avenue
New York, N.Y. 10003
(212) 741-0079

Agencies Handling Romance Publishers

Dorf/MJH
518 Fifth Avenue
New York, N.Y. 10036
(212) 382-2121

Ogilvie & Mather II
230 Park Avenue
New York, N.Y. 10169
(212) 867-8200

Tips for TV

BY VELMA DANIELS

TV host

Promoting your book? Do it with *love!*

Love is a many-splendored thing; we all know this, but the honeymoon can be short-lived if you hit the promotion tour with your head in the clouds and your feet on the pavement. This whole wonderful idea of traveling around the country to sell your book can be the best part of the writing game. But, surprisingly, the majority of the writers come trudging back home like a sore-footed camel babbling incoherently, "Wearily, wearily, I say unto you—no more of this book tour for me!"

Let's change this bad mental attitude with a few easy tips for TV appearances.

Acrostic—LOVERS

L—let the interviewer lead
like the interviewer or at least pretend to
lively answers make points for you
let the camera do the work—don't be twisting and turning
   like a gosling
look at the interviewer when talking
look luscious! "A little paint helps any old barn!"

O—ooze femininity
overstating content can lead to disappointment
originality: tell of hobby, collection, etc.
offhand comments can be silly—answer simply and honestly
opportunity—your chance to sell yourself and your book
oratory—listen to your voice on tape, then keep it low and
   calm
overcome doubt, be yourself

V—vanity has no place on camera
variety—give tips to interviewer before show
vivaciousness is key to selling your book
voice—breathe deep before going on air to keep steady
vulgarity is sign of stupidity
verify all times, dates, etc., before appearance
valentines to interviewer helps—a mere "thank you!" means
   a lot

E—express yourself clearly
early—do not arrive at last minute
enthusiasm for yourself and content of book
equipment: copies of books, recipes, or whatever visuals
   you require
expect interview to go well
ease, sit ladylike
eye contact with interviewer
enjoy yourself

R—radiate
ready for anything
remember your interviewer wants to make you look good
remain who you are; don't be a copycat
roll with the punches if something unexpected comes up
relate some humorous things to interviewer before show
restrain—don't tell everything you know
romance—that's your business, so sell your audience on
   ideas

S—smile!
solid colors: don't wear checks and figures in dress
secret: let interviewer in on some little-known fact
seize every opportunity to appear on TV. Sells books!
set happy mood
shine; show you are special!

signals—be familiar by asking talent coordinator what the hand signals mean so you will know when to stop talking!
simple—keep your answers to the point

Now isn't that easy! Look forward to the author tour that is facing you. You are unique. You are wonderful. You have something to say that no one has ever thought of—say it! Your business is love. You are an ambassador for love! Have fun!

The Author-Publicist Relationship

BY JOAN SCHULHAFER

publicist, Pocket Books

Writers often view publicity as *the* way to sell their books. Granted, the recognition resulting from good TV, radio, and press interviews can be a plus to book sales. However, authors, especially category romance writers, should realize that there are many potential pitfalls involved in this kind of exposure and that not every author is the ideal candidate for an intensive campaign.

Most publishing houses employ professional publicity people whose job it is to decide which authors and titles will benefit most from various kinds of publicity. Time, budgeting, the number of books expected to be sold, and the authors themselves are all key factors in determining the type of publicity to be done. An author tour is not the answer in all cases, a fact many writers misunderstand. Category romance writers are having their books publicized, advertised, and promoted as part of the line they are writing for. Outside of a line, those same titles and authors might not receive as much attention as they now do. For many writing outside of a category, it is often frustrating to think that nothing is being done for their book. The bad news to a writer may be that the publisher is not going to book him or her on a twenty-city tour. But the good news is that there is a great deal being done internally on behalf of the book, and that isn't always obvious to those outside a company.

For instance, in an ideal publishing world, publicity people start talking about a book as soon as it is acquired. Catalogues are produced well ahead of publication, positioning each title for reviewers, columnists, TV and radio contracts, and a variety of editors at newspapers and magazines nationwide. As a rule, publicity professionals are constantly talking to their contacts at national TV and radio programs, as well as to key reviewers at magazines and newspapers. Not every book can be pitched to these people, but the publicist can make sure their contacts know about every book being published. Press releases are done on many books, and this ensures additional exposure for the title and author. Every release does not have to be sent with a review copy of a book, which means hundreds can be sent out, giving reviewers and interviewers an additional chance to express interest in a title. This all adds up to a lot of exposure, especially considering that your publicist is dealing with only one way of reaching consumers. At your publishing house, promotion and sales people have been pushing your book for months before publication directly to the booksellers, the people who are in daily contact with consumers.

In considering the obvious kind of publicity—TV, radio, and press interviews—your publicist has to weigh a number of factors. One is quite simply the number of copies of your title the publisher is selling. An author tour is an expensive investment in terms of both money and time. Other considerations draw on the publicist's expertise and knowledge of what interviewers all over the country are most interested in. Booking novelists for interviews is not an easy task. Many interviewers will not even consider fiction writers. And those who do may well have a choice of established mainstream authors who have already become publishing celebrities. The competition is incredible, and a tour can be a very risky proposition.

Another consideration, and the hardest for both publicist and author to admit to, is that often an author is just not ready for the kind of exposure a tour generates. An author may not have all that much to say that is interesting to an interviewer's audience. How many times can the current state of romance publishing be fascinating? In addition, the author may not have developed the ability to handle the pressure of a tour. The topics and ideas that you and your publicist discuss with enthusiasm may not cut it with an audience not involved in the romance industry. And a bad author tour is far worse than no tour at all, because it can affect both the author's and the publicist's credibility.

Most writers are quite willing to accept the fact that their publicist has voted against touring. The battle doesn't begin until the author, who may agree that touring is not essential, expresses the desire to do some interview locally. The publicist may simply have to say it can't be done. What is often misunderstood is that the advance work—preparing an author biography, excerpting clippings, printing materials, selecting media—takes just as much time and energy as the preparation for a major tour. Publicity departments are not always large; many have a staff of only three or four people. Also, a publicist is usually working on more than one title at a time. It really can be prohibitive for your publicist to put together the kind of presentation that will work best for you. There are alternatives, of course. A few contacts in your area can be selected and a note that simply states your availability for interviews can be sent with your book. Or you can decide to take the task of doing local publicity into your own hands. *Caution:* There is a lot more to this than you may expect. This is where your publicist can help you.

A publicist can advise you on the presentation of your materials, go over your copy, and help you focus on topics that will work to get you interviews. Your publicist is supposed to be a professional and does for a living what you're attempting to do. You should assume the publicist you work with knows what to do. This doesn't mean that if you disagree, you shouldn't get a second opinion from someone whose expertise you value. It does mean you should trust your publicist and take suggestions seriously. Check the people you're approaching with your publicist. Your publicist may be pitching you to national contacts and to trade publications. A conflict can be very embarrassing as well as annoying to the people being approached. And many people do not want to be approached by authors directly.

Once you've decided to take on the task of local publicity there will be a lot of work to do, even if you don't follow all the suggestions mentioned here.

The first matter of business in pursuing interviews is assembling publicity materials. Some of the basics, which can be assembled into a "kit" of sorts using folders available at stationery stores, or simply clipped together are: information about the book and its publication; biographical information; positive reviews or press clippings from interviews you've already done; a "pitch" letter; and suggested interview topics.

You can combine some or all of these items into a single presentation or prepare them separately to be sent in one package. Keep in mind that the people being targeted have a limited amount of time to get your message. Don't "pad" your kit to create an impressive *looking* presentation. Your publicist can advise you on the proper way to present and write these materials and may be able to provide you with samples from other campaigns.

Don't be dismayed as you start trying to think up provocative interview topics. You may suddenly realize the life of a romance novelist is not as exciting as you thought. However, many of you have some great topics you may not have thought of. For instance, author Jude Deveraux often discusses her work with costumes and costume history, which she uses as part of the research for her historical novels. Many writers have been doing successful interviews on the current state of romance publishing—when they've been qualified and well prepared to talk about it. If one of your novels is set in the area you live in, the research you've done may have unearthed some local folklore or points of special interest to interviewers. It might just be the book you need. And, of course, depending on the size of the town in which you live, the simple "local boy/girl makes good" angle may be all that's necessary.

The added bonus of having assembled these materials is that when you do start doing interviews you'll be well prepared and familiar with the ideas you want to discuss.

It may be wise to invest in a photo of yourself for press purposes. For optimum use, it should be black and white, preferably five-by-seven, high contrast and have an uncluttered background. Before you go ahead with this you should decide with your publicist what kind of an image you're trying to convey. Make sure it's an image you're comfortable with. Try a variety of backgrounds and poses until you're satisfied.

Once your materials are assembled, you have to research potential interviewers. Your publicist may be able to advise you based on a variety of media guides available in most publicity offices. However, a lot of these contacts and programs change and, as your publicist does, you'll have to double check them all. Call your local TV and radio stations. Find out which programs use guests, what the program's format is, and the name of the booking contact. Watch and/or listen to the shows. Only select the ones that suit you and the topics you can discuss. Then send in your materials and follow up with a phone call. Don't nag. Call suggesting the interview and using your best angles. If they've said no after you've given it your best shot, drop it. Don't alienate these people. Behave professionally and they may be more responsive the next time around.

At newspapers, find out the names of the book review editor, lifestyle editor, and feature editor. They may be the same person or be called by a different title, but you should be able to locate the contacts you want. Again, become familiar with the publication to find out where a story about you might fit in. Not all book reviewers have the freedom to do interviews, but more feature-oriented editors usually do.

There always exists the possibility that after you've done all this work, you've ended up with few results. Your publicist is probably familiar with this experience, too. But, if you've undertaken this project to help your book sell, and not just to satisfy your own cravings for personal recognition, it really doesn't matter. You've tried to do all you could to help sell your book. When all is said and done, it is the novel you have written that has to stand on its own.

All the publicity in the world can't help a bad book sell once a negative reaction begins to spread among romance fans. And if your book is good, your readers will take over. They'll start the word of mouth that is the best recommendation your book can have, and your circle of fans will grow with each new novel.

PART EIGHT

———— 16 ————
Pink Ink

Listing of Major Romance Publishing Houses

Pink Ink or Pink, Inc., it all adds up to Passion's Paperback Publishers, with New York as the heart of the industry.

This directory has been prepared to help new writers direct their material to the right company and right person.

The recommended reading list was chosen to give new writers some inkling of a company's publishing and editorial policy.

Send a SASE (self-addressed stamped envelope) with your requests for tip sheets from category romance publishers or for submissions.

Category Romances

Candelight Ecstasy
Dell and Ecstasy Supreme
1 Dag Hammarskjold Plaza
New York, N.Y. 10017
(212) 605-3000

Editor: Anne Gisonny
Submission Requirements: Synopsis with first fifty pages, or three chapters, with SASE.

Recommended Reading: As Night Follows Day by Suzanne Simmons, *Passion and Illusion* by Bonnie Drake, *Surrender to the Night* by Shirley Hart, *A Season for Love* by Heather Graham, *Moonlight Rapture* by Prudence Martin, *Conflict of Interest* by Jayne Castle, *White Sand, Wild Sea* by Diana Blayne, *Designing Woman* by Elaine Raco Chase, *Loving Adversaries* by Eileen Bryan, *Passion's Price* by Donna Vitek

Editorial Requirements: A compelling love story that has smoldering love scenes and a convincing, full-dimensioned, and mature love affair. Fantasy grounded in reality. Emphasis is on the seduction of the senses (taste, smell, touch) and an intense, convincing emotional exchange between the protagonists. American heroines depicted are generally older (twenty-five or thirty-five) and confront the normal, often provocative in problems of a modern relationship. Length: 60,000 words. Tip sheets available with SASE.

Harlequin American Romances
919 Third Avenue
New York, N.Y. 10022
(212) 759-1785

Senior Editor: Hilary Cohen
Submission Requirements: Complete manuscripts only. Send a SASE and cover letter.

Editorial Requirements: Mini-mainstream contemporary novels, but with a happy ending. Sensual but never graphic, the plot and characters develop a level of sensuality. The editors are seeking good storytellers. Any kind of realism is okay as long as it fits within the context of the plot. Length: 70,000–75,000 words. Tip sheet available.

For Harlequin Romances and Presents, see Mills & Boon

Harlequin Temptation
225 Duncan Mill Road
Don Mills, Ontario, Canada
M3B 3K9
(416) 445-5860

Senior Editor: Margaret Carney
Submission Requirements: Complete manuscripts only. Send a SASE and cover letter.

Hourglass Romances
Zebra
475 Park Avenue South
New York, N.Y. 10016
(212) 889-2299

Senior Editor: Kathy O'Hehir
Submission Requirements: A
synopsis and fifty pages or
the first three chapters or entire manuscript.

Editorial Requirements: The story should depict women in realistic situations, wrenching drama in the short-novel form. The
heroine, in her late twenties, can be single, married, a working-
woman parent or divorcee. Her relationships with friends and
lover will be fraught with tension, tenderness, compassion,
and irrepressible sensuality. The hero can be either a friend,
husband, lover, engaging stranger, or antagonist who captivates
heroine with his boldness and challenges her professional
abilities, morality, and fortitude and causes her no uncertain
amount of both anguish and pleasure. Length: 50,000–60,000
words. Tip sheets available.

Loveswept
Bantam Books
666 Fifth Avenue
New York, N.Y. 10103
(212) 765-6500

Editor: Carolyn Nichols
Submission Requirements: Published romance writers, synopsis and three chapters.
Unpublished, complete
manuscript.
*Recommended Reading: Surren-
der* by Helen Mittermeyer,
A Love for All Time by
Dorothy Garlock, *Tempta-
tion's Sting* by Helen Conrad, *The Joining Stone* by
Noelle Berry McCue

Editorial Requirements: Mini-mainstream novels. Erotic and
sensual. Good storytelling. Length: 60,000 words.

Mills & Boon
15-16 Brook's Mews
London, W1A IDR, England
01 493-8131

Senior Editor: Jacqui Bianchi
Submission Requirements: A
synopsis and fifty pages or
the first three chapters.

Editorial Requirements: Mills & Boon originates the Harlequin Presents and Harlequin Romance lines, as well as the Doctor-Nurse Romance series, although the latter line tends to rely solely on British authors, because American-written hospital romances don't seem to work with Mills & Boons readers.

Mills & Boon editors are looking for a "genuine love of story telling combined with a freshness and originality of approach. Each author must possess an individual touch, her own particular way of telling the story. Characters should be convincing in both their actions and words. Background is equally important: accurate details about locations, occupations and other settings are crucial." Mills & Boon romances have a standard length of between 50,000 and 60,000 words. Tip sheet available.

Alan Boon's Likes

1. Pose one problem at a time to keep the reader concerned about the heroine, but don't answer one until you've posed another.
2. Keep the action moving all the time.
3. Try to show what the characters are like by what they do and say.
4. Always give your characters a logical reason for everything they do, even if you don't tell it right away.
5. Don't allow hero and heroine to confess their love before the last ten pages.

Mills & Boon publishes its romances in hardcover and then paperback, in England, and a few months later they are reprinted in paperback by Harlequin and distributed worldwide as Harlequin Romances and Presents.

Rapture Romance
NAL/Signet
1633 Broadway
New York, N.Y. 10019
(212) 397-8000

Editor: Mary Anne Gartland
Submission Requirements: A synopsis and fifty pages or the first three chapters. Send a SASE.

Tips from Robin Grunder
former editor, Rapture Romance

I find the most crucial element in writing a romance is establishing a personality for your heroine and hero. It may be tempting to follow past examples, and people your story with stock characters; don't. We have all read the trembling young girl and the overbearing older man a million times, and once you've read Jane Eyre *nothing else is as good.*

Make sure that your heroine and hero are individuals. Before you even start to plot the book, you should have personality profiles that include their past history, their favorite colors, foods, and books, their values, their goals, and their dreams. You may not ever use these details, but when you start writing you will know instinctively what your heroine or hero would do or say in any given situation.

Moreover, knowing their personalities will help to visualize situations that will lead to a plot. For instance, a timid girl who is courageous in the defense of loved ones might be a veterinarian—she wouldn't argue with her boyfriend of long standing, but should come raring to the rescue of an animal she saw being mistreated. Knowing her, you can start to see the kind of conflicts that would come between her and the man she loves. You don't need to rely on hackneyed jealousy and implausible misunderstandings to create tension and conflict. You should create a realistic, believable, and fresh plot that is specific to the two people about whom you are writing.

Remember, vivid personalities make the most unforgettable love stories. Gone With the Wind *comes alive because Scarlett and Rhett are unique people, with faults and virtues, whom we know and care about. Our heroine and hero may not be perfect, but they are perfect for each other. It would be a tragedy if they had not found each other, and your book's romantic tension is the result of the reader's worry that the lovers will not, somehow, resolve their differences and live happily ever after.*

Rapture Romance (*Contd.*)

Recommended Reading: Love So Fearful by Nina Coombs, *River of Love* by Lisa McConnell, *Lovers' Lair* by Jeanette Ernest, *Welcome Intruder* by Charlotte Wisely, *Chesapeake Autumn* by Stephanie Richards, *Tender Rhapsody* by Jennifer Dale, *Summer Storm* by Joan Wolf, *Crystal Dreams* by Diana Morgan, *The Wine-Dark Sea* by Ellie Winslow, *Flower of Desire* by Francine Shore

Editorial Requirements: Highly sensual, entirely believable, but not realistic love stories. All of the traditional elements, but none of the cliché devices of old-style romances. Length: 60,000 words. Tip sheet available.

Second Chance at Love
Jove Publications
200 Madison Avenue
New York, N.Y. 10016
(212) 686-9820

Editor: Ellen Edwards

Submission Requirements: Published authors: complete synopsis and several sample chapters. Unpublished authors: complete manuscript, Query letters are encouraged.

Recommended Reading: Glitter Girl by Jocelyn Day, *The Golden Touch* by Robin James, *Torn Asunder* by Ann Christy, *On Wings of Magic* by Susanna Collins, *Untamed Desire* by Beth Brookes, *Satin and Steele* by Jaelyn Conlee, *Half Way There* by Aimee DuVall, *Return Engagement* by Kay Robbins, *Stormy Reunion* by Jasmine Craig, *Stormy Passage* by Laurel Blake

Editorial Requirements: The plot must involve the heroine's "second chance at love." She must be a divorcee or widowed. In the novel, she will succeed in finding the happiness she missed or lost before. The settings are either contemporary or Regency England. The heroine should be a mature young woman. Explicit, sensual detail may be used to describe the foreplay phase of lovemaking, but a fade-out should occur before actual intercourse. Length: 65,000–70,000 words.

Silhouette
1230 Avenue of the Americas
New York, N.Y. 10026
(212) 586-6151

Submission Requirements: Complete manuscript, or fifty pages and synopsis, with SASE.

Silhouette Romances, Special Edition, Desire, Intimate Moments, Inspiration
Simon and Schuster
1240 Avenue of the Americas
New York, N.Y. 10020
(212) 245-6400

Senior Editor: Karen Solem
Associate Editor: Alicia Condon
Submission Requirements: Complete manuscript, or fifty pages and synopsis. SASE.
Recommended Authors for Silhouette Romances: Dixie Browning, Janet Dailey, Ann Hampson, Nora Roberts, Donna Vitek
Recommended Authors for Silhouette Special Edition: Janet Dailey, Billie Douglas, Pat Wallace
Recommended Author for Intimate Moments: Stephanie James (a.k.a. Jayne Castle)

Editorial Requirements for Silhouette Romances: Sweet romance set in the U.S. and abroad featuring the traditional romance format of a young, inexperienced heroine who meets an older, more sophisticated hero. Length: 50,000–55,000 words. Tip sheet available.

Editorial Requirements for Silhouette Special Edition: Longer and more sophisticated plots, more complex and believable, centering on the developing relationship between the hero and heroine and the problems they must overcome on their way to a happy ending. The heroine (twenty-three to twenty-nine) is intelligent and mature, independent and accomplished, never weepy. The hero (eight to ten years older) is dynamic, virile, self-confident, and supremely masculine. Length: 70,000–75,000 words. Tip sheet available.

Editorial Requirements for Silhouette Desire: The writing should be extremely sensuous, providing vivid, evocative descriptions of lovemaking and concentrating on the characters' emotion-packed reactions to each other and the sexual tension between them. The plot centers on the developing relationship between the heroine (mid-twenties or thirties and worldly), who is mature and capable, and the hero, a realistic, believable, modern male. Length: 60,000 words. Tip sheet available.

Editorial Requirements for Intimate Moments: Larger-than-life romance, with glitzy touches à la Danielle Steel. Length: 80,000 words. Tip sheet available.

Editorial Requirements for Inspiration: Love stories about people who have personally experienced Christianity. Tip sheet available.

Alicia Condon's Tips

1. *Multiple viewpoints can work if used carefully, especially the hero's.*
2. *The hero doesn't necessarily have to be tall, dark, handsome, and wealthy. He should be intelligent, capable, self-confident, sexy—a strong yet tender character.*
3. *There is no one right place for the first love scene and no set number of love scenes per book. The love scenes should come out of the story.*

Superromance
Worldwide Library
Harlequin Books
225 Duncan Mill Road
Don Mills, Ontario, Canada
Canada M3B 359
(416) 445-5860

Senior Editor: Star Helmer
Submission Requirements: A synopsis and fifty pages or the first three chapters.
Recommended Reading: Captive of Desire by Alexandra Sellers, *Fire in the Wind* by

Alexandra Sellers, *Serenade for a Lost Love* by Jocelyn Haley, *Dawn of Passion* by Catherine Kay, *Tender Rhapsody* by Judith Duncan, *Proud Surrender* by June Casey, *Journey into Love* by Polly Foster, *Sweet Temptation* by Shannon Clare, *Song of Desire* by Rosalind Carson, *The Forever Spell* by Robyn Anzelon

Editorial Requirements: The romance and sexual relationship grows believably out of shared experiences, feelings, and

---

George Glay's Likes and Dislikes
former editor, Harlequin

1. *Unique complex plots*
2. *Imaginative writing*
3. *Depth and emotional intensity to the relationship*
4. *Long, sensuous scenes*
5. *Well-motivated conflicts*
6. *Mature, realistic characters*
7. *Lots of dialogue*
8. *Romantic backgrounds—local or foreign*
9. *Touch of humor*
10. *High dramatic or emotional suspense*

1. *Wimpy, naïve heroines*
2. *Brutal, sadistic heroes*
3. *Stereotypes—catty other women or nice, dependable other men*
4. *Contrived plot devices—coincidences, marriages of convenience, simple midunderstandings*
5. *Abrupt endings*
6. *Violence*
7. *Depressing topics*
8. *Elaborate descriptions of heroine's makeup and clothes*
9. *Backgrounds that read like travelogues*
10. *Archeological careers (overdone lately)*

loving commitment, leading to marriage. The story should retain warm, emotional appeal, the locale be interesting, exotic, or romantic. The hero and heroine are mature adults with fully developed characters, engaged in the occupations and interests of today's world. Length: 95,000 words. Tip sheet available.

To Have and To Hold
Second Chance at Love
Berkley/Jove
200 Madison Avenue
New York, N.Y. 10016
(212) 686-9820

Senior Editor: Ellen Edwards
Submission Requirements: Complete manuscripts. Tip sheet available. Length: 60,000 words.

Editorial Requirements: Romances of married couples.

Historical Romances

Avon
1790 Broadway
New York, N.Y. 10019
(212) 262-6255

Editor: Page Cuddy
Submission Requirements: Synopsis and three sample chapters with SASE. Length: 80,000 words or over.
Recommended Authors: Kathleen Woodiwiss, Patricia Gallagher, Shirley Busbee, Alexandra Ripley, Jo Ann Simon

Ballantine
201 E. 50th Street
New York, N.Y. 10022
(212) 751-2600

Editor: Pamela Strickler
Submission Requirements: Complete manuscript of several hundred pages. Synopsis with cover letter. Length: 100,000–150,000 words.
Recommended Authors: Jennifer Wilde, Cynthia Wright, Bertrice Small, Claire Lorrimar, Betty Receveur

Bantam
666 Fifth Avenue
New York, N.Y. 10019
(212) 765-6500

Editors: Linda Price
Submission Requirements: Complete manuscript or several hundred pages. Synopsis

with cover letter. Query first.
Length: 80,000 words or
over.

Recommended Author: Georgette Heyer (historicals and Regencies)

Berkley/Jove
200 Madison Avenue
New York, N.Y. 10016
(212) 686-9820

Editor: Nancy Coffey

Book Creations
Schillings Crossing
Canaan, N.Y. 12029
(518) 781-4171

President: Lyle Kenyon Engel
Submission Requirements: This company is a book packager, and splits the royalties with the author. Professional writers (no agents) contact only, with samples of books and complete résumé. Series idea is given to author by publisher.

Recommended Series: The Australians, Roselynde Chronicles, Royal Dynasty, Kent Family Chronicles, Windhaven, Wagons West, etc.

Dell
1 Dag Hammarskjold Plaza
New York, N.Y. 10017
(212) 605-3000

Editor: Judith Riven
Submission Requirements: Query letter. No length requirement.

Recommended Reading: The Black Swan by Day Taylor, *Bitter Eden* by Sharon Salvato, The Heiress series by Roberta Gellis, *Seize the Dawn* by Vanessa Royall, *Love's Wildest Fire* by Christina Savage, *Palomino* by Danielle Steel, *The Taming* by Aleen Malcolm

Fawcett
Ballantine
201 E. 50th Street
New York, N.Y. 10023
(212) 751-2600

Editor: Leona Nevler
Submission Requirements:
Agent only.
Editorial Requirements: Each
month. Fawcett's three lines
will publish nonformula historicals and Regencies. Quality writing and strong storytelling.
*Recommended Reading: Em-
brace and Conquer* by Jennifer Blake, *Phoenix Rising*
by Frances Patton Statham,
Passion's Child by Fiona
Harrowe, *Proud Surrender*
by Diana Haviland, anything
by Victoria Holt and Natasha
Peters

Robert Hale
Clerkenwell House
45-47 Clerkenwell Green
London, EC1R OHT, England

Managing Director: John Hale
Submission Requirements: Complete manuscript with SASE.
Simultaneous (only in special circumstances) and photocopied manuscripts okay.

Hodder and Stroughton
P.O. Box 703
Mill Road, Dunton Green
Sevenoaks, Kent, TV13 2YE,
England

Editorial Submissions: Synopsis with cover letter.

Pinnacle
1430 Broadway
New York, N.Y. 10018
(212) 719-5900

Editor: Liza Dawson
Submission Requirements:
Query or outline/synopsis with
four sample chapters and
SASE. Simultaneous and
photocopied submissions
okay.
Recommended Authors: Patricia Matthews, Marie de Jourlet, Paula Fairman, Virginia
Lee Hart, Virginia Myers

Pocket Books
1230 Avenue of the Americas
New York, N.Y. 10020
(212) 246-2121

Editor: Beverly Lewis
Submission   Requirements:
    Query with SASE.
Recommended Authors: Jude
    Deveraux, Janet Dailey, Joan
    Dial, Roseanne Kohake

Tapestry
Pocket Books
1230 Avenue of the Americas
New York, N.Y. 10020
(212) 246-2121

Editor: Beverly Lewis
Submission Requirements: Out-
    line and first three chapters.
    More exotic locations than
    U.S. and U.K. Historical
    romances. Length: 85,000
    words. No tip sheet.
*Recommended Reading: Defiant
    Love* by Maura Seger, *Kin-
    dred Spirits* by DeAnn Pat-
    rick, *High Country Pride* by
    Lynn Erickson

Warner
666 Fifth Avenue
New York, N.Y. 10103
(212) 484-2900

Editor: Fredda Isaacson
Submission   Requirements:
    Query with outline or letter,
    also writing credentials
Recommended Authors: Joan
    Aiken, Jennifer Wilde, Jan-
    et Louise Roberts, Valerie
    Sherwood, Lydia Lancaster,
    Rebecca Brandewyne

Zebra
475 Park Avenue South
New York, N.Y. 10016
(212) 889-2299

Editor: Carin Cohen
Submission Requirements: Three
    sample chapters and outline,
    with SASE.
Recommended Authors: Janelle
    Taylor, Eleanora Brownleigh,
    Karen Harper, Valerie Satler,
    Sylvie Sommerfield

Teen Romances

Tip Sheets are available

Caprice
Berkley/Jove
200 Madison Avenue
New York, N.Y. 10016
(212) 686-9820

Editor
Editorial Submission: Complete manuscript or three chapters with an outline, and SASE. Length: 50,000 words.
Recommended Reading: Before Love and *Me and Superman* by Gloria Miklowitz, *Cheer Me On* and *Computer Cupid* by Judith Enderle

First Love
Silhouette
1230 Avenue of the Americas
New York, N.Y. 10020
(212) 586-6151

Editor: Nancy Jackson
Editorial Submission: Complete manuscript with SASE. Length: 55,000 words.
Recommended Authors: Elaine Harper, Caroline Cooney, Dorothy Francis

Sweet Dreams
Bantam
Cloverdale Press
133 Fifth Avenue
New York, N.Y. 10003
(212) 420-1555

Editor: Ben Baglio
Editorial Submission: Query with SASE or submit through agent. Length 55,000 words.
Recommended Reading: P.S. I Love You by Barbara Conklin, *California Sun* by Janet Quin-Harkin, *Laurie's Song* by Suzanne Rand

Wildfire and Wishing Star
Scholastic
50 W. 44th Street
New York, N.Y. 10036
(212) 944-7700

Editor: Ann Reit
Editorial Submission: Synopsis with first three chapters and SASE. Length: 55,000 words.
Recommended Reading: Audrey Johnson, Mary Bringle, Helen Cavanaugh

Ann Reit's Likes and Dislikes

1. *Strong friendships between girls*
2. *Humor*
3. *Realistic plots*
4. *Girls who don't giggle, squeal, toss their heads*
5. *Boys who don't want their girlfriends helpless*
6. *Strong mothers*
7. *Good dialogue*

1. *Boys who treat the girls like simps*
2. *Jealous, mean girls*
3. *Clichés of any kind*
4. *Heroines who let the boy determine the nature of their relationship*
5. *Old-fashioned ideas about dating, families, careers*
6. *Stock characters*

Regency Romances

Avon
1790 Broadway
New York, N.Y. 10019
(212) 262-6255

Editor: Colleen O'Shea
Editorial Submission: Query or outline/synopsis and three sample chapters with SASE.

Ballantine
201 E. 50th Street
New York, N.Y. 10022
(212) 751-2600

Editor: Leona Nevler
Editorial Submission: By agent only.

Bantam
666 Fifth Avenue
New York, N.Y. 10103
(212) 765-6500

Editor: Linda Price
Editorial Submission: Query or outline/synopsis with SASE.
Recommended Authors: Georgette Heyer, Claire D'Arcy

Berkley/Jove
200 Madison Avenue
New York, N.Y. 10016
(212) 686-9820

Editor: Nancy Coffey
Editorial Submission: Query or outline synopsis with SASE.
Recommended Author: Elizabeth Mansfield

NAL/Signet
1633 Broadway
New York, N.Y. 10019
(212) 397-8000

Editor: Hilary Ross
Editorial Submission: Complete manuscript or outline/synopsis and sample chapters with SASE.
Recommended Authors: Catherine Coulter, Diana Brown, April Kihlstrom, Joan Wolf, Julia Jeffries, Sandra Heath

St. Martin's Press
175 Fifth Avenue
New York, N.Y. 10010
(212) 674-5151

Editor: Hope Dellon
Editorial Submission: Query or complete manuscript with SASE.
Recommended Authors: Patricia Veryan, Diana Brown

Starlight Romances
Doubleday
245 Park Avenue
New York, N.Y. 10017
(212) 953-4561

Editor: Veronica Mixon
Editorial Submission: Query letter only. Publishes Regency, historical and category for special hardcover library editions.

Walker & Co.
720 Fifth Avenue
New York, N.Y. 10019
(212) 265-3632

Editor: Ruth Cavin
Editorial Submission: Query or complete manuscript. Conventional Regency length: 50,000–55,000 words. English settings with humor.
Recommended Authors: Norma Lee Clare, Georgette Heyer, Marnie Ellingson, Elizabeth Kidd, Jacqueline Diamond, Clare Darcy

Romantic Suspense and Gothic

Bantam
666 Fifth Avenue
New York, N.Y. 10103
(212) 765-6500

Editor: Carolyn Nichols
Editorial Submission: Query with SASE or submit through agent.
Recommended Reading: Midnight Whispers by Patricia and Clayton Matthews

Zebra Books
475 Park Avenue South
New York, N.Y. 10016
(212) 889-2299

Editor: Leslie Gelbman
Editorial Submission: Query or complete manuscript, or outline/synopsis and sample chapters, with SASE.
Editorial Requirements: Romantic Suspense, no! Gothic, yes!

Contemporary

Avon
1790 Broadway
New York, N.Y. 10019
(212) 262-6255

Editor: Colleen O'Shea
Editorial Submission: 80,000 words or over. Synopsis and three sample chapters, with SASE.

Bantam
666 Fifth Avenue
New York, N.Y. 10103
(212) 765-6500

Editor: Carolyn Nichols
Editorial Submission: Query with SASE or submit through agent.

Berkley/Jove
200 Madison Avenue
New York, N.Y. 10016
(212) 686-9820

Editor: Nancy Coffey
Editorial Submission: Synopsis with three sample chapters, with SASE.

Dell
1 Dag Hammarskjold Plaza
New York, N.Y. 10017
(212) 605-3000

Editor: Judith Riven
Editorial Submission: Four-page synopsis or outline with a cover letter stating previous work published, with SASE.

Science Fiction and Fantasy

Ballantine/Del Rey
201 E. 50th Street
New York, N.Y. 10022
(212) 751-2600

Editor: Judy Lynn Del Rey
Editorial Submission: Complete manuscript.
Recommended Authors: Anne McCaffrey, Carole Nelson Douglas, Andre Norton, Piers Anthony

A Publisher Talks About Romance Fiction

BY RON BUSCH

president, Pocket Books

Gothic romances were the "bread and butter" for some publishers in the late sixties and early seventies. They were steady sellers, sometimes with modest sales, and a clear indication that there was a market for romance novels.

Unfortunately, many publishers took this as a sign that what the consumer wanted was more gothic romances, and so the bookstores were glutted with this type of novel. Of course sales fell, affecting the genre as a whole and convincing many publishers that there was no longer a romance market. At the same time, the idea of brand-name contemporary romances was still being ignored by most U.S. publishers, with the exception of Dell's Candlelight line.

Pocket Books, however, recognized the strong demand for romance novels. We began researching ways of serving this market and formulating our plans for the future.

Meanwhile, the romance field continued to change and expand. In the mid-seventies, several romance novelists broke away from their usual positions on the mid-lists of mass market houses to become major best-sellers. Authors like Danielle Steel, Kathleen Woodiwiss, and Rosemary Rogers proved to publishers that there was a wide readership clearly waiting for bigger and better romance novels. It was time for publishers to turn to the market-place for inspiration about the kinds of books readers were looking for.

Pocket Books began by finding out what the readers of romantic fiction were like. We found them to be intelligent, well informed, and critical of many of the books being published. They became our greatest resource, and we've never stopped listening to them. Now, innovations such as direct marketing, newsletters, and writers' workshops give us much faster feedback than we intially had, allowing our editors to keep pace with the changes in reader's tastes and demands even better than before.

Nineteen eighty was a pivotal year for us. We were preparing to launch our own line of romances. Our research and attention to the readers led us to believe the time was right for a move into category contemporary fiction that answered audience demand for new titles. At the same time, we selected authors who could bring a fresh, new approach to the novels and who could inject a unique, American viewpoint into their writing.

This, of course, became Silhouette Romances, which began publication in May of 1980 and has been successful ever since. Silhouette Books has grown editorially to include not just Silhouette Romances, but Silhouette Special Editions, Silhouette Desire, and a special line of young readers, First Love. And despite the number of books we are publishing now, we believe there is more room for new ideas and quality writing.

Preparation for the launch of Silhouette Romances brought to our attention many things that were being ignored. For instance, the day of the bodice ripper, so much a part of romance publishing in the mid-seventies, was coming to a close. Yet at the end of the seventies they were still being published in great numbers, with no sign of change. While this type of novel still had an audience, the majority of romance readers were looking for something new, novels responsive to their own changing attitudes and values.

Readers were indicating their preference for better-developed stories and more sensuous stories. We looked for the writers already filling those needs. As we found them, the authors, like Janet Dailey, were brought to the forefront of our lists, giving them the necessary support to reach the widest possible audience. Today, we continue to highlight authors like Janet Dailey, Jude Deveraux, Joan Dial, and Diane Antonio, whose novels are as different from each other as their personalities, in order to give them the support they need to reach their fans and to introduce them to a wider range of readers.

Pocket Books continues its response to the changing romance field in other ways as well. In 1982 we perceived that the focus of publishers had shifted so much to contemporary romantic fiction that an entire area of genre, historical romances, had begun to be ignored. Many publishers had started to cut these books from their lists, or were relying solely on established authors and longer books.

We didn't agree with this type of publishing, for several reasons. For one thing, the cover prices on the longer historical titles put them out of reach for many romance buyers. And in many cases good, solid plots were being stretched to provide a "saga" look, causing them to lose their vitality. Published in a format that they simply did not fit, the books lost sales, which in turn lent further weight to the argument that there was no longer a market for historical romances.

We saw a definite need for a change in the way these books were being published. October 1982 marked the launch of Tapestry Romances, a new line of historical novels from Pocket Books. The line does not have tip sheets, and the only guideline is the length of the novel. This allowed us to overcome both of our major complaints about the direction historical romances were taking. We weren't faced with having to stretch plots, and by not doing so we are able to keep the books affordable at $2.50 each.

Tapestry Romances has also given us the opportunity to bring new writers to the attention of readers as well as to provide a new outlet for veteran writers.

I already see Tapestry Romances as a successful entry into the romance field. Reader and bookseller response has been outstanding. As for the future, I'm neither willing to make predictions in this volatile field nor will I disclose projects already being explored. However, I will say that we at Pocket Books have gotten immense satisfaction from discovering and developing new talent. For us, romance publishing remains a fluid, ever-changing field and presents a challenge we can respond to with years of experience and three simple words—"ask the reader."

Publications

Periodicals

Romantic Times*
163 Joralemon Street
Suite 1234C
Brooklyn Heights, N.Y. 11201

(1 Year, 6 issues, $8.95)
Sample Copy—$1.50

A bimonthly magazine for writers and readers of romance novels, contemporary and historical; reviews books, profiles authors, lists forthcoming titles, industry trade news, gossip, how-to write information.

*Romantic Times Writers
  Newsletter*
163 Joralemon Street
Suite 1234C
Brooklyn Heights, N.Y. 11201

(1 Year, 12 issues, $60)
Sample Copy—$5

Monthly newsletter for aspiring and published popular-fiction writers. Covers every aspect of writing and publishing. Special cassette tapes available. Listing of local writers groups.

*Romantic Times Readers
  Newsletter*
163 Joralemon Street
Suite 1234C
Brooklyn Heights, N.Y. 11201

(1 Year, 4 issues, $10)
Sample Copy—$3

Quarterly "fanzine" publication for avid readers. Special reports on readers and trends, a valuable tool for writers. Regular features include book reviews, Q & A, pseudonym research, and letters.

* For Canadian subscribers, send check in U.S. funds and add $3 for additional postage; foreign subscribers must check with each publication and determine if mailing is to be first class or boat rate.

Publishers Weekly*
R. R. Bowker Company
Subscription Department R
P.O. Box 13731
Philadelphia, Pa. 19001

(1 Year, 52 issues, $59)
Sample Copy—$2

Weekly trade magazine of the entire book industry, covers everything from typesetting to profit margins, author profiles, media alerts, book reviews, and trade talk.

Writer's Digest*
Subscription Service R
205 West Center Street
Marion, Oh. 43306

(1 Year, 12 issues, $15)
Sample Copy—$2

A monthly periodical providing interviews with editors and writers, advice on all types of fiction and nonfiction writing.

The Writer*
8 Arlington Street
Boston, Mass. 02216

(1 Year, 12 issues, $15)
Sample Copy—$2

Monthly magazine offering interviews with writers and poets, specific writing techniques, market newsletter for fiction writers.

Romance Section
Publishers Weekly
Att: John Baker
1180 Avenue of the Americas
New York, N.Y. 10036

($3 for 24-page section)

In November 1981, *Publishers Weekly* printed a special romance section giving a comprehensive overview of the industry, including an analysis of the subgenres, reader survey, covers, and interviews with editors and publishers. The guest editor was Kathryn Falk.

Torch Magazine
8353 A Greensboro Drive
McLean, Va. 22102

(Sample Copy—$1.50)

Monthly magazines featuring a complete category romance. New market for unpublished romance authors. Tip sheet available with SASE.

Books

Love's Leading Ladies
Romantic Times
163 Joralemon Street
Suite 1234C
Brooklyn Heights, N.Y. 11201

An intimate look at the women who write the best-selling romance novels. The Who's Who of romance writers, 65 profiles of leading authors,

($8.50, including postage)
Check payable to Romantic Times

including their tips on writing, and complete with photographs, facts, favorite recipes, and listing of titles and pseudonyms. Written by Kathryn Falk, published by Pinnacle Books (1982).

The Romantic Spirit
MJK Enterprises
P.O. Box 5571
San Antonio, Tex. 78201-0571

($11.50, including postage)

Source book of authors' titles and pseudonyms, and numbered/category romances. Privately published. Essential for readers who want to know an author's complete bibliography.

Lovelines
Facts on File
460 Park Avenue South
New York, N.Y. 10016

(Paperback $7.95)

A romance reader's guide. Interviews with editors, illustrators, readers, and booksellers; fascinating facts and trivia. Written by Rosemary Guiley.

Fiction Writer's Market
Writer's Digest Books
9933 Alliance Road
Cincinnati, Ohio 45242

($16.95)

A writer's guide to the entire publishing market, complete with addresses and editorial requirements, special articles, and lists of agents.

The Writer's Handbook
The Writer, Inc.
8 Arlington Street
Boston, Mass. 02116

A comprehensive book containing 82 chapters of practical advice for writing and getting published, including lists of agents and publishers.

One-Liners for Romance Writers
Daring Press R
1308 Harrison Street
Canton, Ohio 44705

A tool for romance writers; over 2,000 one-line descriptions, 28 categories, including heart beats, smiles, kisses, and sex. (Include SASE for information.)

Harlequin's 30th Anniversary Book
Harlequin Book Department
225 Duncan Mills Road
Don Mills, Ontario, M3B 3K9, Canada

($1.25 plus 75¢ postage)

The first 30 years (1949–79) of Harlequin's romance fiction is printed here with complete bibliography and many author profiles.

Conferences

Romantic Book Lovers' Conference
Contact: *Romantic Times*
Suite 1234C
163 Joralemon Street
Brooklyn Heights, N.Y. 11201

Annual New York City gathering of authors, editors, booksellers, and readers. Hospitality suites hosted by leading romance publishers, who provide new writer's tip sheets, sample books, and souvenirs for book lovers. Over 25 workshops for writers and readers, plus a special awards banquet. A three-day event that includes a book fair. Held in October at a New York hotel. Free brochure available.

International Romantic Book Lovers' Conference
Contact: *Romantic Times*
Suite 1234C
163 Joralemon Street
Brooklyn Heights, N.Y. 11201

An international conference held in London, in conjunction with the British Book Fair. Codirector with Kathryn Falk is Marion Chesney, Regency author. Participants can join special tour which visits another country during the trip.

Dixie Council of Authors and Journalists
Contact: Frances Statham
2248 Marann Drive N.E.
Atlanta, Ga. 30345

A three-day conference in June held on St. Simon's Island, Georgia, and attended by many types of fiction writers, editors, and agents. Manuscript appraisal.

Award

The Georgette Heyer Award
The Bodley Head
9 Bow Street
Covenant Garden, London,
  WT2E, 7AL, England

A prize open to full-length un-published novels from any historical period. The winner receives a cash prize and guaranteed hardcover and paperback publication. Entries close every year on August 31, and all submissions should be accompanied by an international postage coupon, to cover return postage, and a self-addressed label.

Cassette Tapes for Romance Writers

Romantic Times Cassettes
163 Joralemon Street
Suite 1234C
Brooklyn Heights, N.Y. 11201

A complete series of tapes from conferences and seminars is available. Please send a SASE (self-addressed stamped envelope) for listing. Tapes cover category and historical romance writing, with special lectures by all the leading editors, authors, and agents. A helpful tool you can listen to over and over until you get romance writing right!

Self-Motivation for Writers
Susan Feldhake
Route 2, Box 142
Watson, Ill. 62473

($5.95 plus $1 postage)

An elemental, down-to-earth presentation that can help the beginning writer cope with getting started.

A Recommended Reading List

COMPILED BY MELINDA HELFER

book reviewer, Romantic Times

Bantam/LOVESWEPT

Carlson, Nancy	*Hard Driving Man*
Curtis, Sharon & Tom	*Lightning That Lingers*
Downing, Joan	*Pfarr Lake Affair*
	Tiger Lady
Green, Billie June	*A Tryst With Mr. Lincoln?*
	A Very Reluctant Knight
Hooper, Kay	*CJ's Fate*
Johansen, Iris	*The Golden Valkyrie*
	The Lady and the Unicorn
	The Reluctant Lark
	A Tempest at Sea
	The Trustworthy Redhead
Michael, Marie	*Irresistible Forces*
Nittermeyer, Helen	*Surrender*
Neggers, Carla	*Heart on a String*
	Matching Wits
Orwig, Sara	*Autumn Flames*
Preston, Fayrene	*For Love of Sami*
	The Seduction of Jason
	Silver Miracles
Reisser, Anne	*Love, Catch a Wild Bird*

NAL/RAPTURE

Chandler, Laurel	*Treasure of Love*
Clark, Marianne	*Apache Tears*
Coombs, Nina	*Passion's Domain*
Kent, Kathryn	*Precious Possession*
McKenzie, Melinda	*Beyond All Stars*
Morgan, Diana	*Amber Dreams*
	Emerald Dreams
Morgan, Leslie	*Against All Odds*
Ransom, Katherine	*O'Hara's Woman*
Richards, Stephanie	*Chesapeake Autumn*

Robb, JoAnn	*Dreamlover*
Wolf, Joan	*Change of Heart*
	Summer Storm

Harlequin/Mills & Boon

Bianchin, Helen	*Bewildered Haven*
Britt, Katrina	*The King of Spades*
Chace, Isobel	*Cadence of Portugal*
Clair, Daphne	*Darling Deceiver*
	A Ruling Passion
Clifford, Kay	*The Duke Wore Jeans*
	Heart of Gold
	The Tycoon's Lady
Collin, Marian	*The Beachcomber*
Corrie, Jane	*The Emerald Eagle*
Craven, Sara	*The Garden of Dreams*
	Sup With the Devil
Dailey, Janet	*Big Sky Country*
	Green Mountain Man
	The Night of the Cotillion
Donald, Robyn	*Bride at Whangatapu*
	Mansion for My Love
Firth, Susanna	*Dark Encounter*
	Lions Walk Alone
George, Catherine	*Dream of Midsummer*
	Gilded Cage
	Reluctant Paragon
Gilbert, Jacqueline	*Autumn in Bangkok*
Gillen, Lucy	*The Runaway Bride*
Gordon, Victoria	*The Sugar Dragon*
Hilliard, Nerina	*Dark Star*
	Dark Intruder
	Land of the Sun
Hunter, Elizabeth	*The Crescent Moon*
James, Vanessa	*Ever After*
Kidd, Flora	*The Dance of Courtship*
	Remedy for Love
	The Summer Wife
Lamb, Charlotte	*Dark Dominion*
	Duel of Desire
	Frustration
	Pagan Encounter

Lorin, Amii	*Candleglow*
Lindsay, Rachel	*Love and Lucy Granger*
McGiveny, Maura	*A Grand Illusion*
MacLean, Jan	*An Island Loving*
Mather, Anne	*Forbidden*
	White Rose of Winter
Mortimer, Carole	*Engaged to Jarrod Stone*
Murrey, Jeneth	*Daughter of the Night*
	Hell Is My Heaven
Oldfield, Elizabeth	*Beloved Stranger*
	Dream Hero
	Submission
Palmer, Beryl	*Man in a Mask*
Steele, Jessica	Innocent Abroad
Stevens, Lynsey	Play Our Song Again
Stratton, Rebecca	*Castles in Spain*
Thorne, Avery	*No Other Chance*
Thorpe, Kay	*An Apple in Eden*
Weale, Anne	*Ecstasy*
	Lord of the Sierras
Wentworth, Sally	*Flying High*
	Man for Hire

Harlequin/Superromance

Anzelon, Robyn	*The Forever Spell*
Bowen, Alyce	*Dangerous Promise*
Church, Emma	*The Heart Remembers*
Clare, Shannon	*Snow Bride*
Collins, Kathryn	*The Wings of Night*
Cott, Christina Hella	*Dangerous Delight*
	Midnight Magic
Haley, Jocely	*Winds of Desire*
Hudson, Meg	*Sweet Dawn of Desire*
Jeffries, Jessica	*A Certain Sunrise*
Jones, Marian	*Bonds of Enchantment*
Logan, Jessica	*Promise to Possess*
McNaught, Judith	*Tender Triumph*
Sellers, Alexandra	*Captive of Desire*
	Fire in the Wind
	Season of Storm
Taylor, Abra	*A Rage to Possess*

Harlequin/American

Ashley, Jacqueline	*Hunting Season*
	Love's Revenge
Brown, Sandra	*Tomorrow's Promise*
Chambers, Ginger	*Game of Hearts*
Francis, Robin	*Memories of Love*
Glenn, Elizabeth	*Taste of Love*
Jeffries, Jessica	*All in the Game*
Lang, Heather	*Thorn in My Side*
Seidel, Kathleen Gilles	*A Risk Worth Taking*
Sommers, Beverly	*City Life, City Love*
	Unscheduled Love

Dell/Ecstasy

Andrews, Barbara	*Stolen Promises*
Black, Jackie	*Autumn Fires*
	Crimson Morning
	Promises in the Night
Blayne, Diana	*A Loving Arrangement*
Bryan, Eileen	*Memory and Desire*
Cameron, Barbara	*An Affair to Remember*
Castle, Jayne	*Conflict of Interest*
	A Man's Protection
	Power Play
	Right of Possession
Chase, Elaine Raco	*Double Occupancy*
	Video Vixen
Copeland, Lori	*Playing for Keeps*
	A Tempting Stanger
Drake, Bonnie	*Sensuous Burgundy*
	Sweet Ember
Fairfax, Gwen	*Lover in Disguise*
Hart, Shirley	*Brand of Passion*
Hooper, Kay	*Breathless Surrender*
	On Wings of Magic
Hudson, Anna	*Design for Desire*
	Kiss the Tears Away
Jennings, Sara	*Reach for the Stars*
Linz, Cathie	*Wildfire*
Lorin, Amii	*Morgan Wade's Woman*

Martin, Prudence	*Love Song*
Morgan, Alice	*Masquerade of Love*
Reisser, Anne	*All's Fair*
	Deceptive Love
Ryan, Rachel	*Love Beyond Reason*
	Prime Time
Woods, Eleanor	*Loving Exile*
	Sensuous Persuasion
	Tempestuous Challenge

Dell/SUPREME

Black, Jackie	*Payment in Full*
Bryan, Eileen	*Crossfire*
Graham, Heather	*Night, Sea and Stars*
	Tempestuous Eden
Hudson, Anna	*Body and Soul*
Martin, Prudence	*Lovers and Pretenders*

Jove/Second Chance

Brookes, Beth	*On Wings of Passion*
Brown, Sandra	*A Relentless Desire*
Conlee, Jaelyn	*Satin and Steele*
Craig, Jasmine	*Imprisoned Heart*
	Stormy Reunion
Cristy, Ann	*Enthralled*
	From the Torrid Past
	Torn Asunder
Damon, Lee	*Laugh With Me, Love With Me*
Duvall, Aimee	*Lover in Blue*
	Loving Touch
Granger, Katherine	*A Man's Persuasion*
Grant, Jeanne	*A Daring Proposition*
	Kisses From Heaven
Harris, Melinda	*The Wind's Embrace*
Hines, Charlotte	*Tender Trap*
Hughes, Cally	*Innocent Seduction*
James, Robin	*The Golden Touch*
Logan, Daisy	*Sweet Bliss*
McKean, Margarett	*Heartthrob*
	This Wild Heart

Mars, Diana   *Sweet Abandon*
Mathews, Jan   *Season of Desire*
Morgan, Faye   *Trial by Fire*
Nolan, Jenny   *Summer Lace*
Phillips, Johanna   *Hidden Dreams*
                               Passion's Song
                               Strange Possession
Rivers, Francine   *Hearts Divided*
Robbins, Kay   *Kissed by Magic*
                               Return Engagement
                               Taken by Storm
Rose, Jennifer   *Twilight Embrace*
Spencer, LaVyrle   *Forsaking All Others*
Thacker, Cathy   *Intimate Scoundrel*

Jove/TO HAVE AND TO HOLD

Bates, Jenny   *Gilded Spring*
Cristy, Ann   *Tread Softly*
Damon, Lee   *Lady Laughing Eyes*
Granger, Katherine   *Moments to Share*
Grant, Jeanne   *Sunburst*
Haskell, Mary   *Hold Fast Till Dawn*
James, Robin   *The Testimony*
Randolph, Melanie   *Heart Full of Rainbows*
Rose, Jennifer   *A Taste of Heaven*

Silhouette/all lines

Barrie, Monica   *Cry Mercy, Cry Love*
                               Gentle Wind
Berk, Ariel   *Silent Beginnings*
Chance, Sara   *Home at Last*
Chase, Elaine Raco   *Calculated Risk*
Clare, Jane   *Old Love, New Love*
Conrad, Constance   *On Wings of Night*
Dailey, Janet   *Terms of Surrender*
                               Western Man
Dixon, Diana   *Mexican Rhapsody*
Douglass, Billie   *Fast Courting*
                               Knightly Love
Eden, Laura   *Mistaken Identity*

Halldorson, Phyllis — *Temporary Bride*
Halston, Carole — *Stand-in Bride*
Hamilton, Lucy — *All's Fair*
— *A Woman's Place*
Hardy, Laura — *Playing With Fire*
Hastings, Brooke — *Playing for Keeps*
— *Rough Diamond*
Hohl, Joan — *Moments Harsh, Moments Gentle*
— *Thorne's Way*
Howard, Linda — *Against the Rules*
— *All That Glitters*
— *An Independent Wife*
James, Kristin — *Dreams of Evening*
James, Stephanie — *Affair of Honor*
— *Body Guard*
— *Lover in Pursuit*
— *Raven's Prey*
— *Serpent in Paradise*
— *Stormy Challenge*
John, Nancy — *Web of Passion*
Joyce, Janet — *Man of the House*
— *Winter Lady*
Lacey, Anne — *Love Feud*
Langan, Ruth — *Hidden Isle*
Lowell, Elizabeth — *The Danvers Touch*
— *Lover in the Rough*
— *Summer Storm*
McKenna, Lindsay — *Captive of Fate*
Major, Ann — *Brand of Diamonds*
Malek, Doreen — *Native Season*
Maxam, Mia — *Lost in Love*
Nicole, Marie — *Tried and True*
Palmer, Diana — *Fire and Ice*
— *Friends and Lovers*
— *Snow Kisses*
Roberts, Nora — *Dance on Dreams*
— *Heart's Victory*
— *Reflections*
— *Song of the West*
— *This Magic Moment*
— *Tonight and Always*
Roszel, Renee — *Wild Flight*

St. Claire, Erin	*Not Even for Love*
St. George, Edith	*Delta River Magic*
	West of the Moon
Simms, Suzanne	*Of Passion Born*
	So Sweet a Madness
Sinclair, Tracy	*Designed for Love*
Stanford, Sondra	*Silver Mist*
Stephens, Jeanne	*Bride in Barbados*
	No Other Love
Summers, Ashley	*A Private Eden*
	Season of Enchantment
Thiels, Kathryn Gorsha	*Texas Rose*
Vitek, Donna	*Valaquez Bride*
Wisdom, Linda	*Dreams From the Past*

Miscellaneous Modern

Dailey, Janet	*Ride the Thunder*
Damon, Lee	*Again the Magic*
Edwards, Andrea	*Now Comes the Spring*
Erickson, Lynn	*Gentle Betrayer*
James, Kristin	*The Golden Sky*
Jones, Nancy	*Jessie's Song*
Jordan, Laura	*The Silken Web*
Sager, Esther	*Only Til Dawn*
Taylor, Abra	*Hold Back the Night*
Trent, Lynda	*Opal Fires*
Weale, Anne	*Antigua Kiss*

Historical Romance

Bale, Karen A.	*The Forever Passion*
Barbieri, Elaine	*Captive Ecstasy*
Barrie, Monica	*Gentle Fury*
Bartlett, Lynn	*Courtly Love*
Blake, Jennifer	*Embrace and Conquer*
	Love's Wild Desire
Brandewynne, Rebecca	*No Gentle Love*
Busbee, Shirlee	*Gypsy Lady*
	Lady Vixen
	While Passion Sleeps
Carrol, Shana	*Paxton Pride*

Cole, Justine	*The Copeland Bride*
Coulter, Catherine	*The Devil's Embrace*
Cruz, Joan Carroll	*Desire of Thy Heart*
DeBlasis, Celeste	*The Tiger's Woman*
Deveraux, Jude	*The Black Lyon*
	The Enchanted Land
	Highland Velvet
	The Velvet Glove
Dunaway, Diane	*Desert Hostage*
DuPont, Diane	*The French Passion*
Foxx, Rosalind	*Winds of Fury, Winds of Fire*
Garlock, Dorothy	*This Loving Land*
Gellis, Roberta	*The Roselynde Chronicles*
Gluyas, Constance	*The King's Brat*
	My Lady Benbrook
Gregory, Lisa	*Bitterleaf*
	The Rainbow Season
Hay, Suzanne	*Savage Destiny*
Ingram, Grace	*Red Adam's Lady*
James, Deana	*Lovestone*
Jordan, Laura	*Hidden Fires*
Joyce, Janet	*Conquer the Memories*
Kamada, Annelise	*A Love So Bold*
Leigh, Susannah	*Glynda*
Lindsey, Johanna	*Heart of Thunder*
	A Pirate's Love
	So Speaks the Heart
McBain, Laurie	*Devil's Desire*
	Tears of Gold
Marsh, Elaine Tanner	*Wrap Me in Splendor*
Marten, Jacqueline	*The English Rose*
Michaels, Fern	*Vixen in Velvet*
Myers, Katherine	*Dark Soldier*
Parker, Laura	*Silks and Sabers*
Rivers, Francine	*Golden Valley*
	Rebel in His Arms
Rogers, Rosemary	*Sweet Savage Love*
	The Wildest Heart
Seger, Maura	*Defiant Love*
	Flame on the Sun
	Forbidden Love
	Rebellious Love

Shaw, Linda	*Ballad in Blue*
Shelley, Elizabeth	*Caravan of Desire*
Shiplett, June Lund	The Wind series
Simon, Jo Ann	*Hold Fast to Love*
	Love Once in Passing
Small, Bertrice	*Love Wild and Fair*
	Skye O'Malley
Spencer, LaVyrle	*The Fulfillment*
	Hummingbird
Statham, Frances Patton	*Flame of New Orleans*
Stephens, Sharon	*The Black Earl*
Taylor, Janelle	The Ecstasy series
Thane, Elswyth	The Williamsburg series
Trent, Lynda	*Shining Nights*
Williams, Caludette	*Blades of Passion*
	Cassandra
	Passion's Pride
Woodiwiss, Kathleen	*The Flame and the Flower*
	The Wolf and the Dove
Wright, Cynthia	*Caroline*
	Spring Fires
Zide, Donna Comeaux	*Savage in Silk*

Regencies

Argers, Helen	*A Lady of Independence*
Ashfield, Helen	*Beau Barron's Lady*
Bourne, Joanne Watkins	*Her Ladyship's Companion*
Brown, Diana	*Come Be My Love*
	The Emerald Necklace
Chater, Elizabeth	*The Gamester*
Clark, Norma Lee	*Lady Jane*
Coulter, Catherine	*An Intimate Deception*
	Lord Harry's Folly
	The Rebel Bride
Cresswell, Jasmine	*The Blackwood Bride*
Darcy, Clare	*Lady Pamela*
	Lydia or Love in Town
Devon, Anne	*Defiant Mistress*
Dunn, Carola	*Lavender Lady*
Ellingson, Manie	*The Wicked Marquis*
Freeman, Joy	*A Suitable Match*

Gallant, Jennie	*Minuet*
Gordon, Susan	*Match of the Season*
Hazard, Barbara	*A Surfeit of Suitors*
Hewitt, Elizabeth	*Broken Vows*
	The Fortune Hunter
Heyer, Georgette	Everything she wrote
Hines, Charlotte	*The Earl's Fancy*
Jeffries, Julia	*The Chadwick Ring*
	The Clergyman's Daughter
Layton, Edith	*The Disdainful Marquis*
	The Duke's Wager
Lindsey, Dawn	*Daughter of Fortune*
	The Duchess of Vidal
Lee, Elsie	*Second Season*
London, Laura	*The Bad Baron's Daughter*
Lorraine, Mariane	*The Ardent Suitor*
	The Mischievous Spinster
Lovelace, Jane	*Eccentric Lady*
Mack, Dorothy	*A Companion in Joy*
MacNeill, Anne	*A Mind of Her Own*
Mansfield, Elizabeth	*The Counterfeit Husband*
Marsh, Lillian	*Love's Masquerade*
Matthews, Laura	*The Aim of a Lady*
	Lord Clayborne's Fancy
	A Very Proper Widow
Metzger, Barbara	*The Earl and the Heiress*
Michaels, Kasey	*The Belligerent Miss Boyston*
	The Rambunctious Lady Royston
	The Tenacious Miss Tamerlaine
Milne, Rosaleen	*Borrowed Plumes*
Morris, Ira	*The Fortune Hunter*
Murray, Frances	*The Heroine's Sister*
Orwig, Sara	*The Fairfax Brew*
	A Spy for Love
Radcliffe, Janette	*Lord Stephen's Lady*
Roberts, Janet Louise	*La Casa Dorada*
	My Lady Mischief
Scott, Amanda	*The Indomitable Miss Scott*
Smith, Joan	*Aunt Sophie's Diamonds*
	Escapade
Stewart, Lucy Phillips	*Bride of Chance*
Stuart, Anne	*Lord Satan's Bride*

Thorpe, Sylvia	*The Silver Nightingale*
Veryan, Patricia	*Love's Duet*
	Mistress of Willowvale
	The Sanguinet series
Walsh, Sheila	*Madalena*
Williams, Claudette	*Spring Gambit*
Wolf, Joan	*The Counterfeit Marriage*
	A Kind of Honor
	His Lordship's Mistress
	A London Season

Romantic Suspense

Badgley, Anne	*The Rembrandt Decisions*
Charles, Theresa	*Fairer Than She*
Cook, Eugenia	*The Forbidden Tower*
Cromie, Alice	*Lucky to Be Alive*
Eyre, Katherine	*The Lute and the Glove*
Gates, Natalie	*Decoy in Diamonds*
Gosling, Paula	*Solo Blues*
	The Zero Trap
Hodge, Jane Aiken	*Last Act*
Holland, Isabelle	*Grenelle*
	Moncrieff
Lee, Elsie	*The Curse of Carranca*
	Season of Evil
McCaffrey, Anne	*The Mark of Merlin*
MacInnes, Helen	*Decision at Delphi*
	The Venetian Affair
Michaels, Barbara	*Ammie, Come Home*
Millhiser, Marlys	*Michael's Wife*
North, Jessica	*The High Valley*
Peters, Elizabeth	*The Camelot Caper/*
	Her Cousin John
	The Dead Sea Cipher
Raynes, Jean	*The Blood Carnelian*
Simmons, Mary Kay	*Megan*
Stevenson, Anne	*Turkish Rondo*
Stewart, Mary	*Madame, Will You Talk?*
	The Moon-spinners
	Nine Coaches Waiting
Thompson, Anne Armstrong	*Message from Absalom*

Westcott, Kathleen   *The Bride of Kilkerran*
Whitney, Phyllis   *Seven Tears for Apollo*

Gothics

Brent, Madeleine   *Moonraker's Bride*
Black, Laura   *Glendraco*
DeBlassis, Celeste   *The Night Child*
Heaven, Constance   *The House of Kuragin*
Hodge, Jane Aiken   *Marry in Haste*
Holt, Victoria   *Mistress of Mellyn*
James, Rebecca   *Tomorrow Is Mine*
Keppel, Charlette   *I Could Be Good to You*
Knight, Alanna   *Castle of Foxes*
Laker, Rosalind   *Ride the Blue Riband*
Leonard, Phyllis G.   *Phantom of the Sacred Well*
Marlowe, Edwina   *Danger at Dahlkari*
Marshall, Joanne   *The Peacock Bed*
Marten, Jacqueline   *Let the Crags Comb Out Her Dainty Hair*
Mayhew, Margaret   *The Master of Aysgarth*
O'Grady, Leslie   *The Artist's Daughter*
Paul, Barbara   *The Frenchwoman*
Peters, Elizabeth   *Crocodile on the Sandbank*
       The Curse of the Pharaohs
Raynes, Jean   *Legacy of the Wolf*
Rigg, Jennifer   *The Slipperdown Chant*
Sheridan, Anne-Marie   *Summoned to Darkness*
Stafford, Caroline   *Moira*
Statham, Frances Patton   *Bright Sun, Dark Moon*

Science Fiction/Fantasy

Bradley, Marion Zimmer   The Darkover series
Bushyager, Linda   *Master of Hawks*
       The Spellstone of Shaltus
Cherryh, C. J.   The Faded Sun trilogy
Cox, Joan   *Star Web*
Cristabel   *The Cruachan and the Killane*
       The Mortal Immortals
Green, Sharon   The Warrior trilogy
Kellog, M. Bradley   *A Rumor of Angels*

Lichtenberg & Lorrah	The Zeor series
Lorrah, Jean	The Savage Empire series
Maxwell, Ann	*Change*
	The Dancer series
	The Singer Enioma
McCaffrey, Anne	The Dragonworld Series
	Restoree
McKillop, Patricia	The Riddlemaster trilogy
Meluch, Rebecca	*The Wind Dancers*
Mezo, Francine	*The Fall of Worlds*
	No Earthly Shore
	Unless She Burn
Morris, Janet	*Cruiser Dreams*
	Dream Dancer
	Earth Dreams
Norton, Andre	The Witch World series
Schmitz, James	*The Witches of Karres*
Springer, Nancy	*The Sable Moon*
	The Silver Sun
	The White Hart

Researching the Historical Novel: A Bibliography

COMPILED BY ROBERTA GELLIS

A bibliography is a list of books. Most often it is a list of those books used as a reference sources to support a scholarly work. In this case, it is provided as a very limited, basic guide to sources that might be useful to the writer of historical fiction. I have divided this bibliography into ten sections:

Books That Tell You Where and How to Look
Books That List Reference Books
Bibliographies
Dictionaries
Encyclopedias
Maps and Atlases
Guides to Periodical Literature
Series Books on History
Biographical Sources
Books on How People Lived

In all cases, the books mentioned are only a bare sampling of those available. They may not even be the best books on the subject. Your library may not have the particular books I mention; however, if you know such books exist and ask for them, the librarian may be able to suggest substitutes or more adequate sources. The important thing is to know that whatever subject you happen to be interested in, someone else was almost certainly also interested and wrote and published information on that subject.

Within the sections, unless specifically stated in that section, the books are not listed in any particular order. Since the sections are short and my time was limited, I just noted them as I remembered them or as I came across them in the sources I myself used to prepare this bibliography.

Books That Tell You Where and How to Look

This is a very limited selection, simply those I know and have used.

Cook, M. G. *The New Library Key*. New York: H. W. Wilson, 1975. Explains library catalogs and classification systems and how to use them; provides lists of general and specific reference books with brief descriptions of contents.

Cordasco, F., and E. S. M. Gatner. *Research and Report Writing*. Totowa, N.J.: Littlefield, Adams, 1974. Paperback. Use of the library and lists of references; briefer than the preceding volumes.

Gates, J. K. *Guide to the Use of Books and Libraries*. New York: McGraw-Hill, 3rd ed., 1974.

Morse, G. W. *Concise Guide to Library Research*. New York: Fleet Academic Editions, 2nd ed., 1975. An extensive list of reference works, listed by subject; comparisons of what is best covered by standard reference works, such as almanacs and encyclopedias.

Books That List Reference Books

Poulton, J. J. *The Historian's Handbook: A Descriptive Guide to Reference Works*. Norman, Okla.: University of Oklahoma Press, 1972.

Reference Books: A Brief Guide. Baltimore: Enoch Pratt Free Library, 400 Cathedral Street, Baltimore, Md. 212101-4484. Write to the publications department.

Winchell, C. M. *Guide to Reference Books*. Chicago: American Library Association, various editions and supplements. Lists books by subject with brief descriptions of content; concentrates on American books.

Walford, A. J. *The Guide to Reference Material*. London: The Library Association, various editions and supplements. Like Winchell, above, but concentrates on British books.

Bibliographies

Bibliographies list books on a particular subject. There are many bibliographies; therefore, several bibliographies of bibliographies have been published. Two of these are listed before those subject bibliographies likely to be useful to a historical novelist. This list is far from exhaustive. There are many useful bibliographies not listed.

The Bibliographical Index. New York: Wilson, 1937 to date. Bibliographies in books, pamphlets, and periodicals.

Besterman, T. *World Bibliography of Bibliographies*. Various editions and publishers. Most comprehensive; books listed by subject.

Beers, H. P. *Bibliographies in American History*. New York: Pageant Books, 1960. Has monographs and manuscript material.

Bibliography of British History. Oxford: Oxford University Press, 1928— . . . Vol. 1, Tudor period; Vol. 2, Stuart period; Vol. 3, eighteenth century.

Biographical Dictionaries and Related Works: A Bibliography. Detroit: Gale Research Co., 1967. Covers nineteenth- and twentieth-century publications.

Guide to Archives and Manuscripts in the United States (P. M. Hamer, ed.). New Haven: Yale University Press, 1960.

Guide to Historical Literature. American Historical Association. New York: Macmillan, 1961.

Writings on British History (A. T. Milne, ed.). New York: Barnes and Nobles, 1937–61.

Dictionaries

Dictionaries are not only for definitions of words. There are dictionaries on every conceivable subject, and some inconceivable ones. A few of those most likely to be useful to the historical novelist are listed.

First are "language" dictionaries; these also contain a wide variety of factual material. If you want to know the date of a person's birth or death, when a word was first used, simple facts about flags or coinage, the date of a saint's day, etc., look it up first in the dictionary; you will often save time.

Funk & Wagnalls New Standard Dictionary of the English Language. Biographical and geographical information included in alphabetical listing.

The Oxford English Dictionary, 12 volumes and supplements. This is the best for etymology (where a word comes from) and when a word was first used. There is an abridged one-volume edition, which I find useful; there is also an unabridged two-volume edition, with which a magnifying glass is provided. I go to the library and use the 12-volume edition.

Webster's International Dictionary of the English Language. I prefer the 2nd edition. Separate biographical and geographical lists.

The following list is of "special" dictionaries that might prove useful. There are many, many others. Check the index of the books mentioned in the first section of this bibliography or ask the research librarian if you want a dictionary on a special subject.

Dictionary of American History (James Truslow Adams, ed.). New York: Scribner, 1942, 6 vols. There is a 1-volume abridgment. This does *not* contain biographical sketches.

Dictionary of Comparative Religion. New York: Scribner. I have not used this. My souce says "compact, covering both living and dead religions."

Eggenberger, D. *Dictionary of Battles.* New York: Crowell, 1967. Lists battles and wars by countries and chronologically.

Grose, F. *A Classical Dictionary of the Vulgar Tongue* (originally published 1796; edited and with commentaries by Eric Partridge). Barnes & Noble, 1963. The date of the original publication says all that is necessary.

Jobes, G. *Dictionary of Mythology, Folklore, and Symbols.* New York: Scarecrow Press, 1961, 63 vols. All cultures, religions, and civilizations from earliest recorded history to the present.

Keller, H. R. *Dictionary of Dates.* New York: Macmillan, 1934. Arranged by countries from antiquity to the thirties.

Patridge, E. *A Dictionary of the Underworld*. New York: Bonanza Books, 1961. Covers the argot of both the British and the American criminal.

Partridge, E. *Today and Yesterday*. London: Routledge; New York: Barnes & Noble. Various editions. Useful for London slang.

Putnam, G. P. *Putnam's Dictionary of Events*. New York: Grosset, 1936. The arrangement is chronological and parallel.

Roget's Thesaurus. Many editions, publishers, editors. This is the classic work for synonyms.

Steinberg, S. H. *Historical Tables*. New York: St. Martin's Press. I have not seen these.

Webster's Biographical Dictionary. Contains upward of 40,000 short entries of a biographical nature.

Webster's Geographical Dictionary. Similar to the biographical dictionary for geography.

Wentworth, H., and S. B. Flexner. *Dictionary of American Slang*. New York: Crowell, 1978. Dates slang.

Encyclopedias

Encyclopedias are almost as various as dictionaries. Only a few of the many available are listed here. More extensive listings can be found in "Books That Tell You Where to Look."

Encyclopedia Britannica. For the purposes of the historical novelist, the 11th edition is best, as it concentrates on biography, history, and geography more than on scientific subjects. The 9th edition is also recommended.

Encyclopedia Americana. This is an excellent encyclopedia but it has the faults of the new *Britannica* in that the concentration is on sciences and technology.

Encyclopedia of Military History. Dupuy, N.Y.: Harper, 1970. Covers 3500 B.C. to present; arranged chronologically and geographically.

Encyclopedia of World History (W. L. Langer, ed.). Boston: Houghton, Mifflin, 1972. From prehistory to early 1970s.

Hastings, J. *Encyclopedia of Religion and Ethnics*. New York: Scribner's, 1908–27, 12 vols. Excellent general reference, but for particular information, there are encyclopedias for each well-known faith.

Larousse Encyclopedia of Ancient and Medieval History (M. Dunan, ed.). New York: Harper, 1963. I have not used or seen this.

Maps and Atlases

An extremely limited listing of general works only. There are atlases on almost all special areas.

Atlas of World History. Hammond, Chicago: Rand McNally, 1961. Available in paperback.

Muir's Historical Atlas: Ancient, Medieval and Modern (R. F. Treharne and H. Fuller, eds.). New York: Barnes & Noble, 1956, 1962. This is in two separate volumes: *Atlas of Ancient and Classical History*, 2nd ed., 1956, and *Historical Atlas, Medieval and Modern*, 9th ed., 1962.

Penguin Atlas of Ancient History and *Penguin Atlas of Medieval History.* Unfortunately, I do not have the full citations on these, but they are paperbacks and reasonable in price.

Shepherd, W. R. *Historical Atlas.* New York: Barnes & Noble, 1964.

Guides to Periodical Literature

Here I will list only those guides that deal with articles written before 1900.

Nineteenth Century Reader's Guide to Periodical Literature. New York: Wilson. Not complete. Intended to cover all articles from 1801 to 1899 but presently only 1880–99 and mostly literary articles.

Poole's Index to Periodical Literature. Reprinted Peter Smith, 1958. Best guide. Covers 450 periodicals from 1802 to 1907.

Series Books on History

I list here only the series name. Each series contains many volumes by individual authors. Each volume is by an authoritative scholar (or scholars) in the particular period it covers, and will provide a reliable and detailed study of political and social events.

The American Nation (A. B. Hart, ed.). New York: Harper, 1904–18. 28 vols. Ends before beginning of World War I.

The Cambridge Ancient History. Cambridge, England: Cambridge University Press. 12 vols. and 5 vols. of plates. Covers prehistoric times to about A.D. 350.

The Cambridge Medieval History, as above. 8 vols. There is a condensation of this work in 2 vols. Covers about A.D. 350 to about 1500.

The New Cambridge Modern History, as above. 13 vols. and atlas. Covers 1493–1945.

The New American Nation (H. S. Commager and R. B. Morris). New York: Harper, 1954–. Not complete. To be 40 vols.

The Oxford History of England. Oxford: Clarendon. 14 vols. This is somewhat less detailed than the following series.

I am not acquainted with either of the series of American history; this is not my field. The reference I am using suggests that the "new" series does not really replace the older one but complements it; that is, details not found in one can be found in the other, owing, I presume, to difference, in emphasis.

Biographical Sources

I list only biographical sources dealing with historical personages, that is, those who are dead.

Dictionary of American Biography. 20 vols. and supplements. Biographical sketches of historical American personages; the length of the biography roughly corresponds to the importance of the individual.

Dictionary of National Biography, Wm. & H. Palmer. 21 vols. and supplements. As above, for British personages.

Who's Who in History. New York: Barnes & Noble, 5 vols. British history. I have never seen or used this, and recommend the use of the *Dictionary of National Biography*, if available.

Books on How People Lived

The Everyday Life Series. London: B. T. Batsford; New York: G. P. Putnam. Like series books on history, this series consists of many volumes by different authors. In general, this is the most useful group of books I have come across for the historical novelist. The books give details of customs, costumes, food, and level of technology (that is, whether the people had horses, saddles for them, whether the wheel had been yet invented in this particular society, etc.). Each volume varies in arrangement and period of time covered. Specific volumes cover life and prehistoric times, ancient Egypt, Babylonia and Assyria, ancient Greece, imperial China, ancient Rome, Britain at all time periods, and others.

A few books on costume and food will be listed also for those who are curious or would like more details. The list given is very limited. Many books on each subject are available.

Costume

Costume Index. New York: Wilson, 1937, 1957. Locates plates and pictures of costumes in books; covers almost all historical periods and all nations.

Davenport, M. *The Book of Costume*. New York: Crown, 1948. A history of dress illustrated by reproductions of sculpture, armor, manuscript illuminations, etc.

Hiler, H. *Bibliography of Costume*. Continental, 1939. I am not familiar with this work, but bibliographies are always useful.

Laver, J. *Costume Through the Ages*. New York: Simon and Schuster, 1963. This is essentially a picture book with reproductions from manuscripts, paintings, and sculpture. There is an introduction but no text.

Yarwood, D. *European Costume*. New York: Larousse, 1975. The illustrations in this book were drawn to accompany the text.

Wilcox, R. T. *Dictionary of Costume*. New York: Scribner, 1969. I am not familiar with this one either.

Food and Drink

Bitting, K. G. *Gastronomic Bibliography*. San Francisco: 1939. *Food and Drink Through the Ages*. Gale, catalogue of books, 1937. I am not familiar with either this book or the previous one listed. However, they are the only general references I could find in English.

Clair, C. *Kitchen Table*. New York: Abelard-Schuman, 1965. Covers from primitive times to about Victorian times with special sections on table settings, drinking vessels, the evolution of the kitchen, and four notable cooks.

Kuper, J. (ed.), *The Anthropologists' Cookbook*. New York: Universe, 1977. This is not essentially a historical text, but it does contain recipes from areas seldom included in ordinary cookbooks and using unusual ingredients, such as puffins, wild greens, and dogs. Each chapter has an introductory text, which gives a brief glance at eating habits in odd places.

Pullar, P. *Consuming Passions*. Boston: Little, Brown, 1970. A violently caustic history of food and eating habits from Roman times to the present. Ms. Pullar doesn't like anyone, but the book has lots of information and (if you don't lose your temper or let your blood pressure rise) is fun to read.

Quayle, E. *Old Cook Books*. New York: Dutton, 1978. Many illustrations and actual recipes.

Researching the Edwardian Novel:
A Bibliography

COMPILED BY ELEANORA BROWNLEIGH

Alpern, Andrew. *Apartments for the Affluent*. New York: McGraw-Hill, 1975.

Batterberry, Michael and Ariane. *On the Town in New York*. New York: Scribner's, 1974.

Birmingham, Stephen. *Life At the Dakota; New York's Most Peculiar Address*. New York: Random House, 1974.

Coleman, Terry. *The Liners, a History of the North Atlantic Crossing*. New York: G. P. Putnam's Sons, 1977.

Cowles, Virginia. *Gay Monarch, The Life and Pleasures of Edward VII*. New York: Harper & Row, 1956.

Crow, Duncan. *The Edwardian Woman*. New York: St. Martin's Press, 1975.

Garland, Madge, and J. Anderson Black. *A History of Fashion*. New York: William Morrow and Company, 1975.

Hardwick, Mollie. *The World of Upstairs/Downstairs*. New York: Holt, Rinehart, & Winston, 1976.

Jackson, Stanley. *The Savoy, The Romance of a Great Hotel*. New York: E. P. Dutton, 1964.

Leslie, Anita. *The Marlborough House Set*. New York: Doubleday, 1973.

Matthew, Christopher. *A Different World, Stories of Great Hotels*. New York: Paddington Press, Ltd., The Two Continents Publishing Group, 1976.

Maxtone-Graham, John. *The Only Way to Cross*. New York: Macmillan, 1972.

Morton, Frederic. *The Rothschilds, A Family of Fortune*. New York: Alfred A. Knopf, 1973.

O'Connor, Richard. *The Golden Summers, an Antic History of Newport*. New York: G. P. Putnam's Sons, 1974.

Seebohm, Caroline. *The Man Who Was* Vogue: *The Life and Time of Condé Nast*. New York: Viking Press, 1982.

Smith, Jane S. *Elsie de Wolfe: A Life in the High Style*. New York: Atheneum, 1982.

Tozier, Josephine. *The Traveler's Handbook: A Manual for Transatlantic Tourists*. New York: Funk & Wagnalls Company, 1905.

Whitehouse, Roger. *New York: Sunshine and Shadow: A Photographic Record of the City and Its People from 1850 to 1915*. New York: Harper & Row, 1974.

*Bibliography of Contributors**

Jennifer Blake (Patricia Maxwell)
AS PATRICIA MAXWELL

SECRET OF MIRROR HOUSE	FAWCETT	1970
STRANGER AT PLANTATION INN	FAWCETT	1971
DARK MASQUERADE	FAWCETT	1974
BRIDE OF A STRANGER	FAWCETT	1974
NOTORIOUS ANGEL	FAWCETT	1977
SWEET PIRACY	FAWCETT	1978
NIGHT OF THE CANDLES	FAWCETT	1978
THE BEWITCHING GRACE	POPULAR LIBRARY	1974
COURT OF THE THORN TREE	POPULAR LIBRARY	1974

*NOTE: Author's real name is in parenthesis.

AS JENNIFER BLAKE

LOVE'S WILD DESIRE	POPULAR LIBRARY	1977
TENDER BETRAYAL	POPULAR LIBRARY	1979
THE STORM AND THE SPLENDOR	FAWCETT	1979
GOLDEN FANCY	FAWCETT	1980
EMBRACE AND CONQUER	FAWCETT	1981
ROYAL SEDUCTION	FAWCETT	1983

AS MAXINE PATRICK

THE ABDUCTED HEART	SIGNET	1978
BAYOU BRIDE	SIGNET	1979
SNOWBOUND HEART	SIGNET	1979

LOVE AT SEA	SIGNET	1980
CAPTIVE KISSES	SIGNET	1980
APRIL OF ENCHANTMENT	SIGNET	1980

AS PATRICIA PONDER

| HAVEN OF FEAR | MANOR BOOKS | 1974 |
| MURDER FOR CHARITY | MANOR BOOKS | 1974 |

AS ELIZABETH TREHEARNE
(WITH CAROL ALBRITTON)

| STORM AT MIDNIGHT | ACE | 1973 |

Diana Brown

THE EMERALD NECKLACE	SIGNET	1981
DEBT OF HONOUR	SIGNET	1982
COME BE MY LOVE	SIGNET	1983

Eleanora Brownleigh (Rhoda Cohen)

AS ELEANORA BROWNLEIGH

| WOMAN OF THE CENTURY | ZEBRA | 1981 |
| HEIRLOOM | ZEBRA | 1983 |

Shirlee Busbee

GYPSY LADY	AVON	1977
LADY VIXEN	AVON	1980
WHILE PASSION SLEEPS	AVON	1983

Mary Canon

O'Hara Dynasty series

THE DEFIANT	WORLDWIDE LIBRARY	1981
THE SURVIVORS	WORLDWIDE LIBRARY	1982
THE RENEGADES	WORLDWIDE LIBRARY	1982
THE EXILED	WORLDWIDE LIBRARY	1983

Barbara Cartland

Barbara Cartland is the world's most prolific female romantic author with over 300 titles. We are listing her titles for 1981 and 1982. Beginning in February 1982 Jove started a new line of Barbara Cartland romance titled Camfield Romances.

LOST LAUGHTER	BANTAM	1981
FROM HELL TO HEAVEN	BANTAM	1981
PRIDE AND THE POOR PRINCESS	BANTAM	1981
THE LIONESS AND THE LILY	BANTAM	1981
THE KISS OF LIFE	BANTAM	1981
AFRAID	BANTAM	1981
LOVE IN THE MOON	BANTAM	1981
THE WALTZ OF HEARTS	BANTAM	1981
DOLLARS FOR THE DUKE	BANTAM	1981
DREAMS DO COME TRUE	BANTAM	1981
A NIGHT OF GAIETY	BANTAM	1981
ENCHANTED	BANTAM	1981
WINGED MAGIC	BANTAM	1981
A PORTRAIT OF LOVE	BANTAM	1981
THE RIVER OF LOVE	BANTAM	1981

GIFT OF THE GODS	BANTAM	1981
AN INNOCENT IN RUSSIA	BANTAM	1981
A SHAFT OF SUNLIGHT	BANTM	1981
LOVE WINS	BANTAM	1982
SECRET HARBOUR	BANTAM	1982
LOOKING FOR LOVE	BANTAM	1982
THE VIBRATIONS OF LOVE	BANTAM	1982
LIES FOR LOVE	BANTAM	1982
LOVE RULES	BANTAM	1982
MOMENTS OF LOVE	BANTAM	1982
MUSIC FROM THE HEART	BANTAM	1982
THE CALL OF THE HIGHLANDS	BANTAM	1982
KNEEL FOR MERCY	BANTAM	1982
WISH FOR LOVE	BANTAM	1982
MISSION TO MONTE CARLO	BANTAM	1982
CAUGHT BY LOVE	BANTAM	1982
LOVE AT THE HELM	BANTAM	1982
PURE AND UNTOUCHED	BANTAM	1982
A MARRIAGE MADE IN HEAVEN	BANTAM	1982
FROM HATE TO LOVE	BANTAM	1982
LOVE ON THE WIND	BANTAM	1982

Jayne Castle (Jayne Krentz)

AS STEPHANIE JAMES

CORPORATE AFFAIR	SILHOUETTE DESIRE	1982
VELVET TOUCH	SILHOUETTE DESIRE	1982
LOVER IN PURSUIT	SILHOUETTE DESIRE	1982
RENAISSANCE MAN	SILHOUETTE DESIRE	1982
A RECKLESS PASSION	SILHOUETTE DESIRE	1982
THE PRICE OF SURRENDER	SILHOUETTE DESIRE	1983
TO TAME THE HUNTER	SILHOUETTE DESIRE	1983
AFFAIR OF HONOR	SILHOUETTE DESIRE	1983
GAMEMASTER	SILHOUETTE DESIRE	1983
THE SILVER SNARE	SILHOUETTE DESIRE	1983
BATTLE PRIZE	SILHOUETTE DESIRE	1983
GAMBLER'S WOMAN	SILHOUETTE DESIRE	1983

AS JAYNE CASTLE

GENTLE PIRATE	CANDLELIGHT ECSTASY	1980
WAGERED WEEKEND	CANDLELIGHT ECSTASY	1981
RIGHT OF POSSESSION	CANDLELIGHT ECSTASY	1981
BARGAIN WITH THE DEVIL	CANDLELIGHT ECSTASY	1981
A MAN'S PROTECTION	CANDLELIGHT ECSTASY	1982
RELENTLESS ADVERSARY	CANDLELIGHT ECSTASY	1982

AFFAIR OF RISK	CANDLE-LIGHT ECSTASY	1982	**A DREAM COMES THROUGH**	CANDLE-LIGHT ECSTASY	1982
A NEGOTIATED SURRENDER	CANDLE-LIGHT ECSTASY	1982	**DOUBLE OCCUPANCY**	CANDLE-LIGHT ECSTASY	1982
POWER PLAY	CANDLE-LIGHT ECSTASY	1982	**DESIGNING WOMAN**	CANDLE-LIGHT ECSTASY	1982
SPELLBOUND	CANDLE-LIGHT ECSTASY	1982	**NO EASY WAY OUT**	CANDLE-LIGHT ECSTASY	1982
CONFLICT OF INTEREST	CANDLE-LIGHT ECSTASY	1983	**VIDEO VIXEN**	CANDLE-LIGHT ECSTASY	1983
			SPECIAL DELIVERY	CANDLE-LIGHT ECSTASY	1983

Ginger Chambers

THE KINDRED SPIRIT	CANDLE-LIGHT ECSTASY	1981	**DARE THE DEVIL**	CANDLE-LIGHT ECSTASY	1983
CALL IT LOVE	CANDLE-LIGHT ECSTASY	1982	**BEST LAID PLANS**	FINDING MR. RIGHT	1983
A FIRE OF THE SOUL	CANDLE-LIGHT ECSTASY	1982	**CALCULATED RISK**	SILHOUETTE DESIRE	1983
SWEET PERSUASION	CANDLE-LIGHT ECSTASY	1982			
GAME OF HEARTS	HARLEQUIN AMERICAN ROMANCE	1983			

Marion Chesney
AS MARION CHESNEY

Elaine Raco Chase

			REGENCY GOLD	FAWCETT	1980
RULES OF THE GAME	CANDLE-LIGHT ECSTASY	1980	**LADY MARGERY'S INTRIGUE**	FAWCETT	1980
			THE CONSTANT COMPANION	FAWCETT	1980
			QUADRILLE	FAWCETT	1981
TENDER YEARNINGS	CANDLE-LIGHT ECSTASY	1981	**MY LORD LADIES AND MARJORIE**	FAWCETT	1981
			THE GHOST AND LADY ALICE	FAWCETT	1982
			LOVE AND LADY LOVELACE	FAWCETT	1982

DUKE'S DIAMONDS	FAWCETT	1982
DOLLY	FAWCETT	1982
THE WESTERBY INHERITANCE	PINNACLE	1982

AS JENNIE TREMAINE

KITTY	DELL	1979
DAISY	DELL	1980
LUCY	DELL	1980
POLLY	DELL	1980
MOLLY	DELL	1980
GINNY	DELL	1980
TILLY	DELL	1981
SUSIE	DELL	1981
POPPY	DELL	1982
SALLY	DELL	1982

AS ANN FAIRFAX

HENRIETTA	JOVE	1979
MY DEAR DUCHESS	JOVE	1979
ANNABELLE	JOVE	1980
PENELOPE	JOVE	1981
THE MARQUESS TAKES A BRIDE	POCKET	1980
THE HIGHLAND COUNTESS	POCKET	1981

Virginia Coffman

MISTRESS OF DEVON	FAWCETT	1973
VERONIQUE	FAWCETT	1975
THE HIGH TERRACE	NAL	1975
THE ICE FOREST	DELL	1975
THE ALPINE COACH	DELL	1976
ENEMY OF LOVE	DELL	1976
CAREEN	DELL	1977
MARSANNE	FAWCETT	1977

FIRE DAWN	FAWCETT	1978
NIGHT AT SEA ABBEY	NAL	1978
THE CLIFF OF DREAD	NAL	1978
THE EVIL AT QUEENS PRIORY	NAL	1978
LEGACY OF FEAR	DELL	1978
THE LOOKING GLASS	DELL	1978
DINAH FAIRE	ARBOR HOUSE	1979
THE GAYNOR WOMEN	FAWCETT	1979
LUCIFER'S COVE	PINNACLE	1979
A FEW FRIENDS TO TEA	PINNACLE	1979
BLACK HEATHER	NAL	1980
PACIFIC CAVALCADE	ARBOR HOUSE	1981
LOMBARD CAVALCADE	ARBOR HOUSE	1982
LOMBARD HOUSE	ARBOR HOUSE	1983

AS JEANNE DUVAL

THE LADY SORENA	NAL	1978
THE RAVISHERS	NAL	1980

Susanna Collins
(Susan Ellen Gross)

THE MIDNIGHT FURY	FAWCETT	1981

AS SUSANNA DE LYONNE

6 DAYS, 5 NITES	FAWCETT	1978

AS SUSANNA COLLINS

FLAMENCO NIGHTS	SECOND CHANCE AT LOVE	1981

Hard to Handle	Second Chance at Love	1981
Destiny's Spell	Second Chance at Love	1981
On Wings of Magic	Second Chance at Love	1982
Breathless Dawn	Second Chance at Love	1983

Janet Dailey

No Quarter Asked	Harlequin	1976
Boss Man from Ogallala	Harlequin	1976
Savage Land	Harlequin	1976
Fire and Ice	Harlequin	1976
Land of Enchantment	Harlequin	1976
The Homeplace	Harlequin	1976
After the Storm	Harlequin	1976
Dangerous Masquerade	Harlequin	1977
Night of the Cotillion	Harlequin	1977
Valley of the Vapors	Harlequin	1977
Fiesta San Antonio	Harlequin	1977
Show Me	Harlequin	1977
Bluegrass King	Harlequin	1977
A Lyon's Share	Harlequin	1977
The Widow and the Wastrel	Harlequin	1977
The Ivory Cane	Harlequin	1978
The Indy Man	Harlequin	1978
Darling Jenny	Harlequin	1978
Reilly's Woman	Harlequin	1978
To Tell the Truth	Harlequin	1978
Sonora Sundown	Harlequin	1978
Big Sky Country	Harlequin	1978
Something Extra	Harlequin	1978
Master Fiddler	Harlequin	1978
Beware of the Stranger	Harlequin	1978
Giant of Mesabi	Harlequin	1978
The Match-makers	Harlequin	1978
For Bitter or Worse	Harlequin	1979
Green Mountain Man	Harlequin	1979
Six White Horses	Harlequin	1979
Summer Mahogany	Harlequin	1979
The Bridge of the Delta Queen	Harlequin	1979
Tidewater Lover	Harlequin	1979
Strange Bedfellow	Harlequin	1979
Low Country Liar	Harlequin	1979
Sweet Promise	Harlequin	1979
For Mike's Sake	Harlequin	1979
Sentimental Journey	Harlequin	1979
Land Called Deseret	Harlequin	1979
Kona Winds	Harlequin Presents	1980
That Boston Man	Harlequin Presents	1980
Bed of Grass	Harlequin Presents	1980
The Thawing of Mara	Harlequin Presents	1980

THE MATING SEASON	HARLEQUIN PRESENTS	1980
LORD OF THE HIGH LONESOME	HARLEQUIN PRESENTS	1980
SOUTHERN NIGHTS	HARLEQUIN PRESENTS	1980
ENEMY IN CAMP	HARLEQUIN PRESENTS	1980
DIFFICULT DECISION	HARLEQUIN PRESENTS	1980
HEART OF STONE	HARLEQUIN PRESENTS	1980
ONE OF THE BOYS	HARLEQUIN PRESENTS	1980
WILD AND WONDERFUL	HARLEQUIN PRESENTS	1981
A TRADITION OF PRIDE	HARLEQUIN PRESENTS	1981
THE TRAVELING KIND	HARLEQUIN PRESENTS	1981
DAKOTA DREAMIN'	HARLEQUIN PRESENTS	1981
THE HOSTAGE BRIDE	SILHOUETTE	1981
THE LANCASTER MEN	SILHOUETTE	1981
FOR THE LOVE OF GOD	SILHOUETTE	1981
TERMS OF SURRENDER	SILHOUETTE	1982
WILDCATTER'S WOMAN	SILHOUETTE	1982
FOXFIRE LIGHT	SILHOUETTE	1982
MISTLETOE AND HOLLY	SILHOUETTE	1982
SEPARATE CABINS	SILHOUETTE	1983
WESTERN MAN	SILHOUETTE	1983
NIGHTWAY	POCKET	1981
TOUCH THE WIND	POCKET	1979
RIDE THE THUNDER	POCKET	1980
THE ROGUE	POCKET	1980

THIS CALDER RANGE	POCKET	1981
THIS CALDER SKY	POCKET	1982
STANDS A CALDER MAN	POCKET	1983
CALDER BORN, CALDER BRED	POCKET	1983

Megan Daniel (Donna Myer)

AMELIA	SIGNET	1980
THE RELUCTANT SUITOR	SIGNET	1981
THE UNLIKELY RIVALS	SIGNET	1981
THE SENSIBLE COURTSHIP	SIGNET	1982

Kathryn Davis
The Dakota series

| BOOK I: AT THE WIND'S EDGE | PINNACLE | 1983 |
| BOOK II: THE ENDLESS SKY | PINNACLE | 1983 |

Celeste De Blasis

THE NIGHT CHILD	FAWCETT	1976
SUFFER A SEA CHANGE	FAWCETT	1979
THE PROUD BREED	FAWCETT	1979
THE TIGER'S WOMAN	FAWCETT	1982

Jude Deveraux (Jude Gilliam White)
AS JUDE DEVERAUX

THE ENCHANTED LAND	AVON	1977
THE BLACK LYON	AVON	1980
CASA GRANDE	AVON	1982

THE VELVET PROMISE	GALLEN/ POCKET	1981		IN HER PRIME	LOVE AND LIFE	1982
HIGHLAND VELVET	POCKET	1982		HER OWN PERSON	LOVE AND LIFE	1982
VELVET SONG	POCKET	1983				
VELVET ANGEL	POCKET	1983		THE BEST MAN	LOVE AND LIFE	1983
SWEETBRIAR	TAPESTRY	1983				

Joan Dial
AS JOAN DIAL

SUSANNA	FAWCETT	1978
LOVERS & WARRIORS	FAWCETT	1978
DEADLY LADY	FAWCETT	1980
ROSES IN WINTER	POCKET	1982
LILIES IN SPRING	POCKET	1983

AS KATHERINE KENT

DRUID'S RETREAT	PINNACLE	1979
DREAMTIDE	GALLEN/ POCKET	1980
WATERS ON EDEN	GALLEN/ POCKET	1981
MIDNIGHT TANGO	GALLEN/ POCKET	1982

AS AMANDA YORK

BELOVED ENEMY	POCKET	1979
SOMEWHERE IN THE WIND	POCKET	1980

Carole Nelson Douglas

AMBERLEIGH	JOVE	1980
FAIR WIND, FIERY STAR	JOVE	1981
SIX OF SWORDS	BALLANTINE/ DEL RAY	1982
EXILES OF THE RYNTH	BALLANTINE/ DEL REY	1982
LADY ROGUE	BALLANTINE	1983

Casey Douglas (June Casey)
AS JUNE CASEY

PROMISES IN THE SAND	CIRCLE OF LOVE	1983

AS CONSTANCE RAVENLOCK

RENDEZVOUS AT GRAMERCY	CANDLE- LIGHT REGENCY	1981

AS CASEY DOUGLAS

INFIDEL OF LOVE	SUPER- ROMANCE	1982
PROUD SURRENDER	SUPER- ROMANCE	1983
DANCE-AWAY LOVER	SUPER- ROMANCE	1983
LOVE'S DARK FANTASIES	SUPER- ROMANCE	1983

Bonnie Drake (Barbara Delinsky)
AS BONNIE DRAKE

THE PASSIONATE TOUCH	CANDLE- LIGHT ECSTASY	1981
SURRENDER BY MOONLIGHT	CANDLE- LIGHT ECSTASY	1981
SWEET EMBER	CANDLE- LIGHT ECSTASY	1981
SENSUOUS BURGUNDY	CANDLE- LIGHT ECSTASY	1981

THE ARDENT PROTECTOR	CANDLELIGHT ECSTASY	1982
WHISPERED PROMISE	CANDLELIGHT ECSTASY	1982
LILAC AWAKENING	CANDLELIGHT ECSTASY	1982
AMBER ENCHANTMENT	CANDLELIGHT ECSTASY	1982
LOVER FROM THE SEA	CANDLELIGHT ECSTASY	1983
THE SILVER FOX	CANDLELIGHT ECSTASY	1983
PASSION AND ILLUSION	CANDLELIGHT ECSTASY	1983

AS BILLIE DOUGLASS

SEARCH FOR A NEW DAWN	SILHOUETTE	1982
A TIME TO LOVE	SILHOUETTE	1982
KNIGHTLY LOVE	SILHOUETTE	1982
FAST COURTING	SILHOUETTE	1983
SWEET SERENITY	SILHOUETTE	1983
FLIP SIDE OF YESTERDAY	SILHOUETTE	1983
BEYOND FANTASY	SILHOUETTE	1983

Julia Fitzgerald
AS JULIA WATSON

THE LOVE CHILD	CORGI	1968
	BANTAM	1968
MEDICI MISTRESS	CORGI	1969
A MISTRESS FOR THE VALOIS	CORGI	1970

THE KING'S MISTRESS	CORGI	1970
THE WOLF AND THE UNICORN	CORGI	1971
WINTER OF THE WITCH	CORGI	1971
	BANTAM	1972
THE TUDOR ROSE	CORGI	1972
SAFFRON	CORGI	1972
LOVE SONG	FUTURA TROUBADOUR	1981

AS JANE DE VERE

THE SCARLET WOMEN	CORGI	1969

AS JULIA HAMILTON

KATHERINE OF ARAGON	SPHERE	1972
	BEAGLE	1972
ANNE OF CLEVES	SPHERE	1972
	BEAGLE	1972
SON OF YORK	SPHERE	1973
HABSBURG *SERIES*	ROBERT HALE	1977–80
THE CHANGELING QUEEN		
THE EMPEROR'S DAUGHTER		
PEARL OF THE HABSBURGS		
THE SNOW QUEEN		
THE HABSBURG INHERITANCE		

AS JULIA FITZGERALD

ROYAL SLAVE	FUTURA TROUBADOUR	1978
	BALLANTINE	1978

SCARLET WOMAN	FUTURA TROUBA-DOUR	1979	THE DRAGON & THE ROSE	PLAYBOY	1977
			THE SWORD & THE SWAN	PLAYBOY	1977
SLAVE LADY	FUTURA TROUBA-DOUR	1980	ROSELYNDE CHRONICLES		
SALAMANDER	FUTURA TROUBA-DOUR	1981	ROSELYNDE	PLAYBOY	1978
			ALINOR	PLAYBOY	1978
			JOANNA	PLAYBOY	1978
FALLEN WOMAN	FUTURA TROUBA-DOUR	1981	GILLIANE	PLAYBOY	1979
			RHIANNON	PLAYBOY	1982
			SYBELLE	PLAYBOY	1983
VENUS RISING	FUTURA TROUBA-DOUR	1981	HEIRESS SERIES		
			THE ENGLISH HEIRESS	DELL	1981

Patricia Gallagher

			THE CORNISH HEIRESS	DELL	1981
SHANNON	AVON	1970	THE KENTISH HEIRESS	DELL	1982
SHADOWS OF PASSION	AVON	1971	THE INDIAN HEIRESS	DELL	1983
SUMMER OF SIGHS	AVON	1971	ROYAL DYNASTY SERIES		
THICKET	AVON	1974			
THE SONS AND THE DAUGHTERS	BANTAM	1975	SIREN SONG	PLAYBOY	1981
CASTLES IN THE AIR	AVON	1976	WINTER SONG	PLAYBOY	1982
ANSWERS TO HEAVEN	AVON	1977			

Audrey P. Johnson

THE FIRES OF BRIMSTONE	AVON	1977	DON'T LOOK BACK	SCHOLASTIC	1981
MYSTIC ROSE	AVON	1977	SISTERS	SCHOLASTIC	1982
NO GREATER LOVE	AVON	1979	I'LL TELL HIM TOMORROW	SCHOLASTIC	1983
ALL FOR LOVE	AVON	1981	HUSH, WINIFRED IS DEAD	THOMAS BOUREGY	1976
ECHOES AND EMBERS	AVON	1982	NURSE OF THE THOUSAND ISLANDS	THOMAS BOUREGY	1978

Roberta Gellis

			THE PET SHOW	GINN & CO.	1972
SING WITCH, SING DEATH	BANTAM	1975			
BOND OF BLOOD	AVON	1976			
KNIGHT'S HONOR	AVON	1976			

Rosanne Kohake

FOR HONOR'S LADY	AVON	1983

Malcolm MacDonald

THE WORLD FROM ROUGH STONES	SIGNET	1976
THE RICH ARE WITH YOU ALWAYS	SIGNET	1977
SONS OF FORTUNE	SIGNET	1979
ABIGAIL	SIGNET	1980
GOLDENEYE	SIGNET	1983

Nelle McFather

WHISPERING ISLAND	ACE	1974
THE RED JAGUAR	ACE	1974
DARK REFUGE	ACE	1976
MISTRESS OF SHADES	MANOR	1977
ECSTASY'S CAPTIVE	TOWER	1979
WOMAN ALIVE	TOWER/ LEISURE	1980

Elizabeth Mansfield (Paula Schwartz)

UNEXPECTED HOLIDAY	DELL	1978
MY LORD MURDERER	BERKLEY	1978
THE PHANTOM LOVER	BERKLEY	1979
A VERY DUTIFUL DAUGHTER	BERKLEY	1979
REGENCY STING	BERKLEY	1980
A REGENCY MATCH	BERKLEY	1980
HER MAN OF AFFAIRS	BERKLEY	1980
DUEL OF HEARTS	BERKLEY	1980

A REGENCY CHARADE	BERKLEY	1981
THE FIFTH KISS	BERKLEY	1981
THE RELUCTANT FLIRT	BERKLEY	1981
THE FROST FAIR	BERKLEY	1982
THE COUNTERFEIT HUSBAND	BERKLEY	1982
HER HEART'S CAPTAIN	BERKLEY	1983
MY JAILOR, MY LOVE	BERKLEY	1983
PASSING FANCIES	BERKLEY	1983

Patricia Matthews

LOVE'S AVENGING HEART	PINNACLE	1977
LOVE'S WILDEST PROMISE	PINNACLE	1977
LOVE, FOREVER MORE	PINNACLE	1977
LOVE'S DARING DREAM	PINNACLE	1978
LOVE'S PAGAN HEART	PINNACLE	1978
LOVE'S MAGIC MOMENT	PINNACLE	1979
LOVE'S GOLDEN DESTINY	PINNACLE	1979
LOVE'S MANY FACES (POEMS)	PINNACLE	1979
LOVE'S RAGING TIDE	PINNACLE	1980
LOVE'S SWEET AGONY	PINNACLE	1980
LOVE'S BOLD JOURNEY	PINNACLE	1980
TIDES OF LOVE	BANTAM	1981
EMBERS OF THE DAWN	BANTAM	1982
FLAMES OF GLORY	BANTAM	1983

DANCER OF DREAMS	BANTAM	1983

AS LAURA WYLIE

THE NIGHT VISITOR	PINNACLE	1979

AS PATRICIA AND CLAYTON MATTHEWS

MIDNIGHT WHISPERS	BANTAM	1981
EMPIRE	BANTAM	1982

Alice Morgan

MASQUERADE OF LOVE	CANDLE-LIGHT ECSTASY	1982
SANDS OF MALIBU	CANDLE-LIGHT ECSTASY	1982
THE IMPETUOUS SURROGATE	CANDLE-LIGHT ECSTASY	1982

Sara Orwig

RUNAWAY DESIRE	MAJOR	1978
FLIGHT TO PARADISE	MAJOR	1978
THE FAIRFAX BREW	HARLEQUIN	1979
THE DUKE'S REVENGE	HARLEQUIN	1980
MAGIC OBSESSION	HARLEQUIN	1983
CAMILLA	MILLS & BOON	1981
LOVE'S TRACE	MILLS & BOON	1983

AS DAISY LOGAN

RECKLESS LONGING	SECOND CHANCE AT LOVE	1982

Maggie Osborne

SALEM'S DAUGHTER	SIGNET	1981
ALEXA	SIGNET	1979
PORTRAIT IN PASSION	SIGNET	1981
YANKEE PRINCESS	SIGNET	1982
ISLAND MISTRESS	SIGNET	1983

Miriam Pace

NEW ORLEANS	ZEBRA	1981
DELTA DESIRE	ZEBRA	1982

Anne N. Reisser

THE FACE OF LOVE	CANDLE-LIGHT ECSTASY	1981
THE CAPTIVE LOVE	CANDLE-LIGHT ECSTASY	1981
DECEPTIVE LOVE	CANDLE-LIGHT ECSTASY	1981
ALL'S FAIR	CANDLE-LIGHT ECSTASY	1982
COME LOVE, CALL MY NAME	CANDLE-LIGHT ECSTASY	1982
BY LOVE BETRAYED	CANDLE-LIGHT ECSTASY	1982

Rosemary Rogers

SWEET SAVAGE LOVE	AVON	1974

THE WILDEST HEART	AVON	1974
DARK FIRES	AVON	1975
WICKED LOVING LIES	AVON	1976
THE CROWD PLEASERS	AVON	1978
THE INSIDERS	AVON	1979
LOST LOVE, LAST LOVE	AVON	1980
LOVE PLAY	AVON	1981
SURRENDER TO LOVE	AVON	1982

Erin Ross

PLEASE STAND BY—YOUR MOTHER'S MISSING	LIBRA	1980
SECOND HARVEST	SILHOUETTE	1982

Vanessa Royall (Mike Hinkemeyer)

FLAMES OF DESIRE	DELL	1978
COME FAITH, COME FIRE	DELL	1979
FIREBRAND'S WOMAN	DELL	1980
WILD WIND WESTWARD	DELL	1982
SEIZE THE DAWN	DELL	1983

Maura Seger

DEFIANT LOVE	TAPESTRY ROMANCE	1982
REBELLIOUS LOVE	TAPESTRY ROMANCE	1983

Suzanne Simms (Suzanne Guntrum)
AS SUZANNE SIMMONS

SUMMER STORM	MACFADDEN ROMANCES	
WINTER WINE	MACFADDEN ROMANCES	
FROM THIS DAY FORWARD	MACFADDEN ROMANCES	
VELVET MORNING	MACFADDEN ROMANCES	
TOUCH THE WIND	MACFADDEN ROMANCES	
THE TEMPTUOUS LOVERS	CANDLELIGHT ECSTASY	1981
NEVER AS STRANGERS	CANDLELIGHT ECSTASY	1982
AS NIGHT FOLLOWS DAY	CANDLELIGHT ECSTASY	1982

AS SUZANNE SIMMS

MOMENT IN TIME	SILHOUETTE	1982
OF PASSION BORN	SILHOUETTE	1982
A WILD, SWEET MAGIC	SILHOUETTE	1983

Bertrice Small

KADIN	AVON	1978
LOVE WILD AND FAIR	AVON	1978
ADORA	BALLANTINE	1980
SKYE O'MALLEY	BALLANTINE	1980
UNCONQUERED	BALLANTINE	1982
BELOVED	BALLANTINE	1983

Danielle Steel (Danielle Steel Traina)

PASSION'S PROMISE	DELL	1977
NOW AND FOREVER	DELL	1978
THE PROMISE	DELL	1978
SEASON OF PASSION	DELL	1979

SUMMER'S END	DELL	1979
TO LOVE AGAIN	DELL	1980
LOVING	DELL	1980
THE RING	DELL	1980
LOVE (POETRY)	DELL	1980
PALOMINO	DELL	1981
REMEMBRANCE	DELL	1981
A PERFECT STRANGER	DELL	1982
CROSSINGS	DELL	1982
GOING HOME	POCKET	1978

Serita Stevens

THIS BITTER ECSTASY	POCKET	1981
A DREAM FOREVER	BALLANTINE	1983

Janelle Taylor

SAVAGE ECSTASY	ZEBRA	1981
DEFIANT ECSTASY	ZEBRA	1982
FORBIDDEN ECSTASY	ZEBRA	1982
BRAZEN ECSTASY	ZEBRA	1983
TENDER ECSTASY	ZEBRA	1983
LOVE ME WITH FURY	ZEBRA	1983
THE VALLEY OF FIRE	HARLEQUIN AMERICAN ROMANCE	1984

Carolyn Thornton

THE HEART NEVER FORGETS	SILHOUETTE	1980
LOVE IS SURRENDER	SILHOUETTE	1982
PRIDE'S RECKONING	SILHOUETTE	1982
LOOKING GLASS LOVE	SILHOUETTE	1983

FOR ERIC'S SAKE	SILHOUETTE	1983
SMILE AND SAY YES	SILHOUETTE	1983
MALE ORDER BRIDE	SILHOUETTE	1983
BY THE BOOK	SILHOUETTE	1984

Brenda Trent (Brenda Trent Himrod)

AS BRENDA TRENT

RISING STAR	SILHOUETTE	1981
WINTER DREAMS	SILHOUETTE	1981
A STRANGER'S WIFE	SILHOUETTE	1981
RUN FROM HEARTACHE	SILHOUETTE	1982
STORMY AFFAIR	SILHOUETTE	1982
RUNAWAY WIFE	SILHOUETTE	1982

AS MEGAN LANE

BITTER VINES	CANDLE-LIGHT ECSTASY	1982

Donna Vitek

AS DONNA ALEXANDER

A LOVER'S QUESTION	MACFADDEN	1979
RED ROSES, WHITE LILIES	MACFADDEN	1979
NO TURNING BACK	MACFADDEN	1979
IN FROM THE STORM	MACFADDEN	1979

AS DONNA VITEK

A DIFFERENT DREAM	SILHOUETTE	1980
SHOWERS OF SUNLIGHT	SILHOUETTE	1980

PROMISES FROM THE PAST	SILHOUETTE	1981
VEIL OF GOLD	SILHOUETTE	1981
WHERE THE HEART IS	SILHOUETTE	1981
A VALAQUEZ BRIDE	SILHOUETTE	1982

AS DONNA KIMEL VITEK

MORNING ALWAYS COMES	CANDLE-LIGHT ECSTASY	1982
PASSION'S PRICE	CANDLE-LIGHT ECSTASY	1983
DANGEROUS EMBRACE	CANDLE-LIGHT ECSTASY	1983
CAUTION TO THE WIND	CANDLE-LIGHT ECSTASY	1983

Lois Walker

AS REBECCA ASHLEY

AN INTRIGUING INNOCENT	DELL	1980
A SEASON OF SURPRISES	DELL	1981
A WILFUL WIDOW	DELL	1981
AN ARROGANT ARISTOCRAT	DELL	1981
AN INTREPID ENCOUNTER	DELL	1982

AS SABRINA MILES

FREEDOM TO LOVE	DELL	1981

AS CANDICE ADAMS

FOR LOVE ALONE	GALLEN/ POCKET	1982

FASCINATION	BALLANTINE	1982
GOING PLACES	BALLANTINE	1982
EXPLORING	BALLANTINE	1983
DIAMOND OF DESIRE	DELL	1983

Jennifer Wilde (Tom E. Huff)

LOVE'S TENDER FURY	WARNER	1976
DARE TO LOVE	WARNER	1978
LOVE ME, MARIETTA	WARNER	1981
ONCE MORE, MIRANDA	BALLANTINE	1983

Violet Winspear

Violet Winspear has written more than sixty category romances for Mills & Boon/Harlequin. Here is a list of her most recent titles.

THE CHATEAU OF ST. AVRELL	HARLEQUIN PRESENTS	1982
THE VALDEZ MARRIAGE	HARLEQUIN PRESENTS	1982
THE AWAKENING OF ALICE	HARLEQUIN PRESENTS	1982
THE LOVED AND THE FEARED	HARLEQUIN PRESENTS	1982
TIME OF THE TEMPTRESS	HARLEQUIN PRESENTS	1982
THE PASSIONATE SINNER	HARLEQUIN PRESENTS	1982
THE CHILD OF JUDAS	HARLEQUIN PRESENTS	1982
THE NOBLE SAVAGE	HARLEQUIN PRESENTS	1982
THE MAN SHE MARRIED	HARLEQUIN PRESENTS	1983
DEAR PURITAN	HARLEQUIN ANTHOLOGY	1983

RAPTURE OF THE DESERT	HARLEQUIN ANTHOLOGY	1983
THE SILVER SLAVE	HARLEQUIN ANTHOLOGY	1983

Kathleen E. Woodiwiss

THE FLAME AND THE FLOWER	AVON	1972
THE WOLF AND THE DOVE	AVON	1974
SHANNA	AVON	1977
ASHES IN THE WIND	AVON	1979
A ROSE IN WINTER	AVON	1982

Cynthia Wright

CAROLINE	BALLANTINE	1977
TOUCH THE SUN	BALLANTINE	1978
SILVER STORM	BALLANTINE	1979
SPRING FIRES	BALLANTINE	1983

AS DEVON LINDSAY

CRIMSON INTRIGUE	GALLEN/ POCKET	1981

Marisa de Zavala

GOLDEN FIRE, SILVER ICE	CANDLELIGHT ECSTASY	1981
SCREAM OF THE PARROT	BERKLEY/ JOVE	1983
KISS GOODNIGHT AND SAY GOODBY	HARLEQUIN AMERICAN ROMANCE	1983

Suzanne Zuckerman

TWO OF A KIND	HEAVENLY ROMANCE	1982
TRYING HARDER	HEAVENLY ROMANCE	1982
MONTAUK SUMMER	HEAVENLY ROMANCE	1983

Index

Accuracy of facts, 163, 165
Active voice, 161–64
Acton, Jay, 368
Advances, 253, 362–64
Advertising, 404
Agents, 253, 362–68
Allen, Hervey, 200
American Indian romances, 176–78
Anderson, Roberta, and Mary
    Kuczkir (Fern Michaels), 324
Associated Press News Features,
    405
Astrology books, 88
Atlases, 218, 460
Auctions, submissions at, 366
Auel, Jean, 286
Austen, Jane, 295
Avon Books, 201–02
    submission and editorial
        requirements, 404, 425, 430
Axelrod, Stephen, 368

Backache, 391
Bagliof, Ben, 332, 429
Ballantine, Betty, 310
Ballantine Books, 202. *See also*
    Fawcett; Love and Life
    submission and editorial
        requirements, 427, 430
Ballantine/Del Rey, 433
Bantam Books, 202, 332. *See
    also* Loveswept; Sweet Dreams
    submission and editorial
        requirements, 430–32
Baron, Maureen, 202
Beginning writer(s). *See also* New
    authors; Tip sheets
    Jacqui Bianchi's advice to, 22–23
    Eleanora Brownleigh's sugges-
        tions for, 55–61

mini-course on category
    romances for, 180–87
Carolyn Nichol's advice to,
    7–9
Anne N. Reisser on her
    experience as, 68–71
Erin Ross's experience as, 168–72
Berkley/Jove, 202, 332, 426. *See
    also* Caprice
submission and editorial
    requirements, 426, 431, 432
Bernstein, Meredith, 368
Bianchi, Jacqui, 14, 419
    interview with, 22–24
Bibliographies, 457. *See also*
    Reference books
    of contributors, 464–79
    for historical romances, 208
Biographical sources, 461
Biographies, 213–19
Black romances, 176–78
Blackmore, Richard D., 195
Blake, Jennifer (Patricia Maxwell)
    bibliography, 464–65
    "Determining the Situation,"
        71–75
Blues, 353
Book clubs, 353
Book Creations, 202, 273–76
    submission and editorial
        requirements, 426
Books. *See* Bibliography;
    Reference books
Boon, Alan, 419
Boucher, Anthony, 298
Brandewyne, Rebecca, 390
Brandt & Brandt, 368
Brown, Curtis, 368
Brown, Diana, "The Demon of
    Writers," 395

Brown, Sandra (Ryan, Rachel), 100
Brownleigh, Eleanora (Rhoda Cohen)
  bibliography, 465
  "The Practical Side of Romance Writing," 55–60
  "Researching the Edwardian Novel: Bibliography," 463–64
Bryant, Sir Arthur, 383
Bulletin board, 61
Bulwer-Lytton, Edward, 196
Busbee, Shirlee
  bibliography, 465
  "Ten Tips for Getting in the Mood for Writing Love Scenes," 231
Busch, Ron, 35
  "A Publisher Talks About Romance Fiction," 433–36
Bonds, Parris Afton, 49

Camhy, Cathy, 425
Candlelight Ecstasy, 14, 151–52, 176
  print run for, 12
  reading list, 445
  submission and editorial requirements, 417
Canon, Mary
  bibliography, 465
  "The O'Hara Dynasty," 271–73
Capital letters, 163
Caprice Romances, 331–32
Careers of heroines, 101
Carney, Margaret, 14, 418
Cartland, Barbara, 368, 391
  bibliography, 465–66
  interview with, 381–89
Casey, June. See Douglas, Casey
Cassette tapes for romantic writers, 441
Castle, Jayne, (Stephanie James)
  bibliography, 466
  "In the Beginning . . .," 115–18
Category romances, 5, 11–20. See also Formula
  characters in. See Characters
  Janet Dailey on, 35–37
  definition of, 354

editors of, 12–14, 417–33
ethnic, 175–78
humor in, 108, 118–23
length of, 10, 12
lines of, 11, 12
mini-course on, 180–87
narrative in, 123–26
opening scenes of, 115–18
plotting, 61–106. See also Plots
print run for, 13
publishers of, 11–13, 417–33
reading list, 2, 443–49
research for, 41–47
setting of, 127–31
sex in, 12–13, 17–20, 30–31, 85–86
submission and editorial requirements, 417–425
suspense in, 132–34
third-person viewpoint in, 81–86
tip sheets for, 8, 13–20
titles of, 100–01
TORTE system for writing, 61
types of, 12
Cavin, Ruth, 431
Chains, 354
Chair, writing, 50
Chambers, Ginger
  bibliography, 467
  "Let the Character's Words Flow," 102–05
Character flaw, of hero, 246–47
Characters, See also Hero; Heroine
  appearance of, 88
  dialogue between. See Dialogue
  credibility of, 166
  Casey Douglas on, 91
  Anne Gisonny on, 180–82
  of historical romances, 207–10, 223–26, 258, 260–66, 279
  identification of readers with. See Identification of reader with heroine.
  Knowing your, 87
  Malcolm MacDonald on, 274
  names of, 88, 98–99
  Maggie Osborne on, 87–91
  reaction to action and stimulus by, 89
  Anne N. Reisser on plotting and, 68

Characters *continued*
 Suzanne Simms on, 65–67
 thoughts of, 89
Chase, Elaine Raco, 191
 bibliography, 467
 "A Pinch of Humor," 120–23
Chesney, Marion, 440
 bibliography, 467
 "A Light-Hearted Plot," 292–94
 "Synopsizing a Novel,"
  346–47
Chronology of events, in
  historical romances, 208
Churchill, Winston, 199
Cinderella legend. *See* Formula
Classes. *See* Courses
Clerkenwell House, submission and
  editorial requirements, 427
Cleveland Plain Dealer, 405
Clothing. *See also* Costume
 of characters, 88–89
 in historical romances, 254
 for stimulating sensuality in the
  writer, 53
Cloverdale Press, 429
Coffee, Nancy, 202, 426, 431,
  432
Coffman, Virginia
 bibliography, 468
 "How to Write Today's
  Gothic," 297–301
Cohen, Carin, 428
Cohen, Hilary, 417
Cohen, Rhoda. *See* Brownleigh,
  Eleanora
Colette, 250–51
Collins, Susanna (Susan Ellen
  Gross)
 bibliography, 468–69
 "The Romantic Setting,"
  127–31
Columbia Literary Associates,
  368
Condon, Alicia, 14, 422
Conferences, 440
Conflict. *See also* Situations
 dialogue expressing, 113
 Casey Douglas on, 91–95
 in historical romances, 232–35
 in opening scene, 115–17
 Brenda Trent on, 76–79
Contemporary romances, 5, 303–10

 authors of, 287–88
 basic features of, 283–85
 editors of, 432–33
 publishers of, 288, 432–33
 reading list, 4, 449
Contractions, 102–03
Contracts, 354, 362–64
Conversations. *See* Dialogue
Cooper, James Fenimore, 196
Copy editors, 162, 360
Costume, reference books on,
  218, 462
Courses, 59
Covers, 355
Crawford, Betty Ann, 332, 429
Creative corner, 49–51
Credibility, straining the reader's,
  166
Cuddy, Page, 202, 425
Curwood, James Oliver, 198

Dailey, Janet, 36, 97, 100, 390,
  403
 bibliography, 469–70
 filmstrip method of, 35,
  36–37, 41
 interview with, 35–37
Daniel, Megan (Donna Meyer)
 bibliography, 470
 "Confessions of a Regency
  Romantic," 289–91
Daniels, Velma, "Tips for TV,",
  409–11
Davis, Kathryn
 bibliography, 470
 "Planning a Multivolume Saga,"
  267–71
Deadline, 354
De Blasis, Celeste, 390
 bibliography, 470
 "The Magic Touch," 260–64
Delinsky, Barbara. *See* Drake,
  Bonnie
Dell. *See also* Candlelight Ecstasy
 submission and editorial
  requirements, 202, 417, 426,
  445
 Dell/Supreme, 446
Dell, Ethel M., 387
Dellon, Hope, 431
Del Rey, Judy Lynn, 433
Desire romances, 135–36

Detroit Free Press, 405

Detroit News, 405

Deveraux, Jude (Jude Gilliam White), 390, 414
  bibliography, 470
  "How I Outlined *Highland Velvet*," 257–60

de Zavala, Marisa
  bibliography, 479
  "The Third-person Viewpoint," 81–86

Dial, Joan
  bibliography, 471
  "Casting the Part of Your Reader in Historical Romance Novels," 219–22

Dialects, 102–05

Dialogue
  Ginger Chambers on, 102–05
  chitchat (small talk), 165
  Bonnie Drake on, 109–15
  Hilary V. Guerin's tips on, 351
  in historical romances, 219–22, 232
  humor in, 118, 120–23
  narrative and, 114, 123
  in opening scene, 115
  Maggie Osborne on, 87
  in Regency romances, 292–94

Dickens, Charles, 182

Dictaphone Dual Display Word Processor, 371–75

Dictating, Barbara Cartland on, 386

Dictionaries, 162, 218, 457–58

Discount for buying your own book, 401

Distributors, 354

Dixie Council of Authors and Journalists, 440

Doctor-Nurse Romance series, 419

Dorf/MJH, 408

Douglas, Carole Nelson, 284, 286
  bibliography, 471
  "My First Sci-Fi Fantasy," 311–13

Douglas, Casey (June Casey)
  bibliography, 371
  "Creating the Hero and Heroine," 91–97

Doyle, Arthur Conan, 195

Drake, Bonnie (Barbara Delinsky), 370
  bibliography, 471
  "The Dialogue of Love," 109–15

Dump, 354

Dutton, E. P., 332
  See also Heavenly Romances

Earn-out, 354

Editors, 354, 417–33
  agents and, 365–67
  of category romances, 12–13, 417–25
  of contemporary romances, 432–33
  copy, 162, 360
  functions of, 361
  of historical romances, 426–28
  line, 360
  of Regency romances, 430–31
  relationship between author and, 360–62
  of romantic suspense and gothic, 432
  of science fiction and fantasy, 433
  of teen romances, 332, 429

Edwards, Ellen, 14, 421

Encyclopedias, 213, 218

Endfield, Cy, 369

Endings, 167
  of sagas, 269–71

Engel, Lyle Kenyon, 202, 426
  "Writing Series and Sagas for Book Creations, Inc.," 273–76

Erickson, Lynn (Molly Swanton and Carla Peltonen), 325

Ethnic romances, 175–78

Evans, Suzan, "Tips for Series and Saga Writers," 270

Everyday Life series, 218, 461

Exclamation points, 163

Exercise, 390–91

Eyes, 392

Falk, Kathryn, 441

Family sagas. *See* Sagas

Fans, mailings to, 403

Fantasy. *See* Science Fiction and fantasy

Farber, Barry, 405

Farnol, Jeffrey, 198
Fawcett (Ballantine), 202
    submission and editorial
        requirements, 427
Fiction Writer's Market (Writer's
    Digest Books), 439
Filler, 354
Filmstrip method, Janet Dailey's,
    35, 36–37, 141
Finishing what you begin, Diana
    Brown on, 395
Finkelstein, Pescha, 202
First Love, 332
    submission and editorial
        requirements, 429
First-person narrative, 204
Fitzgerald, Julia
    bibliography, 472–73
    "Channeling Feelings into
        History," 223–26
Flaxman, Richard, "A Market
    Analysis of the Romance
    Reader for the Romance
    Writer," 136–40
Florid writing, 165
Flowers, 54
Flournoy, Valerie, 177
Food, in historical romances, 254
Food and drink, reference books
    on, 462–63
Foreign rights, 298, 362–64
Forester, C. S., 200
Formula (rules), 136–38, 354
    category romances, 5, 32
    contemporary romances, 5–6
    Anne Gisonny on, 182–84
    historical romances, 5
    Mills & Boon editor on, 106
    Regency romances, 6
    Judy Sullivan on, 33
    teen romances, 333–37
Friday, Nancy, 315

Gallagher, Patricia
    bibliography, 473
    "Jottings from My 'Castles in the
        Air' Notebook Journals,"
        239–43
Galleys, 355
Garon, Jay, 368
Gartland, Mary Anne, 14, 419
Gelbman, Leslie, 432

Gellis, Roberta, 50, 441
    bibliography, 473
    "Researcher's Bibliography,"
        218
    "Researching the Historical Novel:
        A Bibliography," 455–63
    "Researching History, 210–19
Genre, 355
Georgette Heyer Award, the, 441
Geraniums, 54
Gisonny, Anne, 14, 417, 441
    "Category Romance Mini-
        Course," 180–92
Glay, George, 4 424
Glynn, Diane, Publicity and Public
    Relations, Inc., 408
Golightly, Bonnie, "The Outline
    Hurdle," 347–49
Gothic novels, 6
    authors of, 287, 454
    basic features of, 282–83
    Virginia Coffman on, 297–301
    gay, 301–03
    publishers of, 432
    reading list, 454
    suspense in, 132
Graham, Mrs. Billy, 388
Grammar. *See also* Punctuation
    active voice versus passive
        voice, 161–64
Gross, Susan Ellen. *See* Collins,
    Susanna
Grunder, Robin, tips from, 420
Guerin, Hilary V., "What
    Happens to Your Manuscript
    When It Arrives at a
    Publishing House," 349–52
Guntrum, Suzanne. *See* Simms,
    Suzanne

Haggard, Rider, 197
Hager, Jean, 177, 178
Hale, John, 427
Hale, Robert, 427
Hardcover, 355
Harlequin, 11, 139, 419. *See
    also* Mills & Boon/Harlequin
    print run for, 12
Harlequin American Romances, 14,
    445
    submission and editorial
        requirements, 417

Harlequin hero, 355

Harlequin Presents, 14, 418

Harlequin Romance, 11, 12, 14

Harlequin Superromance, 14, 444

Harlequin Temptation, 11, 14, 418

Harlequin's 30th Anniversary Book, 440

Hayden, June, "How We Write Together," 326–28

Heavenly Romances, 332
  submission and editorial requirements, 429

Helfer, Melinda, "A Recommended Reading List," 443

Helmer, Star, 423

Henty, G. A., 197

Hero, 182
  Barbara Cartland on, 386
  character flaw of, 245–47
  Elaine Raco Chase on, 121
  Casey Douglas on creating a, 92, 95–97
  Anne Gisonny on, 190–92
  Harlequin, 355
  of historical romances, 236–38, 240, 244–47
  name of, 97–99
  physical appearance of, 192, 245
  questions to ask about, 172

Heroine, 182
  Elaine Raco Chase on, 120–21
  ethnic, 175
  Anne Gissony on, 187–90
  of historical romances, 224–26, 237–38, 240, 246–48
  job or career of, 101
  name of, 98–99
  Maggie Osborne on, 90
  physical appearance of, 246–47
  questions to ask about, 172
  in Danielle Steel novels, 305–08

Heyer, Georgette, 198, 289, 295

Himrod, Brenda Trent. *See* Trent, Brenda

Hinkemeyer, Mike (Vanessa Royall)
  bibliography, 476

"How Can a Man Write Romance Novels?" 317–20

"My Secret Life: How I Became Vanessa Royall," 316

Hispanic romances, 176–78

Historical dramas, 210–11

Historical fiction, types of, 210–11

Historical romances, 5, 195–280, 449
  advances to authors of, 362–64
  authors of, 449
  for bibliography, 208
  Eleanora Brownleigh on research for, 58–59
  Barbara Cartland on, 385–89
  characters of, 223–26, 257–58, 260–66, 278–79
  chronology of events in, 208
  clothing in, 254
  dialogue in, 220–22
  editors of, 202, 426–28
  feeling in, 223–26
  hero of, 237, 240, 244–47
  heroine of, 224–26, 237–38, 240
  Mike Hinkemeyer (Vanessa Royall) on, 316–20
  housing in, 255
  identification of reader with heroine in, 206
  Fredda Isaacson's recommendations for writers of, 203–05
  Malcolm MacDonald on, 274–80
  Kay Meierbachtol on, 205–07
  narrative of, 277–78
  opening scenes of, 277–78
  outline for, 209, 257–60
  Miriam Pace on getting organized for writing, 207–10
  plot of, 205–07, 209, 232–36, 265, 277
  political intrigue in, 256
  publishers of, 202, 426–28
  reading list, 3, 449–51
  reference material for, 213, 218, 455–63
  research for, 240–43, 268, 272–73
  sagas, 267–76
  sensuality in, 250–52
  setting of, 253–57, 279
  sex in, 200–01, 204–05, 224–31

Historical romances *(continued)*
  social details in, 255
  submission and editorial
    requirements, 426–28
  survey of (1940–71), 200–02
Hodder and Stoughton, submission and editorial requirements,
  427
Hope, Anthony, 199
Hourglass Romances, submission
  and editorial requirements, 418
Housing, in historical romances,
  208–9
Huff, Tom E. (Jennifer Wilde),
  142, 314–15, 320–21, 390–91
  bibliography, 478
  "Writing the Sensual Novel,"
    250–52
Hugo, Victor, 196
Humor
  in category romances, 108,
    118–23
  Elaine Raco Chase on, 120–23
  in dialogue, 118–19,
    121–22
Husbands of authors, 375–80

Identification of reader with
    heroine
  in historical romances, 206,
    219–22
  Maggie Osborne on, 90
Imagery (image-making), 34, 39–40
  exercises for developing,
    39–40
International Romantic Book
    Lovers' Conference, 440
Interviews, 409–11, 412–15
Isaacson, Fredda, 202, 203, 428
  "Recommendations for Begin-
    ning Writers," 203–05
Isham, Frederick, 199
Italics, 163

Jackson, Helen Hunt, 197
Jackson, Nancy, 322, 429
Jeeves, Heather, 202
Johnson, Audrey P., 339
  bibliography, 473
  "The Teenage Formula,"
    333–36
Johnson, Mary, 198

Jourlet, Marie de, 39, 369
Jove Publications. *See* Berkley/
    Jove; Second Chance at Love
Juneman, Karen (Flanne Devlin),
    311

Kingsley, Charles, 195
Kohake, Rosanne, 474
  "How to Write Like Rosemary
    Rogers," 236–37
  "How to Write Like Danielle
    Steel," 305–08
  "How to Write Like Kathleen
    Woodiwiss," 265–67
Krentz, Janye. *See* Castle, Jayne
Kuczkir, Mary, and Roberta
    Anderson (Fern Michaels),
    324, 329

Lamb, Charlotte, 100
Lande, Melissa, Promotions, Inc.,
    408
Lawyers, 362
Lead book, 355
Lectures, 403
Leoni, Adele, 368
Lewis, Beverly, 202, 428
Libraries, 212–13
Lieberman, 135
Line, 355
Line editors, 360
Literary agents. *See* Agents
Locale (location). *See also* Setting
  choice of, 65–66
  questions to ask about, 173
Lorin, Amii, 49
Lopriore, Marianne, "Manuscript
    Preparation," 340–44
Love Beat, PR, 408
Love and Life series, 308–10
  submission and editorial
    requirements, 433
Lovelines (Facts on Files), 439
Lovemaking. *See* Sex
Love's Leading Ladies, 438
Loveswept, 14, 442
  submission and editorial
    requirements, 418–19

Length (word count)
  of category romances, 5, 11–13
  of Harlequin novels, 17
  method of figuring, 8, 342

Lowenstein, Barbara, 368
Luce Clipping Service, 407

McCaffrey, Anne, 310
MacCampbell, Donald, 368
McCutchen, George B., 199
MacDonald, Lonnie, "Creative
    Writing Tips," 394
MacDonald, Malcolm, 50
    bibliography, 474
    interview with, 277–80
McFather, Nelle
    bibliography, 474
    "Suspense in Romance," 132–34
Machismo, 95
Magazines, 57–59, 437–38
    for promotion, 405
Mail-order business, 404
Major, Charles, 199
Mansfield, Elizabeth (Paula
    Schwartz), 441
    bibliography, 474
    "An Explanation of the
    Regency," 294–97
Manuscript
    clean, 354
    edited, 354
    length of. See Length
    mailing your, 343–44
    preparation of, 340–44
    submission of, by agents, 365–66
    submission of, requirements
    for, 417–33
Maps, 460
Marcil, Denise, 14, 441
    "Author-Agent Relationships,"
    365–68
Market size, 139
Market trends, 365
Mass market, 355
Matthews, Clayton and Patricia,
    324–25
Matthews, Patricia, 370
    bibliography, 474–75
    "Building a Novel," 232–36
Maxwell, Patricia. See Blake,
    Jennifer
Media. See Promotion
Media outlets, 405–07
Meierbachtol, Kay, "Improving
    Your Historical Romance
    Plot," 205–07

Meyer, Donna. See Daniel,
    Megan
Michaels, Fern (Roberta Ander-
    son and Mary Kuczkir), 324
Microwriter, 369
Mills & Boon/Harlequin
    reading list, 443
    submission and editorial
    requirements, 419
    tip sheet, 14–17
Miscellaneous Modern, 449
Mitchell, Margaret, 200
Mitchell, S. Weir, 198
Mixon, Veronica, 177, 431
Modernage Photo Service, 401
Morgan, Alice, 108
    bibliography, 475
    "Full-Blown Eroticism," 150–57
Movie rights, 364
Movies, historical romances, 200
Multivolume sagas. See Sagas

NAL/Signet, 202. See also
    Rapture Romances, 442
    submission and editorial
    requirements, 431
Names. See also Pseudonyms
    of characters, 88, 97–99
    famous, 166
Narrative
    dialogue and, 114, 123
    first-person, 204
    of historical romances, 277–78
    Malcolm MacDonald on, 277–79
    of setting, 127
    Lois Walker on, 123–26
Narrative transitions, 125–26
Nevler, Leona, 202, 427, 430
Newsday, 405
Newsletters, 403–04
    for promotion, 405, 415
New writers, 355
    advances to, 362
    creative writing tips for,
    394–95
Nichols, Carolyn, 14, 418, 432
    advice to beginning writers, 8–9
    on common mistakes of
    beginners, 118
Nicknames, 88
Nolan, Betsy, Group Incorporated,
    408

Notebooks
    Patricia Gallagher's, 239–43
    writing by hand in, 56
Notebook system, Phyllis A.
        Whitney's, 43–44

Ogilvie Mather II, 408
O'Herir, Kathy, 332, 418
One-Liners for Romance Writers
        (Daring Press R.), 439
Opening scenes
    Jayne Castle on, 115–18
    of historical romances, 277
    Malcolm MacDonald on, 277
    narrative and dialogue in, 123–24
    suspense in, 133
Orczy, Baroness, 199
Orwig, Sara, 42
    bibliography, 475
    "Organizing Research Material
        for Category Romances,"
        44–47
Osborne, Maggie, 401
    bibliography, 475
    "Breathing Life into Your
        Characters," 87–90
O'Shea, Colleen, 430, 432
Outlines, 39, 342
    Bonnie Golightly on, 347–48
    of historical romances, 209,
        257–59, 279
    Malcolm MacDonald on, 279
Oxier, Debra, "Finding the Right
        Names, Titles, and Careers,"
        97–102

Pace, Miriam
    bibliography, 475
    "Getting Organized," 207–10
Padding (plumping out), 165
Pagination, 355
Partial, 355
Passive voice, 161
Peltonen, Carla, and Molly
        Swanton (Lynn Erickson), 325
People magazine, 405
Periodicals. *See* Magazines
Personal publicity. *See*
        Promotion
Photograph, publicity, 399–401
Physical activity and exercises,
        390–92

Physical appearance
    of characters, 88
    of hero, 192, 244–45
    of heroine, 246
Pinnacle, submission and edito-
        rial requirements, 427
Plots (plotting), 61–106. *See also*
        Formula; Synopsis
    Jennifer Blake on, 71–75
    Barbara Cartland on, 386, 389
    Elaine Raco Chase on, 122
    credibility of, 166
    directing idea and, 185–86
    Casey Douglas on, 91–97
    Anne Gisonny on, 181,
        184–87
    of historical romances, 205–07,
        209, 232–35, 265–66, 274–75
    Malcolm MacDonald on, 277–78
    overloading, 166
    of Regency romances, 289–90
    Anne N. Reisser on, 69–71
    Suzanne Simms on, 65–67
    of Danielle Steel novels,
        305–06
    Serita Stevens on questions to
        ask while developing, 172–75
    synopsis of, 107–09
    Carolyn Thornton on, 62–64
    TORTE system and, 61–62
    Brenda Trent on, 76–79
    "what if" technique for, 63
Pocket Books, 202, 434–36
    submission and editorial
        requirements, 428
Polishing the prose, 107–09
Political intrigue, in historical
        romances, 256
Political statements, in ethnic
        romances, 177
Porter, Jane, 195
Posture, 392
Prescott, Eileen, Company, Inc.,
        408
Press-clipping service, 407
Press kit, 399–401
Press releases, 399, 411–13
Price, Linda, 202, 425, 430
Print run, 355
    for category romances, 13
Professional women, Suzanne
        Simms on writing about, 66

Prolific writers, 356
Promotion (publicity), 359,
    397–15
  advertising, 404
  effectiveness of, 403–04
  interviews, 409–11, 412–15
  lectures, 403
  media outlets, 405–07
  newspapers and magazines for,
    405
  press kit, 399–401
  publicists, 408, 411–15
  radio programs, 401, 405–06
  television programs, 402,
    406–10
Pseudonyms, 5
  of male authors, 321–22
  reasons for using, 7
Psychological aspects of writing,
    394–96
Publication, route from manuscript
    to, 357–59
Publicists, 398, 408, 411–15
Publicity. See Promotion
Public relations (PR), 355
Publishers, 416–36
  of category romances, 12, 13,
    417–25
  of contemporary romances, 432
  of historical romances, 426–28
  publicity agencies handling, 408
  of Regency romances, 430–31
  of romantic suspense and gothic,
    432
  of science fiction and fantasy,
    433
  submission and editorial
    requirements, 417–22
  of teen romances, 331–32, 429
Publishers Weekly, 57, 438
Punctuation, 163

Query letters, 340–41, 344–46
  to agents, 366–67
Questionnaire, for character
    development, 87–88

Radio programs, 401, 405–06
Rainbow method of underlining,
    32, 34
Ramee, Louise de la, 197
Rape, 230–31

Rapp, Joel, 405
Rapture Romance, 14
  submission and editorial
    requirements, 419, 421
  tip sheet, 17–19
Reader identification. See
    Identification of reader with
    heroine
Reader's report, 360
Reading
  magazines, 57–60
  Anne N. Reisser on, 68
Reading list, 2–4, 443–55
  category romances, 443–48
  contemporary romances, 449
  gothics, 454
  historical romances, 449–50
  Regency romances, 451–53
  romantic suspense, 353
  science fiction and fantasy,
    454–55
  series and sagas, 270
Reading out loud
  dialogue writing and, 102–03
  testing your novel by, 175
Real estate, 356
Reference books, 212–13, 218
  on agents, 366
  biographical sources, 461
  on costume, 462
  dictionaries, 457–59
  encyclopedias, 459
  on food and drink, 462–63
  guides to periodical literature,
    460
  for historical romances,
    455–63
  on how people lived, 461–62
  maps and atlases, 460
  on romances and authors,
    438–40
  series books on history,
    460–61
  that list reference books,
    456–57
  that tell you where and how to
    look, 456
Regency romances, 4–6
  authors of, 287, 451
  basic features of, 281–82
  Marion Chesney on, 292–94
  Megan Daniel on, 289–91

Regency romances *(continued)*
  dialogue in, 292–93
  editors of, 430–31
  plots of, 290–91
  publishers of, 288, 430–31
  reading list, 4, 351–53
  research for, 289–90
  sex in, 296
Reisser, Anne, 183
  bibliography, 475
  "How and why," 68–71
Reit, Ann, 335, 430
Repetition, 166
Research, 272. *See also* Reference
  books
  Eleanora Brownleigh on, 58–59
  Barbara Cartland on, 384–85
  for category romances, 42–47
  for Edwardian novels, 463–64
  for historical romances, 204–08,
    210–19, 240–43, 268,
    272–73
  notebook system for, 42–44
  for Regency romances, 289–90
  for sagas, 268–69, 272–73
  Carolyn Thorton on, 62–64
Reversal device, Suzanne Simms
  on, 66
Revisions, 356, 360
Riven, Judith, 202, 426, 432
Rewriting dialogue, 103–04
Rogers, Rosemary, 39, 49, 201,
  247, 390, 391
  bibliography, 475
  how to write like, 236–38
Roman à clef, 284
Romance centers, 256
Romance novels
  Jacqui Bianchi's definition of,
    23
  classification of, 5–7
Romance rules. *See* Formula
Romantic Book Lovers' Conference,
  440
Romantic Spirit, The (MJK
  Enterprises), 439
Romantic suspense novels, 6
  authors of, 287, 453
  basic features of, 283
  publishers of, 288, 432
  reading list, 4, 453
Romantic Times, 437

Romantic Times Cassettes, 441
Romantic Times Readers Newsletter,
  437
Romantic Times Writers Newsletter,
  437
Ross, Erin (Shirley Bennett
  Tallman)
  bibliography, 476
  "The Aches and Pains of
    Writing Your First Romance
    Novel," 168–72
Ross, Hilary, 202, 431
Rotrosen, Jane, 368
Royall, Vanessa. *See* Hinkemeyer,
  Mike
Royalty rates (or points), 356, 362
Royalty statements, 356, 363–64
Rubin, Renée, 441
  "Caveats and Don'ts,"
    164–67
Ryan, Donna, 157–58
  "Beware of the Pillaging
    Mouth," 159–61
  "Tips from a Copy Editor,"
    162–64
Ryan, Rachel (Sandra Brown), 100

Sabatini, Rafael, 200
Sagas, 267–76
  endings of, 269–70
  plot overloading in, 166
  research for, 268–69, 271–73
Sager, Esther, 284
St. Martin's Press, submission and
  editorial requirements, 431
Scarlet Ribbons, 202
Schedule, 256
Scholastic Book Services, 335
Schulhafer, Joan, 403
  "The Author-Publicist Relation-
    ship," 411–15
Schwartz, Paula. *See* Mansfield,
  Elizabeth
Science fiction and fantasy, 7,
  286–87, 310–13
  authors of, 454
  editors of, 433
  publishers of, 288, 433
  reading list, 4, 454–55
Second Chance at Love, 14, 177,
  421, 446
  reading list, 466

Second Chance at Love *(continued)*
  submission and editorial
    requirements, 425
Seduction, 227
Seger, Maura
  bibliography, 476
  "The Tapestry of Historical
    Romance," 253–57
Self-knowledge, 396
Sensuality. *See also* Sex
  in historical romances, 250–52
  Vivian Stephens on ways to
    stimulate, 52–53
  sustained, 357
Sentence structure, Malcolm
    MacDonald on, 278
Separation of hero and heroine,
  questions to ask about, 173,
  174
Series. *See* Saga
Setting. *See also* Location
  of category romances, 127–31
  of historical romances, 253–57,
    279
  Malcolm MacDonald on, 279
Sex (lovemaking; physical
    expression of love)
  in category romances, 5,
    11–13, 17–19, 30–31, 85–86,
    135–58, 70–71
  Marisa de Zavala on, 85–86
  in historical romances, 200–02,
    203–04, 224–31, 251–52
  Alice Morgan on, 150–57
  narrative in scenes of, 126
  questions to ask about, 173–74
  in Rapture Romances, 17–20
  in Regency romances, 6,
    295–96
  Erin Ross on, 170–71
  setting and, 129–31
  suspense and, 134
  Violet Winspear on, 30–31
Sexual tension, 142–49
Sheldon, Sidney, 268–69
Shelf life, 356
Silhouette, 14, 332, 434, 447. *See
    also* First Love
  print run for, 12
  reading list, 447–49
  submission and editorial
    requirements, 422–23

Silhouette Desire, 135, 422–23
Silhouette First Love, 177
Silhouette Inspiration, 422
Silhouette Intimate Moments, 11,
  12, 422–23
Silhouette Romances, 11, 12, 14,
  422–23
Silhouette Special Edition, 63,
  422–23
Simms, Suzanne (Suzanne
    Guntrum,)
  bibliography, 476
  "The Use of Theme," 65–67
Simon and Schuster. *See*
  Silhouette
Singer, June Flaum, 284
Sinkiewicz, Henryk, 197
Sitting position, 50–51
Situations. *See also* Conflict
  Jennifer Blake on, 71–75
  questions to ask about, 172–75
Sizzle, 356
Small, Bertrice, 39, 49–50, 390,
  441
  bibliography, 476
  "Writing the Erotic Love
    Scene, or Sex Sells!" 226–31
Small, George, "Advice to
    Husbands: Don't Bite the Hand
    That Writes," 376–80
Social commentaries, 177
Social details, in historical
  romances, 255–56
Solem, Karen, 422
Spelling, 163
Starlight Romances, submission
  and editorial requirements, 431
Statham, Frances Patton, 134
Steel, Danielle (Danielle Steel
    Traina), 6, 303–08
  bibliography, 476–77
  how to write like, 305–08
Stephens, Vivian, 14, 176
  "Stimulating Sensuality," 52–53
Stevens, Serita
  bibliography, 477
  "Questions to Ask While
    Plotting," 172–75
Stevenson, Robert Louis, 196
Strickler, Pamela, 202, 425
  "Advice on the Contemporary
    Romance Novel," 308–10

Stripping, 356
Strong story, 356
Subsidiary rights, 357, 362–64
Sullivan, Judy, "Finding the Formula," 33
Summerville, Margaret (Barbara and Pam Wilson), 325
Superromance, 11, 12, 14, 432–25
submission and editorial requirements, 432–25
Susann, Jacqueline, 51
Suspense, 132–34
sexual, 142–49
Suspense novels. *See* Romantic supense novels
Swanton, Molly, and Carla Peltonen (Lynn Erickson), 325, 328
Sweet Dreams, 332
submission and editorial requirements, 429
Synopses, 346–47

Tagliarino, Peggy, 408
Tallman, Shirley Bennett. *See* Ross, Erin
Tapestry Romances, 202, 253, 435
submission and editorial requirements, 428
Taylor, Janelle, 370
bibliography, 477
"How to Write a Best-seller on a Dictaphone Word Processor," 371–75
Teal and Watt, 368
Teams, writing, 323–29
Teasing, 166
Teen romances, 330–39
editors of, 429–30
ethnic, 176
publishers of, 429–30
Television programs, 402, 406–10
Tension, Barbara Cartland on sustaining, 388
Theme, Suzanne Simms on, 65–67
Third-person viewpoint, Marisa de Zavala on, 81–86
Thompson, Maurice, 197

Thornton, Carolyn
bibliography, 477
"Mixing Fact with Fiction," 62–64
Thoughts of characters, 89
Tip sheets, 22, 357
for Caprice Romances, 331–32
of category romances, 10, 13–20
for Mills & Boon/Harlequin, 14–17
for Rapture Romance, 17–20
To Have and To Hold, submission and editorial requirements, 425, 447
Tom Selleck, 357
Tonch Magazine, 14, 438
Trade book, 357
Traina, Danielle Steel. *See* Steel, Danielle
Transitions, narrative, 125–26
Trent, Brenda (Brenda Trent Himrod)
bibliography, 477
"Obstacles to Love," 76–79
Trent, Lynda (Dan and Lynda Trent), 325
Twain, Mark, 196
Typewriters, 55–56, 369–70
electronic pocket, 369
Typing, 343
Typing paper, 51, 55–56

Underlining, rainbow method of, 32, 34
Underscored words, 163
Undset, Sigrid, 199
United Press International, 405
Usage, 165

Van Slyke, Helon, 284
Velvet Glove Romances, 11, 14
Viewpoint
Maggie Osborne on, 90
third-person, 81–86
Virga, Vincent, 302–03
Vitek, Donna
bibliography, 477
"Building Sexual Tension," 141–49
Vries, Jan de, 360

Walker Co., submissional and editorial requirements, 431
Walker, Lois
  bibliography, 478
  "Narrowing the Narrative," 123–26
Wallace, Lew, 196
Warehouse, 357
Warner, 202, 203,
  submission and editorial requirements, 428
Webster's New Collegiate Dictionary. 8th ed., 162
Weiner, Cherry, 368
Weronko, Rick, 405
Weyman, Stanley, 198
White, Jude Gilliam. *See* Deveraux, Jude
Whitney, Phyllis A., 42
  notebook system of, 42–44
Wilde, Jennifer. *See* Huff, Tom E.
Wildfire Romances, 334–35
Williams, Ruth, 405
Wilson, Barbara and Pam (Margaret Summerville), 325
Winn, Godfrey, 382
Winsor, Kathleen, 200
Winspear, Violet, 21
  bibliography, 478–79
  "The Meaning of Romance: Notes on the Writing of the Romantic Novel," 25–31
Women's World magazine, 405
Woodiwiss, Kathleen E., 133, 201, 247, 404

bibliography, 479
how to write like, 265–66
"What if" technique, 63
Word count. *See* Length
Word processors, 370, 371–75
Work habits, 394
  creative corner, 49–51
  Janet Dailey's, 35–38
  Danielle Steel's, 303–05
  writing by hand, 56
Worldwide Library, 423
Wren, P. C., 199
Wright, Cynthia
  bibliography, 479
  "How I Create My Heros and Heroines," 201–5
Writer, the, 438
Writer's Digest, 438
Writer's Handbook, the (The Writer, Inc.), 439
Writers House, 368
Writing by hand, 56
Writing habits. *See* Work habits
Writing tools, 368–75

Young, Charles, 176

Zebra, 202
  submission and editorial requirements, 418, 428, 432
Zuckerman, Suzanne
  bibliography, 479
  "Turning Teenage Fantasies into Fiction," 337–39